The Themes That Bind Us

Previous book by Gretchen Oltman, Johnna L. Graff, and Cynthia Wood Maddux

Law Meets Literature: A Novel Approach for the English Classroom

The Themes That Bind Us

Simplifying U.S. Supreme Court Cases for the Social Studies Classroom

Gretchen Oltman
Johnna L. Graff
Cynthia Wood Maddux

ROWMAN & LITTLEFIELD
Lanham • Boulder • New York • London

Published by Rowman & Littlefield
An imprint of The Rowman & Littlefield Publishing Group, Inc.
4501 Forbes Boulevard, Suite 200, Lanham, Maryland 20706
www.rowman.com

Unit A, Whitacre Mews, 26-34 Stannary Street, London SE11 4AB

British Library Cataloguing in Publication Information Available

Library of Congress Cataloging-in-Publication Data

Names: Oltman, Gretchen A., author. | Graff, Johnna L., 1974- author. | Maddux, Cynthia Wood, 1964- author.
Title: The themes that bind us : simplifying U.S. Supreme Court cases for the social studies classroom / Gretchen Oltman, Johnna L. Graff, Cynthia Wood Maddux.
Description: Lanham : Rowman & Littlefield, 2018. | Includes bibliographical references and index.
Identifiers: LCCN 2018006792 (print) | LCCN 2018007390 (ebook) | ISBN 9781475836080 (electronic) | ISBN 9781475836066 (cloth : alk. paper) | ISBN 9781475836073 (pbk. : alk. paper)
Subjects: LCSH: Constitutional law—Study and teaching (Secondary)—United States. | Law--Cases—Study and teaching (Secondary)—United States. | LCGFT: Casebooks.
Classification: LCC KF4208.5.L3 (ebook) | LCC KF4208.5.L3 O44 2018 (print) | DDC 342.730071/2—dc23
LC record available at https://lccn.loc.gov/2018006792

∞ ™ The paper used in this publication meets the minimum requirements of American National Standard for Information Sciences Permanence of Paper for Printed Library Materials, ANSI/NISO Z39.48-1992.

Printed in the United States of America

To our husbands, Ron, Matt, and Pete, for their enthusiastic support of our work.

Special thanks to Pete Maddux for lending us his expertise as a history teacher.

Contents

Chronological Timeline of Cases

Marbury v. Madison, 5 U.S. 137 (1803)
United States v. The Amistad, 40 U.S. 518 (1841)
Swift & Co. v. United States, 196 U.S. 375 (1905)
Meyer v. Nebraska, 262 U.S. 390 (1923)
United States v. 95 Barrels of Vinegar, 265 U.S. 438 (1924)
Whitney v. California, 274 U.S. 357 (1927)
Korematsu v. United States, 323 U.S. 214 (1944)
Adler v. Bd. of Educ. of City of New York, 342 U.S. 485 (1952)
Brown v. Bd. of Educ. of Topeka, 347 U.S. 483 (1954)
Edwards v. South Carolina, 372 U.S. 229 (1963)
Gideon v. Wainwright, 372 U.S. 335 (1963)
Sherbert v. Verner, 374 U.S. 398 (1963)
Miranda v. Arizona, 364 U.S. 436 (1966)
In re Gault, 387 U.S. 1 (1967)
Loving v. Virginia, 388 U.S. 1 (1967)
Tinker v. Des Moines Indep. Comty. Sch. Dist, 393 U.S. 503 (1969)
Brandenburg v. Ohio, 395 U.S. 444 (1969)
Wisconsin v. Yoder, 406 U.S. 205 (1972)
South Carolina v. Gathers, 490 U.S. 805 (1989)
Texas v. Johnson, 491 U.S. 397 (1989)
County of Allegheny v. American Civil Liberties Union, 492 U.S. 573 (1989)
Payne v. Tennessee, 501 U.S. 808 (1991)
United States v. American Library Assn., Inc., 539 U.S. 194 (2003)
Roper v. Simmons, 543 U.S. 551 (2005)
Gonzales v. Raich, 545 U.S. 1 (2005)
Kelo v. City of New London, 545 U.S. 469 (2005)
Medellín v. Texas, 552 U.S. 491 (2008)
United States v. Jones, 565 U.S. 400 (2012)
Maryland v. King, 569 U.S. 435 (2013)
Shelby County v. Holder, 570 U.S. 529 (2013)
Michigan v. Environmental Protection Agency, 576 U.S. ___ (2015)
Maslenjak v. United States, 582 U.S. ___ (2017)

Cases Organized by Big Ideas

Cultural dominance or imperialism: the idea that the United States is unique, special, and functions differently than any other nation in the world.

a. *United States v. The Amistad*, 40 U.S. 518 (1841)
b. *Meyer v. Nebraska,* 262 U.S. 390 (1923)
c. *Korematsu v. United States,* 323 U.S. 214 (1944)
d. *Kelo v. City of New London*, 545 U.S. 469 (2005)
e. *Medellín v. Texas*, 552 U. S. 491 (2008)
f. *Maslenjak v. United States*, 582 U.S. ___ (2017)

Challenging authority: the idea that the nation was founded by people who were fighting authority and today's citizens continue to carry this ideal. Incorporated in this idea could be challenges between federal and state conflicts and those involving individual rights versus government regulation.

a. *Marbury v. Madison,* 5 U.S. 137 (1803)
b. *Whitney v. California*, 274 U.S. 357 (1927)
c. *Korematsu v. United States,* 323 U.S. 214 (1944)
d. *Adler v. Bd. of Educ. of City of New York,* 342 U.S. 485 (1952)
e. *Brown v. Bd. of Educ. of Topeka,* 347 U.S. 483 (1954)
f. *Edwards v. South Carolina*, 372 U.S. 229 (1963)
g. *Gideon v. Wainwrigh*t, 372 U.S. 335 (1963)
h. *Sherbert v. Verner,* 374 U.S. 398 (1963)
i. *Miranda v. Arizona*, 364 U.S. 436 (1966)
j. *In re Gault*, 387 U.S. 1 (1967)
k. *Loving v. Virginia,* 388 U.S. 1 (1967)
l. *Tinker v. Des Moines Indep. Cmnty. Sch. Dist.*, 393 U.S. 503 (1969)
m. *Brandenburg v. Ohio,* 395 U.S. 444 (1969)
n. *Wisconsin v. Yoder*, 406 U.S. 205 (1972)
o. *South Carolina v. Gathers*, 490 U.S. 805 (1989)
p. *Texas v. Johnson*, 491 U.S. 397 (1989)
q. *County of Allegheny v. American Civil Liberties Union*, 492 U.S. 573 (1989)
r. *Payne v. Tennessee*, 501 U.S. 808 (1991)

s. *United States v. American Library Assn., Inc.*, 539 U.S. 194 (2003)
t. *Gonzales v. Raich*, 545 U.S. 1 (2005)
u. *Kelo v. City of New London*, 545 U.S. 469 (2005)
v. *United States v. Jones,* 565 U.S. 400 (2012)
w. *Maryland v. King*, 569 U.S. 435 (2013)
x. *Maslenjak v. United States*, 582 U.S. ___ (2017)

Isolation versus internationalism: whether the United States functions independently, interdependently, or reliant on resources, people, and things from around the world continues to challenge the nation both historically and presently.

a. *United States v. The Amistad*, 40 U.S. 518 (1841)
b. *Meyer v. Nebraska,* 262 U.S. 390 (1923)
c. *Roper v. Simmons,* 543 U.S. 551 (2005)
d. *Medellin v. Texas*, 552 U.S. 491 (2008)
e. *Maslenjak v. United States*, 582 U.S. ___ (2017)

Individual versus industry: weighing the rights and needs of individuals versus the progress of the nation as an industrial, scientifically advanced, and competitive entity.

a. *Swift & Co. v. United States*, 196 U.S. 375 (1905)
b. *United States v. 95 Barrels of Vinegar,* 265 U.S. 438 (1924)
c. *United States v. Jones,* 565 U.S. 400 (2012)
d. *Maryland v. King*, 569 U.S. 435 (2013)
e. *Michigan v. EPA*, 576 U.S. ______ (2015)

Civil rights: the rights of the individual to receive equal treatment.

a. *United States. v. The Amistad*, 40 U.S. 518 (1841)
b. *Korematsu v. United States,* 323 U.S. 214 (1944)
c. *Adler v. Bd. of Educ. of City of New York,* 342 U.S. 485 (1952)
d. *Brown v. Bd. of Educ. of Topeka,* 347 U.S. 483 (1954)
e. *United States v. American Library Assn., Inc.*, 539 U.S. 194 (2003)
f. *United States v. Jones,* 565 U.S. 400 (2012)
g. *Maryland v. King*, 569 U.S. 435 (2013)
h. *Shelby County v. Holder,* 570 U.S. 529 (2013)

Chapter One

Why Teach Students to Read Case Law in the Social Studies Classroom?

Teaching social studies in the twenty-first century is no longer simply rehearsing recitation of historical dates or listing U.S. presidents in chronological order. The complexity facing social studies teachers in today's schools continues to build year after year. From the importance of civics education to historical understanding to application of diverse content in a complex political world, now, more than ever, it is necessary to prepare students as independent and critical thinkers.

United States Supreme Court case law provides a lens through which to view the nation historically and politically. It also provides a backdrop to understand political events, cultural trends, and scientific advancements. The U.S. Supreme Court serves as a thermometer of sorts—one that can measure tolerance of citizens, challenges to long-held beliefs, and trace shifting ethical boundaries. As such, putting case law in the hands of today's students is like handing them a snapshot of history. They are able to hear the voices of real people who lived during different points in the nation's past.

The Library of Congress notes three reasons why students should read primary documents like published cases:

1. To engage students in a personal way through first-person accounts in a real, interesting manner;
2. To develop critical thinking skills by encouraging analytical reading and challenging students' assumptions; and
3. To construct knowledge by basing conclusions to difficult questions on evidence and wrestling with the different perceptions of issues both past and present (Library of Congress, n.d.).

The National Archives' "History in the Raw" describes the importance of this interaction between student and text: "Primary sources fascinate students because they are real and they are personal; history is humanized through them. Using original sources, students touch the lives of the people about whom history is written. They participate in human emotions and in the values and attitudes of the past" (para. 4). Thus, reading primary documents is more than just reading for understanding. It engages a reader in a way to bring history to life, to understand the context of a problem, and to see the humanity in those who have lived generations before us.

Case law, therefore, is more than a judge's opinion about a set of facts. Case law tells stories of real people facing challenging, complex legal issues. These stories present the humanity of problems faced within the country, illustrate an issue, and capture a moment in time when the nation's laws were challenged. Studying case law can be a fascinating glimpse into a time and place in history.

The premise of this book is that case law, particularly those cases from the U.S. Supreme Court, can be taught in nearly every social studies–related classroom. Because the U.S. Supreme Court decides cases on nearly every topic, finding content that applies in economics, civics, psychology, history, or political science *is* possible. In addition, once students learn how to read a case, more complex lessons and applications can be developed. Students can read for argumentation, historical understanding, perceptions of cultural traditions, or application of legislation.

In today's high school social studies textbooks, court cases are rarely published or studied in their original form. This means, in reality, textbook publishers are the ones deciding how cases should be interpreted. This book allows students and teachers to have that interaction. That is, high school students are often taught only using a brief summary of a case, a synopsis of a court's decision, or a short statement of the state of the law today. Students never really get the chance to read the details of an argument, the complexities of a challenge against the government, or a court's rationale when making a decision.

In reality, once students leave high school, they may never encounter the opportunity to read case law again. If we teach students how to access and read case law in high school, we provide them with a lifetime tool—so that as new cases emerge, new legal arguments erupt, and new laws are implemented, students can access the information firsthand and not through news sources or secondhand retellings of events. Teaching case law is more than teaching a social studies lesson; it is giving students a skill set to use in the rest of their lives. It hands the responsibility of understanding the evolving nature of the legal process over to their control. It empowers citizens to be informed and educated regardless of their generation.

WHAT IS AN APPROPRIATE PRIMARY DOCUMENT TO TEACH?

Primary documents include historical pieces throughout U.S. history in their original form. Yale University defines primary documents as "sources that provide firsthand testimony or direct evidence concerning a topic or question under investigation" (Yale University, n.d.). These artifacts illustrate a definitive point in time and are studied in the same condition in which they were created (or even created after an event like an autobiography or oral retelling of an event).

Primary documents include government publications, political cartoons, letters, recordings, diaries, legislation, news accounts, treaties, court decisions, acts, amendments, and other documents. Examples include the U.S. Constitution, the Kansas-Nebraska Act, the decision from *Brown v. Board of Education*, or George Washington's Commission as Commander in Chief. Primary documents should be preserved in as much of their original form as possible so as to allow students to inspect documents as they were created. Sometimes this includes unusual fonts, page structures, or sentence variety. Access to primary documents is easier than ever with electronic sources available from the likes of the Library of Congress and National Archives.

The Colonial Williamsburg Foundation provides a list of considerations when selecting primary documents to use in a classroom. This includes:

- Ensuring copies are legible and clear;
- Reviewing all documents prior to implementation in the classroom;
- Editing "judiciously" or in a way that keeps the original meaning or spirit of a document but might ease reader interaction;
- Defining difficult terms; and
- Using primary sources to promote inquiry and further study (Colonial Williamsburg Foundation, 2006)

Case law, then, is a primary document category that is widely found and accessible within a social studies classroom. For this reason, we argue for moving beyond textbook synopses of major U.S. Supreme Court cases to actually putting the case in the hands of students to read, wrestle with, and consider within the context of a typical classroom environment. Court cases present unique challenges to high school students. The language can be complex, vocabulary archaic, and sometimes one must understand history in order to understand why the Court made a decision at a particular point in time. For this reason, cases in this book are edited to allow for accessibility and readability and are intended to limit distractions and challenges that impair lay readers.

CONNECTING CASE LAW TO THE "BIG IDEAS" IN THE SOCIAL STUDIES CLASSROOM

Incorporating case law need not be an isolated event in the social studies classroom, nor should it be an exclusive method of teaching. Using case law to support the larger themes present in most social studies curricula provides access to primary documents and disciplinary reading skills, and also enhances understanding of the larger concepts present in most historical studies.

For example, the competing desires of individuals versus industry is a repeating pattern throughout U.S. history—from the industrial period to the space race of the 1960s to the more recent developments of Internet privacy—individuals in the United States are constantly challenged by scientific innovation. This theme is present for more than one distinct time period and carries multiple curriculum possibilities. For the purposes of this book, five larger themes were identified that overarch the individual curricular themes and ideas. These "big ideas" include the following:

- Cultural dominance or imperialism—the idea that the United States is unique, special, and functions differently than any other nation in the world
- Challenging authority—the idea that the nation was founded by people who were fighting authority and that today's citizens continue to carry this ideal. Incorporated into this idea is that there could be challenges between federal and state conflicts and those involving individual rights versus government regulation
- Isolation versus internationalism—whether the United States functions independently, interdependently, or is reliant on resources, people, and things from around the world continues to challenge the nation both historically and presently
- Individual versus industry—weighing the rights and needs of individuals versus the progress of the nation as an industrial, scientifically advanced, and competitive entity

- Civil rights—the rights of the individual to receive equal treatment

While these ideas are not universally exclusive and do not capture every element of the social studies curriculum, they are illustrative of how concepts within social studies tend to run throughout multiple periods of time and through different historical events. Therefore, cases in this book might fit additional themes identified by classroom teachers in the same spirit.

THE IMPORTANCE OF TEACHING DISCIPLINARY READING

Disciplinary literacy teaches "Literacy skills specialized to history, science, mathematics, literature, or other subject matter" (Shanahan & Shanahan, 2008, p. 44). This type of teaching emphasizes tools that help students function within a specific discipline rather than adapting generalized reading strategies to the content at hand.

In English class, students might use inference in order to understand an author's purpose, while in math classes, students might use technical vocabulary in order to solve a complex problem. Reading, while assumed to be a universal skill, can also be very different depending on what one is reading. The act of reading a fiction detective novel is much different than reading a science textbook. Students must access and utilize different reading skills in order to read and understand the information that is presented to them. Timothy and Cynthia Shanahan, researchers who specialize in disciplinary literacy, make a solid argument for teaching reading skills that are associated with specific disciplines. They note:

> But what if our purpose is to apprentice students into the disciplinary literacy of historians by teaching them to compare and contrast treatments of the same topic in several primary and secondary sources? Then it might be better to guide students through the process of analyzing multiple texts, including eyewitness accounts of the Dust Bowl, editorial cartoons from the period, and speeches of President Roosevelt, along with some later historical analyses, perhaps including that textbook chapter. It would also seem wise to teach students the skill of sourcing—evaluating and weighing evidence by considering its source. In the study of history, it's just as important to ask questions about the source (Who wrote this? Who was the audience? What was the author's purpose? Is this source reliable?) as it is to determine what the documents say. Rather than balancing content-area reading and disciplinary literacy activities, it makes more sense to think about our instructional purposes and to select the approaches best aligned with those purposes. (Shanahan & Shanahan, 2017, p. 21)

Within the context of studying case law, students need to understand not only the format in which a case is typically presented, but also how and why a judge pens an opinion in a certain voice or tone, and the general audience for which a case is intended. Exercising the skill of how to read a case is just as important as the case itself. Specifically, disciplinary reading with case law requires students to understand the historical context surrounding a case, acknowledge the "voice" of judges writing an opinion, and have a basic knowledge of legal vocabulary and jargon.

THE TEACHER'S ROLE IN TEACHING CASE LAW

Teaching primary documents like case law is more than handing out a photocopied case with a set of fill-in-the-blank comprehension questions. Guiding students through the reading and application of a case takes time, attention, and care. It is a joint adventure in reading.

Neumann (2010) proposed a model methodology for teaching primary sources in his article advocating for preservice teachers to learn how to teach in this fashion. First, he asks teachers to build a conceptual framework surrounding the reading of primary documents; that is, to assist students in interpreting primary sources as "an active, imaginative, 'reconstruction' or the text based on the limited cues at their disposal" (Neumann, 2010, p. 506).

Second, he directs teachers to select primary documents that "strategically support the larger questions and concepts they plan to address in a particular unit" (Neumann, 2010, p. 506). In this selection, he advises teachers to begin with reading documents for which authorship is obvious, and as students build primary document reading skills, to then introduce more complex documents where students must seek the significance for themselves and authorship may not be as overt.

Third, he advises teachers to guide understanding. Teachers should model reading, conduct think-aloud sessions, identify guiding questions throughout the text, and as the year progresses, teachers should allow students more independence.

HOW CASES WERE SELECTED, PREPARED, AND EDITED FOR THIS TEXT

Case law can be messy reading for the average reader. Published cases are typically heavy with citations, legal vocabulary, and historical storytelling that helps establish the justification for a decision. However, in staying with the spirit of the Colonial Williamsburg Foundation, cases within this book have been edited by teacher-lawyers with distinct experience in teaching reading and legal content within the high school classroom. While cases in this text are not in their original, unedited form, they are in a form that is more accessible to students in the following ways:

- Citations and citation phrases that distracted from the flow of reading were edited or removed entirely. The intent of this was not to remove attribution, but to enable students to seamlessly read the content of a case without the frequent stopping required by citations that interrupt the cases. Full cases can be found online in the original form.
- Some historical or argumentative material was removed in order to allow students to focus on the case at hand. These materials, often called *dicta*, or extraneous material, are not necessary to understand the holding or decision of the Court. While this material can be helpful to understand historical contexts or the prior history of a case, when students are reading one case, it is important to allow the focus to remain, as much as possible, on the case being studied. Therefore, cases were edited to remove extraneous information that may have interfered with the reading.
- Majority opinions are presented as the primary teaching method of case law. While dissenting opinions are sometimes valuable in studying argumentation and the rationale for why a Justice may disagree with the U.S. Supreme Court's majority, concurring and dissenting opinions were removed from most of the cases presented in this book. Again, teachers can always find these materials in the free, online published case materials, but for the purposes of teaching case law within a classroom, focusing on the majority opinion helps students understand the importance of the Court's holding and how that decision is argued within the discussion of the decision.

Each chapter in this book focuses on a theme from the publication *National Curriculum Standards for Social Studies* (2010) from the National Council for the Social Studies (NCSS).

To correspond with each of the ten themes, three U.S. Supreme Court cases were selected for each theme, and appropriately edited for classroom use. Within each case are pre-reading questions, questions to consider during reading, and post-reading questions. These questions are intended to assist the teacher in guiding students to important points within the cases and to direct questioning at appropriate points in the cases. Following each case are a set of additional resources to enhance student learning, provide opportunities for further research, and promote connections with current events.

A NOTE FROM THE AUTHORS

Our backgrounds all have one thing in common: we all graduated from law school and entered the field of teaching as a primary profession. While we each did this for different reasons, our passion remains united in the idea that case law can and should be accessible by every person in the United States, including students in social studies classrooms. When we studied the multitude of cases we did in law school, all of us became intrigued by the storytelling involved in case law. Case law is much more than a set of laws and rules—the stories told within case law can be fascinating, enchanting, challenging, and maddening.

As readers, we found ourselves reading case law in the same way we read top-selling novels—with great interest and intrigue. This passion led us to develop a course called "Law and Literature," a high school elective English course pairing literature with legal themes to assist reading and writing development. This next led to us collaboratively writing the book *Law Meets Literature: A Novel Approach for the English Classroom.* Through our experiences sharing the contents of the first book, we met many social studies teachers who asked for our help, most specifically, "How do I teach case law in my classroom?"

This book is our attempt to help solve this problem. It is meant to serve as a teacher's aide in providing not only disciplinary reading tips, but also organization and order to the plethora of cases available for teaching. While we have not presented every single U.S. Supreme Court case here, nor have we included any of the multitude of state or local cases that may present meaningful learning interaction, we do focus on materials that are easy to find and access, cases we have edited through our lens as high school teachers and legal scholars, and links to additional resources commonly sought to support the additional research done in social studies classrooms.

In sum, we do not claim to be the world's greatest experts, but rather invigorated advocates to help social studies teachers put real cases in the hands of today's students. In doing so, we believe a more informed citizenry can develop, particularly one in which citizens are confident in understanding the emerging case law they will encounter the rest of their adult lives outside of the high school classroom.

Chapter Two

How to Use This Book

UNDERSTANDING THE THEMES OF THE NATIONAL CURRICULUM STANDARDS FOR SOCIAL STUDIES

The contents of this book are meant to be interactive and accessible to any classroom teacher. Each chapter contains several helpful elements to assist when teaching one of the identified U.S. Supreme Court cases. In addition, reading questions for pre-, during-, and post-reading are provided as a means to help teachers guide the disciplinary reading process. Each chapter also features additional resources to extend on issues found within each case. Last, teaching advice from the authors is featured in the "Notes From the Authors" section at the end of each chapter.

Cases in this text are organized in several ways. First, as this book's table of contents indicates, the main organization of this book is based on the *National Curriculum Standards for Social Studies: A Framework for Teaching, Learning, and Assessment*, a bulletin published by the National Council for the Social Studies (NCSS). This framework provides "opportunities for professional deliberation and planning about what should occur in a national social studies program in grades pre-K through 12" (NCSS, 2010, p. 3). The standards are arranged around themes, or "ways of categorizing knowledge about the human experience, and they constitute the organizing strands that should thread through a social studies program" (p. 3). The ten themes are broad categories that capture the value and challenges that are natural within the social studies curriculum. The ten themes are as follows:

1. Culture
2. Time, Continuity, and Change
3. People, Places, and Environments
4. Individual Development and Identity
5. Individuals, Groups, and Institutions
6. Power, Authority, and Governance
7. Production, Distribution, and Consumption
8. Science, Technology, and Society
9. Global Connections
10. Civic Ideals and Practices

The ten themes set forth by the NCSS are interconnected and do not stand in isolation. That is, during one unit, students might study culture, power and authority, and global connections at the same time. For the purposes of this book, three U.S. Supreme Court cases, commonly taught in high school social studies classrooms (U.S. history, civics, government, global issues, etc.) were selected to fit within each theme. While some cases may fit more than one theme, care was used to identify how a case fit the theme at hand and how it could be used to best teach to the broad concepts supported within that theme.

A second method of organization of the cases in this text is chronological. That is, teachers may not plan classroom instruction around the NCSS's framework, but rather around a set of state or local standards or curricular expectations. For that reason, there is a chronological case list found in the front matter of this text. Cases are listed in chronological order based on the date of the published decision. Teachers can pull cases from a specific time period or date range to further enhance instruction. Those cases are then found on the identified pages within the larger thematic organization of the text.

Last, cases are also organized around five universal threads found throughout social studies curricula. These threads, or "big ideas," are found in the front matter of this book as well, and list cases as they fit within these larger universal concepts. The five "big ideas" are:

1. Cultural dominance or imperialism—the idea that the United States is unique, special, and functions differently than any other nation in the world
2. Challenging authority—the idea that the nation was founded by people who were fighting authority and that today's citizens continue to carry this ideal. Incorporated in this idea could be challenges between federal and state conflicts and those involving individual rights versus government regulation
3. Isolation versus internationalism—whether the United States functions independently, interdependently, or is reliant on resources, people, and things from around the world continues to challenge the nation both historically and presently
4. Individual versus industry—weighing the rights and needs of individuals versus the progress of the nation as an industrial, scientifically advanced, and competitive entity
5. Civil rights—the rights of the individual to receive equal treatment

Cases used in this book may fit more than one of these "big ideas" and therefore may be listed under several of the larger ideas. Teachers are free, then, to pick and choose the cases that best fit the concept being taught.

In sum, there are multiple ways to use this book: to present appropriately edited cases to students in a guided manner, to accompany the themes identified by the National Council for the Social Studies—within a historical time period—or as enhancements for some of the larger ideas that carry through many social studies classrooms. The cases present a puzzle of sorts—when and where to use the cases to best fit the needs of the students. For the classroom teacher, this book provides multiple opportunities to use any case in several ways. The precise nature of how the cases have been edited for readability in addition to the scaffolding provided by the instructional components of the text should be a complement to any social studies classroom.

TEACHING STUDENTS TO READ A CASE

Teaching students to read case law requires understanding the basic components of every published case. While each case may look a bit different on paper, there are some universal pieces present in every case that students can identify as readers of case law:

- Parties/Litigants: The people, groups, or participants involved in a case. This might include the plaintiff, defendant, petitioner, respondent, Judge, witnesses, jury, lawyers, or advocates.
- Location/Venue: The location where the legal conflict arose. That is, a house, street, city, state, neighborhood, or any other "place" that serves as the setting behind the legal conflict.
- Facts: In the early portions of every opinion, students will find a set of facts telling the story of the legal conflict. This might include how the issue arose, why people are fighting, how one person's claims conflict with the government's assertions, or how a person is challenged by the authority of the government. These fact patterns are the "story" behind the case itself. Having students dive into understanding the people behind a case can increase student engagement with a case.
- Argument: The arguments within a case are what are often portrayed in today's Hollywood movies: a highly emotional debate between lawyers fighting for justice. Each side presents an argument, or why that side should prevail, which is then left to the court to make the final determination. As readers of case law, it is the argument portion of a case that presents persuasive argumentation, emotional appeals, and one-sided discussions of issues.
- Issue: The reason the parties are in court—the problem, argument, reason, or thing that the parties are in conflict over
- Decision: The final determination of a court as to which side prevails
- Rule of Law: The law, statute, custom, or central principle on which a decision is based
- Exploring the Story: These resources help students understand the people behind the cases. The extension exercises include investigations into the human issues presented in the cases, the conflict of existence, and understanding how average people end up in complex legal cases.
- Exploring the Law: These resources expand on the central legal issue in the case. That is, what is the central law or legal issue studied in the case and what else can or should students know about the legal concept?
- Exploring the Effects: These resources ask students to consider the effects of a case and to acknowledge that judicial decisions are not without significant effect. That is, once a case is decided, how does life change for the people of the country? What does the case say about the changing nature of culture and humanity? How did the world change as a result of the decision?
- Activities for Extending the Learning: These ideas are suggestions to extend student research opportunities and provide opportunities for additional content exploration. These activities promote interdisciplinary learning and allow the cases being taught to serve as a springboard for research and further learning.

As students read, it is helpful to have them identify each of these basic case elements before diving into more complex study of disciplinary issues. When using the cases prepared for this book, students can use highlighters or different identification methods to properly identify each of the basic case elements.

HOW CASES WERE PREPARED FOR THIS BOOK

Cases within this book were selected for a variety of reasons. First, cases that are frequently mentioned within major high school social studies textbooks were compiled into a master list. Most textbooks offer only a brief description of judicial decisions, so it was critical that this text provide more than a textbook publisher's interpretation of a decision, but rather to provide student access to the case itself.

Second, cases were selected based on relevance to the ten themes set forth by the National Curriculum Standards for Social Studies.

Last, cases were selected based on the relevance and interest of content to teen readers. While cases were not eliminated because the content was not exciting enough, cases were selected that would pique the interest of today's high school students. Cases were studied for the use of accessible language, high interest legal conflicts, and issues that students in today's world can relate to.

Maintaining the integrity of each case while preparing each case in a readable fashion for high school students was of the utmost importance when selecting cases. Each chapter features three cases that were compiled in original form from public source websites. All U.S. Supreme Court cases are available free, to the public, and can be accessed on a variety of websites.

The cases, in their original form, were then transferred to an editing dock wherein the authors pared away some of the components that distract teen readers. Editing cases included removing citations to additional references beyond the cases, dicta, some dissents, discussion within cases not focused on the case at hand, or distracting information. It is important to note that the original language of the cases was not changed. In an effort to allow students to better access the key feature of a case and to understand the legal issues presented within a case, it became important to prepare each case as a readable document that would not cause students to stumble or quit during reading.

Each case was then paired with a theme, "big idea," and chronological time period. Cases were examined to ensure this book provides a wide range of historical timeframes, application of the larger threads that appear throughout social studies classes, and appropriate relation to the NCSS themes. It is typical that the older cases have more complex vocabulary and language. More recent cases have a more modern tone. Careful attention was given to the language presented by the Justices at any given time period. As authors, we felt it was important to not eliminate cases because the language or issues were particularly challenging, but rather, whether with good teaching and assistance from the prepared reading questions and additional curricular links, students could learn from the experience.

A SAMPLE CASE

Cases in this book are presented in their original language in nearly full form. As noted previously, cases were edited from their original published form to reduce reading stumbling blocks, but to preserve original language and tone. In order to illustrate how a case is presented in this book, *Bethel School Dist. v. Fraser*, a U.S. Supreme Court case dealing with vulgar student speech, is presented here, in the same form as the cases presented throughout this book.

Pre-Reading Questions: Prior to each case is a set of two to four pre-reading questions to activate student interest and inquiry prior to reading the case at hand. These questions might ask students to consider their own opinions of an issue within the case prior to reading or to review a historical time period before reading a case.

CASE #1: *BETHEL SCHOOL DIST. V. FRASER,* 478 U.S. 675 (1986)

CHIEF JUSTICE BURGER delivered the opinion of the Court.

We granted certiorari to decide whether the First Amendment prevents a school district from disciplining a high school student for giving a lewd speech at a school assembly.

During-Reading Questions: Found in italicized text within each case are a series of During-Reading Questions. These questions are used to guide students as they read the text of the case. Teachers can present these questions to students as discussion questions, individual response questions, or reflective contemplation events. For this case specifically, teachers might ask students to consider why the government has any say in what happens in a school assembly. In addition, students might identify the purposes as to why schools hold school assemblies and how those might be linked to the curricula of the schools.

IA

On April 26, 1983, respondent Matthew N. Fraser, a student at Bethel High School in Pierce County, Washington, delivered a speech nominating a fellow student for student elective office. Approximately 600 high school students, many of whom were 14-year-olds, attended the assembly. Students were required to attend the assembly or to report to the study hall. The assembly was part of a school-sponsored educational program in self-government. Students who elected not to attend the assembly were required to report to study hall. During the entire speech, Fraser referred to his candidate in terms of an elaborate, graphic, and explicit sexual metaphor.

Two of Fraser's teachers, with whom he discussed the contents of his speech in advance, informed him that the speech was "inappropriate and that he probably should not deliver it," and that his delivery of the speech might have "severe consequences."

During-Reading Questions: Does it matter that the student talked to teachers before giving the speech and that no one specifically forbade him from doing so? Why or why not?

During Fraser's delivery of the speech, a school counselor observed the reaction of students to the speech. Some students hooted and yelled; some by gestures graphically simulated the sexual activities pointedly alluded to in respondent's speech. Other students appeared to be bewildered and embarrassed by the speech. One teacher reported that on the day following the speech, she found it necessary to forgo a portion of the scheduled class lesson in order to discuss the speech with the class.

A Bethel High School disciplinary rule prohibiting the use of obscene language in the school provides:

"Conduct which materially and substantially interferes with the educational process is prohibited, including the use of obscene, profane language or gestures."

During-Reading Questions: The "law" in question in this case is actually a school policy and how strictly it can be applied in a public school setting in light of the First Amendment's freedom of speech provision. Basically, can schools restrict freedom of speech when it takes place on the school's time and property? What does this mean for students? And what does it mean for freedom of speech?

The morning after the assembly, the Assistant Principal called Fraser into her office and notified him that the school considered his speech to have been a violation of this rule. Fraser was presented with copies of five letters submitted by teachers, describing his conduct at the assembly; he was given a chance to explain his conduct, and he admitted to having given the speech described and that he deliberately used sexual innuendo in the speech. Fraser was then informed that he would be suspended for three days, and that his name would be removed from the list of candidates for graduation speaker at the school's commencement exercises.

During-Reading Questions: How does the student conflict with school authority? What does the First Amendment seem to say about this?

IB

Respondent, by his father as guardian ad litem, then brought this action in the United States District Court for the Western District of Washington. Respondent alleged a violation of his First Amendment right to freedom of speech and sought both injunctive relief and monetary damages under 42 U.S.C. 1983. The District Court held that the school's sanctions violated respondent's right to freedom of speech under the First Amendment to the United States Constitution, that the school's disruptive-conduct rule is unconstitutionally vague and overbroad, and that the removal of respondent's name from the graduation speaker's list violated the Due Process Clause of the Fourteenth Amendment because the disciplinary rule makes no mention of such removal as a possible sanction. The District Court awarded respondent $278 in damages, $12,750 in litigation costs and attorney's fees, and enjoined the School District from preventing respondent from speaking at the commencement ceremonies. Respondent, who had been elected graduation speaker by a write-in vote of his classmates, delivered a speech at the commencement ceremonies on June 8, 1983.

II

This Court acknowledged in *Tinker v. Des Moines Independent Community School Dist.*, that students do not "shed their constitutional rights to freedom of speech or expression at the schoolhouse gate." The Court of Appeals read that case as precluding any discipline of Fraser for indecent speech and lewd conduct in the school assembly. That court appears to have proceeded on the theory that the use of lewd and obscene speech in order to make what the speaker considered to be a point in a nominating speech for a fellow student was essentially the same as the wearing of an armband in *Tinker* as a form of protest or the expression of a political position.

The marked distinction between the political "message" of the armbands in *Tinker* and the sexual content of respondent's speech in this case seems to have been given little weight by the Court of Appeals. In upholding the students' right to engage in a nondisruptive, passive expression of a political viewpoint in *Tinker*, this Court was careful to note that the case did "not concern speech or action that intrudes upon the work of the schools or the rights of other students."

Teaching Note: This is a great case to consider not only Constitutional issues, but also historical ones as well. This case took place in the 1980s. What other events had taken place in U.S. history that might have influenced how outsiders felt about what went on in this case?

III

These fundamental values of "habits and manners of civility" essential to a democratic society must, of course, include tolerance of divergent political and religious views, even when the views expressed may be unpopular. But these "fundamental values" must also take into account consideration of the sensibilities of others, and, in the case of a school, the sensibilities of fellow students. The undoubted freedom to advocate unpopular and controversial views in schools and classrooms must be balanced against the society's countervailing interest in teaching students the boundaries of socially appropriate behavior. Even the most heated political discourse in a democratic society requires consideration for the personal sensibilities of the other participants and audiences.

The First Amendment guarantees wide freedom in matters of adult public discourse. It does not follow, however, that simply because the use of an offensive form of expression may not be prohibited to adults making what the speaker considers a political point, the same latitude must be permitted to children in a public school.

During-Reading Questions: Should public school students have the same rights as adults? Why or why not? Historically, has this always been the case? And how do we balance these interests?

Surely it is a highly appropriate function of public school education to prohibit the use of vulgar and offensive terms in public discourse. Indeed, the "fundamental values necessary to the maintenance of a democratic political system" disfavor the use of terms of debate highly offensive or highly threatening to others. Nothing in the Constitution prohibits the states from insisting that certain modes of expression are inappropriate and subject to sanctions. The inculcation of these values is truly the "work of the schools."

During-Reading Questions: What should the "work of the schools" be? How do we know? What does history tell us about this?

The pervasive sexual innuendo in Fraser's speech was plainly offensive to both teachers and students—indeed to any mature person. By glorifying male sexuality, and in its verbal content, the speech was acutely insulting to teenage girl students. The speech could well be seriously damaging to its less mature audience, many of whom were only 14 years old and on the threshold of awareness of human sexuality. Some students were reported as bewildered by the speech and the reaction of mimicry it provoked.

We hold that petitioner School District acted entirely within its permissible authority in imposing sanctions upon Fraser in response to his offensively lewd and indecent speech. Unlike the sanctions imposed on the students wearing armbands in *Tinker*, the penalties imposed in this case were unrelated to any political viewpoint. The First Amendment does not prevent the school officials from determining that to permit a vulgar and lewd speech such as respondent's would undermine the school's basic educational mission. A high school assembly or classroom is no place for a sexually explicit monologue directed towards an unsuspecting audience of teenage students. Accordingly, it was perfectly appropriate for the school to disassociate itself to make the point to the pupils that vulgar speech and lewd conduct is wholly inconsistent with the "fundamental values" of public school education.

The judgment of the Court of Appeals for the Ninth Circuit is

Reversed.

Post-Reading Questions follow each case and provide an opportunity for synthesis and analysis of the entirety of the case. These questions generally focus on why the Court made the decision it did—that is, the rationale, reasoning, justification, and analysis of the final determination.

RESOURCES BEYOND THE CASE

The thirty cases prepared for this text can serve a variety of purposes: historical illustrations, thematic connections, and instruction on law and the justice system. Social studies classes are where students are often asked to make connections and to conduct further research on concepts studied in class. To assist with these activities, each chapter provides a series of extension opportunities that apply to any social studies classroom. These additional extension activities and suggestions called "Further Explorations" are found following each case and are presented in the following categories:

- Exploring the Story: These resources help students understand the people behind the cases. The extension exercises include investigations into the human issues presented in the cases, the conflict of existence, and understanding how average people end up in complex legal cases.
- Exploring the Law: These resources expand on the central legal issue in the case. That is, what is the central law or legal issue studied in the case and what else can or should students know about the legal concept?
- Exploring the Effects: These resources ask students to consider the effects of a case and to acknowledge that judicial decisions are not without significant effect. That is, once a case is decided, how does life change for the people of the country? What does the case say about the changing nature of culture and humanity? How did the world change as a result of the decision?
- Activities for Extending the Learning: These ideas are suggestions to extend student research opportunities and provide opportunities for additional content exploration. These activities promote interdisciplinary learning and allow the cases being taught to serve as a springboard for research and further learning.

A NOTE FROM THE AUTHORS

As we carefully read and selected cases to include in this book, we challenged ourselves to step into the shoes of our high school readers. That is, if we were to photocopy and hand out a printout of a case to a student, which, granted, is a common practice of many teachers, where would students face difficulties? What would cause them to stop reading? Where would they quit and why? Finally, as lawyers and reading teachers, how could we help?

It was through this experiment where we were reading as those we teach that we carefully worked through each case through the eyes of not only a teen reader, but also a lawyer and teacher intent on protecting the integrity and spirit of the law. Thus, while the cases in this book are edited to clearly focus on the legal issue at hand and to provide scaffolding before, during, and after the reading process, we acknowledge the importance of the classroom teacher. That is, case law is not intended to be an isolated experience for students, but rather an interactive reading event wherein teachers guide and coach the reader through the complexities of the legal reading.

We hope that our careful editing of these cases helps in this process, eases access to cases, and allows more students to read case law rather than textbook interpretations of case law. We believe this is a skill that will serve students throughout their lives and that each summer, as new U.S. Supreme Court cases are published and the legal landscape of American life evolves, students will be engaged and willing readers of the esteemed words of the Justices.

Chapter Three

Culture

> Theme 1: *Social studies programs should include experiences that provide for the study of culture and cultural diversity.*
> —*National Curriculum Standards for Social Studies* (2010), National Council for the Social Studies, p. 14

Theme 1 challenges students to consider the human condition, how culture adapts and changes over time, and how different cultural groups exist in the same communities. Theme 1 asks teachers to help students identify their cultural identities, likenesses, and differences. Students should analyze specific aspects of culture including language, religion, beliefs, and how these aspects of culture influence how the society functions as a whole. Theme 1 asks students to consider the following questions:

> What is culture? What roles does culture play in human and societal development? What are the common characteristics across cultures? How is unity developed within and among cultures? What is the role of diversity and how is it maintained within a culture? How do various aspects of culture such as belief systems, religious faith, or political ideals, influence other parts of a culture such as its institutions or literature, music, and art? How does culture change over time to accommodate different ideas, and beliefs? How does cultural diffusion occur within and across communities, regions, and nations? (NCSS, 2010, p. 14)

The United States has always been a diverse nation made up of many cultures, languages, nationalities, and religions. This diversity has never existed without conflict. Through the past two centuries, the United States Supreme Court (the Court) has studied the impact of how the law interacts with or interferes with the variety of cultures within the country. Under the United States Constitution, the government may not endorse a specific religion, promote one culture over another, or deny protections of any one group in favor of another. The questions facing the Court are sometimes complex and challenge closely held beliefs of the American people.

The three cases included in this chapter represent an intersection of religion, language, culture, and nationality. All of the cases can help students consider the true basis for one's culture and can help students consider how culture and cultural diversity can be a benefit or drawback to the larger functions of the government.

In *Meyer v. Nebraska* (1923), a post–World War I case challenging a law prohibiting the instruction of any language besides English in school classrooms, students will encounter a time in history when language was seen as one way to ensure loyalty of the citizens. As such, questions arose as to whether languages other than English defined or defied the "American way." What does American culture mean?

Brown v. Board of Education of Topeka (1954) helps students consider the notion of "separate but equal," a once legal standard maintaining racial segregation in the nation's public schools. The case, a combination of several cases brought at one time, illustrates that one must consider not only the equality of resources, but whether the "separateness" can ever truly be equal.

In *County of Allegheny v. American Civil Liberties Union* (1989), students are challenged to explore the scope of the First Amendment's religious freedom components when a community's Christmas and Chanukah displays are challenged. Of particular note in this case is the Court's invitation to understand both cultural and historical significance of religious holidays and to recognize that the significance of such events cannot be so easily separated from government endorsement when put on public display.

CASE #1: *MEYER V. STATE OF NEBRASKA*

Pre-Reading Questions

1. How would you define the cultural identity of the United States?
2. What would the value of only allowing English as the official language be to the functions and operations of the government? What are the drawbacks of an English-only requirement?
3. This case was decided shortly after World War I ended. What historic events and cultural changes were occurring that may have warranted a state seeking to instruct its people only in English? Was loyalty to the country an issue?

***Meyer v. State of Nebraska*, 262 U.S. 390 (1923)**

MR. JUSTICE McREYNOLDS delivered the opinion of the Court.

Plaintiff in error was tried and convicted in the District Court for Hamilton County, Nebraska, under an information which charged that on May 25, 1920, while an instructor in Zion Parochial School, he unlawfully taught the subject of reading in the German language to Raymond Parpart, a child of ten years, who had not attained and successfully passed the eighth grade. The information is based upon "An act relating to the teaching of foreign languages in the State of Nebraska," approved April 9, 1919, which follows [Laws 1919, c. 249.]:

> Section 1. No person, individually or as a teacher, shall, in any private, denominational, parochial or public school, teach any subject to any person in any language other than the English language.
>
> Sec. 2. Languages, other than the English language, may be taught as languages only after a pupil shall have attained and successfully passed the eighth grade as evidenced by a certificate of graduation issued by the county superintendent of the county in which the child resides.
>
> Sec. 3. Any person who violates any of the provisions of this act shall be deemed guilty of a misdemeanor and upon conviction, shall be subject to a fine of not less than twenty-five dollars ($25), nor more than one hundred dollars ($100) or be confined in the county jail for any period not exceeding thirty days for each offense.
>
> Sec. 4. Whereas, an emergency exists, this act shall be in force from and after its passage and approval.

During-Reading Question: This law punishes anyone who teaches any language other than English to someone before they are in the eighth grade as a criminal offense. Why do you think this was the penalty?

The Supreme Court of the State affirmed the judgment of conviction. It declared the offense charged and established was "the direct and intentional teaching of the German language as a distinct subject to a child who had not passed the eighth grade," in the parochial school maintained by Zion Evangelical Lutheran Congregation, a collection of Biblical stories being used therefor. And it held that the statute forbidding this did not conflict with the Fourteenth Amendment, but was a valid exercise of the police power. The following excerpts from the opinion sufficiently indicate the reasons advanced to support the conclusion.

> The salutary purpose of the statute is clear. The legislature had seen the baneful effects of permitting foreigners, who had taken residence in this country, to rear and educate their children in the language of their native land. The result of that condition was found to be inimical to our own safety. To allow the children of foreigners, who had emigrated here, to be taught from early childhood the language of the country of their parents was to rear them with that language as their mother tongue. It was to educate them so that they must always think in that language, and, as a consequence, naturally inculcate in them the ideas and sentiments foreign to the best interests of this country. The statute, therefore, was intended not only to require that the education of all children be conducted in the English language, but that, until they had grown into that language and until it had become a part of them, they should not in the schools be taught any other language. The obvious purpose of this statute was that the English language should be and become the mother tongue of all children reared in this state. The enactment of such a statute comes reasonably within the police power of the state.

During-Reading Question: The Court seems to indicate that teaching kids to "think" in English is necessary before teaching them other languages. Why?

> It is suggested that the law is an unwarranted restriction, in that it applies to all citizens of the state and arbitrarily interferes with the rights of citizens who are not of foreign ancestry, and prevents them, without reason, from having their children taught foreign languages in school. That argument is not well taken, for it assumes that every citizen finds himself restrained by the statute. The hours which a child is able to devote to study in the confinement of school are limited. It must have ample time for exercise or play. Its daily capacity for learning is comparatively small. A selection of subjects for its education, therefore, from among the many that might be taught, is obviously necessary. The legislature no doubt had in mind the practical operation of the law. The law affects few citizens, except those of foreign lineage. Other citizens, in their selection of studies, except perhaps in rare instances, have never deemed it of importance to teach their children foreign languages before such children have reached the eighth grade. In the legislative mind, the salutary effect of the statute no doubt outweighed the restriction upon the citizens generally, which, it appears, was a restriction of no real consequence.

The problem for our determination is whether the statute as construed and applied unreasonably infringes the liberty guaranteed to the plaintiff in error by the Fourteenth Amendment. "No State shall . . . deprive any person of life, liberty, or property, without due process of law."

During-Reading Question: How can forcing someone to not learn English be considered a deprivation of life, liberty, or property?

While this Court has not attempted to define with exactness the liberty thus guaranteed, the term has received much consideration and some of the included things have been definitely stated. Without doubt, it denotes not merely freedom from bodily restraint but also the right of the individual to contract, to engage in any of the common occupations of life, to acquire useful knowledge, to marry, establish a home and bring up children, to worship God according to the dictates of his own conscience, and generally to enjoy those privileges long recognized at common law as essential to the orderly pursuit of happiness by free men. The established doctrine is that this liberty may not be interfered with, under the guise of protecting the public interest, by legislative action which is arbitrary or without reasonable relation to some purpose within the competency of the State to effect. Determination by the legislature of what constitutes proper exercise of police power is not final or conclusive but is subject to supervision by the courts.

During-Reading Question: What is "liberty"?

The American people have always regarded education and acquisition of knowledge as matters of supreme importance which should be diligently promoted. The Ordinance of 1787 declares, "Religion, morality, and knowledge being necessary to good government and the happiness of mankind, schools and the means of education shall forever be encouraged." Corresponding to the right of control, it is the natural duty of the parent to give his children education suitable to their station in life; and nearly all the States, including Nebraska, enforce this obligation by compulsory laws.

Practically, education of the young is only possible in schools conducted by especially qualified persons who devote themselves thereto. The calling always has been regarded as useful and honorable, essential, indeed, to the public welfare. Mere knowledge of the German language cannot reasonably be regarded as harmful. Heretofore it has been commonly looked upon as helpful and desirable. Plaintiff in error taught this language in school as part of his occupation. His right thus to teach and the right of parents to engage him so to instruct their children, we think, are within the liberty of the Amendment.

During-Reading Question: What does the Court seem to be saying about the role of teachers in society?

The challenged statute forbids the teaching in school of any subject except in English; also the teaching of any other language until the pupil has attained and successfully passed the eighth grade, which is not usually accomplished before the age of twelve. The Supreme Court of the State has held that "the so-called ancient or dead languages" are not "within the spirit or the purpose of the act." *Nebraska District of Evangelical Lutheran Synod v. McKelvie*. Latin, Greek, Hebrew are not proscribed; but German, French, Spanish, Italian and every other alien speech are within the ban. Evidently the legislature has attempted materially to interfere with the calling of modern language teachers, with the opportunities of pupils to acquire knowledge, and with the power of parents to control the education of their own.

It is said the purpose of the legislation was to promote civic development by inhibiting training and education of the immature in foreign tongues and ideals before they could learn English and acquire American ideals; and "that the English language should be and become the mother tongue of all children reared in this State." It is also affirmed that the foreign born population is very large, that certain communities commonly use foreign words, follow foreign leaders, move in a foreign atmosphere, and that the children are thereby hindered from becoming citizens of the most useful type and the public safety is imperiled.

During-Reading Questions: Would knowing more than one language hinder one's loyalty to the United States? What historical events might make one believe this to be true?

That the State may do much, go very far, indeed, in order to improve the quality of its citizens, physically, mentally and morally, is clear; but the individual has certain fundamental rights which must be respected. The protection of the Constitution extends to all, to those who speak other languages as well as to those born with English on the tongue. Perhaps it would be highly advantageous if all had ready understanding of our ordinary speech, but this cannot be coerced by methods which conflict with the Constitution—a desirable end cannot be promoted by prohibited means.

For the welfare of his Ideal Commonwealth, Plato suggested a law which should provide: "That the wives of our guardians are to be common, and their children are to be common, and no parent is to know his own child, nor any child his parent. . . . The proper officers will take the offspring of the goods parents to the pen or fold, and there they will deposit them with certain nurses who dwell in a separate quarter; but the offspring of the inferior, or of the better when they chance to be deformed, will be put away in some mysterious, unknown place, as they should be." In order to submerge the individual and develop ideal citizens, Sparta assembled the males at seven into barracks and [e]ntrusted their subsequent education and training to official guardians. Although such measures have been deliberately approved by men of great genius, their ideas touching the relation between individual and State were wholly different from those upon which our institutions rest; and it hardly will be affirmed that any legislature could impose such restrictions upon the people of a State without doing violence to both letter and spirit of the Constitution.

The desire of the legislature to foster a homogeneous people with American ideals prepared readily to understand current discussions of civic matters is easy to appreciate. Unfortunate experiences during the late war and aversion toward every characteristic of truculent adversaries were certainly enough to quicken that aspiration. But the means adopted, we think, exceed the limitations upon the power of the State and conflict with rights assured to plaintiff in error. The interference is plain enough and no adequate reason therefor in time of peace and domestic tranquility has been shown.

During-Reading Question: What events does the Court acknowledge might have influenced the development of this law?

The power of the State to compel attendance at some school and to make reasonable regulations for all schools, including a requirement that they shall give instructions in English, is not questioned. Nor has challenge been made of the State's power to prescribe a curriculum for institutions which it supports. Those matters are not within the present controversy. Our concern is with the prohibition approved by the Supreme Court. No emergency has arisen which renders knowledge by a child of some language other than English so clearly harmful as to justify its inhibition with the consequent infringement of rights long freely enjoyed. We are constrained to conclude that the statute as applied is arbitrary and without reasonable relation to any end within the competency of the State.

As the statute undertakes to interfere only with teaching which involves a modern language, leaving complete freedom as to other matters, there seems no adequate foundation for the suggestion that the purpose was to protect the child's health by limiting his mental activities. It is well known that proficiency in a foreign language seldom comes to one not instructed at an early age, and experience shows that this is not injurious to the health, morals or understanding of the ordinary child.

The judgment of the Court below must be reversed and the cause remanded for further proceedings not inconsistent with this opinion.

Reversed.

Post-Reading Questions

1. What was the main reason the Court decided the statute was not Constitutional?
2. What does the Court seem to say are the role of schools in the United States?

Further Explorations

Exploring the Story

The winning lawyer from this case, Arthur Mullen, wrote in his autobiography about his experience arguing the case. An excerpt can be found here in the *Washington Post*: Kopel, D. (2016, February 4). Meyer v. Nebraska: As told by the lawyer who won it. *The Washington Post.* Retrieved from https://www.washingtonpost.com/news/volokh-conspiracy/wp/2016/02/04/meyer-v-nebraska-as-told-by-the-lawyer-who-won-it/?utm_term=.71435a99bc53

The author of the article mentions that the Court defined "eight points of liberty." How do these "points" exist today in American life? What challenges do we face?

Exploring the Law

Immigration and people moving into the United States from other countries has been a contentious issue for centuries. Consider some of the rhetoric from the 2016 U.S. presidential campaign about building a wall to keep people from Mexico from illegally crossing the southern border and President Trump's controversial travel bans. What immigration laws exist today and how do they compare to the law present back in the 1920s in *Meyer?*

Exploring the Effects

There are many states today with English-only laws. Why are these permitted today? Should these laws be deemed unconstitutional? Why or why not? Read some of the following articles on the effects of English-only laws. Do any of these states provide compelling justification for requiring one language as an official state language?

- Mitchell, C. (2017, October 24). Some states with "English-only" laws won't offer tests in other languages. *Education Week.* Retrieved from https://www.edweek.org/ew/articles/2017/10/25/some-states-with-english-only-laws-wont-offer.html
- Schwarz, H. (2014, August 12). States where English is the official language. GovBeat. *The Washington Post.* Retrieved from https://www.washingtonpost.com/blogs/govbeat/wp/2014/08/12/states-where-english-is-the-official-language/?utm_term=.3d351745004a

Activities for Extending the Learning

- This case provides a great opportunity to explore the diversity and cultural history of the United States. Have students investigate laws in other countries regarding how languages are taught or permitted throughout the countries. What rationales are offered for specific language laws in those countries?
- Have students investigate current immigration proposals and those of recent times. Is immigration always discouraged or encouraged? How and why? PBS.org has an excellent set of resources to help students investigate and understand issues related to immigration today. View those at: PBS. (n.d.). For Educators. [a collection of educational resources associated with the television series episode, The New Americans]. In L. Vossen & S. J. Fifer (Executive producers), *Independent Lens*. Retrieved from http://www.pbs.org/independentlens/newamericans/foreducators_index.html

CASE #2: *BROWN V. BOARD OF EDUCATION OF TOPEKA*

Pre-Reading Questions

1. Students will need a general understanding of "separate but equal" under *Plessy v. Ferguson* (1896) in order to understand how *Brown v. Board of Education* changes and applies that prior U.S. Supreme Court case. Discuss how the country changed during the time between the two cases that may have warranted reconsideration by the Court.
2. Is "separate but equal" possible? Ask students to explore how this might be attained in gender-based, age-based, or skill-based schools.

***Brown v. Board of Education of Topeka,* 347 U.S. 483 (1954)**

MR. CHIEF JUSTICE WARREN delivered the opinion of the Court.

[1]

These cases come to us from the States of Kansas, South Carolina, Virginia, and Delaware. They are premised on different facts and different local conditions, but a common legal question justifies their consideration together in this consolidated opinion.

In each of the cases, minors of the Negro race, through their legal representatives, seek the aid of the courts in obtaining admission to the public schools of their community on a nonsegregated basis. In each instance, they had been denied admission to schools attended by white children under laws requiring or permitting segregation according to race. This segregation was alleged to deprive the plaintiffs of the equal protection of the laws under the Fourteenth Amendment. In each of the cases other than the Delaware case, a three-judge federal district court denied relief to the plaintiffs on the so-called "separate but equal" doctrine announced by this Court in *Plessy* v. *Ferguson*, 163 U.S. 537. Under that doctrine, equality of treatment is accorded when the races are provided substantially equal facilities, even though these facilities be separate. In the Delaware case, the Supreme Court of Delaware adhered to that doctrine, but ordered that the plaintiffs be admitted to the white schools because of their superiority to the Negro schools.

During-Reading Question: Plessy v. Ferguson *permitted "separate but equal" on public transportation (railcars). Why do you think the Court is reconsidering its own decision here when the issue moved to public schools?*

The plaintiffs contend that segregated public schools are not "equal" and cannot be made "equal," and that hence they are deprived of the equal protection of the laws. Because of the obvious importance of the question presented, the Court took jurisdiction. Argument was heard in the 1952 Term, and reargument was heard this Term on certain questions propounded by the Court.

[2]

Reargument was largely devoted to the circumstances surrounding the adoption of the Fourteenth Amendment in 1868. It covered exhaustively consideration of the Amendment in Congress, ratification by the states, then existing practices in racial segregation, and the views of proponents and opponents of the Amendment.

During-Reading Question: What does the Fourteenth Amendment say and how does it apply to public schools?

This discussion and our own investigation convince us that, although these sources cast some light, it is not enough to resolve the problem with which we are faced. At best, they are inconclusive. The most avid proponents of the post-War Amendments undoubtedly intended them to remove all legal distinctions among "all persons born or naturalized in the United States." Their opponents, just as certainly, were antagonistic to both the letter and the spirit of the Amendments and wished them to have the most limited effect. What others in Congress and the state legislatures had in mind cannot be determined with any degree of certainty.

An additional reason for the inconclusive nature of the Amendment's history, with respect to segregated schools, is the status of public education at that time. In the South, the movement toward free common schools, supported by general taxation, had not yet taken hold. Education of white children was largely in the hands of private groups. Education of Negroes was almost nonexistent, and practically all of the race were illiterate. In fact, any education of Negroes was forbidden by law in some states. Today, in contrast, many Negroes have achieved outstanding success in the arts and sciences as well as in the business and professional world. It is true that public school education at the time of the Amendment had advanced further in the North, but the effect of the Amendment on Northern States was generally ignored in the congressional debates. Even in the North, the conditions of public education did not approximate those existing today. The curriculum was usually rudimentary; ungraded schools were common in rural areas; the school term was but three months a year in many states; and compulsory school attendance was virtually unknown. As a consequence, it is not surprising that there should be so little in the history of the Fourteenth Amendment relating to its intended effect on public education.

During-Reading Questions: How did the country change after the Fourteenth Amendment? Do you think these were anticipated or unanticipated results of the Amendment?

In the first cases in this Court construing the Fourteenth Amendment, decided shortly after its adoption, the Court interpreted it as proscribing all state-imposed discriminations against the Negro race. The doctrine of "separate but equal" did not make its appearance in this Court until 1896 in the case of *Plessy* v. *Ferguson,* involving not education but transportation. American courts have since labored with the doctrine for over half a century. In this Court, there have been six cases involving the "separate but equal" doctrine in the field of public education. In more recent cases, all on the graduate school level, inequality was found in that specific benefits enjoyed by white students were denied to Negro students of the same educational qualifications. In none of these cases was it necessary to re-examine the doctrine to grant relief to the Negro plaintiff. And in *Sweatt* v. *Painter,* the Court expressly reserved decision on the question whether *Plessy* v. *Ferguson* should be held inapplicable to public education.

In the instant cases, that question is directly presented. Here, unlike *Sweatt* v. *Painter*, there are findings below that the Negro and white schools involved have been equalized, or are being equalized, with respect to buildings, curricula, qualifications and salaries of teachers, and other "tangible" factors. Our decision, therefore, cannot turn on merely a comparison of these tangible factors in the Negro and white schools involved in each of the cases. We must look instead to the effect of segregation itself on public education.

[3]

In approaching this problem, we cannot turn the clock back to 1868 when the Amendment was adopted, or even to 1896 when *Plessy* v. *Ferguson* was written. We must consider public education in the light of its full development and its present place in American life throughout the Nation. Only in this way can it be determined if segregation in public schools deprives these plaintiffs of the equal protection of the laws.

[4]

Today, education is perhaps the most important function of state and local governments. Compulsory school attendance laws and the great expenditures for education both demonstrate our recognition of the importance of education to our democratic society. It is required in the performance of our most basic public responsibilities, even service in the armed forces. It is the very foundation of good citizenship. Today it is a principal instrument in awakening the child to cultural values, in preparing him for later professional training, and in helping him to adjust normally to his environment. In these days, it is doubtful that any child may reasonably be expected to succeed in life if he is denied the opportunity of an education. Such an opportunity, where the state has undertaken to provide it, is a right which must be made available to all on equal terms.

During-Reading Question: The Court seems to place a great deal of weight on the importance of public school education. Why?

[5]

We come then to the question presented: Does segregation of children in public schools solely on the basis of race, even though the physical facilities and other "tangible" factors may be equal, deprive the children of the minority group of equal educational opportunities? We believe that it does.

In *Sweatt* v. *Painter,* in finding that a segregated law school for Negroes could not provide them equal educational opportunities, this Court relied in large part on "those qualities which are incapable of objective measurement but which make for greatness in a law school." In *McLaurin* v. *Oklahoma State Regents,* the Court, in requiring that a Negro admitted to a white graduate school be treated like all other students, again resorted to intangible considerations: ". . . his ability to study, to engage in discussions and exchange views with other students, and, in general, to learn his profession." Such considerations apply with added force to children in grade and high schools. To separate them from others of similar age and qualifications solely because of their race generates a feeling of inferiority as to their status in the community that may affect their hearts and minds in a way unlikely ever to be undone. The effect of this separation on their educational opportunities was well stated by a finding in the Kansas case by a court which nevertheless felt compelled to rule against the Negro plaintiffs:

> Segregation of white and colored children in public schools has a detrimental effect upon the colored children. The impact is greater when it has the sanction of the law; for the policy of separating the races is usually interpreted as denoting the inferiority of the negro group. A sense of inferiority affects the motivation of a child to learn. Segregation with the sanction of law, therefore, has a tendency to [retard] the educational and mental development of negro children and to deprive them of some of the benefits they would receive in a racial[ly] integrated school system.

Whatever may have been the extent of psychological knowledge at the time of *Plessy* v. *Ferguson*, this finding is amply supported by modern authority. Any language in *Plessy* v. *Ferguson* contrary to this finding is rejected.

During-Reading Question: Why does the Court seem to think that public K–12 education is arguably more important than graduate school education?

[6]

We conclude that in the field of public education the doctrine of "separate but equal" has no place. Separate educational facilities are inherently unequal. Therefore, we hold that the plaintiffs and others similarly situated for whom the actions have been brought are, by reason of the segregation complained of, deprived of the equal protection of the laws guaranteed by the Fourteenth Amendment. This disposition makes unnecessary any discussion whether such segregation also violates the Due Process Clause of the Fourteenth Amendment.

Because these are class actions, because of the wide applicability of this decision, and because of the great variety of local conditions, the formulation of decrees in these cases presents problems of considerable complexity. On reargument, the consideration of appropriate relief was necessarily subordinated to the primary question—the constitutionality of segregation in public education. We have now announced that such segregation is a denial of the equal protection of the laws. In order that we may have the full assistance of the parties in formulating decrees, the cases will be restored to the docket, and the parties are requested to present further argument on Questions 4 and 5 previously propounded by the Court for the reargument this Term. The Attorney General of the United States is again invited to participate. The Attorneys General of the states requiring or permitting segregation in public education will also be permitted to appear as *amici curiae* upon request to do so by September 15, 1954, and submission of briefs by October 1, 1954.

It is so ordered.

Post-Reading Questions

1. How did the Court overturn *Plessy v. Ferguson?*
2. How did the Court serve as a protector of citizens? Why?

3. What did the Court determine are the purposes of public education within American life? Are those purposes still in place today? Why or why not?

Further Explorations

Exploring the Story

- The website Voices of History (www.voicesofhistory.org) provides photographs of an all-white public school classroom and a segregated classroom during the time of *Brown* in the following resource: Winborne, W. (ca. 2014). Documents to Examine (A–K). [Handout B within the lesson, Equal Protection and Affirmative Action]. Voices of History. (Documents E, F, and G). Retrieved from https://voicesofhistory.org/wp-content/uploads/2014/12/SCDBQ-005-HandoutB.pdf. Have students view the photographs and compare and contrast the settings—were the settings separate but equal? If so, how? If not, why not?
- Part of the argument in this case was based on the research of child psychologists Kenneth and Mamie Clark, who believed that "separate but equal" would cause psychological damage to children's self-esteem and self-image. Would researchers today say the same thing?
- Thurgood Marshall argued the *Brown v. Board of Education* case on behalf of the NAACP. Have students study his career from lawyer to first African American U.S. Supreme Court Justice.

Exploring the Law

- "Separate but equal" may have ended school segregation, but there are still instances where we separate people today based on their ability, gender, language, or other distinguishing feature. Is this Constitutional under *Brown v. Board of Education?* How?
- Locate the U.S. map documenting segregated schools within the following article at the Khan Academy: Recchiuti, J. (n.d.). Brown v. Board of Education of Topeka. In Kahn Academy. Retrieved from https://www.khanacademy.org/humanities/ap-us-history/period-8/apush-civil-rights-movement/a/brown-v-board-of-education

Exploring the Effects

Public school segregation ended as a result of this case. This took time, however. How did communities integrate schools and how long did it take? How can the effects of this case be seen in today's schools? The fiftieth anniversary of the *Brown v. Board of Education* case was in 2014. Numerous news articles and publications looked into how public education had changed during those five decades. Read some of these articles and have students consider if the country has fully met the Court's desires for public education as expressed in *Brown.*

- Brownstein, R. (2014, April 25). How *Brown v. Board of Education* changed—and didn't change—American education. *The Atlantic*. Retrieved from https://www.theatlantic.com/education/archive/2014/04/two-milestones-in-education/361222/
- Winters, R. (2004, May 10). No longer separate, but not yet equal. *Time, 163*(19). Retrieved from http://content.time.com/time/magazine/article/0,9171,632100,00.html

Activities for Extending the Learning

Brown v. Board of Education is a good springboard for research on the Civil Rights Act of 1964 and the Voting Rights Act of 1965. In addition, one larger learning question might be,

"How does the government protect its citizens?" Have students research and demonstrate the multiple ways the government exercises care to protect its people (or not).

CASE #3: *COUNTY OF ALLEGHENY V. AMERICAN CIVIL LIBERTIES UNION*

Pre-Reading Questions

1. Have students consider the visual display of these holiday events as they occurred at the time. What impressions do students feel prior to reading this case? Photos of the holiday displays involved in this case can be viewed at: Linder, D. (ca. 2011). Religious symbols in public places. In *Exploring Constitutional Conflicts*. Retrieved from http://law2.umkc.edu/faculty/projects/fTrials/conlaw/religioussymbols.htm
2. Outlining the *Lemon* test the Court uses to determine if a government's action violates the Establishment Clause of the First Amendment would be helpful prior to reading this case. The three-pronged test says the government violates the Establishment Clause unless its action can meet all three prongs: 1. The action has a significant secular (i.e., non-religious) purpose; 2. The action does not have the primary effect of advancing or inhibiting religion; and, 3. The action does not foster excessive entanglement between government and religion.

***County of Allegheny v. American Civil Liberties Union*, 492 U.S. 573 (1989)**

JUSTICE HARRY BLACKMUN delivered the opinion of the Court.

IA

The county courthouse is owned by Allegheny County and is its seat of government. It houses the offices of the county commissioners, controller, treasurer, sheriff, and clerk of court. Civil and criminal trials are held there. The "main," "most beautiful," and "most public" part of the courthouse is its Grand Staircase, set into one arch and surrounded by others, with arched windows serving as a backdrop.

Since 1981, the county has permitted the Holy Name Society, a Roman Catholic group, to display a creche in the county courthouse during the Christmas holiday season. Christmas, we note perhaps needlessly, is the holiday when Christians celebrate the birth of Jesus of Nazareth, whom they believe to be the Messiah. Western churches have celebrated Christmas Day on December 25 since the fourth century. As observed in this Nation, Christmas has a secular, as well as a religious, dimension.

The creche in the county courthouse, like other creches, is a visual representation of the scene in the manger in Bethlehem shortly after the birth of Jesus, as described in the Gospels of Luke and Matthew. The creche includes figures of the infant Jesus, Mary, Joseph, farm animals, shepherds, and wise men, all placed in or before a wooden representation of a manger, which has at its crest an angel bearing a banner that proclaims "Gloria in Excelsis Deo!"

During the 1986–1987 holiday season, the creche was on display on the Grand Staircase from November 26 to January 9. It had a wooden fence on three sides and bore a plaque stating: "This Display Donated by the Holy Name Society." Sometime during the week of December 2, the county placed red and white poinsettia plants around the fence. The county also placed a small evergreen tree, decorated with a red bow, behind each of the two endposts of the fence. These trees stood alongside the manger backdrop and were slightly shorter than it was. The angel thus was at the apex of the creche display. Altogether, the creche, the fence, the poinsettias, and the trees occupied a substantial amount of space on the Grand Staircase. No figures of Santa Claus or other decorations appeared on the Grand Staircase.

The county uses the creche as the setting for its annual Christmas-carol program. During the 1986 season, the county invited high school choirs and other musical groups to perform during weekday lunch hours from December 3 through December 23. The county dedicated this program to world peace and to the families of prisoners-of-war and of persons missing in action in Southeast Asia.

Near the Grand Staircase is an area of the county courthouse known as the "gallery forum" used for art and other cultural exhibits. The creche, with its fence-and-floral frame, however, was distinct and not connected with any exhibit in the gallery forum. In addition, various departments and offices within the county courthouse had their own Christmas decorations, but these also are not visible from the Grand Staircase.

IB

The City-County Building is separate and a block removed from the county courthouse and, as the name implies, is jointly owned by the city of Pittsburgh and Allegheny County. The city's portion of the building houses the city's principal offices, including the mayor's. The city is responsible for the building's Grant Street entrance which has three rounded arches supported by columns.

For a number of years, the city has had a large Christmas tree under the middle arch outside the Grant Street entrance. Following this practice, city employees on November, erected a 45-foot tree under the middle arch and decorated it with lights and ornaments. A few days later, the city placed at the foot of the tree a sign bearing the mayor's name and entitled "Salute to Liberty." Beneath the title, the sign stated: "During this holiday season, the city of Pittsburgh salutes liberty. Let these festive lights remind us that we are the keepers of the flame of liberty and our legacy of freedom."

At least since 1982, the city has expanded its Grant Street holiday display to include a symbolic representation of Chanukah, an 8-day Jewish holiday that begins on the 25th day of the Jewish lunar month of Kislev. The 25th of Kislev usually occurs in December, and thus Chanukah is the annual Jewish holiday that falls closest to Christmas Day each year. In 1986, Chanukah began at sundown on December 26.

According to Jewish tradition, on the 25th of Kislev in 164 B.C.E. (before the common era [165 B.C.]), the Maccabees rededicated the Temple of Jerusalem after recapturing it from the Greeks, or, more accurately, from the Greek-influenced Seleucid Empire, in the course of a political rebellion. Chanukah is the holiday which celebrates that event. The early history of the celebration of Chanukah is unclear; it appears that the holiday's central ritual—the lighting of lamps—was well established long before a single explanation of that ritual took hold.

The Talmud explains the lamplighting ritual as a commemoration of an event that occurred during the rededication of the Temple. The Temple housed a seven-branch menorah, which was to be kept burning continuously. When the Maccabees rededicated the Temple, they had only enough oil to last for one day. But, according to the Talmud, the oil miraculously lasted for eight days (the length of time it took to obtain additional oil). To celebrate and publicly proclaim this miracle, the Talmud prescribes that it is a mitzvah (*i.e.*, a religious deed or commandment), for Jews to place a lamp with eight lights just outside the entrance to their homes or in a front window during the eight days of Chanukah. Where practicality or safety from persecution so requires, the lamp may be placed in a window or inside the home. The Talmud also ordains certain blessings to be recited each night of Chanukah before lighting the lamp. One such benediction has been translated into English as "We are blessing God who has sanctified us and commanded us with mitzvot and has told us to light the candles of Hanukkah."

Although Jewish law does not contain any rule regarding the shape or substance of a Chanukah lamp (or "hanukkiyyah"), it became customary to evoke the memory of the Temple menorah. The Temple menorah was of a tree-and-branch design; it had a central candlestick with six branches. In contrast, a Chanukah menorah of tree-and-branch design has eight branches—one for each day of the holiday—plus a ninth to hold the shamash (an extra candle used to light the other eight). Also in contrast to the Temple menorah, the Chanukah menorah is not a sanctified object; it need not be treated with special care.

Lighting the menorah is the primary tradition associated with Chanukah, but the holiday is marked by other traditions as well. One custom among some Jews is to give children Chanukah gelt, or money. Another is for the children to gamble their gelt using a dreidel, a top with four sides. Each of the four sides contains a Hebrew letter; together the four letters abbreviate a phrase that refers to the Chanukah miracle.

Chanukah, like Christmas, is a cultural event as well as a religious holiday. Indeed, the Chanukah story always has had a political or national, as well as a religious, dimension: it tells of national heroism in addition to divine intervention. Also, Chanukah, like Christmas, is a winter holiday; according to some historians, it was associated in ancient times with the winter solstice. Just as some Americans celebrate Christmas without regard to its religious significance, some nonreligious American Jews celebrate Chanukah as an expression of ethnic identity, and "as a cultural or national event, rather than as a specifically religious event."

During-Reading Questions: The Court seems to be acknowledging both religious and cultural implications of holidays. Are Christmas and Chanukah the only holidays with this dual role? What other holidays might be included and why?

The cultural significance of Chanukah varies with the setting in which the holiday is celebrated. In contemporary Israel, the nationalist and military aspects of the Chanukah story receive special emphasis. In this country, the tradition of giving Chanukah gelt has taken on greater importance because of the temporal proximity of Chanukah to Christmas. Indeed, some have suggested that the proximity of Christmas accounts for the social prominence of Chanukah in this country. Whatever the reason, Chanukah is observed by American Jews to an extent greater than its religious importance would indicate: in the hierarchy of Jewish holidays, Chanukah ranks fairly low in religious significance. This socially heightened status of Chanukah reflects its cultural or secular dimension.

On December 22 of the 1986 holiday season, the city placed at the Grant Street entrance to the City-County Building an 18-foot Chanukah menorah of an abstract tree-and-branch design. The menorah was placed next to the city's 45-foot Christmas tree, against one of the columns that supports the arch into which the tree was set. The menorah is owned by Chabad, a Jewish group, but is stored, erected, and removed each year by the city. The tree, the sign, and the menorah were all removed on January 13.

During-Reading Questions: There are two different holiday displays in two different buildings that are in question during this case. What holiday displays seem the most problematic when displayed in a government building? Why?

II

This litigation began on December 10, 1986, when respondents, the Greater Pittsburgh Chapter of the American Civil Liberties Union and seven local residents, filed suit against the county and the city, seeking permanently to enjoin the county from displaying the creche in the county courthouse and the city from displaying the menorah in front of the City-County Building. Respondents claim that the displays of the creche and the menorah each violate the Establishment Clause of the First Amendment, made applicable to state governments by the Fourteenth Amendment. Chabad was permitted to intervene to defend the display of its menorah.

During-Reading Question: What specific part of the Fourteenth Amendment is in question here?

On May 8, 1987, the District Court denied respondents' request for a permanent injunction. Relying on *Lynch* v. *Donnelly*, 465 U.S. 668 (1984), the court stated that "the creche was but part of the holiday decoration of the stairwell and a foreground for the high school choirs which entertained each day at noon." Regarding the menorah, the court concluded that "it was but an insignificant part of another holiday display." The court also found that "the displays had a secular purpose" and "did not create an excessive entanglement of government with religion."

During-Reading Questions: The lower court found that the displays had a secular purpose and were not solely religious displays. Do you agree with that finding? Why or why not?

IIIA

This Nation is heir to a history and tradition of religious diversity that dates from the settlement of the North American Continent. Sectarian differences among various Christian denominations were central to the origins of our Republic. Since then, adherents of religions too numerous to name have made the United States their home, as have those whose beliefs expressly exclude religion.

Precisely because of the religious diversity that is our national heritage, the Founders added to the Constitution a Bill of Rights, the very first words of which declare: "Congress shall make no law respecting an establishment of religion, or prohibiting the free exercise thereof . . ." Perhaps in the early days of the Republic these words were understood to protect only the diversity within Christianity, but today they are recognized as guaranteeing religious liberty and equality to "the infidel, the atheist, or the adherent of a non-Christian faith such as Islam or Judaism." *Wallace* v. *Jaffree*, 472 U.S., at 52. It is settled law that no government official in this Nation may violate these fundamental constitutional rights regarding matters of conscience.

In *Lemon* v. *Kurtzman,* the Court sought to refine these principles by focusing on three "tests" for determining whether a government practice violates the Establishment Clause. Under the *Lemon* analysis, a statute or practice which touches upon religion, if it is to be permissible under the Establishment Clause, must have a secular purpose; it must neither advance nor inhibit religion in its principal or primary effect; and it must not foster an excessive entanglement with religion. This trilogy of tests has been applied regularly in the Court's later Establishment Clause cases.

Of course, the word "endorsement" is not self-defining. Rather, it derives its meaning from other words that this Court has found useful over the years in interpreting the Establishment Clause. Thus, it has been noted that the prohibition against governmental endorsement of religion "preclude[s] government from conveying or attempting to convey a message that religion or a particular religious belief is *favored* or *preferred.*" *Wallace* v. *Jaffree*, 472 U.S., at 70.

During-Reading Questions: What does "endorsement" really mean? What actions does the government "do" to endorse something?

Whether the key word is "endorsement," "favoritism," or "promotion" the essential principle remains the same. The Establishment Clause, at the very least, prohibits government from appearing to take a position on questions of religious belief or from "making adherence to a religion relevant in any way to a person's standing in the political community." *Lynch* v. *Donnelly*, 465 U.S., at 687.

IIIB

We have had occasion in the past to apply Establishment Clause principles to the government's display of objects with religious significance. In *Stone* v. *Graham*, 449 U.S. 39 (1980), we held that the display of a copy of the Ten Commandments on the walls of public classrooms violates the Establishment Clause. Closer to the facts of this litigation is *Lynch* v. *Donnelly,* in which we considered whether the city of Pawtucket, R. I., had violated the Establishment Clause by including a creche in its annual Christmas display, located in a private park within the downtown shopping district. By a 5-to-4 decision in that difficult case, the Court upheld inclusion of the creche in the Pawtucket display, holding, that the inclusion of the creche did not have the impermissible effect of advancing or promoting religion.

IV

We turn first to the county's creche display. There is no doubt, of course, that the creche itself is capable of communicating a religious message. Indeed, the creche in this lawsuit uses words, as well as the picture of the Nativity scene, to make its religious meaning unmistakably clear. "Glory to God in the Highest!" says the angel in the creche—Glory to God because of the birth of Jesus. This praise to God in Christian terms is indisputably religious—indeed sectarian—just as it is when said in the Gospel or in a church service.

During-Reading Question: When displays like this carry the government's message, it is often subtle or implied. Would visitors to these displays have naturally felt the government was the sole voice of the message?

Under the Court's holding in *Lynch*, the effect of a creche display turns on its setting. Here, unlike in *Lynch*, nothing in the context of the display detracts from the creche's religious message. The *Lynch* display comprised a series of figures and objects, each group of which had its own focal point. Santa's house and his reindeer were objects of attention separate from the creche, and had their specific visual story to tell. Similarly, whatever a "talking" wishing well may be, it obviously was a center of attention separate from the creche. Here, in contrast, the creche stands alone: it is the single element of the display on the Grand Staircase.

The floral decoration surrounding the creche cannot be viewed as somehow equivalent to the secular symbols in the overall *Lynch* display. The floral frame, like all good frames, serves only to draw one's attention to the message inside the frame. The floral decoration surrounding the creche contributes to, rather than detracts from, the endorsement of religion conveyed by the creche. It is as if the county had allowed the Holy Name Society to display a cross on the Grand Staircase at Easter, and the county had surrounded the cross with Easter lilies. The county could not say that surrounding the cross with traditional flowers of the season would negate the endorsement of Christianity conveyed by the cross on the Grand Staircase. Its contention that the traditional Christmas greens negate the endorsement effect of the creche fares no better.

Nor does the fact that the creche was the setting for the county's annual Christmas-carol program diminish its religious meaning. First, the carol program in 1986 lasted only from December 3 to December 23 and occupied at most one hour a day. The effect of the creche on those who viewed it when the choirs were not singing—the vast majority of the time—cannot be negated by the presence of the choir program. Second, because some of the carols performed at the site of the creche were religious in nature, those carols were more likely to augment the religious quality of the scene than to secularize it.

Furthermore, the creche sits on the Grand Staircase, the "main" and "most beautiful part" of the building that is the seat of county government. No viewer could reasonably think that it occupies this location without the support and approval of the government. Thus, by permitting the "display of the creche in this particular physical setting," the county sends an unmistakable message that it supports and promotes the Christian praise to God that is the creche's religious message.

During-Reading Questions: What parts of government buildings are considered the "main" parts? Consider a government building in your town. What would be the "main" part of that building where a display like this might have been a problem? Why do you think it would have been a problem?

The fact that the creche bears a sign disclosing its ownership by a Roman Catholic organization does not alter this conclusion. On the contrary, the sign simply demonstrates that the government is endorsing the religious message of that organization, rather than communicating a message of its own. But the Establishment Clause does not limit only the religious content of the government's own communications. It also prohibits the government's support and promotion of religious communications by religious organizations. Indeed, the very concept of "endorsement" conveys the sense of promoting someone else's message. Thus, by prohibiting government endorsement of religion, the Establishment Clause prohibits precisely what occurred here: the government's lending its support to the communication of a religious organization's religious message.

Finally, the county argues that it is sufficient to validate the display of the creche on the Grand Staircase that the display celebrates Christmas, and Christmas is a national holiday. This argument obviously proves too much. It would allow the celebration of the Eucharist inside a courthouse on Christmas Eve. While the county may have doubts about the constitutional status of celebrating the Eucharist inside the courthouse under the government's auspices, this Court does not. The government may acknowledge Christmas as a cultural phenomenon, but under the First Amendment it may not observe it as a Christian holy day by suggesting that people praise God for the birth of Jesus.

In sum, *Lynch* teaches that government may celebrate Christmas in some manner and form, but not in a way that endorses Christian doctrine. Here, Allegheny County has transgressed this line. It has chosen to celebrate Christmas in a way that has the effect of endorsing a patently Christian message: Glory to God for the birth of Jesus Christ. Under *Lynch*, and the rest of our cases, nothing more is required to demonstrate a violation of the Establishment Clause. The display of the creche in this context, therefore, must be permanently enjoined.

VI

The display of the Chanukah menorah in front of the City-County Building may well present a closer constitutional question. The menorah, one must recognize, is a religious symbol: it serves to commemorate the miracle of the oil as described in the Talmud. But the menorah's message is not exclusively religious. The menorah is the primary visual symbol for a holiday that, like Christmas, has both religious and secular dimensions.

Moreover, the menorah here stands next to a Christmas tree and a sign saluting liberty. While no challenge has been made here to the display of the tree and the sign, their presence is obviously relevant in determining the effect of the menorah's display. The necessary result of placing a menorah next to a Christmas tree is to create an "overall holiday setting" that represents both Christmas and Chanukah—two holidays, not one.

The mere fact that Pittsburgh displays symbols of both Christmas and Chanukah does not end the constitutional inquiry. If the city celebrates both Christmas and Chanukah as religious holidays, then it violates the Establishment Clause. The simultaneous endorsement of Judaism and Christianity is no less constitutionally infirm than the endorsement of Christianity alone.

Conversely, if the city celebrates both Christmas and Chanukah as secular holidays, then its conduct is beyond the reach of the Establishment Clause. Because government may celebrate Christmas as a secular holiday, it follows that government may also acknowledge Chanukah as a secular holiday. Simply put, it would be a form of discrimination against Jews to allow Pittsburgh to celebrate Christmas as a cultural tradition while simultaneously disallowing the city's acknowledgment of Chanukah as a contemporaneous cultural tradition.

Accordingly, the relevant question for Establishment Clause purposes is whether the combined display of the tree, the sign, and the menorah has the effect of endorsing both Christian and Jewish faiths, or rather simply recognizes that both Christmas and Chanukah are part of the same winter-holiday season, which has attained a secular status in our society. Of the two interpretations of this particular display, the latter seems far more plausible and is also in line with *Lynch*.

The Christmas tree, unlike the menorah, is not itself a religious symbol. Although Christmas trees once carried religious connotations, today they typify the secular celebration of Christmas. Numerous Americans place Christmas trees in their homes without subscribing to Christian religious beliefs, and when the city's tree stands alone in front of the City-County Building, it is not considered an endorsement of Christian faith. Indeed, a 40-foot Christmas tree was one of the objects that validated the creche in *Lynch*. The widely accepted view of the Christmas tree as the preeminent secular symbol of the Christmas holiday season serves to emphasize the secular component of the message communicated by other elements of an accompanying holiday display, including the Chanukah menorah.

During-Reading Questions: Is the Christmas tree a religious or cultural symbol? How do we know?

The tree, moreover, is clearly the predominant element in the city's display. The 45-foot tree occupies the central position beneath the middle archway in front of the Grant Street entrance to the City-County Building; the 18-foot menorah is positioned to one side. Given this configuration, it is much more sensible to interpret the meaning of the menorah in light of the tree, rather than vice versa. In the shadow of the tree, the menorah is readily understood as simply a recognition that Christmas is not the only traditional way of observing the winter-holiday season. In these circumstances, then, the combination of the tree and the menorah communicates, not a simultaneous endorsement of both the Christian and Jewish faiths, but instead, a secular celebration of Christmas coupled with an acknowledgment of Chanukah as a contemporaneous alternative tradition.

Although the city has used a symbol with religious meaning as its representation of Chanukah, this is not a case in which the city has reasonable alternatives that are less religious in nature. It is difficult to imagine a predominantly secular symbol of Chanukah that the city could place next to its Christmas tree. An 18-foot dreidel would look out of place and might be interpreted by some as mocking the celebration of Chanukah. The absence of a more secular alternative symbol is itself part of the context in which the city's actions must be judged in determining the likely effect of its use of the menorah. Where the government's secular message can be conveyed by two symbols, only one of which carries religious meaning, an observer reasonably might infer from the fact that the government has chosen to use the religious symbol that the government means to promote religious faith. But where, as here, no such choice has been made, this inference of endorsement is not present.

The mayor's sign further diminishes the possibility that the tree and the menorah will be interpreted as a dual endorsement of Christianity and Judaism. The sign states that during the holiday season the city salutes liberty. Moreover, the sign draws upon the theme of light, common to both Chanukah and Christmas as winter festivals, and links that theme with this Nation's legacy of freedom, which allows an American to celebrate the holiday season in whatever way he wishes, religiously or otherwise. While no sign can disclaim an overwhelming message of endorsement, an "explanatory plaque" may confirm that in particular contexts the government's association with a religious symbol does not represent the government's sponsorship of religious beliefs. Here, the mayor's sign serves to confirm what the context already reveals: that the display of the menorah is not an endorsement of religious faith but simply a recognition of cultural diversity.

Given all these considerations, it is not "sufficiently likely" that residents of Pittsburgh will perceive the combined display of the tree, the sign, and the menorah as an "endorsement" or "disapproval . . . of their individual religious choices." *Grand Rapids*, 473 U.S., at 390. While an adjudication of the display's effect must take into account the perspective of one who is neither Christian nor Jewish, as well as of those who adhere to either of these religions, the constitutionality of its effect must also be judged according to the standard of a "reasonable observer." When measured against this standard, the menorah need not be excluded from this particular display. The Christmas tree alone in the Pittsburgh location does not endorse Christian belief; and, on the facts before us, the addition of the menorah "cannot fairly be understood to" result in the simultaneous endorsement of Christian and Jewish faiths. On the contrary, for purposes of the Establishment Clause, the city's overall display must be understood as conveying the city's secular recognition of different traditions for celebrating the winter-holiday season.

During-Reading Questions: Who is a "reasonable observer"? What would that person say about these displays?

VII

Lynch v. *Donnelly* confirms, and in no way repudiates, the longstanding constitutional principle that government may not engage in a practice that has the effect of promoting or endorsing religious beliefs. The display of the creche in the county courthouse has this unconstitutional effect. The display of the menorah in front of the City-County Building, however, does not have this effect, given its "particular physical setting."

The judgment of the Court of Appeals is affirmed in part and reversed in part, and the cases are remanded for further proceedings.

It is so ordered.

Post-Reading Questions

1. The Court seemed to have two different outcomes here. What were these outcomes and why?
2. Did the government "establish" religion through these displays? How or how not?
3. In the dissent for this case, one Justice accuses the Court of having "hostility" toward religion. Do you feel the Court's majority was hostile toward religion? Why or why not?

Further Explorations

Exploring the Story

This case is based on the premise that the United States is a diverse country with many different religions, religious celebrations, and cultural events. Some of these tend to overlap. Consider what other holidays are both cultural and religious. How could the Court distinguish between the religious or cultural implications of the holiday?

Exploring the Law

What issues regarding the separation church and state do we confront in our lives today? Consider both sides to these issues.

Exploring the Effects

There are many examples of religious symbols within government buildings and spaces, including the inclusion of prayer within Congressional sessions, the Ten Commandments carved in the walls of buildings, and references to "God" on the country's currency. How has the landscape for religious symbols changed after this case? How do some of these symbols still exist today? What religious symbols exist that are merely ornamental and not seen as the government endorsing religion?

Activities for Extending the Learning

Read some of the cases still occurring today that seem to present conflicting accounts of what constitutes "endorsement" and what does not. Some sources include:

- CNNAccess. (2003, August 21). Advocates debate the First Amendment, Ten Commandments. [Transcript of a CNN debate]. *CNN.com Law Center*. Retrieved from http://www.cnn.com/2003/LAW/08/21/cnna.commandments.debate/index.html
- Schachar, N. (2015, July 9). Oklahoma's Ten Commandments case is part of an age-old battle in U.S. *Los Angeles Times*. Retrieved from http://www.latimes.com/nation/la-na-ten-commandments-20150709-story.html

A NOTE FROM THE AUTHORS

Culture can be a fascinating topic to explore with students. Every student brings a unique piece to the table—from religion to nationality to family traditions. As unique as every individual is, somehow we still have to exist as a community of people and function as one nation. These cases show that culture is more than just one's religion or national identity; culture really does go to the core of a person's being.

Where does one's culture stem from? How do we identify within one culture? How do we identify among multiple cultures? Why? Students today are growing up in a world where learning about different cultures is part of the curriculum, but what do we teach beyond facts and rote answers? How do we teach students to respect and appreciate differences? What do these cases teach us about some of the uglier parts of our nation's past? And how can we best exist in a multicultural world where differences are embraced? Students can be challenged to study their own cultural backgrounds as well as to learn about those different from their own.

Chapter Four

Time, Continuity, and Change

Theme 2: *Social studies programs should include experiences that provide for the study of the past and its legacy.*
—*National Curriculum Standards for Social Studies* (2010), National Council for the Social Studies, p. 15

The study of the decisions of the United States Supreme Court is the study of what was happening socially and politically in the United States at the time the decisions were made. How did the framers of our country see us when the United States was first formed? How has the United States stayed the same since its inception? How has it changed? By looking at Supreme Court decisions, students will be able to see the transformation of the nation in the words of the decisions, and in the stories and issues behind the cases that brought them before the Court. Students will easily be able to explore many of the questions central to NCSS Theme 2, including:

> What are the roots of our social, political and economic systems? What are our personal roots and how can they be viewed as part of human history? Why is the past important to us today? How has the world changed and how might it change in future? How do perspectives about the past differ, and to what extent do these differences inform contemporary ideas and actions? (NCSS, 2010, p. 15)

The cases provided in this chapter provide an examination of both stable case law and changed case law. *Marbury v. Madison* (1803) is the seminal case where Chief Justice Marshall articulates the role of the Supreme Court as it relates to the United States government. This case is still binding today, and understanding its importance is critical to understanding how the United States' concept of checks and balances works.

Whitney v. California (1927) and *Brandenburg v. Ohio* (1969) consider the Constitutional issues of free speech and assembly. When does the participation in an organization constitute a threat punishable by law? How did the ideas of protected speech change over the course of the twentieth century?

The cases *South Carolina v Gathers* (1989) and *Payne v. Tennessee* (1991) ask students to focus on whose rights are most important when deciding the verdict in a capital criminal case: the criminal defendant or the victim? Students will be able to see the development of victim's rights in the latter part of the twentieth century by analyzing these two cases together.

CASE #1: *MARBURY V. MADISON*

Pre-Reading Questions

1. What does Article 3 of the United States Constitution say about the Supreme Court? Is there anything about judicial review of Constitutional issues in the Constitution? How was the role of the judiciary expanded by the Judiciary Act of 1789?
2. Tension between political rivals is not new in American history, and it was the transition of one presidency to another that brought about the case of *Marbury v. Madison.* What was the story behind this important case? Go to TeachingAmericanHistory.org (http://teachingamerican
history.org) and search for "Marbury v. Madison" to learn more.

Marbury v. Madison, 5 U.S. 137 (1803)

Mr. Chief Justice MARSHALL delivered the opinion of the Court.

At the last term, on the affidavits then read and filed with the clerk, a rule was granted in this case requiring the Secretary of State to show cause why a mandamus should not issue directing him to deliver to William Marbury his commission as a justice of the peace for the county of Washington, in the District of Columbia.

During-Reading Question: What is a writ of mandamus*?*

No cause has been shown, and the present motion is for a mandamus. The peculiar delicacy of this case, the novelty of some of its circumstances, and the real difficulty attending the points which occur in it require a complete exposition of the principles on which the opinion to be given by the Court is founded.

In the order in which the Court has viewed this subject, the following questions have been considered and decided.

1. Has the applicant a right to the commission he demands?

His right originates in an act of Congress passed in February, 1801, concerning the District of Columbia.

It appears from the affidavits that, in compliance with this law, a commission for William Marbury as a justice of peace for the County of Washington was signed by John Adams, then President of the United States, after which the seal of the United States was affixed to it, but the commission has never reached the person for whom it was made out.

During-Reading Questions: Who prevented Marbury from receiving his commission? Why do you think that person failed to deliver it to him?

In order to determine whether he is entitled to this commission, it becomes necessary to inquire whether he has been appointed to the office. For if he has been appointed, the law continues him in office for five years, and he is entitled to the possession of those evidences of office, which, being completed, became his property.

The second section of the second article of the Constitution declares,

"The President shall nominate, and, by and with the advice and consent of the Senate, shall appoint ambassadors, other public ministers and consuls, and all other officers of the United States, whose appointments are not otherwise provided for."

The third section declares, that "He shall commission all the officers of the United States."

An act of Congress directs the Secretary of State to keep the seal of the United States, "to make out and record, and affix the said seal to all civil commissions to officers of the United States to be appointed by the President, by and with the consent of the Senate, or by the President alone; provided that the said seal shall not be affixed to any commission before the same shall have been signed by the President of the United States."

These are the clauses of the Constitution and laws of the United States which affect this part of the case. They seem to contemplate three distinct operations:

1. The nomination. This is the sole act of the President, and is completely voluntary.
2. The appointment. This is also the act of the President, and is also a voluntary act, though it can only be performed by and with the advice and consent of the Senate.
3. The commission. To grant a commission to a person appointed might perhaps be deemed a duty enjoined by the Constitution. "He shall," says that instrument, "commission all the officers of the United States."

It is therefore decidedly the opinion of the Court that, when a commission has been signed by the President, the appointment is made, and that the commission is complete when the seal of the United States has been affixed to it by the Secretary of State.

Where an officer is removable at the will of the Executive, the circumstance which completes his appointment is of no concern, because the act is at any time revocable, and the commission may be arrested if still in the office. But when the officer is not removable at the will of the Executive, the appointment is not revocable, and cannot be annulled. It has conferred legal rights which cannot be resumed.

The discretion of the Executive is to be exercised until the appointment has been made. But having once made the appointment, his power over the office is terminated in all cases, where by law the officer is not removable by him. The right to the office is then in the person appointed, and he has the absolute, unconditional power of accepting or rejecting it.

Mr. Marbury, then, since his commission was signed by the President and sealed by the Secretary of State, was appointed, and as the law creating the office gave the officer a right to hold for five years independent of the Executive, the appointment was not revocable, but vested in the officer legal rights which are protected by the laws of his country.

During-Reading Question: Justice Marshall discusses two distinctions about presidential appointments. The president has the right to terminate some positions—"removable at will"—but when the appointment is not removable by the president he cannot terminate the appointment. Which do you think Marbury says he has?

To withhold the commission, therefore, is an act deemed by the Court not warranted by law, but violative of a vested legal right.

This brings us to the second inquiry, which is:

2. If he has a right, and that right has been violated, do the laws of his country afford him a remedy?

The very essence of civil liberty certainly consists in the right of every individual to claim the protection of the laws whenever he receives an injury. One of the first duties of government is to afford that protection. In Great Britain, the King himself is sued in the respectful form of a petition, and he never fails to comply with the judgment of his court.

During-Reading Questions: Why do you think Justice Marshall is pointing out that even the king in Great Britain can be sued? Who is Marshall implying is subject to the Court in this case?

The Government of the United States has been emphatically termed a government of laws, and not of men. It will certainly cease to deserve this high appellation if the laws furnish no remedy for the violation of a vested legal right.

It behooves us, then, to inquire whether there be in its composition any ingredient which shall exempt from legal investigation or exclude the injured party from legal redress. In pursuing this inquiry, the first question which presents itself is whether this can be arranged with that class of cases which come under the description of damnum absque injuria—a loss without an injury.

This description of cases never has been considered, and, it is believed, never can be considered, as comprehending offices of trust, of honour or of profit. The office of justice of peace in the District of Columbia is such an office; it is therefore worthy of the attention and guardianship of the laws. It has received that attention and guardianship. It has been created by special act of Congress, and has been secured, so far as the laws can give security to the person appointed to fill it, for five years. It is not then on account of the worthlessness of the thing pursued that the injured party can be alleged to be without remedy.

During-Reading Question: Justice Marshall says that in order to have a legal remedy, the object in question must have some value. What does Marshall say is the value of being a justice of the peace?

Is it in the nature of the transaction? Is the act of delivering or withholding a commission to be considered as a mere political act belonging to the Executive department alone, for the performance of which entire confidence is placed by our Constitution in the Supreme Executive, and for any misconduct respecting which the injured individual has no remedy?

During-Reading Question: Again, who is Justice Marshall pointing the finger at for causing this issue to arise?

That there may be such cases is not to be questioned, but that every act of duty to be performed in any of the great departments of government constitutes such a case is not to be admitted.

By the Constitution of the United States, the President is invested with certain important political powers, in the exercise of which he is to use his own discretion, and is accountable only to his country in his political character and to his own conscience. To aid him in the performance of these duties, he is authorized to appoint certain officers, who act by his authority and in conformity with his orders.

In such cases, their acts are his acts; and whatever opinion may be entertained of the manner in which executive discretion may be used, still there exists, and can exist, no power to control that discretion. The subjects are political. They respect the nation, not individual rights, and, being entrusted to the Executive, the decision of the Executive is conclusive. The application of this remark will be perceived by adverting to the act of Congress for establishing the Department of Foreign Affairs. This officer, as his duties were prescribed by that act, is to conform precisely to the will of the President. He is the mere organ by whom that will is communicated. The acts of such an officer, as an officer, can never be examinable by the Courts.

But when the Legislature proceeds to impose on that officer other duties; when he is directed peremptorily to perform certain acts; when the rights of individuals are dependent on the performance of those acts; he is so far the officer of the law, is amenable to the laws for his conduct, and cannot at his discretion, sport away the vested rights of others.

During-Reading Questions: What is the difference, according to the opinion of the Court, whether officers of the president can act solely at the direction of the president? When are these officers required to act differently?

The conclusion from this reasoning is that, where the heads of departments are the political or confidential agents of the Executive, merely to execute the will of the President, or rather to act in cases in which the Executive possesses a constitutional or legal discretion, nothing can be more perfectly clear than that their acts are only politically examinable. But where a specific duty is assigned by law, and individual rights depend upon the performance of that duty, it seems equally clear that the individual who considers himself injured has a right to resort to the laws of his country for a remedy.

The power of nominating to the Senate, and the power of appointing the person nominated, are political powers, to be exercised by the President according to his own discretion. When he has made an appointment, he has exercised his whole power, and his discretion has been completely applied to the case. If, by law, the officer be removable at the will of the President, then a new appointment may be immediately made, and the rights of the officer are terminated. But as a fact which has existed cannot be made never to have existed, the appointment cannot be annihilated, and consequently, if the officer is by law not removable at the will of the President, the rights he has acquired are protected by the law, and are not resumable by the President. They cannot be extinguished by Executive authority, and he has the privilege of asserting them in like manner as if they had been derived from any other source.

It is then the opinion of the Court:

1. That, by signing the commission of Mr. Marbury, the President of the United States appointed him a justice of peace for the County of Washington in the District of Columbia, and that the seal of the United States, affixed thereto by the Secretary of State, is conclusive testimony of the verity of the signature, and of the completion of the appointment, and that the appointment conferred on him a legal right to the office for the space of five years.
2. That, having this legal title to the office, he has a consequent right to the commission, a refusal to deliver which is a plain violation of that right, for which the laws of his country afford him a remedy.

It remains to be inquired whether, 3. He is entitled to the remedy for which he applies.

This depends on:

1. The nature of the writ applied for, and
2. The power of this court.

It is true that the mandamus now moved for is not for the performance of an act expressly enjoined by statute.

It is to deliver a commission, on which subjects the acts of Congress are silent. This difference is not considered as affecting the case. It has already been stated that the applicant has, to that commission, a vested legal right of which the Executive cannot deprive him. He has been appointed to an office from which he is not removable at the will of the Executive, and, being so appointed, he has a right to the commission which the Secretary has received from the President for his use. The act of Congress does not, indeed, order the Secretary of State to send it to him, but it is placed in his hands for the person entitled to it, and cannot be more lawfully withheld by him than by another person.

This, then, is a plain case of a mandamus, either to deliver the commission or a copy of it from the record, and it only remains to be inquired:

Whether it can issue from this Court.

The act to establish the judicial courts of the United States authorizes the Supreme Court "to issue writs of mandamus, in cases warranted by the principles and usages of law, to any courts appointed, or persons holding office, under the authority of the United States."

The Secretary of State, being a person, holding an office under the authority of the United States, is precisely within the letter of the description, and if this Court is not authorized to issue a writ of mandamus to such an officer, it must be because the law is unconstitutional, and therefore absolutely incapable of conferring the authority and assigning the duties which its words purport to confer and assign.

During-Reading Question: To whom is the Court saying it has the power to issue a writ of mandamus?

The Constitution vests the whole judicial power of the United States in one Supreme Court, and such inferior courts as Congress shall, from time to time, ordain and establish. This power is expressly extended to all cases arising under the laws of the United States; and consequently, in some form, may be exercised over the present case, because the right claimed is given by a law of the United States.

In the distribution of this power, it is declared that "The Supreme Court shall have original jurisdiction in all cases affecting ambassadors, other public ministers and consuls, and those in which a state shall be a party. In all other cases, the Supreme Court shall have appellate jurisdiction."

It has been insisted at the bar, that, as the original grant of jurisdiction to the Supreme and inferior courts is general, and the clause assigning original jurisdiction to the Supreme Court contains no negative or restrictive words, the power remains to the Legislature to assign original jurisdiction to that Court in other cases than those specified in the article which has been recited, provided those cases belong to the judicial power of the United States.

If it had been intended to leave it in the discretion of the Legislature to apportion the judicial power between the Supreme and inferior courts according to the will of that body, it would certainly have been useless to have proceeded further than to have defined the judicial power and the tribunals in which it should be vested. The subsequent part of the section is mere surplusage—is entirely without meaning—if such is to be the construction. If Congress remains at liberty to give this court appellate jurisdiction where the Constitution has declared their jurisdiction shall be original, and original jurisdiction where the Constitution has declared it shall be appellate, the distribution of jurisdiction made in the Constitution, is form without substance.

During-Reading Question: What argument does the Court use to say that it has power to decide legal issues and it doesn't need to wait for Congress to give it additional authority?

Affirmative words are often, in their operation, negative of other objects than those affirmed, and, in this case, a negative or exclusive sense must be given to them or they have no operation at all.

It cannot be presumed that any clause in the Constitution is intended to be without effect, and therefore such construction is inadmissible unless the words require it.

To enable this court then to issue a mandamus, it must be shown to be an exercise of appellate jurisdiction, or to be necessary to enable them to exercise appellate jurisdiction.

It has been stated at the bar that the appellate jurisdiction may be exercised in a variety of forms, and that, if it be the will of the Legislature that a mandamus should be used for that purpose, that will must be obeyed. This is true; yet the jurisdiction must be appellate, not original.

It is the essential criterion of appellate jurisdiction that it revises and corrects the proceedings in a cause already instituted, and does not create that case. Although, therefore, a mandamus may be directed to courts, yet to issue such a writ to an officer for the delivery of a paper is, in effect, the same as to sustain an original action for that paper, and therefore seems not to belong to appellate, but to original jurisdiction. Neither is it necessary in such a case as this to enable the Court to exercise its appellate jurisdiction.

The authority, therefore, given to the Supreme Court by the act establishing the judicial courts of the United States to issue writs of mandamus to public officers appears not to be warranted by the Constitution, and it becomes necessary to inquire whether a jurisdiction so conferred can be exercised.

During-Reading Question: The Court says it doesn't have the authority to issue Marbury's writ of mandamus. What reason does it give?

The question whether an act repugnant to the Constitution can become the law of the land is a question deeply interesting to the United States, but, happily, not of an intricacy proportioned to its interest. It seems only necessary to recognise certain principles, supposed to have been long and well established, to decide it.

That the people have an original right to establish for their future government such principles as, in their opinion, shall most conduce to their own happiness is the basis on which the whole American fabric has been erected. The exercise of this original right is a very great exertion; nor can it nor ought it to be frequently repeated. The principles, therefore, so established are deemed fundamental. And as the authority from which they proceed, is supreme, and can seldom act, they are designed to be permanent.

This original and supreme will organizes the government and assigns to different departments their respective powers. It may either stop here or establish certain limits not to be transcended by those departments.

The Government of the United States is of the latter description. The powers of the Legislature are defined and limited; and that those limits may not be mistaken or forgotten, the Constitution is written. To what purpose are powers limited, and to what purpose is that limitation committed to writing, if these limits may at any time be passed by those intended to be restrained? The distinction between a government with limited and unlimited powers is abolished if those limits do not confine the persons on whom they are imposed, and if acts prohibited and acts allowed are of equal obligation. It is a proposition too plain to be contested that the Constitution controls any legislative act repugnant to it, or that the Legislature may alter the Constitution by an ordinary act.

Between these alternatives there is no middle ground. The Constitution is either a superior, paramount law, unchangeable by ordinary means, or it is on a level with ordinary legislative acts, and, like other acts, is alterable when the legislature shall please to alter it.

This theory is essentially attached to a written Constitution, and is consequently to be considered by this Court as one of the fundamental principles of our society. It is not, therefore, to be lost sight of in the further consideration of this subject.

If an act of the Legislature repugnant to the Constitution is void, does it, notwithstanding its invalidity, bind the Courts and oblige them to give it effect? Or, in other words, though it be not law, does it constitute a rule as operative as if it was a law? This would be to overthrow in fact what was established in theory, and would seem, at first view, an absurdity too gross to be insisted on. It shall, however, receive a more attentive consideration.

It is emphatically the province and duty of the Judicial Department to say what the law is. Those who apply the rule to particular cases must, of necessity, expound and interpret that rule. If two laws conflict with each other, the Courts must decide on the operation of each.

So, if a law be in opposition to the Constitution, if both the law and the Constitution apply to a particular case, so that the Court must either decide that case conformably to the law, disregarding the Constitution, or conformably to the Constitution, disregarding the law, the Court must determine which of these conflicting rules governs the case. This is of the very essence of judicial duty.

If, then, the Courts are to regard the Constitution, and the Constitution is superior to any ordinary act of the Legislature, the Constitution, and not such ordinary act, must govern the case to which they both apply.

This doctrine would subvert the very foundation of all written Constitutions. It would declare that an act which, according to the principles and theory of our government, is entirely void, is yet, in practice, completely obligatory. It would declare that, if the Legislature shall do what is expressly forbidden, such act, notwithstanding the express prohibition, is in reality effectual. It would be giving to the Legislature a practical and real omnipotence with the same breath which professes to restrict their powers within narrow limits. It is prescribing limits, and declaring that those limits may be passed at pleasure.

That it thus reduces to nothing what we have deemed the greatest improvement on political institutions—a written Constitution, would of itself be sufficient, in America where written Constitutions have been viewed with so much reverence, for rejecting the construction. But the peculiar expressions of the Constitution of the United States furnish additional arguments in favour of its rejection.

The judicial power of the United States is extended to all cases arising under the Constitution.

During-Reading Question: After the Court decides it cannot issue Marbury's writ of mandamus, what has the Court gone on to declare about what the role of the Supreme Court is?

Could it be the intention of those who gave this power to say that, in using it, the Constitution should not be looked into? That a case arising under the Constitution should be decided without examining the instrument under which it arises?

This is too extravagant to be maintained.

[I]t is apparent that the framers of the Constitution contemplated that instrument as a rule for the government of courts, as well as of the Legislature.

Why otherwise does it direct the judges to take an oath to support it? This oath certainly applies in an especial manner to their conduct in their official character. How immoral to impose it on them if they were to be used as the instruments, and the knowing instruments, for violating what they swear to support!

The oath of office, too, imposed by the Legislature, is completely demonstrative of the legislative opinion on this subject. It is in these words:

> I do solemnly swear that I will administer justice without respect to persons, and do equal right to the poor and to the rich; and that I will faithfully and impartially discharge all the duties incumbent on me as according to the best of my abilities and understanding, agreeably to the Constitution and laws of the United States.

Why does a judge swear to discharge his duties agreeably to the Constitution of the United States if that Constitution forms no rule for his government? [I]f it is closed upon him and cannot be inspected by him?

During-Reading Question: What evidence does the Court use to support the idea that the framers intended for the Supreme Court to decide Constitutional issues?

Thus, the particular phraseology of the Constitution of the United States confirms and strengthens the principle, supposed to be essential to all written Constitutions, that a law repugnant to the Constitution is void, and that courts, as well as other departments, are bound by that instrument.

The rule must be discharged.

Post-Reading Questions

1. After reading this case, why do you think that Chief Justice John Marshall has been called "the father of the Supreme Court"?
2. What happened to Marbury and the other justices who were not given their commissions? Is the importance of this case really about Marbury at all?
3. When many other United States Supreme Court cases have been successfully challenged and overturned, what it is about the decision about the role of the Supreme Court in the United States in *Marbury v. Madison* that has stood the test of time? What could you argue might happen if *Marbury* were overturned?

Further Explorations

Exploring the Story

Learn more about Justice John Marshall by visiting the John Marshall Foundation website at http://www.johnmarshallfoundation.org.

Exploring the Law

Justice Marshall was not acting without some historical support when he made his declaration in *Marbury v. Madison* about the power of the judiciary. Read Alexander Hamilton's Federalist No. 78. The following is one of many sources for this work: Hamilton, A. (1788, May 28). The Judiciary Department. (Essay No. 78). In A. Hamilton, J. Madison, and J. Jay, *The Federalist: A collection of essays, written in favour of the new Constitution, as agreed upon by the Federal Convention.* Retrieved fromhttp://avalon.law.yale.edu/18th_century/fed78.asp

What does Hamilton say about the power of the judiciary? Why did Hamilton think the judiciary was necessary?

Exploring the Effects

Have students research the impacts of the *Marbury* decision and discuss how it enhanced the idea of checks and balances in the United States government.

Activities for Extending the Learning

- Have students do research on the reach of the Supreme Court and what exactly it can review. Students can research the following concepts:
  - Constitutional Interpretation
  - Prudential Consideration
  - Strict Necessity
  - Clear Mistake
  - Extra-Constitutional Tests
  - The Presumption of Constitutionality
  - Statutory Interpretation
- Street Law, Inc. has additional resources and activities that can be used to help teach *Marbury v. Madison*: Street Law, Inc. and the Supreme Court Historical Society. (n.d.) *Marbury v. Madison.* In *Landmark Cases of the U.S. Supreme Court.* Retrieved from http://landmarkcases.org/en/landmark/cases/marbury_v_madison

CASE #2A: *WHITNEY V. CALIFORNIA*

Pre-Reading Questions

1. This case was decided in 1927, but the events that created the case happened in 1919. Do some research into the "Red Scare of 1919" in the United States for some background about the history of the time. Why do you think average Americans might have been worried about people who were members of socialist organizations?
2. When the opinions of the United States Supreme Court are published, one Justice authors the opinion and represents the voice of the entire Court. However, often (as in this case) other Justices will either write their own concurrence or dissents. Do some research into the history of concurrences and dissents. What impacts do they have on Supreme Court cases?

Whitney v. California, 274 U.S. 357 (1927)

MR. JUSTICE SANFORD delivered the opinion of the Court.

By a criminal information filed in the Superior Court of Alameda County, California, the plaintiff in error was charged, in five counts, with violations of the Criminal Syndicalism Act of that State. She was tried, convicted on the first count, and sentenced to imprisonment.

The pertinent provisions of the Criminal Syndicalism Act are:

> Section 1. The term "criminal syndicalism" as used in this act is hereby defined as any doctrine or precept advocating, teaching or aiding and abetting the commission of crime, sabotage (which word is hereby defined as meaning willful and malicious physical damage or injury to physical property), or unlawful acts of force and violence or unlawful methods of terrorism as a means of accomplishing a change in industrial ownership or control, or effecting any political change.
>
> Sec. 2. Any person who: . . . 4. Organizes or assists in organizing, or is or knowingly becomes a member of, any organization, society, group or assemblage of persons organized or assembled to advocate, teach or aid and abet criminal syndicalism is guilty of a felony and punishable by imprisonment.

The first count of the information, on which the conviction was had charged that, on or about November 28, 1919, in Alameda County, the defendant, in violation of the Criminal Syndicalism Act, "did then and there unlawfully, willfully, wrongfully, deliberately and feloniously organize and assist in organizing, and was, is, and knowingly became a member of an organization, society, group and assemblage of persons organized and assembled to advocate, teach, aid and abet criminal syndicalism."

During-Reading Question: What does the Criminal Syndicalism Act define as a crime?

We proceed to the determination, upon the merits, of the constitutional question considered and passed upon by the Court of Appeal. Of course, our review is to be confined to that question, since it does not appear, either from the order of the Court of Appeal or from the record otherwise, that any other federal question was presented in and either expressly or necessarily decided by that court.

The following facts, among many others, were established on the trial by undisputed evidence: the defendant, a resident of Oakland, in Alameda County, California, had been a member of the Local Oakland branch of the Socialist Party. This Local sent delegates to the national convention of the Socialist Party held in Chicago in 1919, which resulted in a split between the "radical" group and the old-wing Socialists. The "radicals"—to whom the Oakland delegates adhered—being ejected, went to another hall, and formed the Communist Labor Party of America. Its Constitution provided for the membership of persons subscribing to the principles of the Party and pledging themselves to be guided by its Platform, and for the formation of state organizations conforming to its Platform as the supreme declaration of the Party. In its "Platform and Program," the Party declared that it was in full harmony with "the revolutionary working class parties of all countries," and adhered to the principles of Communism laid down in the Manifesto of the Third International at Moscow, and that its purpose was "to create a unified revolutionary working class movement in America," organizing the workers as a class in a revolutionary class struggle to conquer the capitalist state for the overthrow of capitalist rule, the conquest of political power and the establishment of a working class government, the Dictatorship of the Proletariat, in place of the state machinery of the capitalists, which should make and enforce the laws, reorganize society on the basis of Communism, and bring about the Communist Commonwealth—advocated, as the most important means of capturing state power, the action of the masses, proceeding from the shops and factories, the use of the political machinery of the capitalist state being only secondary; the organization of the workers into "revolutionary industrial unions"; propaganda pointing out their revolutionary nature and possibilities, and great industrial battles showing the value of the strike as a political weapon—commended the propaganda and example of the Industrial Workers of the World and their struggles and sacrifices in the class war—pledged support and cooperation to "the revolutionary industrial proletariat of America" in their struggles against the capitalist class —cited the Seattle and Winnipeg strikes and the numerous strikes all over the country "proceeding without the authority of the old reactionary Trade Union officials," as manifestations of the new tendency—and recommended that strikes of national importance be supported and given a political character, and that propagandists and organizers be mobilized "who cannot only teach, but actually help to put in practice the principles of revolutionary industrial unionism and Communism."

Shortly thereafter, the Local Oakland withdrew from the Socialist Party and sent accredited delegates, including the defendant, to a convention held in Oakland in November, 1919, for the purpose of organizing a California branch of the Communist Labor Party. The defendant, after taking out a temporary membership in the Communist Labor Party, attended this convention as a delegate and took an active part in its proceedings. She was elected a member of the Credentials Committee, and, as its chairman, made a report to the convention upon which the delegates were seated. She was also appointed a member of the Resolutions Committee, and, as such, signed the following resolution in reference to political action, among others proposed by the Committee:

> The C.L.P. of California fully recognizes the value of political action as a means of spreading communist propaganda; it insists that, in proportion to the development of the economic strength of the working class, it, the working class, must also develop its political power. The C.L.P. of California proclaims and insists that the capture of political power, locally or nationally by the revolutionary working class, can be of tremendous assistance to the workers in their struggle of emancipation. Therefore, we again urge the workers who are possessed of the right of franchise to cast their votes for the party which represents their immediate and final interest—the C.L.P.—at all elections, being fully convinced of the utter futility of obtaining any real measure of justice or freedom under officials elected by parties owned and controlled by the capitalist class.

The minutes show that this resolution, with the others proposed by the committee, was read by its chairman to the convention before the Committee on the Constitution had submitted its report. According to the recollection of the defendant, however, she herself read this resolution. Thereafter, before the report of the Committee on the Constitution had been acted upon, the defendant was elected an alternate member of the State Executive Committee. The Constitution, as finally read, was then adopted. This provided that the organization should be named the Communist Labor Party of California; that it should be "affiliated with" the Communist Labor Party of America, and subscribe to its Program, Platform and Constitution, and, "through this affiliation," be "joined with the Communist International of Moscow;" and that the qualifications for membership should be those prescribed in the National Constitution. The proposed resolutions were later taken, up and all adopted except that on political action, which caused a lengthy debate, resulting in its defeat and the acceptance of the National Program in its place. After this action, the defendant, without, so far as appears, making any protest, remained in the convention until it adjourned. She later attended as an alternate member one or two meetings of the State Executive Committee in San Jose and San Francisco, and stated, on the trial, that she was then a member of the Communist Labor Party. She also testified that it was not her intention that the Communist Labor Party of California should be an instrument of terrorism or violence, and that it was not her purpose or that of the Convention to violate any known law.

During-Reading Question: The defendant, initially a Socialist, joined the Communist Labor Party of California and became a member of the Executive Committee. What is it about the Communist Party in 1919 that would cause people in California to have concerns?

In the light of this preliminary statement, we now take up, insofar as they require specific consideration, the various grounds upon which it is here contended that the Syndicalism Act and its application in this case is repugnant to the due process and equal protection clauses of the Fourteenth Amendment.

1.

While it is not denied that the evidence warranted the jury in finding that the defendant became a member of and assisted in organizing the Communist Labor Party of California, and that this was organized to advocate, teach, aid or abet criminal syndicalism as defined by the Act, it is urged that the Act, as here construed and applied, deprived the defendant of her liberty without due process of law in that it has made her action in attending the Oakland convention unlawful by reason of "a subsequent event brought about against her will by the agency of others," with no showing of a specific intent on her part to join in the forbidden purpose of the association, and merely because, by reason of a lack of "prophetic" understanding, she failed to foresee the quality that others would give to the convention. The argument is, in effect, that the character of the state organization could not be forecast when she attended the convention; that she had no purpose of helping to create an instrument of terrorism and violence; that she "took part in formulating and presenting to the convention a resolution which, if adopted, would have committed the new organization to a legitimate policy of political reform by the use of the ballot;" that it was not until after the majority of the convention turned out to be "contrary-minded, and other less temperate policies prevailed," that the convention could have taken on the character of criminal syndicalism, and that, as this was done over her protest, her mere presence in the convention, however violent the opinions expressed therein, could not thereby become a crime.

This contention, while advanced in the form of a constitutional objection to the Act, is in effect nothing more than an effort to review the weight of the evidence for the purpose of showing that the defendant did not join and assist in organizing the Communist Labor Party of California with a knowledge of its unlawful character and purpose. This question, which is foreclosed by the verdict of the jury—sustained by the Court of Appeal over the specific objection that it was not supported by the evidence—is one of fact merely, which is not open to review in this Court, involving, as it does, no constitutional question whatever. And we may add that the argument entirely disregards the facts: that the defendant had previously taken out a membership card in the National Party, that the resolution which she supported did not advocate the use of the ballot to the exclusion of violent and unlawful means of bringing about the desired changes in industrial and political conditions, and that, after the constitution of the California Party had been adopted, and this resolution had been voted down and the National Program accepted, she not only remained in the convention, without protest, until its close, but subsequently manifested her acquiescence by attending as an alternate member of the State Executive Committee and continuing as member of the Communist Labor Party.

During-Reading Question: The defendant argues that she personally was not interested in the terrorist nature of the organization which she joined, but that other people had later made those policy changes. Do you agree with the Court that she should still bear consequences due to her continued affiliation with the Communist Labor Party?

2.

It is clear that the Syndicalism Act is not repugnant to the due process clause by reason of vagueness and uncertainty of definition.

The Act, plainly, meets the essential requirement of due process that a penal statute be "sufficiently explicit to inform those who are subject to it, what conduct on their part will render them liable to its penalties," and be couched in terms that are not "so vague that men of common intelligence must necessarily guess at its meaning and differ as to its application." *Connally v. General Construction Co.* This statute presents no greater uncertainty or difficulty, in application to necessarily varying facts, than has been repeatedly sanctioned by this court.

So, as applied here, the Syndicalism Act required of the defendant no "prophetic" understanding of its meaning. And similar Criminal Syndicalism statutes of other States, some less specific in their definitions, have been held by the State courts not to be void for indefiniteness.

During-Reading Question: The defendant also argues that the Criminal Syndicalism Act is vague because it forces people to predict what their organization might do. Do you agree with the Court or the defendant?

3.

Neither is the Syndicalism Act repugnant to the equal protection clause on the ground that, as its penalties are confined to those who advocate a resort to violent and unlawful methods as a means of changing industrial and political conditions, it arbitrarily discriminates between such persons and those who may advocate a resort to these methods as a means of maintaining such conditions.

It is, settled by repeated decisions of this Court that the equal protection clause does not take from a State the power to classify in the adoption of police laws, but admits of the exercise of a wide scope of discretion, and avoids what is done only when it is without any reasonable basis, and therefore is purely arbitrary, and that one who assails the classification must carry the burden of showing that it does not rest upon any reasonable basic, but is essentially arbitrary. *Lindsley v. National Carbonic Gas Co.*

A statute does not violate the equal protection clause merely because it is not all-embracing. A State may properly direct its legislation against what it deems an existing evil without covering the whole field of possible abuses. The statute must be presumed to be aimed at an evil where experience shows it to be most felt, and to be deemed by the legislature coextensive with the practical need, and is not to be overthrown merely because other instances may be suggested to which also it might have been applied, that being a matter for the legislature to determine unless the case is very clear. And it is not open to objection unless the classification is so lacking in any adequate or reasonable basis as to preclude the assumption that it was made in the exercise of the legislative judgment and discretion.

The Syndicalism Act is not class legislation; it affects all alike, no matter what their business associations or callings, who come within its terms and do the things prohibited. And there is no substantial basis for the contention that the legislature has arbitrarily or unreasonably limited its application to those advocating the use of violent and unlawful methods to effect changes in industrial and political conditions, there being nothing indicating any ground to apprehend that those desiring to maintain existing industrial and political conditions did or would advocate such methods. That there is a widespread conviction of the necessity for legislation of this character is indicated by the adoption of similar statutes in several other States.

4.

Nor is the Syndicalism Act, as applied in this case, repugnant to the due process clause as a restraint of the rights of free speech, assembly, and association.

That the freedom of speech which is secured by the Constitution does not confer an absolute right to speak, without responsibility, whatever one may choose, or an unrestricted and unbridled license giving immunity for every possible use of language and preventing the punishment of those who abuse this freedom, and that a State in the exercise of its police power may punish those who abuse this freedom by utterances inimical to the public welfare, tending to incite to crime, disturb the public peace, or endanger the foundations of organized government and threaten its overthrow by unlawful means, is not open to question.

During-Reading Question: Do you agree that states should be able to punish people who make statements that could incite others to violence in order to protect the public?

By enacting the provisions of the Syndicalism Act, the State has declared, through its legislative body, that to knowingly be or become a member of or assist in organizing an association to advocate, teach or aid and abet the commission of crimes or unlawful acts of force, violence or terrorism as a means of accomplishing industrial or political changes involves such danger to the public peace and the security of the State, that these acts should be penalized in the exercise of its police power. That determination must be given great weight. Every presumption is to be indulged in favor of the validity of the statute, and it may not be declared unconstitutional unless it is an arbitrary or unreasonable attempt to exercise the authority vested in the State in the public interest.

The essence of the offense denounced by the Act is the combining with others in an association for the accomplishment of the desired ends through the advocacy and use of criminal and unlawful methods. It partakes of the nature of a criminal conspiracy. That such united and joint action involves even greater danger to the public peace and security than the isolated utterances and acts of individuals is clear. We cannot hold that, as here applied, the Act is an unreasonable or arbitrary exercise of the police power of the State, unwarrantably infringing any right of free speech, assembly or association, or that those persons are protected from punishment by the due process clause who abuse such rights by joining and furthering an organization thus menacing the peace and welfare of the State.

During-Reading Question: Do you agree with the Court that membership in an organization with others who may want to effect change using criminal methods is almost like being a part of a criminal conspiracy?

We find no repugnancy in the Syndicalism Act as applied in this case to either the due process or equal protection clauses of the Fourteenth Amendment on any of the grounds upon which its validity has been here challenged.

The order dismissing the writ of error will be vacated and set aside, and the judgment of the Court of Appeal Affirmed.

MR. JUSTICE BRANDEIS, concurring.

During-Reading Questions: Justice Brandeis' concurrence promotes the "clear and present danger" test for the restraint of free speech and assembly. What are Brandeis' requirements for that test? What examples does he use?

Miss Whitney was convicted of the felony of assisting in organizing, in the year 1919, the Communist Labor Party of California, of being a member of it, and of assembling with it. These acts are held to constitute a crime because the party was formed to teach criminal syndicalism. The statute which made these acts a crime restricted the right of free speech and of assembly theretofore existing. The claim is that the statute, as applied, denied to Miss Whitney the liberty guaranteed by the Fourteenth Amendment.

The felony which the statute created is a crime very unlike the old felony of conspiracy or the old misdemeanor of unlawful assembly. The mere act of assisting in forming a society for teaching syndicalism, of becoming a member of it, or of assembling with others for that purpose, is given the dynamic quality of crime. There is guilt although the society may not contemplate immediate promulgation of the doctrine. Thus, the accused is to be punished not for contempt, incitement, or conspiracy, but for a step in preparation, which, if it threatens the public order at all, does so only remotely. The novelty in the prohibition introduced is that the statute aims not at the practice of criminal syndicalism, nor even directly at the preaching of it, but at association with those who propose to preach it.

This Court has not yet fixed the standard by which to determine when a danger shall be deemed clear; how remote the danger may be and yet be deemed present, and what degree of evil shall be deemed sufficiently substantial to justify resort to abridgement of free speech and assembly as the means of protection. To reach sound conclusions on these matters, we must bear in mind why a State is, ordinarily, denied the power to prohibit dissemination of social, economic and political doctrine which a vast majority of its citizens believes to be false and fraught with evil consequence.

Those who won our independence believed that the final end of the State was to make men free to develop their faculties, and that, in its government, the deliberative forces should prevail over the arbitrary. They valued liberty both as an end, and as a means. They believed liberty to be the secret of happiness, and courage to be the secret of liberty. They believed that freedom to think as you will and to speak as you think are means indispensable to the discovery and spread of political truth; that, without free speech and assembly, discussion would be futile; that, with them, discussion affords ordinarily adequate protection against the dissemination of noxious doctrine; that the greatest menace to freedom is an inert people; that public discussion is a political duty, and that this should be a fundamental principle of the American government. They recognized the risks to which all human institutions are subject. But they knew that order cannot be secured merely through fear of punishment for its infraction; that it is hazardous to discourage thought, hope and imagination; that fear breeds repression; that repression breeds hate; that hate menaces stable government; that the path of safety lies in the opportunity to discuss freely supposed grievances and proposed remedies, and that the fitting remedy for evil counsels is good ones. Believing in the power of reason as applied through public discussion, they eschewed silence coerced by law—the argument of force in its worst form. Recognizing the occasional tyrannies of governing majorities, they amended the Constitution so that free speech and assembly should be guaranteed.

Fear of serious injury cannot alone justify suppression of free speech and assembly. Men feared witches and burnt women. It is the function of speech to free men from the bondage of irrational fears. To justify suppression of free speech, there must be reasonable ground to fear that serious evil will result if free speech is practiced. There must be reasonable ground to believe that the danger apprehended is imminent. There must be reasonable ground to believe that the evil to be prevented is a serious one. Every denunciation of existing law tends in some measure to increase the probability that there will be violation of it. Condonation of a breach enhances the probability. Expressions of approval add to the probability. Propagation of the criminal state of mind by teaching syndicalism increases it. Advocacy of law-breaking heightens it still further. But even advocacy of violation, however reprehensible morally, is not a justification for denying free speech where the advocacy falls short of incitement and there is nothing to indicate that the advocacy would be immediately acted on. The wide difference between advocacy and incitement, between preparation and attempt, between assembling and conspiracy, must be borne in mind. In order to support a finding of clear and present danger, it must be shown either that immediate serious violence was to be expected or was advocated, or that the past conduct furnished reason to believe that such advocacy was then contemplated.

Those who won our independence by revolution were not cowards. They did not fear political change. They did not exalt order at the cost of liberty. To courageous, self-reliant men, with confidence in the power of free and fearless reasoning applied through the processes of popular government, no danger flowing from speech can be deemed clear and present unless the incidence of the evil apprehended is so imminent that it may befall before there is opportunity for full discussion. If there be time to expose through discussion the falsehood and fallacies, to avert the evil by the processes of education, the remedy to be applied is more speech, not enforced silence. Only an emergency can justify repression. Such must be the rule if authority is to be reconciled with freedom. Such, in my opinion, is the command of the Constitution. It is therefore always open to Americans to challenge a law abridging free speech and assembly by showing that there was no emergency justifying it.

Moreover, even imminent danger cannot justify resort to prohibition of these functions essential to effective democracy unless the evil apprehended is relatively serious. Prohibition of free speech and assembly is a measure so stringent that it would be inappropriate as the means for averting a relatively trivial harm to society. A police measure may be unconstitutional merely because the remedy, although effective as means of protection, is unduly harsh or oppressive. Thus, a State might, in the exercise of its police power, make any trespass upon the land of another a crime, regardless of the results or of the intent or purpose of the trespasser. It might, also, punish an attempt, a conspiracy, or an incitement to commit the trespass. But it is hardly conceivable that this Court would hold constitutional a statute which punished as a felony the mere voluntary assembly with a society formed to teach that pedestrians had the moral right to cross unenclosed, unposted, wastelands and to advocate their doing so, even if there was imminent danger that advocacy would lead to a trespass. The fact that speech is likely to result in some violence or in destruction of property is not enough to justify its suppression. There must be the probability of serious injury to the State. Among free men, the deterrents ordinarily to be applied to prevent crime are education and punishment for violations of the law, not abridgment of the rights of free speech and assembly.

Whenever the fundamental rights of free speech and assembly are alleged to have been invaded, it must remain open to a defendant to present the issue whether there actually did exist at the time a clear danger; whether the danger, if any, was imminent, and whether the evil apprehended was one so substantial as to justify the stringent restriction interposed by the legislature. The legislative declaration, like the fact that the statute was passed and was sustained by the highest court of the State, creates merely a rebuttable presumption that these conditions have been satisfied.

Whether in 1919, when Miss Whitney did the things complained of, there was in California such clear and present danger of serious evil might have been made the important issue in the case. She might have required that the issue be determined either by the court or the jury. She claimed below that the statute, as applied to her, violated the Federal Constitution; but she did not claim that it was void because there was no clear and present danger of serious evil, nor did she request that the existence of these conditions of a valid measure thus restricting the rights of free speech and assembly be passed upon by the court or a jury. On the other hand, there was evidence on which the court or jury might have found that such danger existed. I am unable to assent to the suggestion in the opinion of the Court that assembling with a political party, formed to advocate the desirability of a proletarian revolution by mass action at some date necessarily far in the future, is not a right within the protection of the Fourteenth Amendment. In the present case, however, there was other testimony which tended to establish the existence of a conspiracy, on the part of members of the International Workers of the World, to commit present serious crimes, and likewise to show that such a conspiracy would be furthered by the activity of the society of which Miss Whitney was a member. Under these circumstances, the judgment of the state court cannot be disturbed.

Post-Reading Questions

1. While Justice Brandeis promotes the "clear and present danger" test in this case, why does he say that it doesn't apply to the defendant, Miss Whitney?
2. Criminal Syndicalism Acts were designed in particular to stop the efforts of labor union groups, particularly the *Wobblies*. What threat did the Wobblies and other labor unions present to the status quo in the early part of the twentieth century?

Further Explorations

Exploring the Story

The defendant in *Whitney v. California*, Charlotte Anita Whitney, has an interesting background and personal history. Have students do further exploration about Whitney and her political impact on the United States.

Exploring the Law

Have students do research on the case *Schenck v. United States* where the idea of a "clear and present danger" was first articulated by Justice Holmes. What is Holmes' famous metaphor on the appropriate limitation of free speech?

Exploring the Effects

To learn more about the impacts of this case on the First Amendment, go to: Hudson, D. L. (2016, January 8). "Free speech" impact of *Whitney v. California*. *Newseum Institute*. Retrieved from http://www.newseuminstitute.org/2016/01/08/free-speech-impact-of-whitney-v-california/

CASE #2B: *BRANDENBURG V. OHIO*

Pre-Reading Questions

1. Why is it good for our society to allow people with whom we disagree to have First Amendment freedom of speech and assembly rights? Are there any people you think shouldn't have those rights? Why?
2. Over forty years passed between the decision in *Whitney v. California* and the decision in *Brandenburg v. Ohio*. Based on your knowledge of the changes in American society from the 1920s to the 1960s, how do you predict the Court might change its decision regarding the First Amendment rights of speech and assembly and restrictions upon those rights? What societal and legal changes could contribute to a different ruling by the Court?

Brandenburg v. Ohio, 395 U.S. 444 (1969)

PER CURIAM.

The appellant, a leader of a Ku Klux Klan group, was convicted under the Ohio Criminal Syndicalism statute for "advocat[ing] . . . the duty, necessity, or propriety of crime, sabotage, violence, or unlawful methods of terrorism as a means of accomplishing industrial or political reform" and for "voluntarily assembl[ing] with any society, group, or assemblage of persons formed to teach or advocate the doctrines of criminal syndicalism."

He was fined $1,000 and sentenced to one to 10 years' imprisonment. The appellant challenged the constitutionality of the criminal syndicalism statute under the First and Fourteenth Amendments to the United States Constitution, but the intermediate appellate court of Ohio affirmed his conviction without opinion. The Supreme Court of Ohio dismissed his appeal sua sponte "for the reason that no substantial constitutional question exists herein." It did not file an opinion or explain its conclusions. Appeal was taken to this Court, and we noted probable jurisdiction.

We reverse.

The record shows that a man, identified at trial as the appellant, telephoned an announcer-reporter on the staff of a Cincinnati television station and invited him to come to a Ku Klux Klan "rally" to be held at a farm in Hamilton County. With the cooperation of the organizers, the reporter and a cameraman attended the meeting and filmed the events. Portions of the films were later broadcast on the local station and on a national network.

The prosecution's case rested on the films and on testimony identifying the appellant as the person who communicated with the reporter and who spoke at the rally. The State also introduced into evidence several articles appearing in the film, including a pistol, a rifle, a shotgun, ammunition, a Bible, and a red hood worn by the speaker in the films.

One film showed 12 hooded figures, some of whom carried firearms. They were gathered around a large wooden cross, which they burned. No one was present other than the participants and the newsmen who made the film. Most of the words uttered during the scene were incomprehensible when the film was projected, but scattered phrases could be understood that were derogatory of Negroes and, in one instance, of Jews. Another scene on the same film showed the appellant, in Klan regalia, making a speech. The speech, in full, was as follows:

> This is an organizers' meeting. We have had quite a few members here today which are—we have hundreds, hundreds of members throughout the State of Ohio. I can quote from a newspaper clipping from the Columbus, Ohio, Dispatch, five weeks ago Sunday morning. The Klan has more

> members in the State of Ohio than does any other organization. We're not a revengent organization, but if our President, our Congress, our Supreme Court, continues to suppress the white, Caucasian race, it's possible that there might have to be some revengeance taken.
>
> We are marching on Congress July the Fourth, four hundred thousand strong. From there, we are dividing into two groups, one group to march on St. Augustine, Florida, the other group to march into Mississippi. Thank you.

The second film showed six hooded figures one of whom, later identified as the appellant, repeated a speech very similar to that recorded on the first film. The reference to the possibility of "revengeance" was omitted, and one sentence was added: "Personally, I believe the nigger should be returned to Africa, the Jew returned to Israel." Though some of the figures in the films carried weapons, the speaker did not.

During-Reading Question: The speech in question was broadcast by a local television station. Does the television station bear any responsibility for sharing the violent message of Brandenburg?

The Ohio Criminal Syndicalism Statute was enacted in 1919. From 1917 to 1920, identical or quite similar laws were adopted by 20 States and two territories. E. Dowell, *A History of Criminal Syndicalism Legislation in the United States*. In 1927, this Court sustained the constitutionality of California's Criminal Syndicalism Act, the text of which is quite similar to that of the laws of Ohio. *Whitney v. California,* 274 U. S. 357. The Court upheld the statute on the ground that, without more, "advocating" violent means to effect political and economic change involves such danger to the security of the State that the State may outlaw it. But *Whitney* has been thoroughly discredited by later decisions. These later decisions have fashioned the principle that the constitutional guarantees of free speech and free press do not permit a State to forbid or proscribe advocacy of the use of force or of law violation except where such advocacy is directed to inciting or producing imminent lawless action and is likely to incite or produce such action. As we said in *Noto v. United States*, "the mere abstract teaching . . . of the moral propriety or even moral necessity for a resort to force and violence is not the same as preparing a group for violent action and steeling it to such action."

During-Reading Question: What does the Court speech have to do in order for a state to restrict and punish a person for saying it?

Measured by this test, Ohio's Criminal Syndicalism Act cannot be sustained. The Act punishes persons who "advocate or teach the duty, necessity, or propriety" of violence "as a means of accomplishing industrial or political reform"; or who publish or circulate or display any book or paper containing such advocacy; or who "justify" the commission of violent acts "with intent to exemplify, spread or advocate the propriety of the doctrines of criminal syndicalism"; or who "voluntarily assemble" with a group formed "to teach or advocate the doctrines of criminal syndicalism." Neither the indictment nor the trial judge's instructions to the jury in any way refined the statute's bald definition of the crime in terms of mere advocacy not distinguished from incitement to imminent lawless action.

Accordingly, we are here confronted with a statute which, by its own words and as applied, purports to punish mere advocacy and to forbid, on pain of criminal punishment, assembly with others merely to advocate the described type of action. Such a statute falls within the condemnation of the First and Fourteenth Amendments. The contrary teaching of *Whitney v. California* cannot be supported, and that decision is therefore overruled.

Reversed.

Post-Reading Questions

1. Some critics of the *Brandenburg* decision think the Court has gone too far, and it allows terrorist groups to plot against innocent people and try to overthrow the government. Do you agree or disagree? What three words are at the center of whether speech or assembly can be made illegal? How easy or difficult do you think that would be to prove?
2. What is the difference between advocacy and incitement? Do you think the Court is correct in this distinction?

Further Explorations

Exploring the Story

Read more about the Ku Klux Klan and other cases that have brought them before the Supreme Court by going to the National Constitution Center's website at constitutioncenter.org/blog and searching for "Three Supreme Court cases involving the Ku Klux Klan."

Exploring the Law

Have students explore how the *Brandenburg* decision could impact their own speech by reading about Michelle Carter's involuntary manslaughter conviction for encouraging her boyfriend to commit suicide: Jacobo, J. (2017, June 21). Can words kill? Guilty verdict in texting suicide trial raises questions. *abcNEWS*. Retrieved from http://abcnews.go.com/US/words-kill-guilty-verdict-texting-suicide-trial-raises/story?id=48093522

Exploring the Effects

Have students research the 2017 Ku Klux Klan rally in Charlottesville, Virginia, where a young woman was struck and killed by one of the white nationalist participants. Using *Brandenburg,* have students debate whether organizers of the rally should be criminally charged for inciting the driver to violence in Charlottesville.

Activities for Extending the Learning

Several different tests have been used by the Supreme Court to determine whether an individual's First Amendment rights have been violated. Have students research and compare the following legal tests:

- The bad tendency test
- The clear and present danger test
- The balancing test
- Imminent lawless action test

Students can analyze the historical similarities and differences, and well as examining how the tests have evolved over time.

CASE #3A: *SOUTH CAROLINA V. GATHERS*

Pre-Reading Questions

1. Do you think victim impact statements and statements supporting people should be read during the sentencing phase of someone convicted of a capital crime? Explain the reasoning behind your answer.
2. In this case, the Court discusses the idea of being "morally culpable" for a crime. What does that mean? Should courts ever allow a jury to listen to anything outside of the "moral culpability" of the defendant during a trial?

South Carolina v. Gathers, 490 U.S. 805 (1989)

JUSTICE BRENNAN delivered the opinion of the Court.

Respondent Demetrius Gathers was convicted of murder and sentenced to death for the killing of Richard Haynes. The evidence at trial showed that Gathers and three companions encountered Haynes, a stranger to them, at a park bench one evening. When Haynes rebuffed Gathers' attempt to initiate a conversation, Gathers and his friends assaulted Haynes, beating and kicking him severely and smashing a bottle over his head. Before leaving the scene, Gathers beat Haynes with an umbrella, which he then inserted into the victim's anus. Some time later, Gathers apparently returned to the scene and stabbed Haynes with a knife.

Richard Haynes was about 31 years old, and unemployed. For two years prior to his death, he had been experiencing "some mental problems" and had been "in and out of [a] mental hospital" three times. Although without formal religious training, Haynes considered himself a preacher, and referred to himself as "Reverend Minister"; his mother testified that he would he would "tal[k] to people all the time about the Lord." He generally carried with him several bags containing articles of religious significance, including two Bibles, rosary beads, plastic statues, olive oil, and religious tracts. Among these items, on the evening of his murder, was a tract entitled "The Game Guy's Prayer." Relying on football and boxing metaphors, it extolled the virtues of the good sport. After Haynes was beaten, his assailants went through his belongings, looking (apparently in vain) for something worth stealing. In rummaging through his personal effects, they scattered on the ground the contents of his wallet and bags, including the just-mentioned tract.

Gathers was tried in the Court of General Sessions for Charleston County, South Carolina. During the guilt phase, the articles found at the scene of the crime were admitted into evidence without objection. The jury found Gathers guilty of murder and first-degree criminal sexual conduct. All of the testimony and exhibits from the guilt phase were readmitted into evidence at the sentencing phase. The State presented no other evidence at the sentencing phase, but the prosecutor's closing argument included the following remarks, which are the basis for the present controversy:

> We know from the proof that Reverend Minister Haynes was a religious person. He had his religious items out there. This defendant strewn [*sic*] them across the bike path, thinking nothing of that.
>
> Among the many cards that Reverend Haynes had among his belongings was this card. It's in evidence. Think about it when you go back there. He had this [*sic*] religious items, his beads. He had a plastic angel. Of course, he is now with the angels now, but this defendant Demetrius Gathers could care little about the fact that he is a religious person. Cared little of the pain and agony he inflicted upon a person who is trying to enjoy one of our public parks.

But look at Reverend Minister Haynes' prayer. It's called the Game Guy's Prayer: Dear God, help me to be a sport in this little game of life. I don't ask for any easy place in this lineup. Play me anywhere you need me. I only ask you for the stuff to give you one hundred percent of what I have got. If all the hard drives seem to come my way, I thank you for the compliment. Help me to remember that you won't ever let anything come my way that you and I together can't handle. And help me to take the bad break as part of the game. Help me to understand that the game is full of knots and knocks and trouble, and make me thankful for them. Help me to be brave, so that the harder they come, the better I like it. And, oh God, help me to always play on the square. No matter what the other players do, help me to come clean. Help me to study the book, so that I'll know the rules, to study and think a lot about the greatest player that ever lived and other players that are portrayed in the book. If they ever found out the best part of the game was helping other guys who are out of luck, help me to find it out, too. Help me to be regular, and also an inspiration with the other players. Finally, oh God, if fate seems to uppercut me with both hands, and I am laid on the shelf in sickness or old age or something, help me to take that as part of the game, too. Help me not to whimper or squeal that the game was a frameup or that I had a raw deal. When, in the falling dusk, I get the final bell, I ask for no lying, complimentary tombstones. I'd only like to know that you feel that I have been a good guy, a good game guy, a saint in the game of life.

Reverend Minister Haynes, we know, was a very small person. He had his mental problems. Unable to keep a regular job. And he wasn't blessed with fame or fortune. And he took things as they came along. He was prepared to deal with tragedies that he came across in his life.

You will find some other exhibits in this case that tell you more about a just verdict. Again this is not easy. No one takes any pleasure from it, but the proof cries out from the grave in this case. Among the personal effects that this defendant could care little about when he went through it is something that we all treasure. Speaks a lot about Reverend Minister Haynes. Very simple, yet very profound. Voting. A voter's registration card.

Reverend Haynes believed in this community. He took part. And he believed that, in Charleston County, in the United States of America, that in this country, you could go to a public park and sit on a public bench and not be attacked by the likes of Demetrius Gathers.

During-Reading Question: What was the prosecutor trying to show about the victim by presenting this evidence during the sentencing phase?

Finding that these "extensive comments to the jury regarding the victim's character were unnecessary to an understanding of the circumstances of the crime," the Supreme Court of South Carolina concluded that the prosecutor's remarks "conveyed the suggestion appellant deserved a death sentence because the victim was a religious man and a registered voter." Relying on our decision in *Booth v. Maryland*, the court reversed Gathers' sentence of death and remanded for a new sentencing proceeding. We granted certiorari, and we now affirm.

Our capital cases have consistently recognized that "[f]or purposes of imposing the death penalty, . . . [the defendant's] punishment must be tailored to his personal responsibility and moral guilt." *Enmund v. Florida*. Two Terms ago, in *Booth v. Maryland*, we addressed the question whether use of "victim impact statements" in capital sentencing proceedings violated this principle that a sentence of death must be related to the moral culpability of the defendant. We held that such statements introduced factors that might be "wholly unrelated to the blameworthiness of a particular defendant." "The statements placed before the jury in *Booth* included descriptions of the victims' personal characteristics, statements concerning the emotional impact of the crime on the victims' family, and the family members' opinions about the crime and the defendant. At issue in the present case is a statement of the first sort—one concerning personal characteristics of the victim. While in this case it was the prosecutor, rather than the victim's survivors, who characterized the victim's personal qualities, the statement is indistinguishable in any relevant respect from that in *Booth*. As in *Booth*, "[a]llowing the jury to rely on [this information] . . . could result in imposing the death sentence because of factors about which the defendant was unaware, and that were irrelevant to the decision to kill."

During-Reading Questions: What is the Court worried about juries doing when listening to positive information about a victim during sentencing? Do you think the Court is correct or incorrect for excluding this type of information?

Our opinion in *Booth*, however, left open the possibility that the kind of information contained in victim impact statements could be admissible if it "relate[d] directly to the circumstances of the crime." South Carolina asserts that such is the case here. It contends that the various personal effects which were "maliciously strewn around [the victim's] body during the event" were "relevant to the circumstances of the crime or reveal certain personal characteristics of the defendant."

We disagree. The fact that Gathers scattered Haynes' personal papers around his body while going through them looking for something to steal was certainly a relevant circumstance of the crime, and thus a proper subject for comment. But the prosecutor's argument in this case went well beyond that fact: he read to the jury at length from the religious tract the victim was carrying, and commented on the personal qualities he inferred from Haynes' possession of the "Game Guy's Prayer" and the voter registration card. The content of these cards, however, cannot possibly have been relevant to the "circumstances of the crime." There is no evidence whatever that the defendant read anything that was printed on either the tract or the voter card. Indeed, it is extremely unlikely that he did so. The testimony at trial was that Gathers went through Haynes' bags very quickly, "just throwing [his belongings] everywhere, looking through things," and that he spent not more than a minute doing so. The crime took place, moreover, at night, along a dark path through a wooded area. Nor did the assailants have flashlights. Under these circumstances, the content of the various papers the victim happened to be carrying when he was attacked was purely fortuitous, and cannot provide any information relevant to the defendant's moral culpability. Notwithstanding that the papers had been admitted into evidence for another purpose, their content cannot be said to relate directly to the circumstances of the crime.

The judgment of the Supreme Court of South Carolina is therefore
Affirmed

Post-Reading Questions

1. What connection to the circumstances of the crime could you have argued to the Court if Gathers had taken time to read through all of the victim's materials and the crime had happened in broad daylight? Does it really make a difference?
2. Sentencing happens after the defendant has already been found guilty. If victim impact statements only go to the punishment of guilty people, why should we care what impact they have on sentencing?

Further Explorations

Exploring the Story

Gathers' death penalty was reversed and he was given life imprisonment based on the exclusion of the victim impact testimony at sentencing. Have students create arguments both for and against the use of victim impact statements for sentencing.

Exploring the Law

Have students research the history of crime victims' rights legislation in the United States. The crime victim rights movement didn't start until the 1970s. What do you think could have contributed to the creation and promotion of the crime victims' rights movement?

Exploring the Effects

South Carolina v. Gathers was decided on a 5-to-4 vote, with the justices voting in this way:

> The majority—John Paul Stevens, William Brennan, Thurgood Marshall, Harry Blackmun, and Byron White; the minority—Sandra Day O'Connor, William Rehnquist, Antonin Scalia, and Anthony Kennedy.

Have the students research the political backgrounds of the Supreme Court Justices to see if they can draw any conclusions about why the Justices decided the way they did.

CASE #3B: *PAYNE V. TENNESSEE*

Pre-Reading Questions

1. Since 1978 in *Locket v. Ohio*, the Supreme Court has held that anyone facing the death penalty has the right to present any mitigating factors about them, and there shouldn't be a limitation on what a defendant can present. Why it is important to provide that right?
2. What is Stare Decisis? How is it legally important?

***Payne v. Tennessee*, 501 U.S. 808 (1991)**

CHIEF JUSTICE REHNQUIST delivered the opinion of the Court.

In this case, we reconsider our holdings in *Booth v. Maryland* and *South Carolina v. Gathers*, that the Eighth Amendment bars the admission of victim impact evidence during the penalty phase of a capital trial.

Petitioner, Pervis Tyrone Payne, was convicted by a jury on two counts of first-degree murder and one count of assault with intent to commit murder in the first degree. He was sentenced to death for each of the murders and to 30 years in prison for the assault.

The victims of Payne's offenses were 28-year-old Charisse Christopher, her 2-year-old daughter Lacie, and her 3-year-old son Nicholas. The three lived together in an apartment in Millington, Tennessee, across the hall from Payne's girlfriend, Bobbie Thomas. On Saturday, June 27, 1987, Payne visited Thomas' apartment several times in expectation of her return from her mother's house in Arkansas, but found no one at home. On one visit, he left his overnight bag, containing clothes and other items for his weekend stay, in the hallway outside Thomas' apartment. With the bag were three cans of malt liquor.

Payne passed the morning and early afternoon injecting cocaine and drinking beer. Later, he drove around the town with a friend in the friend's car, each of them taking turns reading a pornographic magazine. Sometime around 3 p.m., Payne returned to the apartment complex, entered the Christophers' apartment, and began making sexual advances towards Charisse. Charisse resisted, and Payne became violent. A neighbor who resided in the apartment directly beneath the Christophers heard Charisse screaming, "Get out, get out," as if she were telling the children to leave. The noise briefly subsided, and then began, "horribly loud." The neighbor called the police after she heard a "blood curdling scream" from the Christophers' apartment.

When the first police officer arrived at the scene, he immediately encountered Payne, who was leaving the apartment building, so covered with blood that he appeared to be "sweating blood." The officer confronted Payne, who responded, "I'm the complainant." When the officer asked, "What's going on up there?", Payne struck the officer with the overnight bag, dropped his tennis shoes, and fled.

Inside the apartment, the police encountered a horrifying scene. Blood covered the walls and floor throughout the unit. Charisse and her children were lying on the floor in the kitchen. Nicholas, despite several wounds inflicted by a butcher knife that completely penetrated through his body from front to back, was still breathing. Miraculously, he survived, but not until after undergoing seven hours of surgery and a transfusion of 1,700 cc's of blood—400 to 500 cc's more than his estimated normal blood volume. Charisse and Lacie were dead. Charisse's body was found on the kitchen floor on her back, her legs fully extended. She had sustained 42 direct knife wounds and 42 defensive wounds on her arms and hands. The wounds were caused by 41 separate thrusts of a butcher knife. None of the 84 wounds inflicted by Payne were individually fatal; rather, the cause of death was most likely bleeding from all of the wounds.

Lacie's body was on the kitchen floor near her mother. She had suffered stab wounds to the chest, abdomen, back, and head. The murder weapon, a butcher knife, was found at her feet. Payne's baseball cap was snapped on her arm near her elbow. Three cans of malt liquor bearing Payne's fingerprints were found on a table near her body, and a fourth empty one was on the landing outside the apartment door.

Payne was apprehended later that day hiding in the attic of the home of a former girlfriend. As he descended the stairs of the attic, he stated to the arresting officers, "Man, I ain't killed no woman." According to one of the officers, Payne had "a wild look about him. His pupils were contracted. He was foaming at the mouth, saliva. He appeared to be very nervous. He was breathing real rapid." He had blood on his body and clothes and several scratches across his chest. It was later determined that the blood stains matched the victims' blood types. A search of his pockets revealed a packet containing cocaine residue, a hypodermic syringe wrapper, and a cap from a hypodermic syringe. His overnight bag, containing a bloody white shirt, was found in a nearby dumpster.

At trial, Payne took the stand and, despite the overwhelming and relatively uncontroverted evidence against him, testified that he had not harmed any of the Christophers. Rather, he asserted that another man had raced by him as he was walking up the stairs to the floor where the Christophers lived. He stated that he had gotten blood on himself when, after hearing moans from the Christophers' apartment, he had tried to help the victims. According to his testimony, he panicked and fled when he heard police sirens and noticed the blood on his clothes. The jury returned guilty verdicts against Payne on all counts.

During the sentencing phase of the trial, Payne presented the testimony of four witnesses: his mother and father, Bobbie Thomas, and Dr. John T. Hutson, a clinical psychologist specializing in criminal court evaluation work. Bobbie Thomas testified that she met Payne at church, during a time when she was being abused by her husband. She stated that Payne was a very caring person, and that he devoted much time and attention to her three children, who were being affected by her marital difficulties. She said that the children had come to love him very much, and would miss him, and that he "behaved just like a father that loved his kids." She asserted that he did not drink, nor did he use drugs, and that it was generally inconsistent with Payne's character to have committed these crimes.

Dr. Hutson testified that, based on Payne's low score on an IQ test, Payne was "mentally handicapped." Hutson also said that Payne was neither psychotic nor schizophrenic, and that Payne was the most polite prisoner he had ever met. Payne's parents testified that their son had no prior criminal record, and had never been arrested. They also stated that Payne had no history of alcohol or drug abuse, he worked with his father as a painter, he was good with children, and he was a good son.

The State presented the testimony of Charisse's mother, Mary Zvolanek. When asked how Nicholas had been affected by the murders of his mother and sister, she responded: "He cries for his mom. He doesn't seem to understand why she doesn't come home. And he cries for his sister Lacie. He comes to me many times during the week and asks me, Grandmama, do you miss my Lacie. And I tell him yes. He says, I'm worried about my Lacie."

In arguing for the death penalty during closing argument, the prosecutor commented on the continuing effects of Nicholas' experience, stating:

> But we do know that Nicholas was alive. And Nicholas was in the same room. Nicholas was still conscious. His eyes were open. He responded to the paramedics. He was able to follow their directions. He was able to hold his intestines in as he was carried to the ambulance. So he knew what happened to his mother and baby sister.
>
> There is nothing you can do to ease the pain of any of the families involved in this case. There is nothing you can do to ease the pain of Bernice or Carl Payne, and that's a tragedy. There is nothing you can do basically to ease the pain of Mr. and Mrs. Zvolanek, and that's a tragedy. They will have to live with it the rest of their lives. There is obviously nothing you can do for Charisse and Lacie Jo. But there is something that you can do for Nicholas.
>
> Somewhere down the road Nicholas is going to grow up, hopefully. He's going to want to know what happened. And he is going to know what happened to his baby sister and his mother. He is going to want to know what type of justice was done. He is going to want to know what happened. With your verdict, you will provide the answer.

In the rebuttal to Payne's closing argument, the prosecutor stated:

> You saw the videotape this morning. You saw what Nicholas Christopher will carry in his mind forever. When you talk about cruel, when you talk about atrocious, and when you talk about heinous, that picture will always come into your mind, probably throughout the rest of your lives. . . .
>
> . . . No one will ever know about Lacie Jo, because she never had the chance to grow up. Her life was taken from her at the age of two years old. So, no, there won't be a high school principal to talk about Lacie Jo Christopher, and there won't be anybody to take her to her high school prom. And there won't be anybody there—there won't be her mother there or Nicholas' mother there to kiss him at night. His mother will never kiss him good night or pat him as he goes off to bed, or hold him and sing him a lullaby.
>
> [Petitioner's attorney] wants you to think about a good reputation, people who love the defendant and things about him. He doesn't want you to think about the people who love Charisse Christopher, her mother and daddy who loved her. The people who loved little Lacie Jo, the grandparents who are still here. The brother who mourns for her every single day and wants to know where his best little playmate is. He doesn't have anybody to watch cartoons with him, a

> little one. These are the things that go into why it is especially cruel, heinous, and atrocious, the burden that that child will carry forever.

The jury sentenced Payne to death on each of the murder counts.

The Supreme Court of Tennessee affirmed the conviction and sentence. The court rejected Payne's contention that the admission of the grandmother's testimony and the State's closing argument constituted prejudicial violations of his rights under the Eighth Amendment as applied in *Booth v. Maryland*, and *South Carolina v. Gathers*. The court characterized the grandmother's testimony as "technically irrelevant," but concluded that it "did not create a constitutionally unacceptable risk of an arbitrary imposition of the death penalty, and was harmless beyond a reasonable doubt."

The court determined that the prosecutor's comments during closing argument were "relevant to [Payne's] personal responsibility and moral guilt." The court explained that "[w]hen a person deliberately picks a butcher knife out of a kitchen drawer and proceeds to stab to death a twenty-eight-year-old mother, her two and one-half year old daughter, and her three and one-half year old son, in the same room, the physical and mental condition of the boy he left for dead is surely relevant in determining his 'blameworthiness.'"

The court concluded that any violation of Payne's rights under *Booth* and *Gathers* "was harmless beyond a reasonable doubt."

We granted certiorari to reconsider our holdings in *Booth* and *Gathers* that the Eighth Amendment prohibits a capital sentencing jury from considering "victim impact" evidence relating to the personal characteristics of the victim and the emotional impact of the crimes on the victim's family.

In *Booth*, the defendant robbed and murdered an elderly couple. As required by a state statute, a victim impact statement was prepared based on interviews with the victims' son, daughter, son-in-law, and granddaughter. The statement, which described the personal characteristics of the victims, the emotional impact of the crimes on the family, and set forth the family members' opinions and characterizations of the crimes and the defendant, was submitted to the jury at sentencing. The jury imposed the death penalty. The conviction and sentence were affirmed on appeal by the State's highest court.

This Court held by a 5-to-4 vote that the Eighth Amendment prohibits a jury from considering a victim impact statement at the sentencing phase of a capital trial. The Court made clear that the admissibility of victim impact evidence was not to be determined on a case-by-case basis, but that such evidence was per se inadmissible in the sentencing phase of a capital case except to the extent that it "relate[d] directly to the circumstances of the crime." In *Gathers*, decided two years later, the Court extended the rule announced in *Booth* to statements made by a prosecutor to the sentencing jury regarding the personal qualities of the victim.

The *Booth* Court began its analysis with the observation that the capital defendant must be treated as a "uniquely individual human bein[g]," and therefore the Constitution requires the jury to make an individualized determination as to whether the defendant should be executed based on the "'character of the individual and the circumstances of the crime.'" The Court concluded that, while no prior decision of this Court had mandated that only the defendant's character and immediate characteristics of the crime may constitutionally be considered, other factors are irrelevant to the capital sentencing decision unless they have "some bearing on the defendant's 'personal responsibility and moral guilt.'" To the extent that victim impact evidence presents "factors about which the defendant was unaware, and that were irrelevant to the decision to kill," the Court concluded, it has nothing to do with the "blameworthiness of a particular defendant." Evidence of the victim's character, the Court observed, "could well distract the sentencing jury from its constitutionally required task [of] determining whether the death penalty is appropriate in light of the background and record of the accused and the particular circumstances of the crime."

The Court concluded that, except to the extent that victim impact evidence relates "directly to the circumstances of the crime," the prosecution may not introduce such evidence at a capital sentencing hearing, because "it creates an impermissible risk that the capital sentencing decision will be made in an arbitrary manner."

Booth and *Gathers* were based on two premises: that evidence relating to a particular victim or to the harm that a capital defendant causes a victim's family do not in general reflect on the defendant's "blameworthiness," and that only evidence relating to "blameworthiness" is relevant to the capital sentencing decision. However, the assessment of harm caused by the defendant as a result of the crime charged has understandably been an important concern of the criminal law, both in determining the elements of the offense and in determining the appropriate punishment. Thus, two equally blameworthy criminal defendants may be guilty of different offenses solely because their acts cause differing amounts of harm.

"If a bank robber aims his gun at a guard, pulls the trigger, and kills his target, he may be put to death. If the gun unexpectedly misfires, he may not. His moral guilt in both cases is identical, but his responsibility in the former is greater." *Booth*. The same is true with respect to two defendants, each of whom participates in a robbery, and each of whom acts with reckless disregard for human life; if the robbery in which the first defendant participated results in the death of a victim, he may be subjected to the death penalty, but if the robbery in which the second defendant participates does not result in the death of a victim, the death penalty may not be imposed. *Tison v. Arizona*.

The principles which have guided criminal sentencing—as opposed to criminal liability—have varied with the times. The book of Exodus prescribes the Lex talionis, "An eye for an eye, a tooth for a tooth." Exodus 21: 22–23. In England and on the continent of Europe, as recently as the 18th century, crimes which would be regarded as quite minor today were capital offenses. Writing in the 18th century, the Italian criminologist Cesare Beccaria advocated the idea that "the punishment should fit the crime." He said that "[w]e have seen that the true measure of crimes is the injury done to society."

Gradually the list of crimes punishable by death diminished, and legislatures began grading the severity of crimes in accordance with the harm done by the criminal. The sentence for a given offense, rather than being precisely fixed by the legislature, was prescribed in terms of a minimum and a maximum, with the actual sentence to be decided by the judge. With the increasing importance of probation, as opposed to imprisonment, as a part of the penological process, some States such as California developed the "indeterminate sentence," where the time of incarceration was left almost entirely to the penological authorities, rather than to the courts. But more recently, the pendulum has swung back. The Federal Sentencing Guidelines, which went into effect in 1987, provided for very precise calibration of sentences, depending upon a number of factors. These factors relate both to the subjective guilt of the defendant and to the harm caused by his acts.

Wherever judges in recent years have had discretion to impose sentence, the consideration of the harm caused by the crime has been an important factor in the exercise of that discretion:

> The first significance of harm in Anglo-American jurisprudence is, then, as a prerequisite to the criminal sanction. The second significance of harm—one no less important to judges—is as a measure of the seriousness of the offense, and therefore as a standard for determining the severity of the sentence that will be meted out.

Whatever the prevailing sentencing philosophy, the sentencing authority has always been free to consider a wide range of relevant material. In the federal system, we observed that "a judge may appropriately conduct an inquiry broad in scope, largely unlimited either as to the kind of information he may consider, or the source from which it may come." *United States v. Tucker*. Even in the context of capital sentencing, prior to *Booth*, the joint opinion of Justices Stewart, Powell, and Steven in *Gregg v. Georgia* had rejected petitioner's attack on the Georgia statute because of the "wide scope of evidence and argument allowed at presentence hearings." The joint opinion stated:

> We think that the Georgia court wisely has chosen not to impose unnecessary restrictions on the evidence that can be offered at such a hearing and to approve open and far-ranging argument. . . . So long as the evidence introduced and the arguments made at the presentence hearing do not prejudice a defendant, it is preferable not to impose restrictions. We think it desirable for the jury to have as much information before it as possible when it makes the sentencing decision.

The Maryland statute involved in *Booth* required that the presentence report in all felony cases include a "victim impact statement" which would describe the effect of the crime on the victim and his family. Congress and most of the States have, in recent years, enacted similar legislation to enable the sentencing authority to consider information about the harm caused by the crime committed by the defendant. The evidence involved in the present case was not admitted pursuant to any such enactment, but its purpose and effect were much the same as if it had been. While the admission of this particular kind of evidence—designed to portray for the sentencing authority the actual harm caused by a particular crime—is of recent origin, this fact hardly renders it unconstitutional.

We have held that a State cannot preclude the sentencer from considering "any relevant mitigating evidence" that the defendant proffers in support of a sentence less than death. Thus, we have, as the Court observed in *Booth*, required that the capital defendant be treated as a "uniquely individual human bein[g]." But it was never held or even suggested in any of our cases preceding *Booth* that the defendant, entitled as he was to individualized consideration, was to receive that consideration wholly apart from the crime which he had committed. The language quoted from *Woodson* in the *Booth* opinion was not intended to describe a class of evidence that could not be received, but a class of evidence which must be received. This misreading of precedent in *Booth* has, we think, unfairly weighted the scales in a capital trial; while virtually no limits are placed on the relevant mitigating evidence a capital defendant may introduce concerning his own circumstances, the State is barred from either offering "a quick glimpse of the life" which a defendant "chose to extinguish." *Mills v. Maryland*.

During-Reading Question: In the efforts to view criminal defendants as individuals, what does the Court believe has happened to the focus of the crimes?

The *Booth* Court reasoned that victim impact evidence must be excluded because it would be difficult, if not impossible, for the defendant to rebut such evidence without shifting the focus of the sentencing hearing away from the defendant, thus creating a "'mini-trial' on the victim's character." In many cases, the evidence relating to the victim is already before the jury, at least in part because of its relevance at the guilt phase of the trial. But even as to additional evidence admitted at the sentencing phase, the mere fact that, for tactical reasons, it might not be prudent for the defense to rebut victim impact evidence makes the case no different than others in which a party is faced with this sort of a dilemma. As we explained in rejecting the contention that expert testimony on future dangerousness should be excluded from capital trials, "the rules of evidence generally extant at the federal and state levels anticipate that relevant, unprivileged evidence should be admitted and its weight left to the factfinder, who would have the benefit of cross-examination and contrary evidence by the opposing party." *Barefoot v. Estelle.*

Payne echoes the concern voiced in Booth's case that the admission of victim impact evidence permits a jury to find that defendants whose victims were assets to their community are more deserving of punishment than those whose victims are perceived to be less worthy. As a general matter, however, victim impact evidence is not offered to encourage comparative judgments of this kind—for instance, that the killer of a hardworking, devoted parent deserves the death penalty, but that the murderer of a reprobate does not. It is designed to show, instead, each victim's "uniqueness as an individual human being," whatever the jury might think the loss to the community resulting from his death might be. The facts of *Gathers* are an excellent illustration of this: the evidence showed that the victim was an out-of-work, mentally handicapped individual, perhaps not, in the eyes of most, a significant contributor to society, but nonetheless a murdered human being.

During-Reading Question: Go back and look at what the prosecutor said about the victim in South Carolina v. Gathers. *How did the prosecutor give value to a person who was, as the Court said, an "out-of-work, mentally handicapped individual, perhaps not, in the eyes of most, a significant contributor to society"?*

Under our constitutional system, the primary responsibility for defining crimes against state law, fixing punishments for the commission of these crimes, and establishing procedures for criminal trials rests with the States. The state laws respecting crimes, punishments, and criminal procedure are, of course, subject to the overriding provisions of the United States Constitution. Where the State imposes the death penalty for a particular crime, we have held that the Eighth Amendment imposes special limitations upon that process.

> First, there is a required threshold below which the death penalty cannot be imposed. In this context, the State must establish rational criteria that narrow the decisionmaker's judgment as to whether the circumstances of a particular defendant's case meet the threshold. Moreover, a societal consensus that the death penalty is disproportionate to a particular offense prevents a State from imposing the death penalty for that offense. Second, States cannot limit the sentencer's consideration of any relevant circumstance that could cause it to decline to impose the penalty. In this respect, the State cannot challenge the sentencer's discretion, but must allow it to consider any relevant information offered by the defendant. *McCleskey v. Kemp.*

But, as we noted in *California v. Ramos* "[b]eyond these limitations . . . , the Court has deferred to the State's choice of substantive factors relevant to the penalty determination."

The States remain free, in capital cases, as well as others, to devise new procedures and new remedies to meet felt needs. Victim impact evidence is simply another form or method of informing the sentencing authority about the specific harm caused by the crime in question, evidence of a general type long considered by sentencing authorities. We think the *Booth* Court was wrong in stating that this kind of evidence leads to the arbitrary imposition of the death penalty. In the majority of cases, and in this case, victim impact evidence serves entirely legitimate purposes. In the event that evidence is introduced that is so unduly prejudicial that it renders the trial fundamentally unfair, the Due Process Clause of the Fourteenth Amendment provides a mechanism for relief. Courts have always taken into consideration the harm done by the defendant in imposing sentence, and the evidence adduced in this case was illustrative of the harm caused by Payne's double murder.

We are now of the view that a State may properly conclude that, for the jury to assess meaningfully the defendant's moral culpability and blameworthiness, it should have before it at the sentencing phase evidence of the specific harm caused by the defendant.

> [T]he State has a legitimate interest in counteracting the mitigating evidence which the defendant is entitled to put in, by reminding the sentencer that just as the murderer should be considered as an individual, so too the victim is an individual whose death represents a unique loss to society and in particular to his family.

During-Reading Question: How does a victim impact statement help the sentencer assess the "specific harm" caused by a criminal defendant?

By turning the victim into a "faceless stranger at the penalty phase of a capital trial," *Booth* deprives the State of the full moral force of its evidence, and may prevent the jury from having before it all the information necessary to determine the proper punishment for a first-degree murder.

The present case is an example of the potential for such unfairness. The capital sentencing jury heard testimony from Payne's girlfriend that they met at church; that he was affectionate, caring, and kind to her children; that he was not an abuser of drugs or alcohol; and that it was inconsistent with his character to have committed the murders. Payne's parents testified that he was a good son, and a clinical psychologist testified that Payne was an extremely polite prisoner and suffered from a low IQ. None of this testimony was related to the circumstances of Payne's brutal crimes. In contrast, the only evidence of the impact of Payne's offenses during the sentencing phase was Nicholas' grandmother's description—in response to a single question—that the child misses his mother and baby sister. *Payne* argues that the Eighth Amendment commands that the jury's death sentence must be set aside because the jury heard this testimony. But the testimony illustrated quite poignantly some of the harm that Payne's killing had caused; there is nothing unfair about allowing the jury to bear in mind that harm at the same time as it considers the mitigating evidence introduced by the defendant. The Supreme Court of Tennessee in this case obviously felt the unfairness of the rule pronounced by Booth when it said:

> It is an affront to the civilized members of the human race to say that, at sentencing in a capital case, a parade of witnesses may praise the background, character and good deeds of Defendant (as was done in this case), without limitation as to relevancy, but nothing may be said that bears upon the character of, or the harm imposed, upon the victims.

During-Reading Question: If the sentencer had only heard the testimony of the people who supported the defendant in this case, what does the Court fear the sentence may have neglected during the sentencing phase?

In *Gathers*, as indicated above, we extended the holding of Booth barring victim impact evidence to the prosecutor's argument to the jury. Human nature being what it is, capable lawyers trying cases to juries try to convey to the jurors that the people involved in the underlying events are, or were, living human beings, with something to be gained or lost from the jury's verdict. Under the aegis of the Eighth Amendment, we have given the broadest latitude to the defendant to introduce relevant mitigating evidence reflecting on his individual personality, and the defendant's attorney may argue that evidence to the jury. Petitioner's attorney in this case did just that. For the reasons discussed above, we now reject the view—expressed in *Gathers*—that a State may not permit the prosecutor to similarly argue to the jury the human cost of the crime of which the defendant stands convicted. We reaffirm the view expressed by Justice Cardozo in *Snyder v. Massachusetts*: "[J]ustice, though due to the accused, is due to the accuser also. The concept of fairness must not be strained till it is narrowed to a filament. We are to keep the balance true."

We thus hold that, if the State chooses to permit the admission of victim impact evidence and prosecutorial argument on that subject, the Eighth Amendment erects no per se bar. A State may legitimately conclude that evidence about the victim and about the impact of the murder on the victim's family is relevant to the jury's decision as to whether or not the death penalty should be imposed. There is no reason to treat such evidence differently than other relevant evidence is treated.

Payne and his amicus argue that, despite these numerous infirmities in the rule created by *Booth* and *Gathers*, we should adhere to the doctrine of stare decisis and stop short of overruling those cases. Stare decisis is the preferred course, because it promotes the evenhanded, predictable, and consistent development of legal principles, fosters reliance on judicial decisions, and contributes to the actual and perceived integrity of the judicial process. Adhering to precedent "is usually the wise policy, because, in most matters, it is more important that the applicable rule of law be settled than it be settled right." Nevertheless, when governing decisions are unworkable or are badly reasoned, "this Court has never felt constrained to follow precedent." *Smith v. Allwright.*

Stare decisis is not an inexorable command; rather, it "is a principle of policy and not a mechanical formula of adherence to the latest decision." *Helvering v. Hallock.* This is particularly true in constitutional cases, because in such cases "correction through legislative action is practically impossible." *Burnet v. Coronado Oil & Gas Co.* Considerations in favor of stare decisis are at their acme in cases involving property and contract rights, where reliance interests are involved, the opposite is true in cases, such as the present one, involving procedural and evidentiary rules.

During-Reading Question: Why do you think the Court believes that Stare Decisis is important when looking at matters of property and contracts but less important when it deals with procedural and evidentiary rules?

Applying these general principles, the Court has, during the past 20 Terms, overruled in whole or in part 33 of its previous constitutional decisions. *Booth* and *Gathers* were decided by the narrowest of margins, over spirited dissents challenging the basic underpinnings of those decisions. They have been questioned by Members' of the Court in later decisions and have defied consistent application by the lower courts. Reconsidering these decisions now, we conclude, for the reasons heretofore stated, that they were wrongly decided and should be, and now are, overruled. We accordingly affirm the judgment of the Supreme Court of Tennessee.

It is so ordered.

Post-Reading Questions

1. The Court was made up of the same Justices as it was when it decided *South Carolina v. Gathers,* yet this decision was 6 to 3 in favor of allowing testimony from the victim. Why do you think there was this change among the Justices just two years later?
2. Justice Rehnquist refers to the fact that the Court has overruled, either fully or partially, thirty-three of its previous cases in the past twenty years. Do you view this as a positive

or a negative about the Supreme Court? What does it say about both the Court and the Constitution?

Further Explorations

Exploring the Story

Have students view the following video providing a discussion of the impact of the case: Crime Victim Testimony: *Payne v. Tennessee*. [News conference, video and transcript]. (1991, April 27). *C-SPAN*. Retrieved from https://www.c-span.org/video/?17731-1/crime-victim-testimony-payne-v-tennessee

Exploring the Law

Read more about the controversy around victim impact statements in this article from *The Atlantic*: Bandes, S. A. (2016, July 23). What are victim-impact statements for? *The Atlantic*. Retrieved from https://www.theatlantic.com/politics/archive/2016/07/what-are-victim-impact-statements-for/492443/

Both of these cases, *South Carolina v. Gathers* and *Payne v. Tennessee*, deal with the use of victim impact statements in capital murder cases. Do you think victim impact statements should be allowed for other crimes during sentencing? What criminal prosecutions should allow a victim to speak?

Exploring the Effects

United States Justice for All Act of 2004 includes the Crime Victims' Rights Act. Have students research the rights afforded to crime victims under this legislation. A good resource is the National Center for Victims of Crime website at http://victimsofcrime.org.

Activities for Extending the Learning

- Organizations such as Mothers Against Drunk Driving have created victim impact panels where people are required to listen to the firsthand stories of the victims of crimes. Have students attend a victim impact panel in your area, or have them do research on the efficacy of victim impact panels to deter crimes like drunk driving.
- Have students conduct a class debate considering whether victim impact statements are too prejudicial during sentencing or not.

A NOTE FROM THE AUTHORS

This chapter shows the true "being" of the Constitution—that is, not only is it a document that we can look at and use for the interpretation of laws from two hundred years ago, but it can also be used to help the Supreme Court make its interpretation as the nation evolves. Humanity is not static and unchanging, and the Constitution has had to keep pace with that reality. While the actual words in the Constitution do not change, how the U.S. Supreme Court applies and uses those words can change due to the passage of time and or cultural norms.

Constitutional authors did not foresee a country with the Internet, automobiles, or massive economic development, yet it has withstood the test of time. The U.S. Supreme Court rarely reverses its own decisions, but the legal concepts continue to evolve, and how facts are presented to the Court during different time periods can certainly impact an outcome.

What this means is that we are fortunate enough to live in a country where the changes of the people in the country are reflected in laws and policies as interpreted by the U.S. Supreme Court. We do not have to live with the same laws they had in 1776. The U.S. Constitution is a living, breathing document and one that is truly reflective of its people then and now. This also illustrates the transformative nature of the American people and the American experience—during one's lifetime, things will not remain as they always have, and, as emerging adults, we should prepare students to grow and evolve with the nation politically, socially, and economically. This allows us to have peaceful transitions between generations and to progress in ways best for the citizenry.

Chapter Five

People, Places, and Environments

> Theme 3: *Social studies programs should include experiences that provide for the study of people, places, and environments.*
> —*National Curriculum Standards for Social Studies* (2010), National Council for the Social Studies, p. 16

NCSS Theme 3 asks teachers to facilitate thinking about the interaction between people, places, and environments by examining such questions as:

> Why do people decide to live where they do or move to other places? Why is location important? How do people interact with the environment and what are some of the consequences of those interactions? What physical and other characteristics lead to the creation of regions? How do maps, globes, geographic tools and geospatial technologies contribute to the understanding of people, places, and environments? (NCSS, 2010, p. 16)

The Supreme Court answers these questions when the Court examines people's property rights and people's interaction with the environment.

A significant part of the United States' history is the fact that the answer to the question "why do people decide to live where they do" is that they didn't—many people that make up our current population are descendants of those who were enslaved and forced to live in the United States. *The United States v. Amistad* (1841) is a pivotal moment in history that could help students explore why location is important. The case also explores how two different countries define property differently. How does the location of the ship define the consequences of the people on that ship?

Kelo v. City of New London (2005) provides the opportunity to examine the individual's right to property. Students can look at the impact of population growth and "analyze changes in relationships between people, places and environment" (NCSS, 2010, p. 16). The case exists because an individual's right to property is in conflict with the government's interest in economic growth. So, how does the Court decide who or what is the most important interest: money, people, or environment? The case could also be a catalyst for the question, "why do people decide to live where they do or move to other places?" (p. 16).

Michigan v. Environmental Protection Agency (2015) will help students develop "skills at evaluating and recommending public policies" (NCSS, 2010, p. 16) as the Court weighs the impact on the environment along with the health of the people and the cost to the industry. What are the considerations in the development of public policies? How should each of those considerations be weighed? The case also provides the opportunity for students to develop an "interest in and concern for the use and misuse of the physical environment" (p. 16).

CASE #1: *UNITED STATES V. THE AMISTAD*

Pre-Reading Questions

The following is an excerpt from Brant T. Lee's article, "Teaching the Amistad." The issues and questions raised can serve as a useful pre-reading discussion.

> I point out that at the time the case was decided, people could be property. I remind them that the Civil War and the Thirteenth Amendment abolishing slavery is only twenty years in the future from this case. At some point we changed our minds, and now it does not make sense to us anymore. I ask them to consider what there is now that might not make sense to us in the future. What kind of property do we recognize now that might not make sense to us in twenty years or two hundred years?
>
> - How is it that one can own land?
> - The flow of water?
> - Food when people are starving?
> - An idea?
> - The right to buy stock at a particular price upon the occurrence of some event at some undetermined time in the future?
> - The right to build a building?
> - The right to cross someone else's property?
>
> (Lee, B. T., 2002, p. 778)

United States v. The Amistad, 40 U.S. 518 (1841)

MR. JUSTICE STORY delivered the opinion of the Court.

The facts, as they appear upon the transcript of the proceedings [from the Circuit Court of the U.S. for the District of Connecticut], are as follows: on the 27th of June, 1839, the schooner L'Amistad, being the property of Spanish subjects, cleared out from the port of Havana, in the island of Cuba, for Puerto Principe, in the same island. On board of the schooner were the master, Ramon Ferrer, and Jose Ruiz and Pedro Montez, all Spanish subjects. The former had with him a negro boy named Antonio, claimed to be his slave. Jose Ruiz had with him forty-nine negroes claimed by him as his slaves, and stated to be his property in a certain pass or document signed by the Governor General of Cuba. Pedro Montez had with him four other negroes, also claimed by him as his slaves and stated to be his property in a similar pass or document, also signed by the Governor General of Cuba. On the voyage, and before the arrival of the vessel at her port of destination, the negroes rose, killed the master, and took possession of her.

On the 26th of August, the vessel was discovered by Lieutenant Gedney, of the United States brig Washington, at anchor on the high seas at the distance of half a mile from the shore of Long Island. A part of the negroes were then on shore, at Culloden Point, Long Island, who were seized by Lieutenant Gedney and brought on board. The vessel, with the negroes and other persons on board, was brought by Lieutenant Gedney into the district of Connecticut, and there libelled for salvage in the District Court of the United States. A libel for salvage was also filed by Henry Green and Pelatiah Fordham, of Sag Harbor, Long Island.

On the 18th of September, Ruiz and Montez filed claims and libels, in which they asserted their ownership of the negroes as their slaves, and of certain parts of the cargo, and prayed that the same might be "delivered to them, or to the representatives of her Catholic Majesty, as might be most proper." On the 19th of September, the attorney of the United States for the district of Connecticut filed an information or libel setting forth that the Spanish minister had officially presented to the proper department of the Government of the United States a claim for the restoration of the vessel, cargo, and slaves as the property of Spanish subjects which had arrived within the jurisdictional limits of the United States and were taken possession of by the said public armed brig of the United States under such circumstances as made it the duty of the United States to cause the same to be restored to the true proprietors pursuant to the treaty between the United States and Spain, and praying the Court, on its being made legally to appear that the claim of the Spanish minister was well founded, to make such order for the disposal of the vessel, cargo, and slaves as would best enable the United States to comply with their treaty stipulations. But if it should appear that the negroes were persons transported from Africa in violation of the laws of the United States, and brought within the United States contrary to the same laws, he then prayed the Court to make such order for their removal to the cost of Africa, pursuant to the laws of the United States, as it should deem fit.

During-Reading Question: Describe the facts of the case.

The main controversy is whether these negroes are the property of Ruiz and Montez, and ought to be delivered up; and to this, accordingly, we shall first direct our attention.

During-Reading Question: What is the significance of the answer to the question of "whether these negroes are the property of Ruiz and Montez"?

It has been argued on behalf of the United States that the Court are bound to deliver them up according to the treaty of 1795 with Spain, which has in this particular been continued in full force by the treaty of 1819, ratified in 1821. The ninth article provides,

> that all ships and merchandise, of what nature soever, which shall be rescued out of the hands of any pirates or robbers on the high seas shall be brought into some port of either State and shall be delivered to the custody of the officers of that port in order to be taken care of and restored, entire, to the true proprietor as soon as due and sufficient proof shall be made concerning the property thereof.

During-Reading Question: What is the agreement according to the treaty of 1795 with Spain?

This is the article on which the main reliance is placed on behalf of the United States for the restitution of these negroes. To bring the case within the article, it is essential to establish: 1st, That these negroes, under all the circumstances, fall within the description of merchandise, in the sense of the treaty. 2d, That there has been a rescue of them on the high seas, out of the hands of the pirates and robbers, which, in the present case, can only be by showing that they themselves are pirates and robbers; and 3d, That Ruiz and Montez, the asserted proprietors, are the true proprietors, and have established their title by competent proof.

During-Reading Question: What must the Court determine in order to decide if the treaty of 1795 applies?

If these negroes were, at the time, lawfully held as slaves under the laws of Spain and recognised by those laws as property capable of being lawfully bought and sold, we see no reason why they may not justly be deemed, within the intent of the treaty, to be included under the denomination of merchandise, and, as such, ought to be restored to the claimants, for, upon that point, the laws of Spain would seem to furnish the proper rule of interpretation. But, admitting this, it is clear, in our opinion that neither of the other essential facts and requisites has been established in proof, and the onus probandi of both lies upon the claimants to give rise to the casus foederis. It is plain beyond controversy, if we examine the evidence, that these negroes never were the lawful slaves of Ruiz or Montez or of any other Spanish subjects. They are natives of Africa, and were kidnapped there, and were unlawfully transported to Cuba in violation of the laws and treaties of Spain and the most solemn edicts and declarations of that government. By those laws and treaties and edicts, the African slave trade is utterly abolished; the dealing in that trade is deemed a heinous crime; and the negroes thereby introduced into the dominions of Spain are declared to be free. Ruiz and Montez are proved to have made the pretended purchase of these negroes with a full knowledge of all the circumstances. And so cogent and irresistible is the evidence in this respect that the district attorney has admitted in open Court, upon the record, that these negroes were native Africans, and recently imported into Cuba, as alleged in their answers to the libels in the case. The supposed proprietary interest of Ruiz and Montez is completely displaced if we are at liberty to look at the evidence or the admissions of the district attorney.

If then, these negroes are not slaves, but are kidnapped Africans who, by the laws of Spain itself, are entitled to their freedom, and were kidnapped and illegally carried to Cuba, and illegally detained and restrained on board the Amistad, there is no pretence to say that they are pirates or robbers. We may lament the dreadful acts by which they asserted their liberty and took possession of the Amistad and endeavored to regain their native country, but they cannot be deemed pirates or robbers in the sense of the law of nations or the treaty with Spain or the laws of Spain itself, at least, so far as those laws have been brought to our knowledge. Nor do the libels of Ruiz or Montez assert them to be such.

It is also a most important consideration in the present case, which ought not to be lost sight of, that, supposing these African negroes not to be slaves, but kidnapped and free negroes, the treaty with Spain cannot be obligatory upon them, and the United States are bound to respect their rights as much as those of Spanish subjects. The conflict of rights between the parties under such circumstances becomes positive and inevitable, and must be decided upon the eternal principles of justice and international law. If the contest were about any goods on board of this ship, to which American citizens asserted a title which was denied by the Spanish claimants, there could be no doubt of the right to such American citizens to litigate their claims before any competent American tribunal, notwithstanding the treaty with Spain. A fortiori, the doctrine must apply where human life and human liberty are in issue, and constitute the very essence of the controversy. The treaty with Spain never could have intended to take away the equal rights of all foreigners who should contest their claims before any of our Courts to equal justice, or to deprive such foreigners of the protection given them by other treaties or by the general law of nations. Upon the merits of the case, then, there does not seem to us to be any ground for doubt that these negroes ought to be deemed free, and that the Spanish treaty interposes no obstacle to the just assertion of their rights.

Upon the whole, our opinion is that the decree of the Circuit Court, affirming that of the District Court, ought to be affirmed except so far as it directs the negroes to be delivered to the President, to be transported to Africa in pursuance of the Act of the 3d of March 1819, and, as to this, it ought to be reversed, and that the said negroes be declared to be free, and be dismissed from the custody of the Court, and go without day.

Post-Reading Questions

1. How does the Court reason in order to find that the "negroes be declared to be free, and be dismissed from the custody of the Court"?
2. How could the abolitionists of the time use the Court's reasoning to further their cause?

Further Explorations

Exploring the Story

If teaching the movie *Amistad* (1997), consult the American Studies Journal website for resources. The following article from the American Studies Journal website includes tasks to complete with different scenes: Meissner, C. (2009). Teaching American history and the movie *Amistad. American Studies Journal, 53.* Retrieved from http://www.asjournal.org/53-2009/teaching-american-history-and-the-movie-amistad/

Exploring the Law

The following website has questions and answers that explore the legal basis for the Supreme Court's decision, the naval officers' claim, and other questions that allow the students to explore the Court's decision: Supplemental materials for *Amistad.* [Collection of educational resources]. *Teach with Movies.* Retrieved from http://www.teachwithmovies.org/guides/amistad-files/amistad-supplemental-materials.html

Exploring the Effects

To understand the historical event, have students read the following article from Education World: Hopkins, G. (Ed.) The *Amistad* comes to life. *Education World.* Retrieved from http://www.educationworld.com/a_lesson/lesson043.shtml. The site also includes many other lessons and activities.

Activities for Extending the Learning

- For a "document-based question" which asks students to explore the significance of *Amistad,* see: Rothschild, E. (n.d.). The significance of the *Amistad* case—A document-based question. [Unit of instruction in a course]. In Federal Judicial Center and American Bar Association's Division for Public Education (Eds.) *Teaching Judicial History Project.* Retrieved from https://www.fjc.gov/sites/default/files/trials/amistad_dbq_0.pdf
- For use in conjunction with *Amistad,* see: Ragsdale, Bruce A. (2002) *Amistad*: The federal courts and the challenge to slavery. In *Federal Trials and Great Debates in United States History.* Washington, DC: Federal Judicial Center. Retrieved from https://www.fjc.gov/sites/default/files/trials/amistad.pdf

CASE #2: *KELO V. CITY OF NEW LONDON*

Pre-Reading Questions

1. The Takings Clause addresses the power of eminent domain. What is eminent domain? Why is this a power that the founders thought was important to include in the Constitution? What are the government's interests versus the rights of the individual?
2. The Takings Clause limits the power of eminent domain by requiring that "just compensation" be paid if private property is taken for public use. Brainstorm the pros and cons of this government power.
3. What is "public use"? May the government take the property and turn it over to a private developer?
4. The Court has said physical occupation constitutes a taking, but what else might constitute a "taking" by the government?
5. In *Berman v. Parker* 348 U.S. 26 (1954), the Court upheld a redevelopment plan targeting a blighted area of Washington, D.C., that contained housing for five thousand occupants that was beyond repair. The plan would condemn the area and part of it would be used for the construction of streets, schools, and other public facilities. The remainder of the land would be sold to private parties for redevelopment including low-cost housing. Plaintiff was the owner of a department store that was not blighted, arguing that a more attractive community wasn't a valid public use. The Court stated that the concept of public welfare is broad and inclusive, and the plan should be judged as a whole; therefore, the taking was considered for "public use." What are the pros and cons of considering a plan as a whole?

Kelo v. City of New London, 545 U.S. 469 (2005)

Justice Stevens delivered the opinion of the Court.

In 2000, the city of New London approved a development plan that, in the words of the Supreme Court of Connecticut, was "projected to create in excess of 1,000 jobs, to increase tax and other revenues, and to revitalize an economically distressed city, including its downtown and waterfront areas." In assembling the land needed for this project, the city's development agent has purchased property from willing sellers and proposes to use the power of eminent domain to acquire the remainder of the property from unwilling owners in exchange for just compensation. The question presented is whether the city's proposed disposition of this property qualifies as a "public use" within the meaning of the Takings Clause of the Fifth Amendment to the Constitution.

During-Reading Question: Restate, in your own words, the question the Court is addressing. What do you think "public use" should mean?

I

The city of New London (hereinafter City) sits at the junction of the Thames River and the Long Island Sound in southeastern Connecticut. Decades of economic decline led a state agency in 1990 to designate the City a "distressed municipality." In 1996, the Federal Government closed the Naval Undersea Warfare Center, which had been located in the Fort Trumbull area of the City and had employed over 1,500 people. In 1998, the City's unemployment rate was nearly double that of the State, and its population of just under 24,000 residents was at its lowest since 1920.

These conditions prompted state and local officials to target New London, and particularly its Fort Trumbull area, for economic revitalization. To this end, respondent New London Development Corporation (NLDC), a private nonprofit entity established some years earlier to assist the City in planning economic development, was reactivated. In January 1998, the State authorized a \$5.35 million bond issue to support the NLDC's planning activities and a \$10 million bond issue toward the creation of a Fort Trumbull State Park. In February, the pharmaceutical company Pfizer Inc. announced that it would build a \$300 million research facility on a site immediately adjacent to Fort Trumbull; local planners hoped that Pfizer would draw new business to the area, thereby serving as a catalyst to the area's rejuvenation. After receiving initial approval from the city council, the NLDC continued its planning activities and held a series of neighborhood meetings to educate the public about the process. In May, the city council authorized the NLDC to formally submit its plans to the relevant state agencies for review. Upon obtaining state-level approval, the NLDC finalized an integrated development plan focused on 90 acres of the Fort Trumbull area.

During-Reading Question: What are the City's interests in redeveloping the Fort Trumbull area?

The Fort Trumbull area is situated on a peninsula that juts into the Thames River. The area comprises approximately 115 privately owned properties, as well as the 32 acres of land formerly occupied by the naval facility (Trumbull State Park now occupies 18 of those 32 acres). The development plan encompasses seven parcels. Parcel 1 is designated for a waterfront conference hotel at the center of a "small urban village" that will include restaurants and shopping. This parcel will also have marinas for both recreational and commercial uses. A pedestrian "riverwalk" will originate here and continue down the coast, connecting the waterfront areas of the development. Parcel 2 will be the site of approximately 80 new residences organized into an urban neighborhood and linked by public walkway to the remainder of the development, including the state park. This parcel also includes space reserved for a new U. S. Coast Guard Museum. Parcel 3, which is located immediately north of the Pfizer facility, will contain at least 90,000 square feet of research and development office space. Parcel 4A is a 2.4-acre site that will be used either to support the adjacent state park, by providing parking or retail services for visitors, or to support the nearby marina. Parcel 4B will include a renovated marina, as well as the final stretch of the riverwalk. Parcels 5, 6, and 7 will provide land for office and retail space, parking, and water-dependent commercial uses.

The NLDC intended the development plan to capitalize on the arrival of the Pfizer facility and the new commerce it was expected to attract. In addition to creating jobs, generating tax revenue, and helping to "build momentum for the revitalization of downtown New London," (Supreme Court of Connecticut in *Kelo v. New London*) the plan was also designed to make the City more attractive and to create leisure and recreational opportunities on the waterfront and in the park.

The city council approved the plan in January 2000, and designated the NLDC as its development agent in charge of implementation. The city council also authorized the NLDC to purchase property or to acquire property by exercising eminent domain in the City's name. The NLDC successfully negotiated the purchase of most of the real estate in the 90-acre area, but its negotiations with petitioners failed. As a consequence, in November 2000, the NLDC initiated the condemnation proceedings that gave rise to this case.

During-Reading Question: Make an illustration of NLDC's proposed plan for the development.

II

Petitioner Susette Kelo has lived in the Fort Trumbull area since 1997. She has made extensive improvements to her house, which she prizes for its water view. Petitioner Wilhelmina Dery was born in her Fort Trumbull house in 1918 and has lived there her entire life. Her husband Charles (also a petitioner) has lived in the house since they married some 60 years ago. In all, the nine petitioners own 15 properties in Fort Trumbull—4 in parcel 3 of the development plan and 11 in parcel 4A. Ten of the parcels are occupied by the owner or a family member; the other five are held as investment properties. There is no allegation that any of these properties is blighted or otherwise in poor condition; rather, they were condemned only because they happen to be located in the development area.

In December 2000, petitioners brought this action in the New London Superior Court. They claimed, among other things, that the taking of their properties would violate the "public use" restriction in the Fifth Amendment.

During-Reading Questions: The Supreme Court of Connecticut held that all takings were valid. Do you agree? Why or why not?

III

Two polar propositions are perfectly clear. On the one hand, it has long been accepted that the sovereign may not take the property of A for the sole purpose of transferring it to another private party B, even though A is paid just compensation. On the other hand, it is equally clear that a State may transfer property from one private party to another if future "use by the public" is the purpose of the taking; the condemnation of land for a railroad with common-carrier duties is a familiar example. Neither of these propositions, however, determines the disposition of this case.

As for the first proposition, the City would no doubt be forbidden from taking petitioners' land for the purpose of conferring a private benefit on a particular private party. Nor would the City be allowed to take property under the mere pretext of a public purpose, when its actual purpose was to bestow a private benefit. The takings before us, however, would be executed pursuant to a "carefully considered" development plan. The trial judge and all the members of the Supreme Court of Connecticut agreed that there was no evidence of an illegitimate purpose in this case. Therefore, as was true of the statute challenged in *Hawaii Housing Authority v. Midkiff*, the City's development plan was not adopted "to benefit a particular class of identifiable individuals."

On the other hand, this is not a case in which the City is planning to open the condemned land—at least not in its entirety—to use by the general public. Nor will the private lessees of the land in any sense be required to operate like common carriers, making their services available to all comers. But although such a projected use would be sufficient to satisfy the public use requirement, this "Court long ago rejected any literal requirement that condemned property be put into use for the general public" (*Hawaii Housing Authority v. Midkiff*). Indeed, while many state courts in the mid-19th century endorsed "use by the public" as the proper definition of public use, that narrow view steadily eroded over time. Not only was the "use by the public" test difficult to administer (e.g., what proportion of the public need have access to the property? at what price?), but it proved to be impractical given the diverse and always evolving needs of society. Accordingly, when this Court began applying the Fifth Amendment to the States at the close of the 19th century, it embraced the broader and more natural interpretation of public use as "public purpose." Thus, in a case upholding a mining company's use of an aerial bucket line to transport ore over property it did not own, Justice Holmes' opinion for the Court stressed "the inadequacy of use by the general public as a universal test." *Strickley v. Highland Boy Gold Mining Company*. We have repeatedly and consistently rejected that narrow test ever since.

During-Reading Question: How would you generalize the Court's definition of public use?

The disposition of this case therefore turns on the question whether the City's development plan serves a "public purpose." Without exception, our cases have defined that concept broadly, reflecting our longstanding policy of deference to legislative judgments in this field.

Viewed as a whole, our jurisprudence has recognized that the needs of society have varied between different parts of the Nation, just as they have evolved over time in response to changed circumstances. Our earliest cases in particular embodied a strong theme of federalism, emphasizing the "great respect" that we owe to state legislatures and state courts in discerning local public needs. For more than a century, our public use jurisprudence has wisely eschewed rigid formulas and intrusive scrutiny in favor of affording legislatures broad latitude in determining what public needs justify the use of the takings power.

During-Reading Question: Under this "test," predict what uses wouldn't qualify as "public use."

IV

Those who govern the City were not confronted with the need to remove blight in the Fort Trumbull area, but their determination that the area was sufficiently distressed to justify a program of economic rejuvenation is entitled to our deference. The City has carefully formulated an economic development plan that it believes will provide appreciable benefits to the community, including—but by no means limited to—new jobs and increased tax revenue. As with other exercises in urban planning and development, the City is endeavoring to coordinate a variety of commercial, residential, and recreational uses of land, with the hope that they will form a whole greater than the sum of its parts. To effectuate this plan, the City has invoked a state statute that specifically authorizes the use of eminent domain to promote economic development. Given the comprehensive character of the plan, the thorough deliberation that preceded its adoption, and the limited scope of our review, it is appropriate for us, as it was in Berman v. Parker, to resolve the challenges of the individual owners, not on a piecemeal basis, but rather in light of the entire plan. Because that plan unquestionably serves a public purpose, the takings challenged here satisfy the public use requirement of the Fifth Amendment.

The judgement of the Supreme Court of Connecticut is affirmed.

It is so ordered.

Post-Reading Questions

1. In Justice O'Conner's dissent, she states that "all private property is now vulnerable to being taken and transferred to another owner, so long as it might be upgraded—i.e., given to an owner who will use it in a way that the legislature deems more beneficial to the public—in the process." Respond to Justice O'Conner as if you are part of the majority opinion.
2. What criteria would you use to assess "public use"? How does the Court in *Kelo v. New London* expand the definition of "public use"?

Further Explorations

Exploring the Story

Kelo v. New London is a story of people being forced to sell their homes. If students want to further explore the human element of the story, check out the following article on the Institute of Justice's website: Kramer, J. (n.d.). Kelo eminent domain: Eminent domain without limits? *Institute of Justice*. Retrieved from http://ij.org/case/kelo/

The article includes a timeline, case documents, news clips from the time, and information about the plaintiffs in the case.

Exploring the Law

To better understand "public use," have students explore: Bill of Rights Institute. (2004). What is public use? [Collection of educational resources]. In *National Constitution Center, Lesson Plans*. Retrieved from https://constitutioncenter.org/learn/educational-resources/lesson-plans/what-is-public-use

Exploring the Effects

- The Fort Trumbull project was a failure. To further explore the aftermath, have students examine the following resource: McKeehan, P. (2009, November 12). Pfizer to leave city that won land-use case. *The New York Times*. Retrieved from http://www.nytimes.com/2009/11/13/nyregion/13pfizer.html
- After *Kelo v. New London*, states enacted legislation and changed constitutions to offer stronger property rights. To further explore how each state responded to the Court's decision, have students explore the following report on the Institute of Justice's website: Castle Coalition. (2007, August). 50 state report card: Tracking eminent domain reform legislation since *Kelo*. In *Institute of Justice, Report, Legal and Policy Studies*. Retrieved from http://ij.org/wp-content/uploads/2015/03/50_State_Report.pdf

Activities for Extending the Learning

For a "document-based question" which asks students to evaluate the Court's decision in Kelo, visit: Bill of Rights Institute. (n.d.). *Kelo v New London* (2005). In *Landmark Supreme Court Cases eLessons*. Retrieved from https://billofrightsinstitute.org/educate/educator-resources/lessons-plans/landmark-supreme-court-cases-elessons/kelo-v-new-london-2005/

CASE #3: *MICHIGAN V. ENVIRONMENTAL PROTECTION AGENCY*

Pre-Reading Questions

1. What impacts are we having on our environment? What is government's role in mitigating that impact?
2. Research the Clean Air Act. What is the purpose of the Act? What are the interests the government has to consider in passing such a law?

Michigan v. Environmental Protection Agency, 576 U.S. ___ (2015)

Justice Scalia delivered the opinion of the Court.

The Clean Air Act directs the Environmental Protection Agency to regulate emissions of hazardous air pollutants from power plants if the Agency finds regulation "appropriate and necessary." We must decide whether it was reasonable for EPA to refuse to consider cost when making this finding.

During-Reading Question: What criteria would you use to determine what was "appropriate and necessary" to regulate emissions of hazardous air pollutants from power plants?

I

The Clean Air Act establishes a series of regulatory programs to control air pollution from stationary sources (such as refineries and factories) and moving sources (such as cars and airplanes).

At the same time, Congress established a unique procedure to determine the applicability of the program to fossil-fuel-fired power plants. Quite apart from the hazardous-air-pollutants program, the Clean Air Act Amendments of 1990 subjected power plants to various regulatory requirements. The parties agree that these requirements were expected to have the collateral effect of reducing power plants' emissions of hazardous air pollutants, although the extent of the reduction was unclear. Congress directed the Agency to "perform a study of the hazards to public health reasonably anticipated to occur as a result of emissions by [power plants] of [hazardous air pollutants] after imposition of the requirements of this chapter." If the Agency "finds . . . regulation is appropriate and necessary after considering the results of the study," it "shall regulate [power plants]."

During-Reading Question: What are the interests that Congress must consider when regulating sources to control pollution?

EPA completed the study in 1998, and concluded that regulation of coal- and oil-fired power plants was "appropriate and necessary" in 2000. In 2012, it reaffirmed the appropriate-and-necessary finding, divided power plants into subcategories, and promulgated floor standards. The Agency found regulation "appropriate" because (1) power plants' emissions of mercury and other hazardous air pollutants posed risks to human health and the environment and (2) controls were available to reduce these emissions. It found regulation "necessary" because the imposition of the Act's other requirements did not eliminate these risks. EPA concluded that "costs should not be considered" when deciding whether power plants should be regulated.

During-Reading Questions: Why did the EPA decide the regulation of coal- and oil-fired power plants was "appropriate and necessary"? Do you agree?

In accordance with Executive Order, the Agency issued a "Regulatory Impact Analysis" alongside its regulation. This analysis estimated that the regulation would force power plants to bear costs of $9.6 billion per year. The Agency could not fully quantify the benefits of reducing power plants' emissions of hazardous air pollutants; to the extent it could, it estimated that these benefits were worth $4 to $6 million per year. The costs to power plants were thus between 1,600 and 2,400 times as great as the quantifiable benefits from reduced emissions of hazardous air pollutants. The Agency continued that its regulations would have ancillary benefits—including cutting power plants' emissions of particulate matter and sulfur dioxide, substances that are not covered by the hazardous-air-pollutants program. Although the Agency's appropriate-and-necessary finding did not rest on these ancillary effects, the regulatory impact analysis took them into account, increasing the Agency's estimate of the quantifiable benefits of its regulation to $37 to $90 billion per year. EPA concedes that the regulatory impact analysis "played no role" in its appropriate-and-necessary finding.

Petitioners (who include 23 States) sought review of EPA's rule in the Court of Appeals for the D. C. Circuit. As relevant here, they challenged the Agency's refusal to consider cost when deciding whether to regulate power plants. The Court of Appeals upheld the Agency's decision not to consider cost.

During-Reading Question: What is the issue the Court is deciding?

II

Federal administrative agencies are required to engage in "reasoned decisionmaking." *Allentown Mack Sales & Service, Inc.v. NLRB*. "Not only must an agency's decreed result be within the scope of its lawful authority, but the process by which it reaches that result must be logical and rational." *Ibid.* It follows that agency action is lawful only if it rests "on a consideration of the relevant factors." *Motor Vehicle Mfrs. Assn. of United States, Inc. v. State Farm Mut. Automobile Ins. Co.*

EPA's decision to regulate power plants allowed the Agency to reduce power plants' emissions of hazardous air pollutants and thus to improve public health and the environment. But the decision also ultimately cost power plants, according to the Agency's own estimate, nearly $10 billion a year. EPA refused to consider whether the costs of its decision outweighed the benefits. The Agency gave cost no thought at all, because it considered cost irrelevant to its initial decision to regulate.

EPA's disregard of cost rested on its interpretation, which, to repeat, directs the Agency to regulate power plants if it "finds such regulation is appropriate and necessary."

We review this interpretation under the standard set out in *Chevron U. S. A. Inc. v. Natural Resources Defense Council, Inc.* Chevron directs courts to accept an agency's reasonable resolution of an ambiguity in a statute that the agency administers. Even under this deferential standard, however, "agencies must operate within the bounds of reasonable interpretation." *Utility Air Regulatory Group v. EPA*. EPA strayed far beyond those bounds when it read [The Clean Air Act] to mean that it could ignore cost when deciding whether to regulate power plants.

During-Reading Question: The Court determines that the EPA's exclusion of cost in its determination was not a reasonable interpretation of the statute. Make an argument that the EPA should not have to consider cost.

A

Congress instructed EPA to add power plants to the program if (but only if) the Agency finds regulation "appropriate and necessary." One does not need to open up a dictionary in order to realize the capaciousness of this phrase. In particular, "appropriate" is "the classic broad and all-encompassing term that naturally and traditionally includes consideration of all the relevant factors." 10th Circuit opinion of Kavanaugh, J. in *U.S. v Kamahele*. Although this term leaves agencies with flexibility, an agency may not "entirely fai[l] to consider an important aspect of the problem" when deciding whether regulation is appropriate.

Read naturally in the present context, the phrase "appropriate and necessary" requires at least some attention to cost. One would not say that it is even rational, never mind "appropriate," to impose billions of dollars in economic costs in return for a few dollars in health or environmental benefits. In addition, "cost" includes more than the expense of complying with regulations; any disadvantage could be termed a cost. EPA's interpretation precludes the Agency from considering any type of cost—including, for instance, harms that regulation might do to human health or the environment. The Government concedes that if the Agency were to find that emissions from power plants do damage to human health, but that the technologies needed to eliminate these emissions do even more damage to human health, it would still deem regulation appropriate. No regulation is "appropriate" if it does significantly more harm than good.

During-Reading Question: The Court's example considers only the effect on humans' health. How do you weigh cost versus damage to human health?

There are undoubtedly settings in which the phrase "appropriate and necessary" does not encompass cost. But this is not one of them. Agencies have long treated cost as a centrally relevant factor when deciding whether to regulate. Consideration of cost reflects the understanding that reasonable regulation ordinarily requires paying attention to the advantages and the disadvantages of agency decisions. It also reflects the reality that "too much wasteful expenditure devoted to one problem may well mean considerably fewer resources available to deal effectively with other (perhaps more serious) problems." *Entergy Corp. v. Riverkeeper, Inc.* Against the backdrop of this established administrative practice, it is unreasonable to read an instruction to an administrative agency to determine whether "regulation is appropriate and necessary" as an invitation to ignore cost.

D

Our reasoning so far establishes that it was unreasonable for EPA to read [The Clean Air Act] to mean that cost is irrelevant to the initial decision to regulate power plants. The Agency must consider cost—including, most importantly, cost of compliance—before deciding whether regulation is appropriate and necessary. We need not and do not hold that the law unambiguously required the Agency, when making this preliminary estimate, to conduct a formal cost-benefit analysis in which each advantage and disadvantage is assigned a monetary value. It will be up to the Agency to decide (as always, within the limits of reasonable interpretation) how to account for cost.

We hold that EPA interpreted [The Clean Air Act] unreasonably when it deemed cost irrelevant to the decision to regulate power plants. We reverse the judgment of the Court of Appeals for the D. C. Circuit and remand the cases for further proceedings consistent with this opinion.
It is so ordered.

Post-Reading Questions

1. The decision in this case was 5–4. Write a dissenting opinion in response to the majority. Identify the majority's weaknesses.
2. If the agency is to consider the cost, it most likely will favor the industry; therefore how should cost be considered in determining whether a regulation is "appropriate and necessary"?

Further Explorations

Exploring the Story

To understand the interests of each party from a local perspective, have students read this article published in Detroit about the case prior to the Court's decision: Burke, M. N. (2015, March 24). Michigan case pits health against power reliability. *The Detroit News.* Retrieved from http://www.detroitnews.com/story/business/2015/03/24/michigan-case-pits-health-power-reliability/70413482/

Exploring the Law

To better understand the Clean Air Act, have students explore the EPA's guide to the Clean Air Act: United States Environmental Protection Agency. (2007, April). The plain English guide to the Clean Air Act. (Publication No. EPA-456/K-07-001) [pdf]. Research Triangle Park, NC: Office of Air Quality Planning and Standards. Retrieved from https://www.epa.gov/sites/production/files/2015-08/documents/peg.pdf

Exploring the Effects

Have students write an editorial style position paper on the Clean Air Act. For examples using other cases, see: Supreme Court lesson plans and teaching methods. [Collection of educational resources]. (n.d.). In *Street Law.* Retrieved from http://streetlaw.org/en/Page/37/Supreme_Court_Lesson_Plans__Teaching_Methods

Activities for Extending the Learning

This case provides an opportunity to incorporate environmental based lesson plans. See the following website for ideas: United States Environmental Protection Agency. (n.d.). Learning and teaching about the environment. Retrieved from https://www.epa.gov/students

A NOTE FROM THE AUTHORS

This theme really focuses on people and their relationships—relationships with others, with the government, and with the environment. This is the crux of being human and one thing students can take away is that relationships are complex—there are not always easy answers or solutions to problems. Questions arise around other issues in social studies:

- How do people new to the country choose a place to live and why?
- What is the citizen's role in preserving an environment for generations they will never live to see?
- Who is ultimately responsible for the community—the government or its citizenry?

Use these teachable moments to help students understand their role as citizens of more than just a city or county, but of a world and environment. The demand for addressing these questions is more than immediate, but has long-term consequences for future generations. In addition, help students see the careful balance between the needs of the government to balance the demands of its citizens and the status quo of being a citizen with expectations of individualism and personal rights.

Chapter Six

Individual Development and Identity

Theme 4: *Social studies programs should include experiences that provide for the study of individual development and identity.*
—*National Curriculum Standards for Social Studies* (2010), National Council for the Social Studies, p. 17

Theme 4 asks teachers to facilitate thinking about individual development and identity by examining the following questions:

> How do individuals grow and change physically, emotionally and intellectually? Why do individuals behave as they do? What influences how people learn, perceive, and grow? How do people meet their basic needs in a variety of contexts? How do individuals develop over time? How do social, political, and cultural interactions support the development of identity? How are development and identity defined at other times and in other places? (NCSS, 2010, p. 17)

The Supreme Court has to consider such questions when dealing with growth as individuals and as a culture.

In *In re Gault* (1967), the Court must examine how an individual's development influences his or her procedural rights. How do rights differ between an adult and juvenile? At the center of the case is the question: "How are development and identity defined at other times and in other places?" (NCSS, 2010, p. 17). The case offers the opportunity to discuss "why do individuals behave as they do?" (p. 17). Students can examine the development of a juvenile versus an adult and how an individual's development influences the way he/she behaves when in custody. Knowing these differences, how should police officers' interactions change or not change?

Loving v. Virginia (1967) provides an opportunity to see how a law hinders the development of an individual. The case challenges a law that defines a social interaction—a person of one race cannot marry a person of another race. Students can examine the question of how the change in law can move an individual's and a society's development. How does a culture's definition of different identities influence rights? Is a purpose of society's laws to encourage individual development?

In *Wisconsin v. Yoder* (1972), the state mandates education, a law that seems to encourage an individual's development and defines cultural interactions. Mandatory education clearly says something about a country's cultural values. Yet, the First Amendment makes clear that religion and religious freedom are also important values. Ultimately, how does the Court balance these value—what interactions seem to be most important to the Court? How does the Court value "what influences how people learn, perceive and grow" (NCSS, 2010, p. 17)?

CASE #1: *IN RE GAULT*

Pre-Reading Questions

1. What are an adult's due process rights?
2. Which of these rights should apply to a juvenile? Why or why not?
3. How does a juvenile differ from an adult taken into custody?

In re Gault, 387 U.S. 1 (1967)

I

On Monday, June 8, 1964, at about 10 a.m., Gerald Francis Gault and a friend, Ronald Lewis, were taken into custody by the Sheriff of Gila County. The police action on June 8 was taken as the result of a verbal complaint by a neighbor of the boys, Mrs. Cook, about a telephone call made to her in which the caller or callers made lewd or indecent remarks. It will suffice for purposes of this opinion to say that the remarks or questions put to her were of the irritatingly offensive, adolescent, sex variety.

At the time Gerald was picked up, his mother and father were both at work. No notice that Gerald was being taken into custody was left at the home. No other steps were taken to advise them that their son had, in effect, been arrested. Gerald was taken to the Children's Detention Home. When his mother arrived home at about 6 o'clock, Gerald was not there. Gerald's older brother was sent to look for him at the trailer home of the Lewis family. He apparently learned then that Gerald was in custody. He so informed his mother. The two of them went to the Detention Home. The deputy probation officer, Flagg, who was also superintendent of the Detention Home, told Mrs. Gault "why Jerry was there," and said that a hearing would be held in Juvenile Court at 3 o'clock the following day, June 9.

Officer Flagg filed a petition with the court on the hearing day, June 9, 1964. It was not served on the Gaults. Indeed, none of them saw this petition until the habeas corpus hearing on August 17, 1964.

On June 9, Gerald, his mother, his older brother, and Probation Officers Flagg and Henderson appeared before the Juvenile Judge in chambers. Gerald's father was not there. He was at work out of the city. Mrs. Cook, the complainant, was not there. No one was sworn at this hearing. No transcript or recording was made. No memorandum or record of the substance of the proceedings was prepared. Our information about the proceedings and the subsequent hearing on June 15, derives entirely from the testimony of the Juvenile Court Judge, Mr. and Mrs. Gault and Officer Flagg at the habeas corpus proceeding conducted two months later. From this, it appears that, at the June 9 hearing, Gerald was questioned by the judge about the telephone call. There was conflict as to what he said. His mother recalled that Gerald said he only dialed Mrs. Cook's number and handed the telephone to his friend, Ronald. Officer Flagg recalled that Gerald had admitted making the lewd remarks. Judge McGhee testified that Gerald "admitted making one of these [lewd] statements." At the conclusion of the hearing, the judge said he would "think about it." Gerald was taken back to the Detention Home. He was not sent to his own home with his parents. On June 11 or 12, after having been detained since June 8, Gerald was released and driven home. There is no explanation in the record as to why he was kept in the Detention Home or why he was released. At 5 p.m. on the day of

Gerald's release, Mrs. Gault received a note signed by Officer Flagg. It was on plain paper, not letterhead. Its entire text was as follows:

> Mrs. Gault:
> Judge McGHEE has set Monday June 15, 1964 at 11:00 A.M. as the date and time for further Hearings on Gerald's delinquency
> /s/Flagg

At the appointed time on Monday, June 15, Gerald, his father and mother, Ronald Lewis and his father, and Officers Flagg and Henderson were present before Judge McGhee. Witnesses at the habeas corpus proceeding differed in their recollections of Gerald's testimony at the June 15 hearing. Mr. and Mrs. Gault recalled that Gerald again testified that he had only dialed the number, and that the other boy had made the remarks. Officer Flagg agreed that, at this hearing Gerald did not admit making the lewd remarks. But Judge McGhee recalled that "there was some admission again of some of the lewd statements. He didn't admit any of the more serious lewd statements." Again, the complainant, Mrs. Cook, was not present. Mrs. Gault asked that Mrs. Cook be present "so she could see which boy that done the talking, the dirty talking over the phone." The Juvenile Judge said "she didn't have to be present at that hearing." The judge did not speak to Mrs. Cook or communicate with her at any time. Probation Officer Flagg had talked to her once—over the telephone on June 9.

At this June 15 hearing a "referral report" made by the probation officers was filed with the court, although not disclosed to Gerald or his parents. This listed the charge as "Lewd Phone Calls." At the conclusion of the hearing, the judge committed Gerald as a juvenile delinquent to the State Industrial School "for the period of his minority [that is, until 21], unless sooner discharged by due process of law." An order to that effect was entered. It recites that "after a full hearing and due deliberation the Court finds that said minor is a delinquent child, and that said minor is of the age of 15 years."

During-Reading Question: What were the steps the State had to take in order to commit Gerald as a juvenile delinquent?

II

Under our Constitution, the condition of being a boy does not justify a kangaroo court. The traditional ideas of Juvenile Court procedure, indeed, contemplated that time would be available and care would be used to establish precisely what the juvenile did and why he did it—was it a prank of adolescence or a brutal act threatening serious consequences to himself or society unless corrected? Under traditional notions, one would assume that, in a case like that of Gerald Gault, where the juvenile appears to have a home, a working mother and father, and an older brother, the Juvenile Judge would have made a careful inquiry and judgment as to the possibility that the boy could be disciplined and dealt with at home, despite his previous transgressions. Indeed, so far as appears in the record before us, except for some conversation with Gerald about his school work and his "wanting to go to . . . Grand Canyon with his father," the points to which the judge directed his attention were little different from those that would be involved in determining any charge of violation of a penal statute. The essential difference between Gerald's case and a normal criminal case is that safeguards available to adults were discarded in Gerald's case. The summary procedure as well as the long commitment was possible because Gerald was 15 years of age instead of over 18.

During-Reading Questions: What is the State's interest in providing fewer safeguards to a juvenile? What is the role of juvenile court?

If Gerald had been over 18, he would not have been subject to Juvenile Court proceedings. For the particular offense immediately involved, the maximum punishment would have been a fine of $5 to $50, or imprisonment in jail for not more than two months. Instead, he was committed to custody for a maximum of six years. If he had been over 18 and had committed an offense to which such a sentence might apply, he would have been entitled to substantial rights under the Constitution of the United States as well as under Arizona's laws and constitution. The United States Constitution would guarantee him rights and protections with respect to arrest, search and seizure, and pretrial interrogation. It would assure him of specific notice of the charges and adequate time to decide his course of action and to prepare his defense. He would be entitled to clear advice that he could be represented by counsel, and, at least if a felony were involved, the State would be required to provide counsel if his parents were unable to afford it. If the court acted on the basis of his confession, careful procedures would be required to assure its voluntariness. If the case went to trial, confrontation and opportunity for cross-examination would be guaranteed. So wide a gulf between the State's treatment of the adult and of the child requires a bridge sturdier than mere verbiage, and reasons more persuasive than cliche can provide.

We now turn to the specific issues which are presented to us in the present case.

III

NOTICE OF CHARGES.

Appellants allege that the Arizona Juvenile Code is unconstitutional, or, alternatively, that the proceedings before the Juvenile Court were constitutionally defective because of failure to provide adequate notice of the hearings. No notice was given to Gerald's parents when he was taken into custody on Monday, June 8. On that night, when Mrs. Gault went to the Detention Home, she was orally informed that there would be a hearing the next afternoon and was told the reason why Gerald was in custody. The only written notice Gerald's parents received at any time was a note on plain paper from Officer Flagg delivered on Thursday or Friday, June 11 or 12, to the effect that the judge had set Monday, June 15, "for further Hearings on Gerald's delinquency."

A "petition" was filed with the court on June 9 by Officer Flagg, reciting only that he was informed and believed that "said minor is a delinquent minor and that it is necessary that some order be made by the Honorable Court for said minor's welfare." The applicable Arizona statute provides for a petition to be filed in Juvenile Court, alleging in general terms that the child is "neglected, dependent or delinquent." The statute explicitly states that such a general allegation is sufficient, "without alleging the facts." There is no requirement that the petition be served, and it was not served upon, given to, or shown to Gerald or his parents.

The "initial hearing" in the present case was a hearing on the merits. Notice at that time is not timely, and even if there were a conceivable purpose served by the deferral proposed by the court below, it would have to yield to the requirements that the child and his parents or guardian be notified, in writing, of the specific charge or factual allegations to be considered at the hearing, and that such written notice be given at the earliest practicable time, and, in any event, sufficiently in advance of the hearing to permit preparation. Due process of law requires notice of the sort we have described—that is, notice which would be deemed constitutionally adequate in a civil or criminal proceeding. It does not allow a hearing to be held in which a youth's freedom and his parents' right to his custody are at stake without giving them timely notice, in advance of the hearing, of the specific issues that they must meet. Nor, in the circumstances of this case, can it reasonably be said that the requirement of notice was waived.

During-Reading Questions: What right does the Court give to juveniles in section III? Why is this an important right of due process, i.e., what are the reasons it would be important to know the charges prior to the hearing?

IV

RIGHT TO COUNSEL

Appellants charge that the Juvenile Court proceedings were fatally defective because the court did not advise Gerald or his parents of their right to counsel, and proceeded with the hearing, the adjudication of delinquency, and the order of commitment in the absence of counsel for the child and his parents or an express waiver of the right thereto.

We conclude that the Due Process Clause of the Fourteenth Amendment requires that, in respect of proceedings to determine delinquency which may result in commitment to an institution in which the juvenile's freedom is curtailed, the child and his parents must be notified of the child's right to be represented by counsel retained by them, or, if they are unable to afford counsel, that counsel will be appointed to represent the child.

During-Reading Questions: Here the Court gives juveniles the right to counsel in proceedings to determine delinquency. But, what is the State's interest in adjudicating juveniles? How is it different than convicting adults? Make an argument that juveniles should not have the right to counsel.

V

CONFRONTATION, SELF-INCRIMINATION, CROSS-EXAMINATION

Appellants urge that the writ of habeas corpus should have been granted because of the denial of the rights of confrontation and cross-examination in the Juvenile Court hearings, and because the privilege against self-incrimination was not observed. The Juvenile Court Judge testified at the habeas corpus hearing that he had proceeded on the basis of Gerald's admissions at the two hearings. Appellants attack this on the ground that the admissions were obtained in disregard of the privilege against self-incrimination.

We conclude that the constitutional privilege against self-incrimination is applicable in the case of juveniles as it is with respect to adults. We appreciate that special problems may arise with respect to waiver of the privilege by or on behalf of children, and that there may well be some differences in technique—but not in principle—depending upon the age of the child and the presence and competence of parents.

During-Reading Question: The Court finds that the Constitution protects juveniles against self-incrimination. Write a response that supports that finding. Write a response that disagrees with that finding.

The recommendations in the Children's Bureau's "Standards for Juvenile and Family Courts" are in general accord with our conclusions. They state that testimony should be under oath and that only competent, material and relevant evidence under rules applicable to civil cases should be admitted in evidence. The New York Family Court Act contains a similar provision. As we said in *Kent v. United States,* with respect to waiver proceedings, "there is no place in our system of law for reaching a result of such tremendous consequences without ceremony . . . ." We now hold that, absent a valid confession, a determination of delinquency and an order of commitment to a state institution cannot be sustained in the absence of sworn testimony subjected to the opportunity for cross-examination in accordance with our law and constitutional requirements.

During-Reading Question: Summarize the Court's reasoning in granting juveniles the right to cross examine witnesses .

For the reasons stated, the judgment of the Supreme Court of Arizona is reversed, and the cause remanded for further proceedings not inconsistent with this opinion.

It is so ordered.

Post-Reading Questions

1. Do you think the sentence that Gault received was "fair"? Did the severity of Gault's sentence influence the Court's decision? Find evidence in the case to support your conclusion.
2. What is the purpose of the juvenile court system? How does the Court's decision further that purpose? How does it hinder that purpose?

Further Explorations

Exploring the Story

Listen to the following NPR interview with Gerry Gault, the fourteen-year-old subject of the case, and the lawyer who represented Gault: Adler, M. (2007, May 19). *Gault* case changed juvenile law. [Interview, audio recording and transcript]. *NPR*. Retrieved from https://www.npr.org/templates/story/story.php?storyId=10279166.

Gault discusses being detained without talking to his parents and the experience. The interview also discusses the reforms, and lack thereof, since *Gault*.

Exploring the Law

In order to critically think about the Court's decision, students should analyze the purposes of the juvenile justice system and how they are different than the purposes of the adult criminal system. To learn and teach more about the juvenile justice system, explore the following educational resources on the *Teach Civics* website: Swinney, R. (n.d.). Juvenile justice introduction. [Unit of instruction within a course.] In *Teaching Civics*. Retrieved from https://teachingcivics.org/lesson/juvenile-justice-introduction/

Exploring the Effects

For further information about the law since *In re Gault*, see the following article in *Social Education*: Tanenhaus, D. (2016, November/December). Equal justice for juveniles? *In re Gault* after a half century. *Social Education, (80)*6, 321–324. Retrieved from https://www.americanbar.org/content/dam/aba/images/public_education/publications/November December2016_InreGault.pdf

Activities for Extending the Learning

To have students apply their knowledge from *In re Gault*, have them apply the law in the case to other fact patterns. For fact patterns, see the American Constitution Society's Sixth Amendment Lesson: American Constitution Society for Law and Policy. (2005). Sixth Amendment Lesson Plan: Right to Counsel. [pdf, lesson plan for a unit of instruction in a course] In M. Ahranjani, G. Ferguson, and J. B. Raskin (Eds.), *Youth Justice in America*. Thousand Oaks, CA: CQ Press. Retrieved from https://www.acslaw.org/files/pdf/HighSchool_ACS%20Sixth_Amd_Lesson_Plan.pdf

CASE #2: *LOVING V. VIRGINIA*

Pre-Reading Questions

1. Discuss the rights articulated in the Fourteenth Amendment:

> All persons born or naturalized in the United States and subject to the jurisdiction thereof, are citizens of the United States and of the State wherein they reside. No State shall make or enforce any law which shall abridge the privileges or immunities of citizens of the United States; nor shall any State deprive any person of life, liberty, or property, without due process of law; nor deny to any person within its jurisdiction the equal protection of the laws. (U.S. Const. amend. XIV, § 1)

2. This case resulted from a challenge to miscegenation laws or laws that forbid the marriage or cohabitation between a man and a woman of different races. What was the State's interest in forbidding unions between different races? In today's society, how is the right to marry limited? What are the State's interests in limiting the right to marry?

Loving v. Virginia, 388 U.S. 1 (1967)

MR. CHIEF JUSTICE WARREN delivered the opinion of the Court.

This case presents a constitutional question never addressed by this Court: whether a statutory scheme adopted by the State of Virginia to prevent marriages between persons solely on the basis of racial classifications violates the Equal Protection and Due Process Clauses of the Fourteenth Amendment. For reasons which seem to us to reflect the central meaning of those constitutional commands, we conclude that these statutes cannot stand consistently with the Fourteenth Amendment.

In June, 1958, two residents of Virginia, Mildred Jeter, a Negro woman, and Richard Loving, a white man, were married in the District of Columbia pursuant to its laws. Shortly after their marriage, the Lovings returned to Virginia and established their marital abode in Caroline County. At the October Term, 1958, of the Circuit Court of Caroline County, a grand jury issued an indictment charging the Lovings with violating Virginia's ban on interracial marriages. On January 6, 1959, the Lovings pleaded guilty to the charge, and were sentenced to one year in jail; however, the trial judge suspended the sentence for a period of 25 years on the condition that the Lovings leave the State and not return to Virginia together for 25 years. He stated in an opinion that:

> Almighty God created the races white, black, yellow, malay and red, and he placed them on separate continents. And, but for the interference with his arrangement, there would be no cause

> for such marriage. The fact that he separated the races shows that he did not intend for the races to mix.

The two statutes under which appellants were convicted and sentenced are part of a comprehensive statutory scheme aimed at prohibiting and punishing interracial marriages.

During-Reading Question: What was the trial judge's justification for convicting Jeter and Loving of violating Virginia's ban on interracial marriage?

The Lovings were convicted of violating § 258 of the Virginia Code:

> *Leaving State to evade law.*—If any white person and colored person shall go out of this State, for the purpose of being married, and with the intention of returning, and be married out of it, and afterwards return to and reside in it, cohabiting as man and wife, they shall be punished as provided in § 20–59, and the marriage shall be governed by the same law as if it had been solemnized in this State. The fact of their cohabitation here as man and wife shall be evidence of their marriage.

Section 259, which defines the penalty for miscegenation, provides:

> *Punishment for marriage.*—If any white person intermarry with a colored person, or any colored person intermarry with a white person, he shall be guilty of a felony and shall be punished by confinement in the penitentiary for not less than one nor more than five years.

Other central provisions in the Virginia statutory scheme are § 20–57, which automatically voids all marriages between "a white person and a colored person" without any judicial proceeding, and §§ 20–54 and 1–14 which, (Page 388 U. S. 5) respectively, define "white persons" and "colored persons and Indians" for purposes of the statutory prohibitions. The Lovings have never disputed in the course of this litigation that Mrs. Loving is a "colored person" or that Mr. Loving is a "white person" within the meanings given those terms by the Virginia statutes. (Page 388 U. S. 6)

During-Reading Question: Explain the statutes (laws) with which the Lovings were convicted.

Virginia is now one of 16 States which prohibit and punish marriages on the basis of racial classifications.

There can be no question but that Virginia's miscegenation statutes rest solely upon distinctions drawn according to race. The statutes proscribe generally accepted conduct if engaged in by members of different races. Over the years, this Court has consistently repudiated "[d]istinctions between citizens solely because of their ancestry" as being "odious to a free people whose institutions are founded upon the doctrine of equality" *Hirabayashi v. United States*. At the very least, the Equal Protection Clause demands that racial classifications, especially suspect in criminal statutes, be subjected to the "most rigid scrutiny" *Korematsu v. United States*, and, if they are ever to be upheld, they must be shown to be necessary to the accomplishment of some permissible state objective, independent of the racial discrimination which it was the object of the Fourteenth Amendment to eliminate. Indeed, two members of this Court have already stated that they "cannot conceive of a valid legislative purpose . . . which makes the color of a person's skin the test of whether his conduct is a criminal offense" *McLaughlin v. Florida*.

There is patently no legitimate overriding purpose independent of invidious racial discrimination which justifies this classification. The fact that Virginia prohibits only interracial marriages involving white persons demonstrates that the racial classifications must stand on their own justification, as measures designed to maintain White Supremacy. We have consistently denied the constitutionality of measures which restrict the rights of citizens on account of race. There can be no doubt that restricting the freedom to marry solely because of racial classifications violates the central meaning of the Equal Protection Clause.

During-Reading Question: What is the Court's reasoning for reversing the lower court?

II

These statutes also deprive the Lovings of liberty without due process of law in violation of the Due Process Clause of the Fourteenth Amendment. The freedom to marry has long been recognized as one of the vital personal rights essential to the orderly pursuit of happiness by free men.

Marriage is one of the "basic civil rights of man," fundamental to our very existence and survival" *Skinner v. Oklahoma*. To deny this fundamental freedom on so unsupportable a basis as the racial classifications embodied in these statutes, classifications so directly subversive of the principle of equality at the heart of the Fourteenth Amendment, is surely to deprive all the State's citizens of liberty without due process of law. The Fourteenth Amendment requires that the freedom of choice to marry not be restricted by invidious racial discriminations. Under our Constitution, the freedom to marry, or not marry, a person of another race resides with the individual, and cannot be infringed by the State.

During-Reading Question: Why is the right to marry part of the Fourteenth Amendment?

These convictions must be reversed. *It is so ordered.*

Post-Reading Questions

1. What are the effects on people of color by forbidding interracial marriage?
2. What are the effects on the society?
3. What are current laws that might have the same effects on people of color or society as a whole?

Further Explorations

Exploring the Story

Loving v. Virginia is the story of people being prosecuted for marrying one another. To further explore that story, including a timeline of the story, check out the following article on Encyclopedia Virginia's website: Newbeck, P., & Wolfe, B. (2015, October 26). *Loving v. Virginia* (1967). In *Encyclopedia Virginia*. Retrieved from http://www.EncyclopediaVirginia.org/Loving_v_Virginia_1967

Exploring the Law

To better understand the history of anti-miscegenation laws, have students explore the following blog on the New York Public Library's website: Frederick, C. (2016, November 3).

'Loving' and the history of anti-miscegenation laws in Virginia and Washington. [Blog]. *New York Public Library*. Retrieved from https://www.nypl.org/blog/2016/11/03/loving-and-history

To listen to moments from the case, go to the following article on NPR's website: Peñaloza, M. (2017, June 12). [Article and audio recordings]. "Illicit cohabitation": Listen to 6 stunning moments from *Loving V. Virginia*. NPR. Retrieved from https://www.npr.org/2017/06/12/532123349/illicit-cohabitation-listen-to-6-stunning-moments-from-loving-v-virginia

Exploring the Effects

For a connection to today's world, have students research Supreme Court cases dealing with sexual orientation and gay rights.

Activities for Extending the Learning

Teach the film, *The Loving Story*, using this teaching guide: Southern Poverty Law Center. (n.d.). The loving story: A teacher's guide. [pdf]. In *Teaching Tolerance*. Retrieved fromhttp://www.tolerance.org/sites/default/files/general/The%20Loving%20Story%20Study%20Guide_0.pdf

The guide also includes many resources and lessons that could be used to explore the story behind the case.

CASE #3: *WISCONSIN V. YODER*

Pre-Reading Questions

1. Read the First Amendment. What rights are protected?
2. Brainstorm limits on an individual's exercise of his or her religious beliefs.

Wisconsin v. Yoder, 406 U.S. 205 (1972)

MR. CHIEF JUSTICE BURGER delivered the opinion of the Court.

On petition of the State of Wisconsin, we granted the writ of certiorari in this case to review a decision of the Wisconsin Supreme Court holding that respondents' convictions of violating the State's compulsory school attendance law were invalid under the Free Exercise Clause of the First Amendment to the United States Constitution, made applicable to the States by the Fourteenth Amendment. For the reasons hereafter stated, we affirm the judgment of the Supreme Court of Wisconsin.

Respondents Jonas Yoder and Wallace Miller are members of the Old Order Amish religion, and respondent Adin Yutzy is a member of the Conservative Amish Mennonite Church. They and their families are residents of Green County, Wisconsin. Wisconsin's compulsory school attendance law required them to cause their children to attend public or private school until reaching age 16, but the respondents declined to send their children, ages 14 and 15, to public school after they completed the eighth grade. The children were not enrolled in any private school, or within any recognized exception to the compulsory attendance law, and they are conceded to be subject to the Wisconsin statute.

During-Reading Questions: What is the State's interest in requiring children to go to school? What are the parents' interests in not sending them to school?

On complaint of the school district administrator for the public schools, respondents were charged, tried, and convicted of violating the compulsory attendance law in Green County Court, and were fined the sum of $5 each. Respondents defended on the ground that the application of the compulsory attendance law violated their rights under the First and Fourteenth Amendments. The trial testimony showed that respondents believed, in accordance with the tenets of Old Order Amish communities generally, that their children's attendance at high school, public or private, was contrary to the Amish religion and way of life. They believed that, by sending their children to high school, they would not only expose themselves to the danger of the censure of the church community, but, as found by the county court, also endanger their own salvation and that of their children. The State stipulated that respondents' religious beliefs were sincere.

During-Reading Questions: Make a list of the State's reasons for requiring education. Make a list of the individuals' (the Amish) reasons for not wanting to educate their children past the eighth grade. How does the Court judge the sincerity of one's beliefs?

In support of their position, respondents presented as expert witnesses scholars on religion and education whose testimony is uncontradicted. They expressed their opinions on the relationship of the Amish belief concerning school attendance to the more general tenets of their religion, and described the impact that compulsory high school attendance could have on the continued survival of Amish communities as they exist in the United States today.

A related feature of Old Order Amish communities is their devotion to a life in harmony with nature and the soil, as exemplified by the simple life of the early Christian era that continued in America during much of our early national life.

Once a child has learned basic reading, writing, and elementary mathematics, these traits, skills, and attitudes admittedly fall within the category of those best learned through example and "doing," rather than in a classroom. And, at this time in life, the Amish child must also grow in his faith and his relationship to the Amish community if he is to be prepared to accept the heavy obligations imposed by adult baptism. In short, high school attendance with teachers who are not of the Amish faith—and may even be hostile to it—interposes a serious barrier to the integration of the Amish child into the Amish religious community.

The Amish do not object to elementary education through the first eight grades as a general proposition, because they agree that their children must have basic skills in the "three R's" in order to read the Bible, to be good farmers and citizens, and to be able to deal with non-Amish people when necessary in the course of daily affairs. They view such a basic education as acceptable because it does not significantly expose their children to worldly values or interfere with their development in the Amish community during the crucial adolescent period.

During-Reading Question: How much should the fact that the Court views the Amish people as "good" play a part in its decision?

I

There is no doubt as to the power of a State, having a high responsibility for education of its citizens, to impose reasonable regulations for the control and duration of basic education. Thus, a State's interest in universal education, however highly we rank it, is not totally free from a balancing process when it impinges on fundamental rights and interests, such as those specifically protected by the Free Exercise Clause of the First Amendment, and the traditional interest of parents with respect to the religious upbringing of their children so long as they, in the words of *Pierce v. Society of Sisters,* "prepare [them] for additional obligations."

It follows that, in order for Wisconsin to compel school attendance beyond the eighth grade against a claim that such attendance interferes with the practice of a legitimate religious belief, it must appear either that the State does not deny the free exercise of religious belief by its requirement or that there is a state interest of sufficient magnitude to override the interest claiming protection under the Free Exercise Clause. Long before there was general acknowledgment of the need for universal formal education, the Religion Clauses had specifically and firmly fixed the right to free exercise of religious beliefs, and buttressing this fundamental right was an equally firm, even if less explicit, prohibition against the establishment of any religion by government. The values underlying these two provisions relating to religion have been zealously protected, sometimes even at the expense of other interests of admittedly high social importance.

During-Reading Question: What is the standard the Court imposes on the State to deny the free exercise of a legitimate religious belief?

II

We come then to the quality of the claims of the respondents concerning the alleged encroachment of Wisconsin's compulsory school attendance statute on their rights and the rights of their children to the free exercise of the religious beliefs they and their forebears have adhered to for almost three centuries. In evaluating those claims, we must be careful to determine whether the Amish religious faith and their mode of life are, as they claim, inseparable and interdependent. A way of life, however virtuous and admirable, may not be interposed as a barrier to reasonable state regulation of education if it is based on purely secular considerations; to have the protection of the Religion Clauses, the claims must be rooted in religious belief.

The conclusion is inescapable that secondary schooling, by exposing Amish children to worldly influences in terms of attitudes, goals, and values contrary to beliefs, and by substantially interfering with the religious development of the Amish child and his integration into the way of life of the Amish faith community at the crucial adolescent stage of development, contravenes the basic religious tenets and practice of the Amish faith, both as to the parent and the child.

The impact of the compulsory attendance law on respondents' practice of the Amish religion is not only severe, but inescapable, for the Wisconsin law affirmatively compels them, under threat of criminal sanction, to perform acts undeniably at odds with fundamental tenets of their religious beliefs.

In sum, the unchallenged testimony of acknowledged experts in education and religious history, almost 300 years of consistent practice, and strong evidence of a sustained faith pervading and regulating respondents' entire mode of life support the claim that enforcement of the State's requirement of compulsory formal education after the eighth grade would gravely endanger, if not destroy, the free exercise of respondents' religious beliefs.

III

Wisconsin concedes that, under the Religion Clauses, religious beliefs are absolutely free from the State's control, but it argues that "actions," even though religiously grounded, are outside the protection of the First Amendment. But our decisions have rejected the idea that religiously grounded conduct is always outside the protection of the Free Exercise Clause. It is true that activities of individuals, even when religiously based, are often subject to regulation by the States in the exercise of their undoubted power to promote the health, safety, and general welfare, or the Federal Government in the exercise of its delegated powers. This case, therefore, does not become easier because respondents were convicted for their "actions" in refusing to send their children to the public high school; in this context, belief and action cannot be neatly confined in logic-tight compartments.

Nor can this case be disposed of on the grounds that Wisconsin's requirement for school attendance to age 16 applies uniformly to all citizens of the State and does not, on its face, discriminate against religions or a particular religion, or that it is motivated by legitimate secular concerns. A regulation neutral on its face may, in its application, nonetheless offend the constitutional requirement for governmental neutrality if it unduly burdens the free exercise of religion.

We turn, then, to the State's broader contention that its interest in its system of compulsory education is so compelling that even the established religious practices of the Amish must give way. Where fundamental claims of religious freedom are at stake, however, we cannot accept such a sweeping claim; despite its admitted validity in the generality of cases, we must searchingly examine the interests that the State seeks to promote by its requirement for compulsory education to age 16, and the impediment to those objectives that would flow from recognizing the claimed Amish exemption.

The State advances two primary arguments in support of its system of compulsory education. It notes, as Thomas Jefferson pointed out early in our history, that some degree of education is necessary to prepare citizens to participate effectively and intelligently in our open political system if we are to preserve freedom and independence. Further, education prepares individuals to be self-reliant and self-sufficient participants in society. We accept these propositions.

However, the evidence adduced by the Amish in this case is persuasively to the effect that an additional one or two years of formal high school for Amish children in place of their long-established program of informal vocational education would do little to serve those interests. Respondents' experts testified at trial, without challenge, that the value of all education must be assessed in terms of its capacity to prepare the child for life. It is one thing to say that compulsory education for a year or two beyond the eighth grade may be necessary when its goal is the preparation of the child for life in modern society as the majority live, but it is quite another if the goal of education be viewed as the preparation of the child for life in the separated agrarian community that is the keystone of the Amish faith.

IV

Finally, the State, on authority of *Prince v. Massachusetts,* argues that a decision exempting Amish children from the State's requirement fails to recognize the substantive right of the Amish child to a secondary education, and fails to give due regard to the power of the State as *parens patriae* to extend the benefit of secondary education to children regardless of the wishes of their parents.

This case, of course, is not one in which any harm to the physical or mental health of the child or to the public safety, peace, order, or welfare has been demonstrated or may be properly inferred. The record is to the contrary, and any reliance on that theory would find no support in the evidence.

V

For the reasons stated we hold, with the Supreme Court of Wisconsin, that the First and Fourteenth Amendments prevent the State from compelling respondents to cause their children to attend formal high school to age 16.

Affirmed.

MR. JUSTICE POWELL and MR. JUSTICE REHNQUIST took no part in the consideration or decision of this case.

Post-Reading Questions

1. What is the three-part test the Court uses?
2. In this case, the parents are exerting their Constitutional rights over their children. Should the desires of the children play a part in the Court's decision?
3. Apply the Court's reasoning to a different religion. What do you think the Court would decide? Why?

Further Explorations

Exploring the Story

If students want to better understand both the history and current living of the Amish, students can watch this short video from Aeon that offers a sincere glimpse into the way of life: Bloom, P. (Director). (2013, November 9). *An Amish Man.* [Streaming video]. United States: Aeon. Retrieved from http://philipbloom.net/blog/an-amish-man/

Exploring the Law

To explore religious liberty and deepen the students' understanding of these principles, Newseum provides a series of lesson plans that does include documents that could be used: McFall, S., and Hynes, C. C. (Eds.). (2009). Living with our deepest differences: Religious liberty in a pluralistic society. First Amendment Center. Retrieved from https://newseumed.org/idea/religious-liberty-lesson-plans-teachers/

Exploring the Effects

To have students apply the Court's ruling to other scenarios, check out these lesson plans provided by PBS, which use three videos of a Muslim prayer, Ramadan observance, and exploring religious America as a springboard for discussion of religion and the First Amendment: Religion and the First Amendment. [Lesson plan]. (n.d.). *PBS Learning Media.* Retrieved from https://net.pbslearningmedia.org/resource/islam08.socst.world.glob.lpfirstame/religion-and-the-first-amendment/#.WicJHbA-ccg

Activities for Extending the Learning

For students to explore the religious freedoms in today's society, see the lesson plan provided by Teaching Tolerance, which allows students to "use the case of Park51's Islamic Cultural Center as a starting point for a discussion about whether religious freedom is absolute and if religious freedom requires respect for other religions.": The First Amendment and freedom of religion. [Lesson plan]. (n.d.). In *Teaching Tolerance*. Retrieved from https://www.tolerance.org/classroom-resources/tolerance-lessons/the-first-amendment-and-freedom-of-religion

A NOTE FROM THE AUTHORS

High school students have a lot of interest in the concept of identity and individual freedoms, so the cases in this chapter tend to be high-interest cases. This conversation opens the door to discussions on the balance between government interests versus individual rights (like, what is the government's interest in giving a juvenile adult rights?). One interesting facet is the question of whether the government's interest is in promoting or hindering public progress—that is, is it the Supreme Court's job to push social progress or to maintain the status quo until the law catches up with society's norms?

A couple of these cases have juveniles as parties to the cases. Students can apply some of the concepts in these "older" cases to today's issues, such as: how does the reasoning of *Loving* impact our thinking about same-sex marriage? How does *In re Gault* influence our perception of the government as our "protector"?

One main question that frequently arises is, what makes a juvenile different than an adult? And, how does that change the way the government treats him or her? Think about issues like the death penalty, medical care, the use of alcohol—all of these arenas have specific guidance on what it means to be a juvenile, but what does that really mean? And is it rational? Last, in actuality, with today's society the way it is, who is a juvenile and why? And why does it matter?

Chapter Seven

Individuals, Groups, and Institutions

Theme 5: *Social studies programs should include experiences that provide for the study of interactions among individuals, groups, and institution.*
—*National Curriculum Standards for Social Studies* (2010), National Council for the Social Studies, p. 18

Theme 5 requires teachers to have students consider how institutions have an impact on their lives—how they engage with institutions, what impact institutions have on their lives, and how institutions change over time:

> Schools, religious institutions, families, government agencies, and the courts all play an integral role in our lives. They are organizational embodiments of the core social values of those who comprise them, and play a variety of important roles in socializing individuals and meeting their needs, as well as in the promotion of societal continuity, the mediation of conflict, and the consideration of public issues. (NCSS, 2010, p. 18)

The Supreme Court, an institution itself, regularly considers individual interactions with groups and institutions, particularly how an individual's affiliation with a group or institution can have an impact on other aspects of an individual's life.

Specifically, Theme 5 asks students to consider these questions: "What is the role of institutions in this and other societies? How am I influenced by institutions? How do institutions change? What is my role in institutional change?" Further, students should be prepared to recognize "the tensions that occur when the goals, values, and principles of two or more institutions or groups conflict" (NCSS, 2010, p. 18).

The cases in this chapter all address the rights of individuals who find themselves before the Court because of tensions that have arisen between two affiliations. These cases allow students to consider three affiliation areas—racial, political, and religious—to analyze how these often emotion-laden categories have been dealt with by the Supreme Court when they come into conflict with contrary laws and regulations.

Korematsu v. United States (1944) addresses a time in United States history when American citizens were removed from their homes and imprisoned because they were of Japanese descent. Students will consider the need for military restrictions during times of war. Is a potential threat to national security sufficient to deny an individual's rights?

Adler v. Board of Education of City of New York (1952) is a case analyzing what organizations teachers may risk losing their jobs over if they are members. At what point does a teacher, in order to keep his or her job, stop being an individual with the right to join groups?

Finally, *Sherbert v. Verner* (1963) considers the tensions between the free expression of religion and the needs of an employer to have an employee who is able to meet the employer's schedule. How flexible must businesses be in accommodating employees? If an employee is fired due to a religious conflict, should the terminated employee be able to receive unemployment benefits?

CASE #1: *KOREMATSU V. UNITED STATES*

Pre-Reading Questions

1. *Korematsu* was a case that resulted from the forced internment of Japanese Americans ordered by President Roosevelt shortly after the Japanese attack on Pearl Harbor. At the time, the United States was at war with all of the Axis powers—Germany, Italy, and Japan. While the Alien Enemies Act allowed aliens from all three countries to be detained, only Japanese American citizens were detained during the war. Explore the reasons for this.
2. What rights do you think Americans should reasonably be expected to give up for the purposes of national safety?

Korematsu v. United States, 323 U.S. 214 (1944)

MR. JUSTICE BLACK delivered the opinion of the Court.

The petitioner, an American citizen of Japanese descent, was convicted in a federal district court for remaining in San Leandro, California, a "Military Area," contrary to Civilian Exclusion Order No. 34 of the Commanding General of the Western Command, U.S. Army, which directed that, after May 9, 1942, all persons of Japanese ancestry should be excluded from that area. No question was raised as to petitioner's loyalty to the United States. The Circuit Court of Appeals affirmed, and the importance of the constitutional question involved caused us to grant certiorari.

It should be noted, to begin with, that all legal restrictions which curtail the civil rights of a single racial group are immediately suspect. That is not to say that all such restrictions are unconstitutional. It is to say that courts must subject them to the most rigid scrutiny. Pressing public necessity may sometimes justify the existence of such restrictions; racial antagonism never can.

During-Reading Questions: Why do you think Justice Black says "that all legal restrictions which curtail the civil rights of a single racial group are immediately suspect"? Looking at the history of the United States at the time of this decision, was this a uniformly agreed upon legal ideal?

In the instant case, prosecution of the petitioner was begun by information charging violation of an Act of Congress, of March 21, 1942, 56 Stat. 173, which provides that

> [W]hoever shall enter, remain in, leave, or commit any act in any military area or military zone prescribed, under the authority of an Executive order of the President, by the Secretary of War, or by any military commander designated by the Secretary of War, contrary to the restrictions appli-

> cable to any such area or zone or contrary to the order of the Secretary of War or any such military commander, shall, if it appears that he knew or should have known of the existence and extent of the restrictions or order and that his act was in violation thereof, be guilty of a misdemeanor and upon conviction shall be liable to a fine of not to exceed $5,000 or to imprisonment for not more than one year, or both, for each offense.

Exclusion Order No. 34, which the petitioner knowingly and admittedly violated, was one of a number of military orders and proclamations, all of which were substantially based upon Executive Order No. 9066, 7 Fed. Reg. 1407. That order, issued after we were at war with Japan, declared that "the successful prosecution of the war requires every possible protection against espionage and against sabotage to national defense material, national defense premises, and national defense utilities. . . ."

One of the series of orders and proclamations, a curfew order, which, like the exclusion order here, was promulgated pursuant to Executive Order 9066, subjected all persons of Japanese ancestry in prescribed West Coast military areas to remain in their residences from 8 p.m. to 6 a.m. As is the case with the exclusion order here, that prior curfew order was designed as a "protection against espionage and against sabotage." In *Hirabayashi v. United States*, 320 U. S. 81, we sustained a conviction obtained for violation of the curfew order. The *Hirabayashi* conviction and this one thus rest on the same 1942 Congressional Act and the same basic executive and military orders, all of which orders were aimed at the twin dangers of espionage and sabotage.

The 1942 Act was attacked in the *Hirabayashi* case as an unconstitutional delegation of power; it was contended that the curfew order and other orders on which it rested were beyond the war powers of the Congress, the military authorities, and of the President, as Commander in Chief of the Army, and, finally, that to apply the curfew order against none but citizens of Japanese ancestry amounted to a constitutionally prohibited discrimination solely on account of race. To these questions, we gave the serious consideration which their importance justified. We upheld the curfew order as an exercise of the power of the government to take steps necessary to prevent espionage and sabotage in an area threatened by Japanese attack.

In the light of the principles we announced in the *Hirabayashi* case, we are unable to conclude that it was beyond the war power of Congress and the Executive to exclude those of Japanese ancestry from the West Coast war area at the time they did. True, exclusion from the area in which one's home is located is a far greater deprivation than constant confinement to the home from 8 p.m. to 6 a.m. Nothing short of apprehension by the proper military authorities of the gravest imminent danger to the public safety can constitutionally justify either. But exclusion from a threatened area, no less than curfew, has a definite and close relationship to the prevention of espionage and sabotage. The military authorities, charged with the primary responsibility of defending our shores, concluded that curfew provided inadequate protection and ordered exclusion. They did so, as pointed out in our Hirabayashi opinion, in accordance with Congressional authority to the military to say who should, and who should not, remain in the threatened areas.

During-Reading Questions: To what extent to do you think the military should be allowed to exclude people from their homes? Should it just be allowed in times of actively declared war, or are there other circumstances where you can see it would be necessary? Do you think it was truly necessary to exclude Mr. Korematsu from his home?

In this case, the petitioner challenges the assumptions upon which we rested our conclusions in the *Hirabayashi* case. He also urges that, by May, 1942, when Order No. 34 was promulgated, all danger of Japanese invasion of the West Coast had disappeared. After careful consideration of these contentions, we are compelled to reject them.

Here, as in the *Hirabayashi* case,

> [W]e cannot reject as unfounded the judgment of the military authorities and of Congress that there were disloyal members of that population, whose number and strength could not be precisely and quickly ascertained. We cannot say that the war-making branches of the Government did not have ground for believing that, in a critical hour, such persons could not readily be isolated and separately dealt with, and constituted a menace to the national defense and safety which demanded that prompt and adequate measures be taken to guard against it.

Like curfew, exclusion of those of Japanese origin was deemed necessary because of the presence of an unascertained number of disloyal members of the group, most of whom we have no doubt were loyal to this country. It was because we could not reject the finding of the military authorities that it was impossible to bring about an immediate segregation of the disloyal from the loyal that we sustained the validity of the curfew order as applying to the whole group. In the instant case, temporary exclusion of the entire group was rested by the military on the same ground. The judgment that exclusion of the whole group was, for the same reason, a military imperative answers the contention that the exclusion was in the nature of group punishment based on antagonism to those of Japanese origin. That there were members of the group who retained loyalties to Japan has been confirmed by investigations made subsequent to the exclusion. Approximately five thousand American citizens of Japanese ancestry refused to swear unqualified allegiance to the United States and to renounce allegiance to the Japanese Emperor, and several thousand evacuees requested repatriation to Japan.

We uphold the exclusion order as of the time it was made and when the petitioner violated it. In doing so, we are not unmindful of the hardships imposed by it upon a large group of American citizens. But hardships are part of war, and war is an aggregation of hardships. All citizens alike, both in and out of uniform, feel the impact of war in greater or lesser measure. Citizenship has its responsibilities, as well as its privileges, and, in time of war, the burden is always heavier. Compulsory exclusion of large groups of citizens from their homes, except under circumstances of direst emergency and peril, is inconsistent with our basic governmental institutions. But when, under conditions of modern warfare, our shores are threatened by hostile forces, the power to protect must be commensurate with the threatened danger.

During-Reading Questions: Do you agree with Justice Black's statement that "all citizens alike, both in and out of uniform, feel the impact of war in greater or lesser measure. Citizenship has its responsibilities, as well as its privileges, and, in time of war, the burden is always heavier"? Why or why not?

It is argued that, on May 30, 1942, the date the petitioner was charged with remaining in the prohibited area, there were conflicting orders outstanding, forbidding him both to leave the area and to remain there. Of course, a person cannot be convicted for doing the very thing which it is a crime to fail to do. But the outstanding orders here contained no such contradictory commands.

There was an order issued March 27, 1942, which prohibited petitioner and others of Japanese ancestry from leaving the area, but its effect was specifically limited in time "until and to the extent that a future proclamation or order should so permit or direct." That "future order," the one for violation of which petitioner was convicted, was issued May 3, 1942, and it did "direct" exclusion from the area of all persons of Japanese ancestry before 12 o'clock noon, May 9; furthermore, it contained a warning that all such persons found in the prohibited area would be liable to punishment under the March 21, 1942, Act of Congress. Consequently, the only order in effect touching the petitioner's being in the area on May 30, 1942, the date specified in the information against him, was the May 3 order which prohibited his remaining there, and it was that same order which he stipulated in his trial that he had violated, knowing of its existence. There is therefore no basis for the argument that, on May 30, 1942, he was subject to punishment, under the March 27 and May 3 orders, whether he remained in or left the area.

It does appear, however, that, on May 9, the effective date of the exclusion order, the military authorities had already determined that the evacuation should be effected by assembling together and placing under guard all those of Japanese ancestry at central points, designated as "assembly centers," in order "to insure the orderly evacuation and resettlement of Japanese voluntarily migrating from Military Area No. 1, to restrict and regulate such migration."

Public Proclamation No. 4, 7 Fed.Reg. 2601. And on May 19, 1942, eleven days before the time petitioner was charged with unlawfully remaining in the area, Civilian Restrictive Order No. 1, 8 Fed.Reg. 982, provided for detention of those of Japanese ancestry in assembly or relocation centers. It is now argued that the validity of the exclusion order cannot be considered apart from the orders requiring him, after departure from the area, to report and to remain in an assembly or relocation center. The contention is that we must treat these separate orders as one and inseparable; that, for this reason, if detention in the assembly or relocation center would have illegally deprived the petitioner of his liberty, the exclusion order and his conviction under it cannot stand.

We are thus being asked to pass at this time upon the whole subsequent detention program in both assembly and relocation centers, although the only issues framed at the trial related to petitioner's remaining in the prohibited area in violation of the exclusion order. Had petitioner here left the prohibited area and gone to an assembly center, we cannot say, either as a matter of fact or law, that his presence in that center would have resulted in his detention in a relocation center. Some who did report to the assembly center were not sent to relocation centers, but were released upon condition that they remain outside the prohibited zone until the military orders were modified or lifted. This illustrates that they pose different problems, and may be governed by different principles. The lawfulness of one does not necessarily determine the lawfulness of the others. This is made clear when we analyze the requirements of the separate provisions of the separate orders. These separate requirements were that those of Japanese ancestry (1) depart from the area; (2) report to and temporarily remain in an assembly center; (3) go under military control to a relocation center, there to remain for an indeterminate period until released conditionally or unconditionally by the military authorities. Each of these requirements, it will be noted, imposed distinct duties in connection with the separate steps in a complete evacuation program. Had Congress directly incorporated into one Act the language of these separate orders, and provided sanctions for their violations, disobedience of any one would have constituted a separate offense. There is no reason why violations of these orders, insofar as they were promulgated pursuant to Congressional enactment, should not be treated as separate offenses.

Since the petitioner has not been convicted of failing to report or to remain in an assembly or relocation center, we cannot in this case determine the validity of those separate provisions of the order. It is sufficient here for us to pass upon the order which petitioner violated. To do more would be to go beyond the issues raised, and to decide momentous questions not contained within the framework of the pleadings or the evidence in this case. It will be time enough to decide the serious constitutional issues which petitioner seeks to raise when an assembly or relocation order is applied or is certain to be applied to him, and we have its terms before us.

It is said that we are dealing here with the case of imprisonment of a citizen in a concentration camp solely because of his ancestry, without evidence or inquiry concerning his loyalty and good disposition towards the United States. Our task would be simple, our duty clear, were this a case involving the imprisonment of a loyal citizen in a concentration camp because of racial prejudice. Regardless of the true nature of the assembly and relocation centers—and we deem it unjustifiable to call them concentration camps, with all the ugly connotations that term implies—we are dealing specifically with nothing but an exclusion order. To cast this case into outlines of racial prejudice, without reference to the real military dangers which were presented, merely confuses the issue. Korematsu was not excluded from the Military Area because of hostility to him or his race. He was excluded because we are at war with the Japanese Empire, because the properly constituted military authorities feared an invasion of our West Coast and felt constrained to take proper security measures, because they decided that the military urgency of the situation demanded that all citizens of Japanese ancestry be segregated from the West Coast temporarily, and, finally, because Congress, reposing its confidence in this time of war in our military leaders—as inevitably it must—determined that they should have the power to do just this. There was evidence of disloyalty on the part of some, the military authorities considered that the need for action was great, and time was short. We cannot—by availing ourselves of the calm perspective of hindsight—now say that, at that time, these actions were unjustified.

Affirmed.

During-Reading Questions: Why do you think the Court wants to draw a very specific distinction between the Japanese American internment camps and the concentration camps mentioned in the case? What are the dangers of drawing parallels with other countries?

MR. JUSTICE MURPHY, dissenting.

This exclusion of "all persons of Japanese ancestry, both alien and non-alien," from the Pacific Coast area on a plea of military necessity in the absence of martial law ought not to be approved. Such exclusion goes over "the very brink of constitutional power," and falls into the ugly abyss of racism.

In dealing with matters relating to the prosecution and progress of a war, we must accord great respect and consideration to the judgments of the military authorities who are on the scene and who have full knowledge of the military facts. The scope of their discretion must, as a matter of necessity and common sense, be wide. And their judgments ought not to be overruled lightly by those whose training and duties ill-equip them to deal intelligently with matters so vital to the physical security of the nation.

At the same time, however, it is essential that there be definite limits to military discretion, especially where martial law has not been declared. Individuals must not be left impoverished of their constitutional rights on a plea of military necessity that has neither substance nor support. Thus, like other claims conflicting with the asserted constitutional rights of the individual, the military claim must subject itself to the judicial process of having its reasonableness determined and its conflicts with other interests reconciled.

"What are the allowable limits of military discretion, and whether or not they have been overstepped in a particular case, are judicial questions." *Sterling v. Constantin.*

I dissent, therefore, from this legalization of racism. Racial discrimination in any form and in any degree has no justifiable part whatever in our democratic way of life. It is unattractive in any setting, but it is utterly revolting among a free people who have embraced the principles set forth in the Constitution of the United States. All residents of this nation are kin in some way by blood or culture to a foreign land. Yet they are primarily and necessarily a part of the new and distinct civilization of the United States. They must, accordingly, be treated at all times as the heirs of the American experiment, and as entitled to all the rights and freedoms guaranteed by the Constitution.

During-Reading Questions: It is true, as Justice Murphy says, that the vast majority of Americans "are kin in some way by blood or culture to a foreign land"? If this is the case, after how many generations of residence should we start identifying someone as "truly" American?

MR. JUSTICE JACKSON, dissenting.

Korematsu was born on our soil, of parents born in Japan. The Constitution makes him a citizen of the United States by nativity, and a citizen of California by residence. No claim is made that he is not loyal to this country. There is no suggestion that, apart from the matter involved here, he is not law-abiding and well disposed. Korematsu, however, has been convicted of an act not commonly a crime. It consists merely of being present in the state whereof he is a citizen, near the place where he was born, and where all his life he has lived.

Even more unusual is the series of military orders which made this conduct a crime. They forbid such a one to remain, and they also forbid him to leave. They were so drawn that the only way Korematsu could avoid violation was to give himself up to the military authority. This meant submission to custody, examination, and transportation out of the territory, to be followed by indeterminate confinement in detention camps.

A citizen's presence in the locality, however, was made a crime only if his parents were of Japanese birth. Had Korematsu been one of four—the others being, say, a German alien enemy, an Italian alien enemy, and a citizen of American-born ancestors, convicted of treason but out on parole—only Korematsu's presence would have violated the order. The difference between their innocence and his crime would result, not from anything he did, said, or thought, different than they, but only in that he was born of different racial stock.

Now, if any fundamental assumption underlies our system, it is that guilt is personal and not inheritable. Even if all of one's antecedents had been convicted of treason, the Constitution forbids its penalties to be visited upon him, for it provides that "no attainder of treason shall work corruption of blood, or forfeiture except during the life of the person attainted." But here is an attempt to make an otherwise innocent act a crime merely because this prisoner is the son of parents as to whom he had no choice, and belongs to a race from which there is no way to resign. If Congress, in peacetime legislation, should enact such a criminal law, I should suppose this Court would refuse to enforce it.

But the "law" which this prisoner is convicted of disregarding is not found in an act of Congress, but in a military order. Neither the Act of Congress nor the Executive Order of the President, nor both together, would afford a basis for this conviction. It rests on the orders of General DeWitt. And it is said that, if the military commander had reasonable military grounds for promulgating the orders, they are constitutional, and become law, and the Court is required to enforce them. There are several reasons why I cannot subscribe to this doctrine.

It would be impracticable and dangerous idealism to expect or insist that each specific military command in an area of probable operations will conform to conventional tests of constitutionality. When an area is so beset that it must be put under military control at all, the paramount consideration is that its measures be successful, rather than legal. The armed services must protect a society, not merely its Constitution. The very essence of the military job is to marshal physical force, to remove every obstacle to its effectiveness, to give it every strategic advantage. Defense measures will not, and often should not, be held within the limits that bind civil authority in peace. No court can require such a commander in such circumstances to act as a reasonable man; he may be unreasonably cautious and exacting. Perhaps he should be. But a commander, in temporarily focusing the life of a community on defense, is carrying out a military program; he is not making law in the sense the courts know the term. He issues orders, and they may have a certain authority as military commands, although they may be very bad as constitutional law.

But if we cannot confine military expedients by the Constitution, neither would I distort the Constitution to approve all that the military may deem expedient. That is what the Court appears to be doing, whether consciously or not. I cannot say, from any evidence before me, that the orders of General DeWitt were not reasonably expedient military precautions, nor could I say that they were. But even if they were permissible military procedures, I deny that it follows that they are constitutional. If, as the Court holds, it does follow, then we may as well say that any military order will be constitutional, and have done with it.

During-Reading Question: What is Justice Jackson's argument against military necessity? Do you agree or disagree with him?

Post-Reading Questions

1. What events in recent American history bring up some of the same issues as are found in the *Korematsu* case? How are these events the same? How are they different?
2. Actor George Takei of *Star Trek* fame was interned in a detention camp during World War II. He has written and produced a musical called *Allegiance* about his experiences, and has given a large number of interviews on the subject. What do Takei and others who lived internment camps say about the experience?

Further Explorations

Exploring the Story

To learn more about Fred T. Korematsu, his story, and his life after the Supreme Court case, go to the Fred T. Korematsu Institute at www.korematsuinstitute.org.

Exploring the Law

To learn more about the *Korematsu* case, its impact, and other learning extensions, visit the website Landmark Cases of the U.S. Supreme Court, at www.landmarkcases.org, and look for the *Korematsu* case. There is a wealth of resources for teachers to use in class on the site.

Exploring the Effects

Given the heightened national security since 9/11, have students research changes that have been made in the United States since 9/11 in the name of national security. Then have students debate whether or not they think a situation like the one faced by Fred Korematsu could happen in the United States in the twenty-first century.

Activities for Extending the Learning

The United States Courts website has an excellent classroom activity where students can do a courtroom simulation: United States Courts. (n.d.). Courtroom simulation roles and responsibilities—*Korematsu v. U.S.* [Lesson plan]. Retrieved from http://www.uscourts.gov/educational-resources/educational-activities/courtroom-simulation-roles-and-responsibilities

Search this site for many other classroom resources.

CASE #2: *ADLER V. BOARD OF EDUCATION OF CITY OF NEW YORK*

Pre-Reading Questions

1. This case is about public school teachers and organizations the Supreme Court has said it is okay for their employer (in this case, the Board of Regents; in your school it may be the state or local school board) to say the teachers cannot be a member of. Why would it be important to monitor the personal affiliations or memberships of teachers? What groups do you think might be controversial?
2. Are there any other professions where personal memberships or affiliations should be monitored as a part of the job? If yes, what professions are these and why? If no, why should teaching be considered a unique profession? What about other professions that work with young people?

***Adler v. Board of Education of City of New York,* 342 U.S. 485 (1952)**

MR. JUSTICE MINTON delivered the opinion of the Court.

Appellants brought a declaratory judgment action in the Supreme Court of New York, Kings County, praying that § 12-a of the Civil Service Law, as implemented by the so-called Feinberg Law, be declared unconstitutional, and that action by the Board of Education of the City of New York thereunder be enjoined. On motion for judgment on the pleadings, the court held that subdivision (c) of § 12-a, the Feinberg Law, and the Rules of the State Board of Regents promulgated thereunder violated the Due Process Clause of the Fourteenth Amendment, and issued an injunction. The Appellate Division of the Supreme Court reversed, and the Court of Appeals affirmed the judgment of the Appellate Division. The appellants come here by appeal under 28 U.S.C. § 1257.

The preamble of the Feinberg Law, § 1, makes elaborate findings that members of subversive groups, particularly of the Communist Party and its affiliated organizations, have been infiltrating into public employment in the public schools of the State; that this has occurred and continues notwithstanding the existence of protective statutes designed to prevent the appointment to or retention in employment in public office, and particularly in the public schools, of members of any organizations which teach or advocate that the government of the United States or of any state or political subdivision thereof shall be overthrown by force or violence or by any other unlawful means. As a result, propaganda can be disseminated among the children by those who teach them and to whom they look for guidance, authority, and leadership. The Legislature further found that the members of such groups use their positions to advocate and teach their doctrines, and are frequently bound by oath, agreement, pledge, or understanding to follow, advocate and teach a prescribed party line or group dogma or doctrine without regard to truth or free inquiry. This propaganda, the Legislature declared, is sufficiently subtle to escape detection in the classroom; thus, the menace of such infiltration into the classroom is difficult to measure. Finally, to protect the children from such influence, it was thought essential that the laws prohibiting members of such groups, such as the Communist Party or its affiliated organizations, from obtaining or retaining employment in the public schools be rigorously enforced. It is the purpose of the Feinberg Law to provide for the disqualification and removal of superintendents of schools, teachers, and employees in the public schools in any city or school district of the State who advocate the overthrow of the Government by unlawful means or who are members of organizations which have a like purpose.

During-Reading Question: Look at the date of this case. What was going on politically in the United States and the world at this time that makes this issue particularly relevant to the time?

Section 3022 of the Education Law, added by the Feinberg Law, provides that the Board of Regents, which has charge of the public school system in the State of New York, shall, after full notice and hearing, make a listing of organizations which it finds advocate, advise, teach, or embrace the doctrine that the government should be overthrown by force or violence or any other unlawful means, and that such listing may be amended and revised from time to time.

It will be observed that the listings are made only after full notice and hearing. In addition, the Court of Appeals construed the statute in conjunction with Article 78 of the New York Civil Practice Act, Gilbert-Bliss' N.Y. Civ. Prac., Vol. 6B, so as to provide listed organizations a right of review.

The Board of Regents is further authorized to provide in rules and regulations, and has so provided, that membership in any listed organization, after notice and hearing, "shall constitute prima facie evidence for disqualification for appointment to or retention in any office or position in the school system"; but before one who is an employee or seeks employment is severed from or denied employment, he likewise must be given a full hearing with the privilege of being represented by counsel and the right to judicial review. It is § 1-a of the Civil Service Law, as implemented by the Feinberg Law as above indicated, that is under attack here.

It is first argued that the Feinberg Law and the rules promulgated thereunder constitute an abridgment of the freedom of speech and assembly of persons employed or seeking employment in the public schools of the State of New York.

It is clear that such persons have the right under our law to assemble, speak, think and believe as they will. It is equally clear that they have no right to work for the State in the school system on their own terms. They may work for the school system upon the reasonable terms laid down by the proper authorities of New York. If they do not choose to work on such terms, they are at liberty to retain their beliefs and associations and go elsewhere. Has the State thus deprived them of any right to free speech or assembly? We think not. Such persons are or may be denied, under the statutes in question, the privilege of working for the school system of the State of New York because, first, of their advocacy of the overthrow of the government by force or violence, or, secondly, by unexplained membership in an organization found by the school authorities, after notice and hearing, to teach and advocate the overthrow of the government by force or violence, and known by such persons to have such purpose.

During-Reading Questions: Why is it reasonable for the State to impose freedom of speech restrictions on teachers? What alternatives do teachers have if they don't like the restrictions, according to the Supreme Court?

The constitutionality of the first proposition is not questioned here. As to the second, it is rather subtly suggested that we should not follow our recent decision in *Garner v. Los Angeles Board*. We there said: "We think that a municipal employer is not disabled because it is an agency of the State from inquiring of its employees as to matters that may prove relevant to their fitness and suitability for the public service. Past conduct may well relate to present fitness; past loyalty may have a reasonable relationship to present and future trust. Both are commonly inquired into in determining fitness for both high and low positions in private industry, and are not less relevant in public employment."

We adhere to that case. A teacher works in a sensitive area in a school room. There he shapes the attitude of young minds towards the society in which they live. In this, the state has a vital concern. It must preserve the integrity of the schools. That the school authorities have the right and the duty to screen the officials, teachers, and employees as to their fitness to maintain the integrity of the schools as a part of ordered society, cannot be doubted. One's associates, past and present, as well as one's conduct, may properly be considered in determining fitness and loyalty. From time immemorial, one's reputation has been determined in part by the company he keeps. In the employment of officials and teachers of the school system, the state may very properly inquire into the company they keep, and we know of no rule, constitutional or otherwise, that prevents the state, when determining the fitness and loyalty of such persons, from considering the organizations and persons with whom they associate.

During-Reading Question: The Court says "One's associates, past and present, as well as one's conduct, may properly be considered in determining fitness and loyalty." How far do you think school authorities should be able to go into investigating the past of a teacher?

If, under the procedure set up in the New York law, a person is found to be unfit and is disqualified from employment in the public school system because of membership in a listed organization, he is not thereby denied the right of free speech and assembly. His freedom of choice between membership in the organization and employment in the school system might be limited, but not his freedom of speech or assembly, except in the remote sense that limitation is inherent in every choice. Certainly such limitation is not one the state may not make in the exercise of its police power to protect the schools from pollution and thereby to defend its own existence.

It is next argued by appellants that the provision in § 3022 directing the Board of Regents to provide in rules and regulations that membership in any organization listed by the Board after notice and hearing, with provision for review in accordance with the statute, shall constitute prima facie evidence of disqualification, denies due process, because the fact found bears no relation to the fact presumed. In other words, from the fact found that the organization was one that advocated the overthrow of government by unlawful means and that the person employed or to be employed was a member of the organization and knew of its purpose, to presume that such member is disqualified for employment is so unreasonable as to be a denial of due process of law. We do not agree.

During-Reading Questions: Prima facie *as a legal term means that it is presumed to be true, unless it is disproven. The Appellants are arguing that just saying that someone is a member of the Communist Party should not mean that it should also be accepted that the member wants to overthrow the government, and assuming that denies teachers due process. Part of firing a tenured teacher requires that the teacher is given due process, which means that the teacher is entitled to a hearing and that the charges against the teacher must be proved. Why do you think it is important that teachers be given due process before they are fired? Do you agree with the Court that, because someone is a Communist, this automatically means they want to overthrow the government?*

Membership in a listed organization found to be within the statute and known by the member to be within the statute is a legislative finding that the member by his membership supports the thing the organization stands for, namely, the overthrow of government by unlawful means. We cannot say that such a finding is contrary to fact or that "generality of experience" points to a different conclusion. Disqualification follows therefore as a reasonable presumption from such membership and support. Nor is there here a problem of procedural due process. The presumption is not conclusive, but arises only in a hearing where the person against whom it may arise has full opportunity to rebut it. The holding of the Court of Appeals below is significant in this regard:

> The statute also makes it clear that . . . proof of such membership "shall constitute prima facie evidence of disqualification" for such employment. But, as was said in Potts v. Pardee: "The presumption growing out of a prima facie case . . . remains only so long as there is no substantial evidence to the contrary. When that is offered the presumption disappears, and unless met by further proof there is nothing to justify a finding based solely upon it."
>
> Thus, the phrase "prima facie evidence of disqualification," as used in the statute, imports a hearing at which one who seeks appointment to or retention in a public school position shall be afforded an opportunity to present substantial evidence contrary to the presumption sanctioned by the prima facie evidence for which subdivision 2 of section 3022 makes provision. Once such contrary evidence has been received, however, the official who made the order of ineligibility has thereafter the burden of sustaining the validity of that order by a fair preponderance of the evidence. Civil Service Law, § 12-a, subd. [d]. Should an order of ineligibility then issue, the party aggrieved thereby may avail himself of the provisions for review prescribed by the section of the statute last cited above. In that view there here arises no question of procedural due process.

Where, as here, the relation between the fact found and the presumption is clear and direct and is not conclusive, the requirements of due process are satisfied.

Without raising in the complaint or in the proceedings in the lower courts the question of the constitutionality of § 3021 of the Education Law of New York, appellants urge here for the first time that this section is unconstitutionally vague. The question is not before us. We will not pass upon the constitutionality of a state statute before the state courts have had an opportunity to do so.

It is also suggested that the use of the word "subversive" is vague and indefinite. But the word is first used in § 1 of the Feinberg Law, which is the preamble to the Act and not in a definitive part thereof. When used in subdivision 2 of § 3022, the word has a very definite meaning, namely, an organization that teaches and advocates the overthrow of government by force or violence.

We find no constitutional infirmity in § 12-a of the Civil Service Law of New York or in the Feinberg Law which implemented it, and the judgment is

Affirmed.

MR. JUSTICE DOUGLAS, with whom MR. JUSTICE BLACK concurs, dissenting.

The law inevitably turns the school system into a spying project. Regular loyalty reports on the teachers must be made out. The principals become detectives; the students, the parents, the community become informers. Ears are cocked for tell-tale signs of disloyalty. The prejudices of the community come into play in searching out the disloyal. This is not the usual type of supervision which checks a teacher's competency; it is a system which searches for hidden meanings in a teacher's utterances.

During-Reading Questions: What is Justice Douglas arguing this ruling does? How might the "prejudices of the community" be a problem when looking into the background of teachers?

What was the significance of the reference of the art teacher to socialism? Why was the history teacher so openly hostile to Franco Spain? Who heard overtones of revolution in the English teacher's discussion of the *Grapes of Wrath*? What was behind the praise of Soviet progress in metallurgy in the chemistry class? Was it not "subversive" for the teacher to cast doubt on the wisdom of the venture in Korea?

What happens under this law is typical of what happens in a police state. Teachers are under constant surveillance; their pasts are combed for signs of disloyalty; their utterances are watched for clues to dangerous thoughts. A pall is cast over the classrooms. There can be no real academic freedom in that environment. Where suspicion fills the air and holds scholars in line for fear of their jobs, there can be no exercise of the free intellect. Supineness and dogmatism take the place of inquiry. A "party line"—as dangerous as the "party line" of the Communists—lays hold. It is the "party line" of the orthodox view, of the conventional thought, of the accepted approach. A problem can no longer be pursued with impunity to its edges. Fear stalks the classroom. The teacher is no longer a stimulant to adventurous thinking; she becomes instead a pipeline for safe and sound information. A deadening dogma takes the place of free inquiry. Instruction tends to become sterile; pursuit of knowledge is discouraged; discussion often leaves off where it should begin.

This, I think, is what happens when a censor looks over a teacher's shoulder. This system of spying and surveillance, with its accompanying reports and trials, cannot go hand in hand with academic freedom. It produces standardized thought, not the pursuit of truth. Yet it was the pursuit of truth which the First Amendment was designed to protect. A system which directly or inevitably has that effect is alien to our system, and should be struck down. Its survival is a real threat to our way of life. We need be bold and adventuresome in our thinking to survive. A school system producing students trained as robots threatens to rob a generation of the versatility that has been perhaps our greatest distinction. The Framers knew the danger of dogmatism; they also knew the strength that comes when the mind is free, when ideas may be pursued wherever they lead. We forget these teachings of the First Amendment when we sustain this law.

Of course, the school systems of the country need not become cells for Communist activities, and the classrooms need not become forums for propagandizing the Marxist creed. But the guilt of the teacher should turn on overt acts. So long as she is a law-abiding citizen, so long as her performance within the public school system meets professional standards, her private life, her political philosophy, her social creed should not be the cause of reprisals against her.

During-Reading Questions: Why does Justice Douglas think overt acts are better for determining the fitness of a teacher? Do you agree?

Post-Reading Questions

1. In 1967 in the case *Keyishian v. Board of Regents*, this subject was revisited when college professors were asked to sign statements saying they had never been members of the Communist Party or be subject to dismissal. The Court in a 5 to 4 decision found

this requirement to be unconstitutional and stated that "the classroom is peculiarly the marketplace of ideas.'" While this effectively overturned the *Adler* decision, the Appellants in *Adler* were high school teachers, while the appellants in *Keyishian* were college professors. Do you think a distinction should be drawn between the two types of teachers? Why or why not?

2. It's been over sixty years since the *Adler* decision. Since that time, social media has exploded, letting us get an insight into the past thoughts, opinions, and affiliations of people as far back as their early teen years. Do you think social media posts made by prospective or current teachers should have an impact and whether someone is hired or stays a teacher? Why or why not? If you think it should be considered when looking at person's fitness for a job, how far back in a person's past should you be allowed to consider?

Further Explorations

Exploring the Story

Irving Adler, the teacher at the center of this case who was fired for his membership in the Communist Party, was a prolific author who died at age ninety-nine in 2012. To learn about teachers who were impacted by the Feinberg Law, see the website *dreamers & fighters: the NYC teacher purges* at http://dreamersandfighters.com. This website contains multimedia resources on Adler and other members of the New York City Teachers' Union.

Exploring the Law

The 1967 case *Keyishian v. Board of Regents,* 385 U.S. 589, overturned the Court's decision in *Adler*. What do you think made the Court reverse its decision? Do some research into *Keyishian* to compare the two cases.

Exploring the Effects

The *Adler* case is not the only one that impacts teachers. Do some research on the following cases to see how they affect teachers and students:

- *Shelton v. Tucker*, 364 U. S. 479 (1960)
- *Pickering v. Board of Education*, 391 U.S. 563 (1968)
- *Russo v. Central School District No. 1.,* 469 F.2d 623 (1972) (This is a Second Circuit Court of Appeals case, but the Supreme Court decline to hear the appeal, so the decision of the Second Circuit stands. However it is only binding on those states that are a part of the Second Circuit.)

Activities for Extending the Learning

Have students research cases of other types of government employees and how their employment can have an impact on their First Amendment rights. The Newseum site at www.newseuminstitute.org is a wonderful resource for investigating this topic further. Have students search Newseum's site for more information on First Amendment rights. The following Newseum article is particularly relevant: Nott, L. & Moniz, M. (2017, April 24). Government employees and First Amendment overview. In *First Amendment Center, Newseum Institute.* Retrieved from http://www.newseuminstitute.org/first-amendment-center/topics/freedom-of-speech-2/free-speech-and-government-employees-overview/

CASE #3: *SHERBERT V. VERNER*

Pre-Reading Questions

1. *Sherbert v. Verner* deals with the Free Exercise Clause of the First Amendment. What are the two provisions of the Free Exercise Clause? What does each of the provisions mean?
2. How far do you think an employer should have to go to accommodate someone's religious beliefs when it comes to scheduling? Should the nature of the work or the person have something to do with it, or not?

Sherbert v. Verner, 374 U.S. 398 (1963)

MR. JUSTICE BRENNAN delivered the opinion of the Court.

Appellant, a member of the Seventh-day Adventist Church, was discharged by her South Carolina employer because she would not work on Saturday, the Sabbath Day of her faith. When she was unable to obtain other employment because, from conscientious scruples, she would not take Saturday work, she filed a claim for unemployment compensation benefits under the South Carolina Unemployment Compensation Act. That law provides that, to be eligible for benefits, a claimant must be "able to work and . . . available for work"; and, further, that a claimant is ineligible for benefits "[i]f . . . The has failed, without good cause . . . to accept available suitable work when offered him by the employment office or the employer. . . ."

The appellee Employment Security Commission, in administrative proceedings under the statute, found that appellant's restriction upon her availability for Saturday work brought her within the provision disqualifying for benefits insured workers who fail, without good cause, to accept "suitable work when offered . . . by the employment office or the employer . . . ." The Commission's finding was sustained by the Court of Common Pleas for Spartanburg County. That court's judgment was, in turn, affirmed by the South Carolina Supreme Court, which rejected appellant's contention that, as applied to her, the disqualifying provisions of the South Carolina statute abridged her right to the free exercise of her religion secured under the Free Exercise Clause of the First Amendment through the Fourteenth Amendment. The State Supreme Court held specifically that appellant's ineligibility infringed no constitutional liberties because such a construction of the statute "places no restriction upon the appellant's freedom of religion, nor does it in any way prevent her in the exercise of her right and freedom to observe her religious beliefs in accordance with the dictates of her conscience."

We reverse the judgment of the South Carolina Supreme Court and remand for further proceedings not inconsistent with this opinion.

During-Reading Questions: What was the complaint of Sherbert that brought her before the Supreme Court? What was she being denied and what was the reason for the denial?

I

The door of the Free Exercise Clause stands tightly closed against any governmental regulation of religious beliefs as such. Government may neither compel affirmation of a repugnant belief, nor penalize or discriminate against individuals or groups because they hold religious views abhorrent to the authorities, nor employ the taxing power to inhibit the dissemination of particular religious views. On the other hand, the Court has rejected challenges under the Free

Exercise Clause to governmental regulation of certain overt acts prompted by religious beliefs or principles, for "even when the action is in accord with one's religious convictions, [it] is not totally free from legislative restrictions." The conduct or actions so regulated have invariably posed some substantial threat to public safety, peace or order.

Plainly enough, appellant's conscientious objection to Saturday work constitutes no conduct prompted by religious principles of a kind within the reach of state legislation. If, therefore, the decision of the South Carolina Supreme Court is to withstand appellant's constitutional challenge, it must be either because her disqualification as a beneficiary represents no infringement by the State of her constitutional rights of free exercise, or because any incidental burden on the free exercise of appellant's religion may be justified by a "compelling state interest in the regulation of a subject within the State's constitutional power to regulate. . . ." *NAACP v. Button.*

II

We turn first to the question whether the disqualification for benefits imposes any burden on the free exercise of appellant's religion. We think it is clear that it does. In a sense, the consequences of such a disqualification to religious principles and practices may be only an indirect result of welfare legislation within the State's general competence to enact; it is true that no criminal sanctions directly compel appellant to work a six-day week. But this is only the beginning, not the end, of our inquiry. For "[i]f the purpose or effect of a law is to impede the observance of one or all religions or is to discriminate invidiously between religions, that law is constitutionally invalid even though the burden may be characterized as being only indirect." *Braunfeld v. Brown.*

Here, not only is it apparent that appellant's declared ineligibility for benefits derives solely from the practice of her religion, but the pressure upon her to forego that practice is unmistakable. The ruling forces her to choose between following the precepts of her religion and forfeiting benefits, on the one hand, and abandoning one of the precepts of her religion in order to accept work, on the other hand. Governmental imposition of such a choice puts the same kind of burden upon the free exercise of religion as would a fine imposed against appellant for her Saturday worship.

Nor may the South Carolina court's construction of the statute be saved from constitutional infirmity on the ground that unemployment compensation benefits are not appellant's "right," but merely a "privilege." It is too late in the day to doubt that the liberties of religion and expression may be infringed by the denial of or placing of conditions upon a benefit or privilege. For example, in *Flemming v. Nestor*, the Court recognized with respect to Federal Social Security benefits that "[t]he interest of a covered employee under the Act is of sufficient substance to fall within the protection from arbitrary governmental action afforded by the Due Process Clause."

In *Speiser v. Randall*, we emphasized that conditions upon public benefits cannot be sustained if they so operate, whatever their purpose, to inhibit or deter the exercise of First Amendment freedoms. We there struck down a condition which limited the availability of a tax exemption to those members of the exempted class who affirmed their loyalty to the state government granting the exemption. While the State was surely under no obligation to afford such an exemption, we held that the imposition of such a condition upon even a gratuitous benefit inevitably deterred or discouraged the exercise of First Amendment rights of expression, and thereby threatened to "produce a result which the State could not command directly." "To deny an exemption to claimants who engage in certain forms of speech is, in effect, to penalize them for such speech." Likewise, to condition the availability of benefits upon this appellant's willingness to violate a cardinal principle of her religious faith effectively penalizes the free exercise of her constitutional liberties.

Significantly, South Carolina expressly saves the Sunday worshipper from having to make the kind of choice which we here hold infringes the Sabbatarian's religious liberty. When, in times of "national emergency," the textile plants are authorized by the State Commissioner of Labor to operate on Sunday,

> [N]o employee shall be required to work on Sunday . . . who is conscientiously opposed to Sunday work, and if any employee should refuse to work on Sunday on account of conscientious . . . objections, he or she shall not jeopardize his or her seniority by such refusal or be discriminated against in any other manner.

No question of the disqualification of a Sunday worshipper for benefits is likely to arise, since we cannot suppose that an employer will discharge him in violation of this statute. The unconstitutionality of the disqualification of the Sabbatarian is thus compounded by the religious discrimination which South Carolina's general statutory scheme necessarily effects.

During-Reading Question: What special exemption does the State of South Carolina give to people who worship on Sunday that contradicts the idea that the State is being unduly punitive to Sherbert?

III

We must next consider whether some compelling state interest enforced in the eligibility provisions of the South Carolina statute justifies the substantial infringement of appellant's First Amendment right. It is basic that no showing merely of a rational relationship to some colorable state interest would suffice; in this highly sensitive constitutional area, "[o]nly the gravest abuses, endangering paramount interests, give occasion for permissible limitation."

No such abuse or danger has been advanced in the present case. The appellees suggest no more than a possibility that the filing of fraudulent claims by unscrupulous claimants feigning religious objections to Saturday work might not only dilute the unemployment compensation fund, but also hinder the scheduling by employers of necessary Saturday work. But that possibility is not apposite here, because no such objection appears to have been made before the South Carolina Supreme Court, and we are unwilling to assess the importance of an asserted state interest without the views of the state court. Nor, if the contention had been made below, would the record appear to sustain it; there is no proof whatever to warrant such fears of malingering or deceit as those which the respondents now advance. Even if consideration of such evidence is not foreclosed by the prohibition against judicial inquiry into the truth or falsity of religious beliefs, *United States v. Ballard*, 322 U. S. 78—a question as to which we intimate no view, since it is not before us—it is highly doubtful whether such evidence would be sufficient to warrant a substantial infringement of religious liberties. For even if the possibility of spurious claims did threaten to dilute the fund and disrupt the scheduling of work, it would plainly be incumbent upon the appellees to demonstrate that no alternative forms of regulation would combat such abuses without infringing First Amendment rights.

During-Reading Questions: What argument does the State of South Carolina give as a reason for a "compelling State interest"? Do you agree with the argument of the State or the reasoning of the United States Supreme Court?

In these respects, then, the state interest asserted in the present case is wholly dissimilar to the interests which were found to justify the less direct burden upon religious practices in *Braunfeld v. Brown*. The Court recognized that the Sunday closing law which that decision sustained undoubtedly served "to make the practice of [the Orthodox Jewish merchants'] . . . religious beliefs more expensive." But the statute was nevertheless saved by a countervailing factor which finds no equivalent in the instant case—a strong state interest in providing one uniform day of rest for all workers. That secular objective could be achieved, the Court found, only by declaring Sunday to be that day of rest. Requiring exemptions for Sabbatarians, while theoretically possible, appeared to present an administrative problem of such magnitude, or to afford the exempted class so great a competitive advantage, that such a requirement would have rendered the entire statutory scheme unworkable. In the present case, no such justifications underlie the determination of the state court that appellant's religion makes her ineligible to receive benefits.

IV

In holding as we do, plainly we are not fostering the "establishment" of the Seventh-day Adventist religion in South Carolina, for the extension of unemployment benefits to Sabbatarians in common with Sunday worshippers reflects nothing more than the governmental obligation of neutrality in the face of religious differences, and does not represent that involvement of religious with secular institutions which it is the object of the Establishment Clause to forestall. Nor does the recognition of the appellant's right to unemployment benefits under the state statute serve to abridge any other person's religious liberties. Nor do we, by our decision today, declare the existence of a constitutional right to unemployment benefits on the part of all persons whose religious convictions are the cause of their unemployment. This is not a case in which an employee's religious convictions serve to make him a nonproductive member of society. Finally, nothing we say today constrains the States to adopt any particular form or scheme of unemployment compensation. Our holding today is only that South Carolina may not constitutionally apply the eligibility provisions so as to constrain a worker to abandon his religious convictions respecting the day of rest. This holding but reaffirms a principle that we announced a decade and a half ago, namely that no State may "exclude individual Catholics, Lutherans, Mohammedans, Baptists, Jews, Methodists, Non-believers, Presbyterians, or the members of any other faith, because of their faith, or lack of it, from receiving the benefits of public welfare legislation."

In view of the result we have reached under the First and Fourteenth Amendments' guarantee of free exercise of religion, we have no occasion to consider appellant's claim that the denial of benefits also deprived her of the equal protection of the laws in violation of the Fourteenth Amendment.

The judgment of the South Carolina Supreme Court is reversed, and the case is remanded for further proceedings not inconsistent with this opinion.

It is so ordered.

MR. JUSTICE HARLAN, whom MR. JUSTICE WHITE joins, dissenting.

Today's decision is disturbing both in its rejection of existing precedent and in its implications for the future. The significance of the decision can best be understood after an examination of the state law applied in this case.

South Carolina's Unemployment Compensation Law was enacted in 1936 in response to the grave social and economic problems that arose during the depression of that period. As stated in the statute itself:

> Economic insecurity due to unemployment is a serious menace to health, morals and welfare of the people of this State; involuntary unemployment is therefore a subject of general interest and concern . . . ; the achievement of social security requires protection against this greatest hazard of our economic life; this can be provided by encouraging the employers to provide more stable employment and by the systematic accumulation of funds during periods of employment to provide benefits for periods of unemployment, thus maintaining purchasing power and limiting the serious social consequences of poor relief assistance.

Thus, the purpose of the legislature was to tide people over, and to avoid social and economic chaos, during periods when work was unavailable. But, at the same time, there was clearly no intent to provide relief for those who, for purely personal reasons, were or became unavailable for work. In accordance with this design, the legislature provided, in § 68–113, that "[a]n unemployed insured worker shall be eligible to receive benefits with respect to any week only if the Commission finds that . . . [h]e is able to work and is available for work. . . ."

The South Carolina Supreme Court has uniformly applied this law in conformity with its clearly expressed purpose. It has consistently held that one is not "available for work" if his unemployment has resulted not from the inability of industry to provide a job, but rather from personal circumstances, no matter how compelling. The reference to "involuntary unemployment" in the legislative statement of policy, whatever a sociologist, philosopher, or theologian might say, has been interpreted not to embrace such personal circumstances.

In the present case, all that the state court has done is to apply these accepted principles. Since virtually all of the mills in the Spartanburg area were operating on a six-day week, the appellant was "unavailable for work," and thus ineligible for benefits, when personal considerations prevented her from accepting employment on a full-time basis in the industry and locality in which she had worked. The fact that these personal considerations sprang from her religious convictions was wholly without relevance to the state court's application of the law. Thus, in no proper sense can it be said that the State discriminated against the appellant on the basis of her religious beliefs or that she was denied benefits because she was a Seventh-day Adventist. She was denied benefits just as any other claimant would be denied benefits who was not "available for work" for personal reasons.

With this background, this Court's decision comes into clearer focus. What the Court is holding is that, if the State chooses to condition unemployment compensation on the applicant's availability for work, it is constitutionally compelled to carve out an exception—and to provide benefits—for those whose unavailability is due to their religious convictions. Such a holding has particular significance in two respects.

First, despite the Court's protestations to the contrary, the decision necessarily overrules *Braunfeld v. Brown*, which held that it did not offend the "Free Exercise" Clause of the Constitution for a State to forbid a Sabbatarian to do business on Sunday. The secular purpose of the statute before us today is even clearer than that involved in *Braunfeld*. And just as in Braunfeld—where exceptions to the Sunday closing laws for Sabbatarians would have been inconsistent with the purpose to achieve a uniform day of rest and would have required case-by-case inquiry into religious beliefs—so here, an exception to the rules of eligibility based on religious convictions would necessitate judicial examination of those convictions and would be at odds with the limited purpose of the statute to smooth out the economy during periods of industrial instability. Finally, the indirect financial burden of the present law is far less than that involved in *Braunfeld*. Forcing a store owner to close his business on Sunday may well have the effect of depriving him of a satisfactory livelihood if his religious convictions require him to close on Saturday as well. Here we are dealing only with temporary benefits, amounting to a fraction of regular weekly wages and running for not more than 22 weeks. Clearly, any differences between this case and *Braunfeld* cut against the present appellant.

During-Reading Questions: Justice Harlan would have preferred that the Court follow the ruling in Braunfeld v. Brown *where a person who worshipped on Saturday was not allowed a religious exception to open his business on Sunday, at a historical time when no businesses were allowed to be open on a Sunday. What are the differences between the* Sherbert *case and the* Braunfeld *case? Why does Justice Harlan think the decision in the* Braunfeld *case was actually more restrictive than in the* Sherbert *case?*

Second, the implications of the present decision are far more troublesome than its apparently narrow dimensions would indicate at first glance. The meaning of today's holding, as already noted, is that the State must furnish unemployment benefits to one who is unavailable for work if the unavailability stems from the exercise of religious convictions. The State, in other words, must single out for financial assistance those whose behavior is religiously motivated, even though it denies such assistance to others whose identical behavior (in this case, inability to work on Saturdays) is not religiously motivated. It has been suggested that such singling out of religious conduct for special treatment may violate the constitutional limitations on state action. My own view, however, is that, at least under the circumstances of this case, it would be a permissible accommodation of religion for the State, if it chose to do so, to create an exception to its eligibility requirements for persons like the appellant. The constitutional obligation of "neutrality," is not so narrow a channel that the slightest deviation from an absolutely straight course leads to condemnation. There are too many instances in which no such course can be charted, too many areas in which the pervasive activities of the State justify some special provision for religion to prevent it from being submerged by an all-embracing secularism. The State violates its obligation of neutrality when, for example, it mandates a daily religious exercise in its public schools, with all the attendant pressures on the school children that such an exercise entails. But there is, I believe, enough flexibility in the Constitution to permit a legislative judgment accommodating an unemployment compensation law to the exercise of religious beliefs such as appellant's.

For very much the same reasons, however, I cannot subscribe to the conclusion that the State is constitutionally compelled to carve out an exception to its general rule of eligibility in the present case. Those situations in which the Constitution may require special treatment on account of religion are, in my view, few and far between, and this view is amply supported by the course of constitutional litigation in this area. Such compulsion in the present case is particularly inappropriate in light of the indirect, remote, and insubstantial effect of the decision below on the exercise of appellant's religion and in light of the direct financial assistance to religion that today's decision requires.

For these reasons I respectfully dissent from the opinion and judgment of the Court.

During-Reading Questions: According to Justice Harlan's argument, what is the effect on non-religious people of allowing Sherbert to benefit from a religious exemption? Do you agree or disagree with his position?

Post-Reading Questions

1. This case created what is known as the "Sherbert Test," which has two parts. First, the court must decide whether the person has a claim involving a "sincere religious belief." Second, the court must determine whether the government action is a "substantial

burden" on the person's ability to act on that belief. What historically has been determined to be a "sincere religious belief"? Is there anything that has been determined not to be a sincere religious belief?
2. In the case *Employment Division v. Smith* (1990), the Court held that employers could prohibit the religious use of sacramental peyote. In the case, the plaintiffs were fired for misconduct after they failed a drug test. Under the two-part test, how would the firing of the employees be allowed?

Further Explorations

Exploring the Story

To learn more about the Constitutional religious freedoms of individuals, visit the American Civil Liberties Union at www.aclu.org, and look under the Religious Liberties tab.

Exploring the Law

To learn more about the Free Exercise of Religion Clause and to explore other cases, lessons, and hypothetical situations, visit the Constitutional Rights Foundation website at http://www.crf-usa.org. A particularly relevant article on their website is: Constitutional Rights Foundation. (n.d.). The free exercise of religion in America. Retrieved from http://www.crf-usa.org/resources/the-free-exercise-of-religion-in-america.

For another resource for learning more about the free exercise of religion is the Newseum Institute at www.newseuminstitute.org; go to the Religious Freedom Center tab.

Exploring the Effects

To read more about the Free Exercise Clause and how it has evolved in the courts in recent years, read the following article: Epps, G. (2016, April 4). The strange career of free exercise. *The Atlantic*. Retrieved from https://www.theatlantic.com/politics/archive/2016/04/the-strange-career-of-free-exercise/476712/

Activities for Extending the Learning

The Free Exercise Clause was regularly considered by the Supreme Court during the twentieth century. Have students go to the Bill of Rights Institute's website at https://billofrightsinstitute.org and compile a timeline of landmark twentieth-century Supreme Court cases and the decisions made in each case. How have these decisions impacted United States citizens and the religions they choose to practice?

A NOTE FROM THE AUTHORS

This chapter shows how we are communal creatures. It demonstrates our affiliations with other people, groups, and ideas, and how these play an important role in our lives, and also how our "identities" still have an impact on how one relates to the government. Everything we do (joining a political party, choosing a religion, the personal identity you hold) has a potential political impact.

The concepts of nationality, religion, and political affiliation are all very personal decisions, some of which are chosen by us, and some of which are chosen for us. Is it right to treat people differently for things they don't have a choice over? Or should we treat everyone the same regardless of who makes the choice? When it comes to something like religion, even if you choose it, how far do we need to change our lives to accommodate other people's religious beliefs? When does that become overly intrusive? Within our schools today, we have multiple religions within one building with different traditions, dress, prayer habits, and expectations. How do these impact others? And what rights do those with no religion have in light of a nation that respects religious independence?

These cases highlight different times in history—times where politically charged feelings influenced the government's actions, but yet looking at history, we see the government often has trends of politically charged reactionary politics. Is this fair? When else has it happened? Are travel bans or other post-9/11 policies similar to that in *Korematsu?* How can students be aware, as citizens, of reactionary politics and how those influence the communal creatures we are? For young people who are deciding who they are and who they want to be, they should be cognizant of the long-term impact of the law as they makes those choices for their lives.

Chapter Eight

Power, Authority, and Governance

Theme 6: *Social studies programs should include experiences that provide for the study of how people create, interact with, and change structures of power, authority, and governance.*
—*National Curriculum Standards for Social Studies* (2010), National Council for the Social Studies, p. 19

Theme 6 examines the relationship between individuals and the government by examining such questions as:

> What are the purposes and functions of government? Under what circumstances is the exercise of political power legitimate? What are the proper scope and limits of authority? How are individual rights protected and challenged within the context of majority rule? What conflicts exist among fundamental principles and values of constitutional democracy? What are the rights and responsibilities of citizens in a constitutional democracy? (NCSS, 2010, p. 19)

The Supreme Court is the key decider in where the power of the government ends and the power of the individual begins.

The *Gideon v. Wainwright* (1963) decision serves as an example of the persistence in addressing an issue and promoting social change. From a prison cell, writing in pencil on prison stationery, Clarence Earl Gideon changed the application of the Sixth Amendment. Students can explore the difference between a right on paper and a right in practice. How does the right to counsel continue to be protected?

In *Miranda v. Arizona* (1966), the Court clearly defines a limit of authority and a protection of individual rights. The case also provides the opportunity to discuss the question: "What conflicts exist among fundamental principles and values of constitutional democracy?" Knowing the foundation of the Miranda warnings, students can explore the balancing of the rights of an individual and the needs of a social group. How does a just society balance those rights? (NCSS, 2010, p. 19).

Tinker v. Des Moines Independent Community School District (1969) is the exploration of one's freedom of speech and the power of the government to limit one's individual right to that freedom. This case also provides the opportunity to examine the value of this right in a democracy, i.e., why political speech is entitled to more protection. How are rights and responsibilities impacted by context? Since the case is about high school students in a high school, it will allow students to see the direct impact of the judicial branch's exercise of power.

CASE #1: *GIDEON V. WAINWRIGHT*

Pre-Reading Questions

1. Discuss the right to counsel articulated in the Sixth Amendment.
2. Discuss the Due Process Clause.

Gideon v. Wainwright, 372 U.S. 335 (1963)

MR. JUSTICE BLACK delivered the opinion of the Court.

Petitioner was charged in a Florida state court with having broken and entered a poolroom with intent to commit a misdemeanor. This offense is a felony under Florida law. Appearing in court without funds and without a lawyer, petitioner asked the court to appoint counsel for him, whereupon the following colloquy took place:

> The COURT: Mr. Gideon, I am sorry, but I cannot appoint Counsel to represent you in this case. Under the laws of the State of Florida, the only time the Court can appoint Counsel to represent a Defendant is when that person is charged with a capital offense. I am sorry, but I will have to deny your request to appoint Counsel to defend you in this case.
>
> The DEFENDANT: The United States Supreme Court says I am entitled to be represented by Counsel.

Put to trial before a jury, Gideon conducted his defense about as well as could be expected from a layman. He made an opening statement to the jury, cross-examined the State's witnesses, presented witnesses in his own defense, declined to testify himself, and made a short argument "emphasizing his innocence to the charge contained in the Information filed in this case." The jury returned a verdict of guilty, and petitioner was sentenced to serve five years in the state prison. Later, petitioner filed in the Florida Supreme Court this habeas corpus petition attacking his conviction and sentence on the ground that the trial court's refusal to appoint counsel for him denied him rights "guaranteed by the Constitution and the Bill of Rights by the United States Government." Treating the petition for habeas corpus as properly before it, the State Supreme Court, "upon consideration thereof" but without an opinion, denied all relief. Since 1942, when *Betts v. Brady* was decided by a divided Court, the problem of a defendant's federal constitutional right to counsel in a state court has been a continuing source of controversy and litigation in both state and federal courts. To give this problem another review here, we granted certiorari. 370 U.S. 908. Since Gideon was proceeding *in forma pauperis,* we appointed counsel to represent him and requested both sides to discuss in their briefs and oral arguments the following: "Should this Court's holding in *Betts v. Brady* be reconsidered?"

During-Reading Question: What does in forma pauperis *mean? What is the State's interest in having a defendant have the representation of a lawyer?*

I

The facts upon which Betts claimed that he had been unconstitutionally denied the right to have counsel appointed to assist him are strikingly like the facts upon which Gideon here bases his federal constitutional claim. Betts was indicted for robbery in a Maryland state court. On arraignment, he told the trial judge of his lack of funds to hire a lawyer and asked the court to appoint one for him. Betts was advised that it was not the practice in that county to appoint counsel for indigent defendants except in murder and rape cases. He then pleaded not guilty, had witnesses summoned, cross-examined the State's witnesses, examined his own, and chose not to testify himself. He was found guilty by the judge, sitting without a jury, and sentenced to eight years in prison. Like Gideon, Betts sought release by habeas corpus, alleging that he had been denied the right to assistance of counsel in violation of the Fourteenth Amendment. Betts was denied any relief, and, on review, this Court affirmed. It was held that a refusal to appoint counsel for an indigent defendant charged with a felony did not necessarily violate the Due Process Clause of the Fourteenth Amendment, which, for reasons given, the Court deemed to be the only applicable federal constitutional provision. The Court said:

> Asserted denial [of due process] is to be tested by an appraisal of the totality of facts in a given case. That which may, in one setting, constitute a denial of fundamental fairness, shocking to the universal sense of justice, may, in other circumstances, and in the light of other considerations, fall short of such denial.

Treating due process as "a concept less rigid and more fluid than those envisaged in other specific and particular provisions of the Bill of Rights," the Court held that refusal to appoint counsel under the particular facts and circumstances in the *Betts* case was not so "offensive to the common and fundamental ideas of fairness" as to amount to a denial of due process. Since the facts and circumstances of the two cases are so nearly indistinguishable, we think the *Betts v. Brady* holding, if left standing, would require us to reject Gideon's claim that the Constitution guarantees him the assistance of counsel.

Upon full reconsideration, we conclude that *Betts v. Brady* should be overruled.

During-Reading Question: Summarize the Court's reasoning in Betts *that not appointing counsel for indigent clients in felony cases did not violate the Due Process Clause.*

II

The Sixth Amendment provides, "In all criminal prosecutions, the accused shall enjoy the right . . . to have the Assistance of Counsel for his defence." We have construed this to mean that, in federal courts, counsel must be provided for defendants unable to employ counsel unless the right is competently and intelligently waived. Betts argued that this right is extended to indigent defendants in state courts by the Fourteenth Amendment. In response, the Court stated that, while the Sixth Amendment laid down

> no rule for the conduct of the States, the question recurs whether the constraint laid by the Amendment upon the national courts expresses a rule so fundamental and essential to a fair trial, and so, to due process of law, that it is made obligatory upon the States by the Fourteenth Amendment.

In order to decide whether the Sixth Amendment's guarantee of counsel is of this fundamental nature, the Court in *Betts* set out and considered "[r]elevant data on the subject . . . afforded by constitutional and statutory provisions subsisting in the colonies and the States prior to the inclusion of the Bill of Rights in the national Constitution, and in the constitutional, legislative, and judicial history of the States to the present date." On the basis of this historical data, the Court concluded that "appointment of counsel is not a fundamental right, essential to a fair trial." It was for this reason the *Betts* Court refused to accept the contention that the Sixth Amendment's guarantee of counsel for indigent federal defendants was extended to or, in the words of that Court, "made obligatory upon, the States by the Fourteenth Amendment."

Plainly, had the Court concluded that appointment of counsel for an indigent criminal defendant was "a fundamental right, essential to a fair trial," it would have held that the Fourteenth Amendment requires appointment of counsel in a state court, just as the Sixth Amendment requires in a federal court.

We think the Court in *Betts* had ample precedent for acknowledging that those guarantees of the Bill of Rights which are fundamental safeguards of liberty immune from federal abridgment are equally protected against state invasion by the Due Process Clause of the Fourteenth Amendment.

During-Reading Question: What makes a guarantee of the Bill of Rights' "fundamental safeguards of liberty"?

We accept *Betts v. Brady*'s assumption, based as it was on our prior cases, that a provision of the Bill of Rights which is "fundamental and essential to a fair trial" is made obligatory upon the States by the Fourteenth Amendment. We think the Court in *Betts* was wrong, however, in concluding that the Sixth Amendment's guarantee of counsel is not one of these fundamental rights. Ten years before *Betts v. Brady,* this Court, after full consideration of all the historical data examined in *Betts,* had unequivocally declared that "the right to the aid of counsel is of this fundamental character" *Powell v. Alabama.* While the Court, at the close of its *Powell* opinion, did, by its language, as this Court frequently does, limit its holding to the particular facts and circumstances of that case, its conclusions about the fundamental nature of the right to counsel are unmistakable. Several years later, in 1936, the Court reemphasized what it had said about the fundamental nature of the right to counsel in this language:

> We concluded that certain fundamental rights, safeguarded by the first eight amendments against federal action, were also safeguarded against state action by the due process of law clause of the Fourteenth Amendment, and among them the fundamental right of the accused to the aid of counsel in a criminal prosecution. *Grosjean v. American Press Co.*

The fact is that, in deciding as it did—that "appointment of counsel is not a fundamental right, essential to a fair trial"—the Court in *Betts v. Brady* made an abrupt break with its own well considered precedents. In returning to these old precedents, sounder, we believe, than the new, we but restore constitutional principles established to achieve a fair system of justice. Not only these precedents, but also reason and reflection, require us to recognize that, in our adversary system of criminal justice, any person haled into court, who is too poor to hire a lawyer, cannot be assured a fair trial unless counsel is provided for him. This seems to us to be an obvious truth. Governments, both state and federal, quite properly spend vast sums of money to establish machinery to try defendants accused of crime. Lawyers to prosecute are everywhere deemed essential to protect the public's interest in an orderly society. Similarly, there are few defendants charged with crime, few indeed, who fail to hire the best lawyers they can get to prepare and present their defenses. That government hires lawyers to prosecute and defendants who have the money hire lawyers to defend are the strongest indications of the widespread belief that lawyers in criminal courts are necessities, not luxuries. The right of one charged with crime to counsel may not be deemed fundamental and essential to fair trials in some countries, but it is in ours. From the very beginning, our state and national constitutions and laws have laid great emphasis on procedural and substantive safeguards designed to assure fair trials before impartial tribunals in which every defendant stands equal before the law. This noble ideal cannot be realized if the poor man charged with crime has to face his accusers without a lawyer to assist him. A defendant's need for a lawyer is nowhere better stated than in the moving words of Mr. Justice Sutherland in *Powell v. Alabama:*

> The right to be heard would be, in many cases, of little avail if it did not comprehend the right to be heard by counsel. Even the intelligent and educated layman has small and sometimes no skill in the science of law. If charged with crime, he is incapable, generally, of determining for himself whether the indictment is good or bad. He is unfamiliar with the rules of evidence. Left without the aid of counsel, he may be put on trial without a proper charge, and convicted upon incompetent evidence, or evidence irrelevant to the issue or otherwise inadmissible. He lacks both the skill and knowledge adequately to prepare his defense, even though he have a perfect one. He requires the guiding hand of counsel at every step in the proceedings against him. Without it, though he be not guilty, he faces the danger of conviction because he does not know how to establish his innocence.

The Court in *Betts v. Brady* departed from the sound wisdom upon which the Court's holding in *Powell v. Alabama* rested. Florida, supported by two other States, has asked that *Betts v. Brady* be left intact. Twenty-two States, as friends of the Court, argue that *Betts* was "an anachronism when handed down," and that it should now be overruled. We agree.

During-Reading Question: What is the Court's reasoning?

The judgment is reversed, and the cause is remanded to the Supreme Court of Florida for further action not inconsistent with this opinion.

Reversed.

Post-Reading Questions

1. Why is it important to have a lawyer if on trial for crime?
2. Although *Gideon* gave indigent defendants charged with a felony the right to counsel, what issues do you think have arisen as a result of that right?

Further Explorations

Exploring the Story

In order to bring the story to life, have students complete the readers theater with a scripted re-enactment, which can be found at the following website: United States Courts. (n.d.). Scripted Re-Enactment—*Gideon v. Wainwright*. Retrieved from http://www.uscourts.gov/educational-resources/educational-activities/scripted-re-enactment-gideon-v-wainwright

Exploring the Law

To explore the Sixth Amendment and the right to counsel, explore the following lesson plan from the National Constitution Center, which can be found at: National Constitution Center. (2006). Key Constitutional Concepts: Right to Counsel. [pdf, Lesson plan]. In *Annenberg Classroom*. Retrieved from http://www.annenbergclassroom.org/Files/Documents/LessonPlans/RigthToCounselLessonPlan.pdf

In the accompanying video resource, use the second part of the video along with lesson plans and student activities: Leonore Annenberg Institute for Civics. (n.d.). Key Constitutional Concepts. [Streaming video]. In *Annenberg Classroom*. Retrieved from http://www.annenbergclassroom.org/page/key-constitutional-concepts

Exploring the Effects

To further explore the issues of providing effective assistance of counsel, see: Street Law, Inc. (2013). Chasing Gideon: Issues in public defense. [Lesson plan]. Retrieved from http://streetlaw.org/en/newsroom/Article/415/Chasing_Gideon__Lesson_Plan

Activities for Extending the Learning

Gideon provides the right to counsel in criminal cases, but it does not apply to civil cases. Have students argue for or against—using the reasoning in *Gideon*—the right to counsel in civil cases.

CASE #2: *MIRANDA V. ARIZONA*

Pre-Reading Questions

Read the Fifth Amendment. What rights are articulated in it? How could those rights be protected in society today?

Miranda v. Arizona, 364 U.S. 436 (1966)

MR. CHIEF JUSTICE WARREN delivered the opinion of the Court.

The cases before us raise questions which go to the roots of our concepts of American criminal jurisprudence: the restraints society must observe consistent with the Federal Constitution in prosecuting individuals for crime. More specifically, we deal with the admissibility of statements obtained from an individual who is subjected to custodial police interrogation and the necessity for procedures which assure that the individual is accorded his privilege under the Fifth Amendment to the Constitution not to be compelled to incriminate himself.

We granted certiorari in these cases in order further to explore some facets of the problems thus exposed of applying the privilege against self-incrimination to in-custody interrogation, and to give concrete constitutional guidelines for law enforcement agencies and courts to follow.

Our holding will be spelled out with some specificity in the pages which follow, but, briefly stated, it is this: the prosecution may not use statements, whether exculpatory or inculpatory, stemming from custodial interrogation of the defendant unless it demonstrates the use of procedural safeguards effective to secure the privilege against self-incrimination. By custodial interrogation, we mean questioning initiated by law enforcement officers after a person has been taken into custody or otherwise deprived of his freedom of action in any significant way. As for the procedural safeguards to be employed, unless other fully effective means are devised to inform accused persons of their right of silence and to assure a continuous opportunity to exercise it, the following measures are required. Prior to any questioning, the person must be warned that he has a right to remain silent, that any statement he does make may be used as evidence against him, and that he has a right to the presence of an attorney, either retained or appointed. The defendant may waive effectuation of these rights, provided the waiver is made voluntarily, knowingly and intelligently. If, however, he indicates in any manner and at any stage of the process that he wishes to consult with an attorney before speaking, there can be no questioning. Likewise, if the individual is alone and indicates in any manner that he does not wish to be interrogated, the police may not question him. The mere fact that he may have answered some questions or volunteered some statements on his own does not deprive him of the right to refrain from answering any further inquiries until he has consulted with an attorney and thereafter consents to be questioned.

During-Reading Question: Analyze each of the rights that the Court articulates in the summary of the case and describe what it means.

I

The constitutional issue we decide in each of these cases is the admissibility of statements obtained from a defendant questioned while in custody or otherwise deprived of his freedom of action in any significant way. In each, the defendant was questioned by police officers, detectives, or a prosecuting attorney in a room in which he was cut off from the outside world. In none of these cases was the defendant given a full and effective warning of his rights at the outset of the interrogation process. In all the cases, the questioning elicited oral admissions, and in three of them, signed statements as well which were admitted at their trials. They all thus share salient features—incommunicado interrogation of individuals in a police-dominated atmosphere, resulting in self-incriminating statements without full warnings of constitutional rights.

An understanding of the nature and setting of this in-custody interrogation is essential to our decisions today.

From . . . representative samples of interrogation techniques, the setting prescribed by the manuals and observed in practice becomes clear. In essence, it is this: to be alone with the subject is essential to prevent distraction and to deprive him of any outside support. The aura of confidence in his guilt undermines his will to resist. He merely confirms the preconceived story the police seek to have him describe. Patience and persistence, at times relentless questioning, are employed. To obtain a confession, the interrogator must "patiently maneuver himself or his quarry into a position from which the desired objective may be attained." When normal procedures fail to produce the needed result, the police may resort to deceptive stratagems such as giving false legal advice. It is important to keep the subject off balance, for example, by trading on his insecurity about himself or his surroundings. The police then persuade, trick, or cajole him out of exercising his constitutional rights.

Even without employing brutality, the "third degree" or the specific stratagems described above, the very fact of custodial interrogation exacts a heavy toll on individual liberty, and trades on the weakness of individuals.

In the cases before us today, given this background, we concern ourselves primarily with this interrogation atmosphere and the evils it can bring. In No. 759, *Miranda v. Arizona*, the police arrested the defendant and took him to a special interrogation room, where they secured a confession. In No. 760, *Vignera v. New York*, the defendant made oral admissions to the police after interrogation in the afternoon, and then signed an inculpatory statement upon being questioned by an assistant district attorney later the same evening. In No. 761, *Westover v. United States*, the defendant was handed over to the Federal Bureau of Investigation by local authorities after they had detained and interrogated him for a lengthy period, both at night and the following morning. After some two hours of questioning, the federal officers had obtained signed statements from the defendant. Lastly, in No. 584, *California v. Stewart*, the local police held the defendant five days in the station and interrogated him on nine separate occasions before they secured his inculpatory statement.

In these cases, we might not find the defendants' statements to have been involuntary in traditional terms. Our concern for adequate safeguards to protect precious Fifth Amendment rights is, of course, not lessened in the slightest. In each of the cases, the defendant was thrust into an unfamiliar atmosphere and run through menacing police interrogation procedures. The potentiality for compulsion is forcefully apparent, for example, in *Miranda*, where the indigent Mexican defendant was a seriously disturbed individual with pronounced sexual fantasies, and in *Stewart*, in which the defendant was an indigent Los Angeles Negro who had dropped out of school in the sixth grade. To be sure, the records do not evince overt physical coercion or patent psychological ploys. The fact remains that in none of these cases did the officers undertake to afford appropriate safeguards at the outset of the interrogation to insure that the statements were truly the product of free choice.

It is obvious that such an interrogation environment is created for no purpose other than to subjugate the individual to the will of his examiner. This atmosphere carries its own badge of intimidation. To be sure, this is not physical intimidation, but it is equally destructive of human dignity. The current practice of incommunicado interrogation is at odds with one of our Nation's most cherished principles—that the individual may not be compelled to incriminate himself. Unless adequate protective devices are employed to dispel the compulsion inherent in custodial surroundings, no statement obtained from the defendant can truly be the product of his free choice.

From the foregoing, we can readily perceive an intimate connection between the privilege against self-incrimination and police custodial questioning. It is fitting to turn to history and precedent underlying the Self-Incrimination Clause to determine its applicability in this situation.

During-Reading Question: Describe the Court's vision of what the interrogation environment looks like. Why is this important to the Court?

II

We sometimes forget how long it has taken to establish the privilege against self-incrimination, the sources from which it came, and the fervor with which it was defended. Its roots go back into ancient times.

Thus, we may view the historical development of the privilege as one which groped for the proper scope of governmental power over the citizen. As a "noble principle often transcends its origins," the privilege has come rightfully to be recognized in part as an individual's substantive right, a "right to a private enclave where he may lead a private life. That right is the hallmark of our democracy" *United States v. Grunewald*. We have recently noted that the privilege against self-incrimination—the essential mainstay of our adversary system—is founded on a complex of values. All these policies point to one overriding thought: the constitutional foundation underlying the privilege is the respect a government—state or federal—must accord to the dignity and integrity of its citizens. To maintain a "fair state-individual balance," to require the government "to shoulder the entire load," to respect the inviolability of the human personality, our accusatory system of criminal justice demands that the government seeking to punish an individual produce the evidence against him by its own independent labors, rather than by the cruel, simple expedient of compelling it from his own mouth. In sum, the privilege is fulfilled only when the person is guaranteed the right "to remain silent unless he chooses to speak in the unfettered exercise of his own will" *Malloy v. Hogan.*

The question in these cases is whether the privilege is fully applicable during a period of custodial interrogation.

During-Reading Questions: Why is the right against self-incrimination so important? Would these reasons be applicable during a period of custodial interrogation?

In this Court, the privilege has consistently been accorded a liberal construction. We are satisfied that all the principles embodied in the privilege apply to informal compulsion exerted by law enforcement officers during in-custody questioning. An individual swept from familiar surroundings into police custody, surrounded by antagonistic forces, and subjected to the techniques of persuasion described above cannot be otherwise than under compulsion to speak. As a practical matter, the compulsion to speak in the isolated setting of the police station may well be greater than in courts or other official investigations, where there are often impartial observers to guard against intimidation or trickery.

Our holding in *Malloy v. Hogan* stressed the fact that the police had not advised the defendant of his constitutional privilege to remain silent at the outset of the interrogation, and we drew attention to that fact at several points in the decision. This was no isolated factor, but an essential ingredient in our decision. The entire thrust of police interrogation there, as in all the cases today, was to put the defendant in such an emotional state as to impair his capacity for rational judgment. The abdication of the constitutional privilege—the choice on his part to speak to the police—was not made knowingly or competently because of the failure to apprise him of his rights; the compelling atmosphere of the in-custody interrogation, and not an independent decision on his part, caused the defendant to speak.

During-Reading Question: Describe what the Court thinks is important in a defendant's right to speak.

A different phase of the *Escobedo* decision was significant in its attention to the absence of counsel during the questioning. There, as in the cases today, we sought a protective device to dispel the compelling atmosphere of the interrogation. In *Escobedo*, however, the police did not relieve the defendant of the anxieties which they had created in the interrogation rooms. Rather, they denied his request for the assistance of counsel. This heightened his dilemma, and made his later statements the product of this compulsion. The denial of the defendant's request for his attorney thus undermined his ability to exercise the privilege—to remain silent if he chose or to speak without any intimidation, blatant or subtle. The presence of counsel, in all the cases before us today, would be the adequate protective device necessary to make the process of police interrogation conform to the dictates of the privilege. His presence would insure that statements made in the government-established atmosphere are not the product of compulsion.

It was in this manner that *Escobedo* explicated another facet of the pretrial privilege, noted in many of the Court's prior decisions: the protection of rights at trial. That counsel is present when statements are taken from an individual during interrogation obviously enhances the integrity of the fact-finding processes in court. The presence of an attorney, and the warnings delivered to the individual, enable the defendant under otherwise compelling circumstances to tell his story without fear, effectively, and in a way that eliminates the evils in the interrogation process. Without the protections flowing from adequate warnings and the rights of counsel,

> all the careful safeguards erected around the giving of testimony, whether by an accused or any other witness, would become empty formalities in a procedure where the most compelling possible evidence of guilt, a confession, would have already been obtained at the unsupervised pleasure of the police. *Mapp v. Ohio.*

During-Reading Questions: What interests of a person in custody are the Court trying to protect? How does the presence of counsel help protect those interests?

III

Today, then, there can be no doubt that the Fifth Amendment privilege is available outside of criminal court proceedings, and serves to protect persons in all settings in which their freedom of action is curtailed in any significant way from being compelled to incriminate themselves. We have concluded that, without proper safeguards, the process of in-custody interrogation of persons suspected or accused of crime contains inherently compelling pressures which work to undermine the individual's will to resist and to compel him to speak where he would not otherwise do so freely. In order to combat these pressures and to permit a full opportunity to exercise the privilege against self-incrimination, the accused must be adequately and effectively apprised of his rights, and the exercise of those rights must be fully honored.

Therefore, in accordance with the foregoing, the judgments of the Supreme Court [o]f Arizona in No. 759, of the New York Court of Appeals in No. 760, and of the Court of Appeals for the Ninth Circuit in No. 761, are reversed. The judgment of the Supreme Court of California in No. 584 is affirmed.

It is so ordered.

Post-Reading Questions

1. The Court goes on to articulate what we now know as the Miranda rights and responds to the argument that "society's need for interrogation outweighs the privilege." Articulate the argument that the *Miranda* decision does handicap law enforcement officers and extends the right against self-incrimination too far.
2. The Court states that the *Miranda* decision applies to "all settings in which their freedom of action is curtailed in any significant way from being compelled to incriminate themselves." Apply the *Miranda* decision to the following scenarios and determine if an officer would have to give Miranda warnings.

    a. Billie is walking down the street and matches the description of a suspect in a recent burglary. Officer Down stops him and starts to ask him questions. Is Billie "in custody"? What if five police cars pull up and all the officers are surrounding Billie?
    b. Sam feels guilty about stealing an iPhone from a store so he goes to the police station voluntarily and confesses. What if Sam was stopped by the security guards at the store and taken into a back room to talk?

Further Explorations

Exploring the Story

To further explore the case, have students watch the following video: Leonore Annenberg Institute for Civics. (n.d.). The right to remain silent: *Miranda v. Arizona*. [Streaming video]. In *Annenberg Classroom*. Retrieved from http://www.annenbergclassroom.org/page/the-right-to-remain-silent-miranda-v-arizona

Exploring the Law

Further information about the meaning of "custodial interrogation" and scenarios can be found within the following article: Rydholm, J. (n.d.). *Miranda*: The meaning of "custodial interrogation." Retrieved from https://www.nolo.com/legal-encyclopedia/miranda-the-meaning-custodial-interrogation.html

Exploring the Effects

This PBS lesson plan allows students to apply *Miranda* to subsequent cases: PBS Learning Media. (n.d.). Understanding and Applying the *Miranda* Decision. [Lesson plan]. Retrieved from https://net.pbslearningmedia.org/resource/bf09.socst.us.const.lpmirzona/understanding-and-applying-the-miranda-decision/#.WjqNbRM-dAY

Activities for Extending the Learning

For a "document-based question" that asks students to evaluate how decisions of the Warren Court (including *Miranda*) affected American society, see: White Plains Public Schools. (2009). Part III: Document-based question. [Lesson plan on the Warren Court's effect on American society]. Retrieved from https://www.whiteplainspublicschools.org/cms/lib/NY01000029/Centricity/Domain/353/DBQ%20Warren%20Court.pdf

CASE #3: *TINKER V. DES MOINES INDEPENDENT COMMUNITY SCHOOL DISTRICT*

Pre-Reading Questions

1. What rights does the First Amendment protect?
2. Why would the Court want to protect political speech above other speech?

Tinker v. Des Moines Independent Community School District, 393 U.S. 503 (1969)

JUSTICE ABE FORTAS delivered the opinion of the Court.

Petitioner John F. Tinker, 15 years old, and petitioner Christopher Eckhardt, 16 years old, attended high schools in Des Moines, Iowa. Petitioner Mary Beth Tinker, John's sister, was a 13-year-old student in junior high school.

In December 1965, a group of adults and students in Des Moines held a meeting at the Eckhardt home. The group determined to publicize their objections to the hostilities in Vietnam and their support for a truce by wearing black armbands during the holiday season and by fasting on December 16 and New Year's Eve. Petitioners and their parents had previously engaged in similar activities, and they decided to participate in the programs.

The principals of the Des Moines schools became aware of the plan to wear armbands.

On December 14, 1965, they met and adopted a policy that any student wearing an armband to school would be asked to remove it, and if he refused he would be suspended until he returned without the armband. Petitioners were aware of the regulation that the school authorities adopted.

On December 16, Mary Beth and Christopher wore black armbands to their schools. John Tinker wore his armband the next day. They were all sent home and suspended from school until they would come back without their armbands. They did not return to school until after the planned period for wearing armbands had expired—that is, until after New Year's Day.

During-Reading Question: Describe the facts of the case (include the "who," "what," "why," "where," and "when").

I

First Amendment rights, applied in light of the special characteristics of the school environment, are available to teachers and students. It can hardly be argued that either students or teachers shed their constitutional rights to freedom of speech or expression at the schoolhouse gate. This has been the unmistakable holding of this Court for almost 50 years.

In *West Virginia v. Barnette,* this Court held that under the First Amendment, the student in public school may not be compelled to salute the flag.

On the other hand, the Court has repeatedly emphasized the need for affirming the comprehensive authority of the States and of school officials, consistent with fundamental constitutional safeguards, to prescribe and control conduct in the schools.

During-Reading Question: Compare and contrast the Court's previous rulings regarding the First Amendment rights in schools. What interests are to be considered in these cases?

Our problem lies in the area where students in the exercise of First Amendment rights collide with the rules of the school authorities.

During-Reading Question: What criteria would you use to assess whether the students' First Amendment rights were violated?

II

The school officials banned and sought to punish petitioners for a silent, passive expression of opinion, unaccompanied by any disorder or disturbance on the part of petitioners. There is here no evidence whatever of petitioners' interference, actual or nascent, with the schools' work or of collision with the rights of other students to be secure and to be let alone. Accordingly, this case does not concern speech or action that intrudes upon the work of the schools or the rights of other students.

Only a few of the 18,000 students in the school system wore the black armbands. Only five students were suspended for wearing them. There is no indication that the work of the schools or any class was disrupted. Outside the classrooms, a few students made hostile remarks to the children wearing armbands, but there were no threats or acts of violence on school premises.

During-Reading Question: List the factors that the Court is considering in this case.

The District Court concluded that the action of the school authorities was reasonable because it was based upon their fear of a disturbance from the wearing of the armbands. But, in our system, undifferentiated fear or apprehension of disturbance is not enough to overcome the right to freedom of expression. Any departure from absolute regimentation may cause trouble. Any variation from the majority's opinion may inspire fear. Any word spoken, in class, in the lunchroom, or on the campus, that deviates from the views of another person may start an argument or cause a disturbance. But our Constitution says we must take this risk, and our history says that it is this sort of hazardous freedom—this kind of openness—that is the basis of our national strength and of the independence and vigor of Americans who grow up and live in this relatively permissive, often disputatious, society.

During-Reading Question: Explain the reasoning of the District Court when it decided that the school's punishment of the students was constitutional.

In order for the State in the person of school officials to justify prohibition of a particular expression of opinion, it must be able to show that its action was caused by something more than a mere desire to avoid the discomfort and unpleasantness that always accompany an unpopular viewpoint. Certainly where there is no finding and no showing that engaging in the forbidden conduct would "materially and substantially interfere with the requirements of appropriate discipline in the operation of the school," the prohibition cannot be sustained.

During-Reading Questions: What is the rule of law? What are examples that you think the Court would consider "a substantial disruption"?

In the present case, the District Court made no such finding, and our independent examination of the record fails to yield evidence that the school authorities had reason to anticipate that the wearing of the armbands would substantially interfere with the work of the school or impinge upon the rights of other students. Even an official memorandum prepared after the suspension that listed the reasons for the ban on wearing the armbands made no reference to the anticipation of such disruption.

On the contrary, the action of the school authorities appears to have been based upon an urgent wish to avoid the controversy which might result from the expression, even by the silent symbol of armbands, of opposition to this Nation's part in the conflagration in Vietnam. It is revealing, in this respect, that the meeting at which the school principals decided to issue the contested regulation was called in response to a student's statement to the journalism teacher in one of the schools that he wanted to write an article on Vietnam and have it published in the school paper.

During-Reading Question: What type of evidence would the school have had to present to justify the punishment of the students?

It is also relevant that the school authorities did not purport to prohibit the wearing of all symbols of political or controversial significance. The record shows that students in some of the schools wore buttons relating to national political campaigns, and some even wore the Iron Cross, traditionally a symbol of Nazism. The order prohibiting the wearing of armbands did not extend to these. Instead, a particular symbol—black armbands worn to exhibit opposition to this Nation's involvement in Vietnam—was singled out for prohibition. Clearly, the prohibition of expression of one particular opinion, at least without evidence that it is necessary to avoid material and substantial interference with schoolwork or discipline, is not constitutionally permissible.

In our system, state-operated schools may not be enclaves of totalitarianism. School officials do not possess absolute authority over their students. Students in school as well as out of school are "persons" under our Constitution. They are possessed of fundamental rights which the State must respect, just as they themselves must respect their obligations to the State. In our system, students may not be regarded as closed-circuit recipients of only that which the State chooses to communicate. They may not be confined to the expression of those sentiments that are officially approved. In the absence of a specific showing of constitutionally valid reasons to regulate their speech, students are entitled to freedom of expression of their views. As Judge Gewin, speaking for the Fifth Circuit, said, school officials cannot suppress "expressions of feelings with which they do not wish to contend" *Burnside v. Byars*.

During-Reading Questions: Explain, in your own words, what the Court is saying. What seems to be important to the Court? What do the Justices value?

Under our Constitution, free speech is not a right that is given only to be so circumscribed that it exists in principle but not in fact. Freedom of expression would not truly exist if the right could be exercised only in an area that a benevolent government has provided as a safe haven for crackpots. The Constitution says that Congress (and the States) may not abridge the right to free speech. This provision means what it says. We properly read it to permit reasonable regulation of speech-connected activities in carefully restricted circumstances. But we do not confine the permissible exercise of First Amendment rights to a telephone booth or the four corners of a pamphlet, or to supervised and ordained discussion in a school classroom.

During-Reading Question: What is considered "speech"?

If a regulation were adopted by school officials forbidding discussion of the Vietnam conflict, or the expression by any student of opposition to it anywhere on school property except as part of a prescribed classroom exercise, it would be obvious that the regulation would violate the constitutional rights of students, at least if it could not be justified by a showing that the students' activities would materially and substantially disrupt the work and discipline of the school. In the circumstances of the present case, the prohibition of the silent, passive "witness of the armbands," as one of the children called it, is no less offensive to the Constitution's guarantees.

During-Reading Question: Predict the outcome if the record would have shown that other students were yelling at the students wearing the armbands in the hallway. Support your answer with evidence from the case.

As we have discussed, the record does not demonstrate any facts which might reasonably have led school authorities to forecast substantial disruption of or material interference with school activities, and no disturbances or disorders on the school premises in fact occurred. These petitioners merely went about their ordained rounds in school. Their deviation consisted only in wearing on their sleeve a band of black cloth, not more than two inches wide. They wore it to exhibit their disapproval of the Vietnam hostilities and their advocacy of a truce, to make their views known, and, by their example, to influence others to adopt them. They neither interrupted school activities nor sought to intrude in the school affairs or the lives of others. They caused discussion outside of the classrooms, but no interference with work and no disorder. In the circumstances, our Constitution does not permit officials of the State to deny their form of expression.

Reversed and remanded.

Post-Reading Questions

1. The students weren't saying anything, so why is the wearing of armbands protected as speech? What are other ways people "speak" without saying anything?
2. Using the *Tinker* standard, brainstorm a list of T-shirts that the school could forbid. Brainstorm a list of T-shirts that would be protected.

Further Explorations

Exploring the Story

Tinker is a story about high school students taking a stand at school. If students want to explore the students who took a stand, check out the podcast from Newseum that interviews Mary Beth Tinker, one of the plaintiffs: NewseumED. (2015, June 18). Podcast with Mary Beth Tinker. In *Living History with Mary Beth Tinker*. [Lesson plan]. Retrieved from http://www.newseum.org/2015/06/18/first-amendment-class-mary-beth-tinker/

Exploring the Law

To explore students' First Amendment rights with scenarios, look to the "You Can't Say That in School?!" lesson plan on the Newseum website: NewseumED. (2015, June 18). You can't say that in school?! [Lesson plan]. In *Living History with Mary Beth Tinker*. Retrieved from http://www.newseum.org/wp-content/uploads/2015/06/education_LCO_YCSTinschoolLP.pdf

Exploring the Effects

If students want to explore the impact of *Tinker*, have them read the following article: Waggoner, C. R. (2013). The impact of symbolic speech in public schools: A selective case analysis from *Tinker* to *Zamecnik*. *Administrative Issues Journal, 3*(1). doi:10.5929/2013.3.1.4

Activities for Extending the Learning

For a "document-based question," which is—evaluate the extent to which the First Amendment should protect symbolic speech, and the degree to which that protection should be guaranteed to students in public school—consult the following resource: Bill of Rights Institute. (n.d.). *Tinker v. Des Moines* DBQ Document 5. Retrieved from https://www.billofrightsinstitute.org/tinker-v-des-moines-dbq-document-5/

A NOTE FROM THE AUTHORS

The balancing of authority versus individual rights is a compelling discussion topic. It is important for students to understand both sides of an issue—and the challenges that occur when an individual's rights conflict with the right of the authority on an issue. Society cannot exist without a balance, but in order to achieve this balance, both sides have to compromise. Add into this mix multiple individuals with diverse viewpoints, and the issues become even more difficult to resolve. These are relevant questions for today's students in that, as they mature into adults, their rights expand and these issues become more complex. These cases apply to a multitude of issues that are reflected in current events, including the right of students to kneel during the National Anthem or questions about dress code. Since the rights within these cases address issues relevant to the lives of students today, this is a way to gain interest and investment in the study of case law.

Chapter Nine

Production, Distribution, and Consumption

Theme 7: *Social studies programs should include experiences that provide for the study of how people organize for the production, distribution, and consumption of goods and services.*
—*National Curriculum Standards for Social Studies* (2010), National Council for the Social Studies, p. 20

The United States is a country of production and distribution, and Theme 7 addresses the issues that arise from United States citizens trying to get what they want. The NCSS asks students to consider the following questions: "What is to be produced? How is production to be organized? How are goods and services to be distributed and to whom? What is the most effective allocation of the factors of production (land, labor, capital, and entrepreneurship)?" (NCSS, 2010, p. 20).

Historically, the Supreme Court has intervened in order to protect the consumer, whether it be to protect the marketplace or to protect the consumer from harmful substances. In this chapter, students have a variety of cases dealing with both businesses and individuals and how the regulation of the production of goods and services can be both beneficial and restrictive, depending on your perspective. Ultimately, in this chapter's cases students will explore this guiding question from NCSS: "What factors influence decision-making on issues of the production, distribution and consumption of goods?" (NCSS, 2010, p. 20).

The *Swift & Co v. United States* (1905) decision is a response to the meatpacking, production, and distribution in the United States at the turn of the twentieth century. The Court applied the provisions of the Sherman Antitrust Act to prevent complete control of the industry in the United States. Students will be able to examine an unusual decision that is vague on its face as the Court breaks up the monopolistic practices of the appellants.

United States v. 95 Barrels of Vinegar (1924) is a short case with the Court applying the provisions of the Pure Food and Drugs Act of 1906 in reference to truth in labeling. Students should easily be able to make connections between this case and the multitude of items on the market that do not seek FDA approval. How can we protect ourselves as consumers?

Gonzales v. Raich (2005) questions whether the Commerce Clause supports the use of a federal law against individuals when states have created laws giving individuals the right to use federally illegal substances. This case can be considered and used in examining whether the federal government has the right to prosecute individuals who use marijuana legally under state law.

CASE #1: *SWIFT & CO. V. UNITED STATES*

Pre-Reading Questions

1. Why are monopolies a bad thing? Why would the government want to restrict the creation and functioning of monopolies?
2. The following case occurred as a result of the enforcement of the Sherman Antitrust Act of 1890. What is the historical background of the Sherman Antitrust Act? Why was it created and what purpose was the Act to serve for the U.S. economy?

Swift & Co. v. United States, 196 U.S. 375 (1905)

MR. JUSTICE HOLMES delivered the opinion of the court.

This is an appeal from a decree of the Circuit Court, on demurrer, granting an injunction against the appellants' commission of alleged violations of the act of July 2, 1890 "to protect trade and commerce against unlawful restraints and monopolies." It will be necessary to consider both the bill and the decree. The bill is brought against a number of corporations, firms and individuals of different States, and makes the following allegations:

1. The defendants (appellants) are engaged in the business of buying livestock at the stockyards in Chicago, Omaha, St. Joseph, Kansas City, East St. Louis, and St. Paul, and slaughtering such livestock at their respective plants in places named, in different States, and converting the livestock into fresh meat for human consumption.

2. The defendants "are also engaged in the business of selling such fresh meats, at the several places where they are so prepared, to dealers and consumers in divers States and Territories of the said United States other than those wherein the said meats are so prepared and sold as aforesaid, and in the District of Columbia, and in foreign countries, and shipping the same meats, when so sold from the said places of their preparation, over the several lines of transportation of the several railroad companies serving the same as common carriers, to such dealers and consumers, pursuant to such sales."

3. The defendants also are engaged in the business of shipping such fresh meats to their respective agents at the principal markets in other States, etc., for sale by those agents in those markets to dealers and consumers.

4. The defendants together control about six-tenths of the whole trade and commerce in fresh meats among the States, Territories and District of Columbia, and,

5. but for the acts charged, would be in free competition with one another.

6. In order to restrain competition among themselves as to the purchase of livestock, defendants have engaged in, and intend to continue, a combination for requiring and do and will require their respective purchasing agents at the stockyards mentioned, where defendants buy their livestock (the same being stock produced and owned principally in other States and shipped to the yards for sale) to refrain from bidding against each other, "except perfunctorily and without good faith," and by this means compelling the owners of such stock to sell at less prices than they would receive if the bidding really was competitive.

7. For the same purposes, the defendants combine to bid up, through their agents, the prices of livestock for a few days at a time, "so that the market reports will show prices much higher than the state of the trade will warrant," thereby inducing stock owners in other States to make large shipments to the stockyards, to their disadvantage.

8. For the same purposes, and to monopolize the commerce protected by the statute, the defendants combine "to arbitrarily, from time to time raise, lower, and fix prices, and to maintain uniform prices at which they will sell" to dealers throughout the States. This is

effected by secret periodical meetings, where are fixed prices to be enforced until changed at a subsequent meeting. The prices are maintained directly, and by collusively restricting the meat shipped by the defendants, whenever conducive to the result, by imposing penalties for deviations, by establishing a uniform rule for the giving of credit to dealers, etc., and by notifying one another of the delinquencies of such dealers and keeping a black list of delinquents, and refusing to sell meats to them.

9. The defendants also combine to make uniform charges for cartage for the delivery of meats sold to dealers and consumers in the markets throughout the States, etc., shipped to them by the defendants through the defendants' agents at the markets, when no charges would have been made but for the combination.

10. Intending to monopolize the said commerce and to prevent competition therein, the defendants "have all and each engaged in and will continue" arrangements with the railroads whereby the defendants received, by means of rebates and other devices, rates less than the lawful rates for transportation, and were exclusively to enjoy and share this unlawful advantage to the exclusion of competition and the public. By force of the consequent inability of competitors to engage or continue in such commerce, the defendants are attempting to monopolize, have monopolized, and will monopolize the commerce in livestock and fresh meats among the States and Territories, and with foreign countries, and,

11. the defendants are and have been in conspiracy with each other, with the railroad companies and others unknown, to obtain a monopoly of the supply and distribution of fresh meats throughout the United States, etc. And, to that end, defendants artificially restrain the commerce and put arbitrary regulations in force affecting the same from the shipment of the livestock from the plains to the final distribution of the meats to the consumers. There is a prayer for an injunction of the most comprehensive sort against all the foregoing proceedings and others, for discovery of books and papers relating directly or indirectly to the purchase or shipment of livestock, and the sale or shipment of fresh meat, and for an answer under oath.

During-Reading Questions: What is the issue with the appellants, in the view of the government? What are they doing and what is happening as a result of their action? Why does the government want to interfere?

To sum up the bill more shortly, it charges a combination of a dominant proportion of the dealers in fresh meat throughout the United States not to bid against each other in the livestock markets of the different States, to bid up prices for a few days in order to induce the cattle men to send their stock to the stockyards, to fix prices at which they will sell, and to that end to restrict shipments of meat when necessary, to establish a uniform rule of credit to dealers and to keep a blacklist, to make uniform and improper charges for cartage, and finally, to get less than lawful rates from the railroads to the exclusion of competitors. It is true that the last charge is not clearly stated to be a part of the combination. But, as it is alleged that the defendants have each and all made arrangements with the railroads, that they were exclusively to enjoy the unlawful advantage, and that their intent in what they did was to monopolize the commerce and to prevent competition, and in view of the general allegation to which we shall refer, we think that we have stated correctly the purport of the bill. It will be noticed further that the intent to monopolize is alleged for the first time in the eighth section of the bill as to raising, lowering and fixing prices. In the earlier sections, the intent alleged is to restrain competition among themselves. But after all the specific charges, there is a general allegation that the defendants are conspiring with one another, the railroads and others, to monopolize the supply and distribution of fresh meats throughout the United States, etc., as has been stated above, and it seems to us that this general allegation of intent colors and applies to all the specific charges of the bill. Whatever may be thought concerning the proper construction of the statute, a bill in equity is not to be read and construed as an indictment would have been read and construed a hundred years ago, but it is to be taken to mean what it fairly conveys to a dispassionate reader by a fairly exact use of English speech. Thus, read, this bill seems to us intended to allege successive elements of a single connected scheme.

The general objection is urged that the bill does not set forth sufficient definite or specific facts. This objection is serious, but it seems to us inherent in the nature of the case. The scheme alleged is so vast that it presents a new problem in pleading. If, as we must assume, the scheme is entertained, it is, of course, contrary to the very words of the statute. Its size makes the violation of the law more conspicuous, and yet the same thing makes it impossible to fasten the principal fact to a certain time and place. The elements, too, are so numerous and shifting, even the constituent parts alleged are, and from their nature must be, so extensive in time and space, that something of the same impossibility applies to them. The law has been upheld, and therefore we are bound to enforce it notwithstanding these difficulties. On the other hand, we equally are bound by the first principles of justice not to sanction a decree so vague as to put the whole conduct of the defendants' business at the peril of a summons for contempt. We cannot issue a general injunction against all possible breaches of the law. We must steer between these opposite difficulties as best we can.

During-Reading Questions: What is the appellants' (the business people's) major concern with the case as presented by the Court? What is the Court's response to the concern? What do you think of the Court's reaction?

The scheme as a whole seems to us to be within reach of the law. The constituent elements, as we have stated them, are enough to give to the scheme a body and, for all that we can say, to accomplish it. Moreover, whatever we may think of them separately when we take them up as distinct charges, they are alleged sufficiently as elements of the scheme. It is suggested that the several acts charged are lawful, and that intent can make no difference. But they are bound together as the parts of a single plan. The plan may make the parts unlawful. The statute gives this proceeding against combinations in restraint of commerce among the States and against attempts to monopolize the same. Intent is almost essential to such a combination, and is essential to such an attempt. Where acts are not sufficient in themselves to produce a result which the law seeks to prevent—for instance, the monopoly—but require further acts in addition to the mere forces of nature to bring that result to pass, an intent to bring it to pass is necessary in order to produce a dangerous probability that it will happen. But when that intent and the consequent dangerous probability exist, this statute, like many others and like the common law in some cases, directs itself against that dangerous probability as well as against the completed result. What we have said disposes incidentally of the objection to the bill as multifarious. The unity of the plan embraces all the parts.

During-Reading Question: The Plaintiffs argue that the Court cannot make a crime out of something that isn't a crime in and of itself. Can you think of other crimes where elements of the criminal process aren't criminal if they stand alone?

One further observation should be made. Although the combination alleged embraces restraint and monopoly of trade within a single State, its effect upon commerce among the States is not accidental, secondary, remote or merely probable. On the allegations of the bill, the latter commerce no less, perhaps even more, than commerce within a single State is an object of attack. Moreover, it is a direct object, it is that for the sake of which the several specific acts and courses of conduct are done and adopted. Therefore the case is not like *United States v. E. C. Knight Co.*, where the subject matter of the combination was manufacture and the direct object monopoly of manufacture within a State. However likely monopoly of commerce among the States in the article manufactured was to follow from the agreement, it was not a necessary consequence nor a primary end. Here, the subject matter is sales, and the very point of the combination is to restrain and monopolize commerce among the States in respect of such sales. The two cases are near to each other, as sooner or later always must happen where lines are to be drawn, but the line between them is distinct.

So, again, the line is distinct between this case and *Hopkins v. United States*. All that was decided there was that the local business of commission merchants was not commerce among the States, even if what the brokers were employed to sell was an object of such commerce. The brokers were not like the defendants before us, themselves the buyers and sellers. They only furnished certain facilities for the sales. Therefore, there again the effects of the combination of brokers upon the commerce was only indirect, and not within the act. Whether the case would have been different if the combination had resulted in exorbitant charges was left open. In *Anderson v. United States*, the defendants were buyers and sellers at the stockyards, but their agreement was merely not to employ brokers, or to recognize yard-traders, who were not members of their association. Any yard-trader could become a member of the association on complying with the conditions, and there was said to be no feature of monopoly in the case. It was held that the combination did not directly regulate commerce between the States, and, being formed with a different intent, was not within the act. The present case is more like *Montague & Co. v. Lowry.*

For the foregoing reasons we are of opinion that the carrying out of the scheme alleged, by the means set forth, properly may be enjoined, and that the bill cannot be dismissed.

So far, it has not been necessary to consider whether the facts charged in any single paragraph constitute commerce among the States or show an interference with it. There can be no doubt, we apprehend, as to the collective effect of all the facts, if true, and if the defendants entertain the intent alleged. We pass now to the particulars, and will consider the corresponding parts of the injunction at the same time. The first question arises on the sixth section. That charges a combination of independent dealers to restrict the competition of their agents when purchasing stock for them in the stockyards. The purchasers and their slaughtering establishments are largely in different States from those of the stockyards, and the sellers of the cattle, perhaps it is not too much to assume, largely in different States from either. The intent of the combination is not merely to restrict competition among the parties, but, as we have said, by force of the general allegation at the end of the bill, to aid in an attempt to monopolize commerce among the States.

It is said that this charge is too vague, and that it does not set forth a case of commerce among the States. Taking up the latter objection first, commerce among the States is not a technical legal conception, but a practical one, drawn from the course of business. When cattle are sent for sale from a place in one State, with the expectation that they will end their transit, after purchase, in another, and when, in effect, they do so, with only the interruption necessary to find a purchaser at the stockyards, and when this is a typical, constantly recurring course, the current thus existing is a current of commerce among the States, and the purchase of the cattle is a part and incident of such commerce. What we say is true at least of such a purchase by residents in another State from that of the seller and of the cattle. And we need not trouble ourselves at this time as to whether the statute could be escaped by any arrangement as to the place where the sale, in point of law, is consummated. But the sixth section of the bill charges an interference with such sales, a restraint of the parties by mutual contract and a combination not to compete in order to monopolize. It is immaterial if the section also embraces domestic transactions.

During-Reading Questions: Usually in Supreme Court decisions, the court is very specific about the elements that relate to its decision; however, in this case Justice Holmes says it's not necessary to be specific. Do you find his reasoning convincing? Why or why not?

The injunction, however, refers not to trade among the States in cattle, concerning which there can be no question of original packages, but to trade in fresh meats, as the trade forbidden to be restrained, and it is objected that the trade in fresh meats described in the second and third sections of the bill is not commerce among the States, because the meat is sold at the slaughtering places, or, when sold elsewhere, may be sold in less than the original packages. But the allegations of the second section, even if they import a technical passing of title at the slaughtering places, also import that the sales are to persons in other States, and that the shipments to other States are part of the transaction—"pursuant to such sales"—and the third section imports that the same things which are sent to agents are sold by them, and sufficiently indicates that some, at least, of the sales are of the original packages. Moreover, the sales are by persons in one State to persons in another. But we do not mean to imply that the rule which marks the point at which state taxation or regulation becomes permissible necessarily is beyond the scope of interference by Congress in cases where such interference is deemed necessary for the protection of commerce among the States. Nor do we mean to intimate that the statute under consideration is limited to that point. Beyond what we have said above, we leave those questions as we find them. They were touched upon in the *Northern Securities Company*'s case.

We are of opinion, further, that the charge in the sixth section is not too vague. The charge is not of a single agreement, but of a course of conduct intended to be continued. Under the act, it is the duty of the court, when applied to, to stop the conduct. The thing done and intended to be done is perfectly definite: with the purpose mentioned, directing the defendants' agents and inducing each other to refrain from competition in bids. The defendants cannot be ordered to compete, but they properly can be forbidden to give directions or to make agreements not to compete. The injunction follows the charge. No objection was made on the ground that it is not confined to the places specified in the bill. It seems to us, however, that it ought to set forth more exactly the transactions in which such directions and agreements are forbidden. The trade in fresh meat referred to should be defined somewhat as it is in the bill, and the sales of stock should be confined to sales of stock at the stockyards named, which stock is sent from other States to the stockyards for sale or is bought at those yards for transport to another State.

After what we have said, the seventh, eighth and ninth sections need no special remark except that the cartage referred to in section nine is not an independent matter, such as was dealt with in *Pennsylvania R.R. Co. v. Knight*, but a part of the contemplated transit—cartage for delivery of the goods. The general words of the injunction "or by any other method or device, the purpose and effect of which is to restrain commerce as aforesaid," should be stricken out. The defendants ought to be informed as accurately as the case permits what they are forbidden to do. Specific devices are mentioned in the bill, and they stand prohibited. The words quoted are a sweeping injunction to obey the law, and are open to the objection which we stated at the beginning that it was our duty to avoid. To the same end of definiteness, so far as attainable, the words "as charged in the bill," should be inserted between "dealers in such meats," and "the effect of which rules," and two lines lower, as to charges for cartage, the same words should be inserted between "dealers and consumers" and "the effect of which."

The acts charged in the tenth section, apart from the combination and the intent, may, perhaps, not necessarily be unlawful, except for the adjective which proclaims them so. At least we may assume, for purposes of decision, that they are not unlawful. The defendants, severally, lawfully may obtain less than the regular rates for transportation if the circumstances are not substantially similar to those for which the regular rates are fixed. It may be that the regular rates are fixed for carriage in cars furnished by the railroad companies, and that the defendants furnish their own cars and other necessities of transportation. We see nothing to hinder them from combining to that end. We agree, as we already have said, that such a combination may be unlawful as part of the general scheme set forth in the bill, and that this scheme, as a whole, might be enjoined. Whether this particular combination can be enjoined, as it is, apart from its connection with the other elements, if entered into with the intent to monopolize, as alleged, is a more delicate question. The question is how it would stand if the tenth section were the whole bill. Not every act that may be done with intent to produce an unlawful result is unlawful, or constitutes an attempt. It is a question of proximity and degree. The distinction between mere preparation and attempt is well known in the criminal law. We are of opinion, however, that such a combination is within the meaning of the statute. It is obvious that no more powerful instrument of monopoly could be used than an advantage in the cost of transportation. And even if the advantage is one which the act of 1887 permits, which is denied, perhaps inadequately, by the adjective "unlawful," still a combination to use it for the purpose prohibited by the act of 1890 justifies the adjective and takes the permission away.

During-Reading Question: What is the missing adjective that Justice Holmes is referring to in this paragraph in relationship to the companies?

It only remains to add that the foregoing question does not apply to the earlier sections, which charge direct restraints of trade within the decisions of the court, and that the criticism of the decree, as if it ran generally against combinations in restraint of trade or to monopolize trade, ceases to have any force when the clause against "any other method or device" is stricken out. So modified, it restrains such combinations only to the extent of certain specified devices, which the defendants are alleged to have used and intend to continue to use

Decree modified and affirmed.

Post-Reading Questions

1. The Clayton Antitrust Act was decided in 1914. How did this Act expand on the provisions of the Sherman Antitrust Act? What provisions did the Clayton Act help to protect for employees not covered under the Sherman Antitrust Act?
2. After the *Swift* decision, the Supreme Court had decided whether other companies have violated the Sherman Antitrust Act. Do some research into the following cases that have come before the Court. What business was involved? What was the impact on consumers? What did the Court eventually decide in these cases?

    a. Standard Oil (1911)
    b. Paramount Pictures (1947)
    c. AT&T (1982)

d. Microsoft (2001)

3. How were antitrust arguments used in the 2017 decision to end net neutrality? Do you think they will work?

Further Explorations

Exploring the Story

Do some research on "The Beef Trust" of 1902 that helped bring about the *Swift* decision.

Exploring the Law

The *Swift* case created the theory of a "stream of commerce," where commerce in the United States is seen as a "continual stream." Using the information from *Swift*, draw your own "stream of commerce" visual showing how the different parts of the beef industry all flowed together, according to the Court.

Exploring the Effects

- For information about the tensions between government and industry, visit Professor Doug Lindner's website, Exploring Constitutional Law at http://law2.umkc.edu/faculty/projects/ftrials/conlaw/home.html.
- For consideration of other commerce clause cases, go to the following page on Lindner's website: Lindner, D. (n.d.). The federal commerce power—The issues: How far do the powers of Congress extend under the Commerce Clause of Article I? In *Exploring Constitutional Conflicts*. Retrieved from http://law2.umkc.edu/faculty/projects/ftrials/conlaw/federalcommercepower.html

Activities for Extending the Learning

Historically, Theodore Roosevelt was known as the "trust-busting" president, but he actually broke up far fewer trusts than his presidential successor, William Taft. Have students research the antitrust activity of both presidents and then analyze why Roosevelt ultimately won the reputation for being tough on business.

CASE #2: *UNITED STATES V. 95 BARRELS OF VINEGAR*

Pre-Reading Questions

1. Why do we care whether items for sale are labeled correctly or not? Do you even read the labels of the things you purchase?
2. Explore the history behind the Food and Drugs Act of 1906. What prompted the creation of this federal legislation?

***United States v. 95 Barrels of Vinegar*, 265 U.S. 438 (1924)**

MR. JUSTICE BUTLER delivered the opinion of the Court.

This case arises under Food and Drugs Act June 30, 1906. The United States filed information in the District Court for the Northern District of Ohio, Eastern Division, for the condemnation of 95 barrels of vinegar. Every barrel seized was labeled:

> Douglas Packing Company
> Excelsior Brand Apple Cider Vinegar Made
> from Selected Apples
> Reduced to 4 Percentum
> Rochester, N.Y.

The information alleged that the vinegar was adulterated, in violation of § 7 of the act. It also alleged that the vinegar was made from dried or evaporated apples, and was misbranded in violation of § 8, in that the statements on the label were false and misleading, and in that it was an imitation of, and offered for sale under, the distinctive name of another article, namely, apple cider vinegar.

The Douglas Packing Company appeared as claimant, and by its answer admitted that the vinegar was labeled as alleged, and that evaporated apples had been used in its manufacture. It averred that nevertheless it was pure cider vinegar, and denied adulteration and misbranding. A jury was waived, and the case was submitted on the pleadings and an agreed statement of facts. The court found that the charge of adulteration was not sustained, but held that the vinegar was misbranded. Claimant appealed, and the circuit court of appeals reversed the judgment.

The question for decision is whether the vinegar was misbranded.

The substance of the agreed statement of facts may be set forth briefly. Claimant is engaged in the manufacture of food products from evaporated and unevaporated apples. During the apple season, from about September 25 to December 15, it makes apple cider and apple cider vinegar from fresh or unevaporated apples. During the balance of the year, it makes products which it designates as "apple cider" and "apple cider vinegar" from evaporated apples. The most approved process for dehydrating apples is used, and, in applying it, small quantities of sulphur fumes are employed to prevent rot, fermentation, and consequent discoloration. The principal result of dehydration is the removal of about 80 percent of the water. Whether and to what extent any other constituents of the apple are removed is not beyond controversy; in the present state of chemical science, no accepted test or method of analysis is provided for the making of such determination. Only mature fruit, free from rot and ferment, can be used economically and advantageously.

In manufacturing, claimant places in a receptacle a quantity of evaporated apples to which an amount of pure water substantially equivalent to that removed in the evaporating process has been added. A heavy weight is placed on top of the apples and a stream of water is introduced at the top of the receptacle through a pipe and is applied until the liquid, released through a vent at the bottom, has carried off in solution such of the constituents of the evaporated apples as are soluble in cold water and useful in the manufacture of vinegar. Such liquid, which is substantially equivalent in quantity to that which would have been obtained had unevaporated apples been used, carries a small and entirely harmless quantity of sulphur dioxide, which is removed during the process of fining and filtration by the addition of barium carbonate or some other proper chemical agent. The liquid is then subjected to alcoholic and subsequent acetic fermentation in the same manner as that followed by the manufacturer of apple cider vinegar made from the liquid content of unevaporated apples. Claimant employs the same receptacles, equipment, and process of manufacturing for evaporated as for unevaporated apples, except that, in the case of evaporated apples, pure water is added as above described, and in the process of fining and filtration, an additional chemical is used to precipitate any sulphur compounds present and resulting from dehydration.

During-Reading Questions: Why is it necessary for the Court to go into exacting detail about the process of making the apple cider vinegar? Could the Court have come to its decision without this level of detail?

The resulting liquid, upon chemical analysis, gives results similar to those obtained from an analysis of apple cider made from unevaporated apples, except that it contains a trace of barium incident to the process of manufacture. Vinegar so made is similar in taste and in composition to the vinegar made from unevaporated apples, except that the vinegar made from evaporated apples contains a trace of barium incident to the process of manufacture. There is no claim by libelant that this trace of barium renders it deleterious or injurious to health. It was conceded that the vinegar involved in these proceedings was vinegar made from dried or evaporated apples by substantially the process above described. There is no claim by the libelant that the vinegar was inferior to that made from fresh or unevaporated apples.

Since 1906, claimant has sold throughout the United States its product manufactured from unevaporated as well as from evaporated apples as "apple cider" and "apple cider vinegar," selling its vinegar under the brand above quoted, or under the brand "Sun Bright brand apple cider vinegar made from selected apples." Its output of vinegar is about 100,000 barrels a year. Before and since the passage of the Food and Drugs Act, vinegar in large quantities, and to a certain extent a beverage, made from evaporated apples were sold in various parts of the United States as "apple cider vinegar" and "apple cider," respectively, by many manufacturers. Claimant, in manufacturing and selling such products so labeled, acted in good faith. The Department of Agriculture has never sanctioned this labeling, and its attitude with reference thereto is evidenced by the definition of "apple cider vinegar" set forth in Circulars 13, 17, 19 and 136, and Food Inspection Decision 140. It is stipulated that the juice of unevaporated apples, when subjected to alcoholic and subsequent acetous fermentation, is entitled to the name "apple cider vinegar."

Section 6 of the act provides that:

> The term "food," as used herein, shall include all articles used for food, drink, confectionery, or condiment by man or other animals, whether simple, mixed, or compound.

Section 8 provides:

> That the term "misbranded," as used herein, shall apply to all . . . articles of food, or articles which enter into the composition of food, the package or label of which shall bear any statement, design, or device regarding such article, or the ingredients or substances contained therein which shall be false or misleading in any particular . . . . That, for the purposes of this act, an article shall also be deemed to be misbranded: . . . In the case of food: First. If it be an imitation of or offered for sale under the distinctive name of another article. Second. If it be labeled or branded so as to deceive or mislead the purchaser. . . . Fourth. If the package containing it or its label shall bear any statement, design, or device regarding the ingredients or the substances contained therein, which . . . shall be false or misleading in any particular . . .

The statute is plain and direct. Its comprehensive terms condemn every statement, design, and device which may mislead or deceive. Deception may result from the use of statements not technically false or which may be literally true. The aim of the statute is to prevent that resulting from indirection and ambiguity, as well as from statements which are false. It is not difficult to choose statements, designs, and devices which will not deceive. Those which are ambiguous and liable to mislead should be read favorably to the accomplishment of the purpose of the act. The statute applies to food, and the ingredients and substances contained therein. It was enacted to enable purchasers to buy food for what it really is.

The vinegar made from dried apples was not the same as that which would have been produced from the apples without dehydration. The dehydration took from them about 80 percent of the water content—an amount in excess of two-thirds of the total of their constituent elements. The substance removed was a part of their juice from which cider and vinegar would have been made if the apples had been used in their natural state. That element was not replaced. The substance extracted from dried apples is different from the pressed out juice of apples. Samples of cider fermented and unfermented made from fresh and evaporated apples, and vinegar made from both kinds of cider were submitted to and examined by the district judge who tried the case. He found that there were slight differences in appearance and taste, but that all had the appearance and taste of cider and vinegar. While the vinegar in question made from dried apples was like or similar to that which would have been produced by the use of fresh apples, it was not the identical product. The added water, constituting an element amounting to more than one-half of the total of all ingredients of the vinegar, never was a constituent element or part of the apples. The use of dried apples necessarily results in a different product.

If an article is not the identical thing that the brand indicates it to be, it is misbranded. The vinegar in question was not the identical thing that the statement, "Excelsior Brand Apple Cider Vinegar made from selected apples," indicated it to be. These words are to be considered in view of the admitted facts and others of which the court may take judicial notice. The words "Excelsior Brand," calculated to give the impression of superiority, may be put to one side as not liable to mislead. But the words, "apple cider vinegar made from selected apples" are misleading. Apple cider vinegar is made from apple cider. Cider is the expressed juice of apples, and is so popularly and generally known. It was stipulated that the juice of unevaporated apples when subjected to alcoholic and subsequent acetous fermentation is entitled to the name "apple cider vinegar." The vinegar in question was not the same as if made from apples without dehydration. The name "apple cider vinegar" included in the brand did not represent the article to be what it really was, and, in effect, did represent it to be what it was not—vinegar made from fresh or unevaporated apples. The words "made from selected apples" indicate that the apples used were chosen with special regard to their fitness for the purpose of making apple cider vinegar. They give no hint that the vinegar was made from dried apples, or that the larger part of the moisture content of the apples was eliminated and water substituted therefor. As used on the label, they said the misrepresentation made by the words "apple cider vinegar."

The misrepresentation was in respect of the vinegar itself, and did not relate to the method of production merely. When considered independently of the product, the method of manufacture is not material. The act requires no disclosure concerning it. And it makes no difference whether vinegar made from dried apples is or is not inferior to apple cider vinegar.

During-Reading Questions: This case initially arose from a complaint made to the American Cider and Vinegar Manufacturer's Association. Why do you think the Association would care whether vinegar was made from fresh or dehydrated apples? What would be the impact of mislabeling on the vinegar industry?

The label was misleading as to the vinegar, its substance, and ingredients. The facts admitted sustain the charge of misbranding.

Judgment reversed.

Post-Reading Questions

1. As a result of the decision of the Supreme Court, the ninety-five barrels of not-really-apple-cider vinegar were ordered to be destroyed. Do you think this is the correct result?
2. To this day, for any vinegar not directly made from a specific fruit juice, the label must read in this manner: "Apple Cider 'Flavored' Vinegar." Can you think of other products you use that are just "flavored," without the real fruit item?

Further Explorations

Exploring the Story

Until 1937, the Food and Drug Administration (FDA) could only deal with products that had been mislabeled; however, after 1937 the FDA gained the right to examine products before they went on the market. Do some research to learn what caused the expansion of the FDA's powers.

Exploring the Law

In this case, the United States government "sued" inanimate objects—in this instance, barrels of vinegar. To find out the reasoning behind why the U.S. government does this and to see other similar cases, read the following article: Northrup, L. (2017, July 6). Why does the U.S. government sue inanimate objects? *Consumerist*. Retrieved from https://consumerist.com/2017/07/06/why-does-the-u-s-government-sue-inanimate-objects/

Exploring the Effects

- With the creation of the Food and Drugs Act, labeling of products has become required for some products, but not for others. Go to the Food and Drug Administration site at www.fda.gov and research what items need to be labeled, the requirements for the labels, and what the FDA does to help keep people safe.
- To learn about another case of interest in this area, read about *The United States Government v. Forty Barrels, Twenty Kegs Coca-Cola* (1916) in the following article: Benjamin, L. T. (2009). Pop psychology: The man who saved Coca-Cola. *Monitor on Psychology, 40*(2), 18. Retrieved from http://www.apa.org/monitor/2009/02/coca-cola.aspx

Activities for Extending the Learning

Have students compile and analyze print advertisements for items that are both FDA approved and non–FDA approved. What is similar about them? What is different? Which items seem more attractive just at face value? Why do we buy items approved by the FDA? Why would anyone want to buy an item not approved by the FDA?

CASE #3: *GONZALES V. RAICH*

Pre-Reading Questions

1. Research the history of the use of medical marijuana. What is the historical tension between its use as a medicine and its recreational use?
2. What are some historical arguments that people have used to restrict the use of the Commerce Clause by the federal government? Which side do you agree with—the state's rights side or the "need for federal control" side?

Gonzales v. Raich, 545 U. S. 1 (2005)

Justice Stevens delivered the opinion of the Court.

California is one of at least nine States that authorize the use of marijuana for medicinal purposes. The question presented in this case is whether the power vested in Congress by Article I, §8, of the Constitution "[t]o make all Laws which shall be necessary and proper for carrying into Execution" its authority to "regulate Commerce with foreign Nations, and among the several States" includes the power to prohibit the local cultivation and use of marijuana in compliance with California law.

I

California has been a pioneer in the regulation of marijuana. In 1913, California was one of the first States to prohibit the sale and possession of marijuana, and at the end of the century, California became the first State to authorize limited use of the drug for medicinal purposes. In 1996, California voters passed Proposition 215, now codified as the Compassionate Use Act of 1996. The proposition was designed to ensure that "seriously ill" residents of the State have access to marijuana for medical purposes, and to encourage Federal and State Governments to take steps towards ensuring the safe and affordable distribution of the drug to patients in need. The Act creates an exemption from criminal prosecution for physicians, as well as for patients and primary caregivers who possess or cultivate marijuana for medicinal purposes with the recommendation or approval of a physician. A "primary caregiver" is a person who has consistently assumed responsibility for the housing, health, or safety of the patient.

Respondents Angel Raich and Diane Monson are California residents who suffer from a variety of serious medical conditions and have sought to avail themselves of medical marijuana pursuant to the terms of the Compassionate Use Act. They are being treated by licensed, board-certified family practitioners, who have concluded, after prescribing a host of conventional medicines to treat respondents' conditions and to alleviate their associated symptoms, that marijuana is the only drug available that provides effective treatment. Both women have been using marijuana as a medication for several years pursuant to their doctors' recommendation, and both rely heavily on cannabis to function on a daily basis. Indeed, Raich's physician believes that foregoing cannabis treatments would certainly cause Raich excruciating pain and could very well prove fatal.

Respondent Monson cultivates her own marijuana, and ingests the drug in a variety of ways including smoking and using a vaporizer. Respondent Raich, by contrast, is unable to cultivate her own, and thus relies on two caregivers, litigating as "John Does," to provide her with locally grown marijuana at no charge. These caregivers also process the cannabis into hashish or keif, and Raich herself processes some of the marijuana into oils, balms, and foods for consumption.

On August 15, 2002, county deputy sheriffs and agents from the federal Drug Enforcement Administration (DEA) came to Monson's home. After a thorough investigation, the county officials concluded that her use of marijuana was entirely lawful as a matter of California law. Nevertheless, after a 3-hour standoff, the federal agents seized and destroyed all six of her cannabis plants.

Respondents thereafter brought this action against the Attorney General of the United States and the head of the DEA seeking injunctive and declaratory relief prohibiting the enforcement of the federal Controlled Substances Act (CSA), 84 Stat. 1242, 21 U. S. C. §801 et seq., to the extent it prevents them from possessing, obtaining, or manufacturing cannabis for their personal medical use. In their complaint and supporting affidavits, Raich and Monson described the severity of their afflictions, their repeatedly futile attempts to obtain relief with conventional medications, and the opinions of their doctors concerning their need to use marijuana. Respondents claimed that enforcing the CSA against them would violate the Commerce Clause, the Due Process Clause of the Fifth Amendment, the Ninth and Tenth Amendments of the Constitution, and the doctrine of medical necessity.

The District Court denied respondents' motion for a preliminary injunction. Although the court found that the federal enforcement interests "wane[d]" when compared to the harm that California residents would suffer if denied access to medically necessary marijuana, it concluded that respondents could not demonstrate a likelihood of success on the merits of their legal claims.

A divided panel of the Court of Appeals for the Ninth Circuit reversed and ordered the District Court to enter a preliminary injunction. The court found that respondents had "demonstrated a strong likelihood of success on their claim that, as applied to them, the CSA is an unconstitutional exercise of Congress' Commerce Clause authority." The Court of Appeals distinguished prior Circuit cases upholding the CSA in the face of Commerce Clause challenges by focusing on what it deemed to be the "separate and distinct class of activities" at issue in this case: "the intrastate, noncommercial cultivation and possession of cannabis for personal medical purposes as recommended by a patient's physician pursuant to valid California state law." The court found the latter class of activities "different in kind from drug trafficking" because interposing a physician's recommendation raises different health and safety concerns, and because "this limited use is clearly distinct from the broader illicit drug market—as well as any broader commercial market for medicinal marijuana—insofar as the medicinal marijuana at issue in this case is not intended for, nor does it enter, the stream of commerce."

The majority placed heavy reliance on our decisions in *United States v. Lopez* and *United States v. Morrison* as interpreted by recent Circuit precedent, to hold that this separate class of purely local activities was beyond the reach of federal power. In contrast, the dissenting judge concluded that the CSA, as applied to respondents, was clearly valid under Lopez and Morrison; moreover, he thought it "simply impossible to distinguish the relevant conduct surrounding the cultivation and use of the marijuana crop at issue in this case from the cultivation and use of the wheat crop that affected interstate commerce in *Wickard v. Filburn*."

The obvious importance of the case prompted our grant of certiorari. The case is made difficult by respondents' strong arguments that they will suffer irreparable harm because, despite a congressional finding to the contrary, marijuana does have valid therapeutic purposes. The question before us, however, is not whether it is wise to enforce the statute in these circumstances; rather, it is whether Congress' power to regulate interstate markets for medicinal substances encompasses the portions of those markets that are supplied with drugs produced and consumed locally. Well-settled law controls our answer. The CSA is a valid exercise of federal power, even as applied to the troubling facts of this case. We accordingly vacate the judgment of the Court of Appeals.

II

Shortly after taking office in 1969, President Nixon declared a national "war on drugs." As the first campaign of that war, Congress set out to enact legislation that would consolidate various drug laws on the books into a comprehensive statute, provide meaningful regulation over legitimate sources of drugs to prevent diversion into illegal channels, and strengthen law enforcement tools against the traffic in illicit drugs. That effort culminated in the passage of the Comprehensive Drug Abuse Prevention and Control Act of 1970.

This was not, however, Congress' first attempt to regulate the national market in drugs. Rather, as early as 1906 Congress enacted federal legislation imposing labeling regulations on medications and prohibiting the manufacture or shipment of any adulterated or misbranded drug traveling in interstate commerce. Aside from these labeling restrictions, most domestic drug regulations prior to 1970 generally came in the guise of revenue laws, with the Department of the Treasury serving as the Federal Government's primary enforcer. For example, the primary drug control law, before being repealed by the passage of the CSA, was the Harrison Narcotics Act of 1914. The Harrison Act sought to exert control over the possession and sale of narcotics, specifically cocaine and opiates, by requiring producers, distributors, and purchasers to register with the Federal Government, by assessing taxes against parties so registered, and by regulating the issuance of prescriptions.

Marijuana itself was not significantly regulated by the Federal Government until 1937 when accounts of marijuana's addictive qualities and physiological effects, paired with dissatisfaction with enforcement efforts at state and local levels, prompted Congress to pass the Marihuana Tax Act. Like the Harrison Act, the Marihuana Tax Act did not outlaw the possession or sale of marijuana outright. Rather, it imposed registration and reporting requirements for all individuals importing, producing, selling, or dealing in marijuana, and required the payment of annual taxes in addition to transfer taxes whenever the drug changed hands. Moreover, doctors wishing to prescribe marijuana for medical purposes were required to comply with rather burdensome administrative requirements. Noncompliance exposed traffickers to severe federal penalties, whereas compliance would often subject them to prosecution under state law. Thus, while the Marihuana Tax Act did not declare the drug illegal per se, the onerous administrative requirements, the prohibitively expensive taxes, and the risks attendant on compliance practically curtailed the marijuana trade.

Then in 1970, after declaration of the national "war on drugs," federal drug policy underwent a significant transformation. A number of noteworthy events precipitated this policy shift. First, in *Leary v. United States*, this Court held certain provisions of the Marihuana Tax Act and other narcotics legislation unconstitutional. Second, at the end of his term, President Johnson fundamentally reorganized the federal drug control agencies. The Bureau of Narcotics, then housed in the Department of Treasury, merged with the Bureau of Drug Abuse Control, then housed in the Department of Health, Education, and Welfare (HEW), to create the Bureau of Narcotics and Dangerous Drugs, currently housed in the Department of Justice. Finally, prompted by a perceived need to consolidate the growing number of piecemeal drug laws and to enhance federal drug enforcement powers, Congress enacted the Comprehensive Drug Abuse Prevention and Control Act.

Title II of that Act, the CSA, repealed most of the earlier antidrug laws in favor of a comprehensive regime to combat the international and interstate traffic in illicit drugs. The main objectives of the CSA were to conquer drug abuse and to control the legitimate and illegitimate traffic in controlled substances. Congress was particularly concerned with the need to prevent the diversion of drugs from legitimate to illicit channels.

To effectuate these goals, Congress devised a closed regulatory system making it unlawful to manufacture, distribute, dispense, or possess any controlled substance except in a manner authorized by the CSA. The CSA categorizes all controlled substances into five schedules. The drugs are grouped together based on their accepted medical uses, the potential for abuse, and their psychological and physical effects on the body. Each schedule is associated with a distinct set of controls regarding the manufacture, distribution, and use of the substances listed therein. The CSA and its implementing regulations set forth strict requirements regarding registration, labeling and packaging, production quotas, drug security, and recordkeeping.

In enacting the CSA, Congress classified marijuana as a Schedule I drug. This preliminary classification was based, in part, on the recommendation of the Assistant Secretary of HEW "that marihuana be retained within schedule I at least until the completion of certain studies now underway." Schedule I drugs are categorized as such because of their high potential for abuse, lack of any accepted medical use, and absence of any accepted safety for use in medically supervised treatment. These three factors, in varying gradations, are also used to categorize drugs in the other four schedules. For example, Schedule II substances also have a high potential for abuse which may lead to severe psychological or physical dependence, but unlike Schedule I drugs, they have a currently accepted medical use. By classifying marijuana as a Schedule I drug, as opposed to listing it on a lesser schedule, the manufacture, distribution, or possession of marijuana became a criminal offense, with the sole exception being use of the drug as part of a Food and Drug Administration pre-approved research study.

The CSA provides for the periodic updating of schedules and delegates authority to the Attorney General, after consultation with the Secretary of Health and Human Services, to add, remove, or transfer substances to, from, or between schedules. Despite considerable efforts to reschedule marijuana, it remains a Schedule I drug.

During-Reading Questions: Section II of the case gives a history of the regulations over marijuana in the twentieth century. When did it become a prohibited drug? What happened before that time that kept the marijuana trade in check?

III

Respondents in this case do not dispute that passage of the CSA, as part of the Comprehensive Drug Abuse Prevention and Control Act, was well within Congress' commerce power. Nor do they contend that any provision or section of the CSA amounts to an unconstitutional exercise of congressional authority. Rather, respondents' challenge is actually quite limited; they argue that the CSA's categorical prohibition of the manufacture and possession of marijuana as applied to the intrastate manufacture and possession of marijuana for medical purposes pursuant to California law exceeds Congress' authority under the Commerce Clause.

In assessing the validity of congressional regulation, none of our Commerce Clause cases can be viewed in isolation. As charted in considerable detail in *United States v. Lopez,* our understanding of the reach of the Commerce Clause, as well as Congress' assertion of authority thereunder, has evolved over time. The Commerce Clause emerged as the Framers' response to the central problem giving rise to the Constitution itself: the absence of any federal commerce power under the Articles of Confederation. For the first century of our history, the primary use of the Clause was to preclude the kind of discriminatory state legislation that had once been permissible. Then, in response to rapid industrial development and an increasingly interdependent national economy, Congress "ushered in a new era of federal regulation under the commerce power," beginning with the enactment of the Interstate Commerce Act in 1887, and the Sherman Antitrust Act in 1890.

Cases decided during that "new era," which now spans more than a century, have identified three general categories of regulation in which Congress is authorized to engage under its commerce power. First, Congress can regulate the channels of interstate commerce. Second, Congress has authority to regulate and protect the instrumentalities of interstate commerce, and persons or things in interstate commerce. Third, Congress has the power to regulate activities that substantially affect interstate commerce. Only the third category is implicated in the case at hand.

Our case law firmly establishes Congress' power to regulate purely local activities that are part of an economic "class of activities" that have a substantial effect on interstate commerce. *Wickard v. Filburn.* As we stated in *Wickard*, "even if appellee's activity be local and though it may not be regarded as commerce, it may still, whatever its nature, be reached by Congress if it exerts a substantial economic effect on interstate commerce." We have never required Congress to legislate with scientific exactitude. When Congress decides that the "'total incidence'" of a practice poses a threat to a national market, it may regulate the entire class.In this vein, we have reiterated that when "'a general regulatory statute bears a substantial relation to commerce, the de minimis character of individual instances arising under that statute is of no consequence.'"

Our decision in *Wickard* is of particular relevance. In *Wickard*, we upheld the application of regulations promulgated under the Agricultural Adjustment Act of 1938, 52 Stat. 31, which were designed to control the volume of wheat moving in interstate and foreign commerce in order to avoid surpluses and consequent abnormally low prices. The regulations established an allotment of 11.1 acres for Filburn's 1941 wheat crop, but he sowed 23 acres, intending to use the excess by consuming it on his own farm. Filburn argued that even though we had sustained Congress' power to regulate the production of goods for commerce, that power did not authorize "federal regulation [of] production not intended in any part for commerce but wholly for consumption on the farm." Justice Jackson's opinion for a unanimous Court rejected this submission. He wrote:

> The effect of the statute before us is to restrict the amount which may be produced for market and the extent as well to which one may forestall resort to the market by producing to meet his own needs. That appellee's own contribution to the demand for wheat may be trivial by itself is not enough to remove him from the scope of federal regulation where, as here, his contribution, taken together with that of many others similarly situated, is far from trivial.

Wickard thus establishes that Congress can regulate purely intrastate activity that is not itself "commercial," in that it is not produced for sale, if it concludes that failure to regulate that class of activity would undercut the regulation of the interstate market in that commodity.

During-Reading Questions: What was the issue in Wickard v. Filburn*? What does the farmer in the case want to do? What historical significance does that case have that could differential it from the case that the Court is now deciding?*

The similarities between this case and *Wickard* are striking. Like the farmer in *Wickard,* respondents are cultivating, for home consumption, a fungible commodity for which there is an established, albeit illegal, interstate market. Just as the Agricultural Adjustment Act was designed "to control the volume [of wheat] moving in interstate and foreign commerce in order to avoid surpluses" and consequently control the market price, id., at 115, a primary purpose of the CSA is to control the supply and demand of controlled substances in both lawful and unlawful drug markets. In *Wickard*, we had no difficulty concluding that Congress had a rational basis for believing that, when viewed in the aggregate, leaving home-consumed wheat outside the regulatory scheme would have a substantial influence on price and market conditions. Here too, Congress had a rational basis for concluding that leaving home-consumed marijuana outside federal control would similarly affect price and market conditions.

More concretely, one concern prompting inclusion of wheat grown for home consumption in the 1938 Act was that rising market prices could draw such wheat into the interstate market, resulting in lower market prices. The parallel concern making it appropriate to include marijuana grown for home consumption in the CSA is the likelihood that the high demand in the interstate market will draw such marijuana into that market. While the diversion of homegrown wheat tended to frustrate the federal interest in stabilizing prices by regulating the volume of commercial transactions in the interstate market, the diversion of homegrown marijuana tends to frustrate the federal interest in eliminating commercial transactions in the interstate market in their entirety. In both cases, the regulation is squarely within Congress' commerce power because production of the commodity meant for home consumption, be it wheat or marijuana, has a substantial effect on supply and demand in the national market for that commodity.

Nonetheless, respondents suggest that *Wickard* differs from this case in three respects: (1) the Agricultural Adjustment Act, unlike the CSA, exempted small farming operations; (2) *Wickard* involved a "quintessential economic activity"—a commercial farm—whereas respondents do not sell marijuana; and (3) the *Wickard* record made it clear that the aggregate production of wheat for use on farms had a significant impact on market prices. Those differences, though factually accurate, do not diminish the precedential force of this Court's reasoning.

The fact that Wickard's own impact on the market was "trivial by itself" was not a sufficient reason for removing him from the scope of federal regulation. 317 U. S., at 127. That the Secretary of Agriculture elected to exempt even smaller farms from regulation does not speak to his power to regulate all those whose aggregated production was significant, nor did that fact play any role in the Court's analysis. Moreover, even though Wickard was indeed a commercial farmer, the activity he was engaged in—the cultivation of wheat for home consumption—was not treated by the Court as part of his commercial farming operation. And while it is true that the record in the *Wickard* case itself established the causal connection between the production for local use and the national market, we have before us findings by Congress to the same effect.

In assessing the scope of Congress' authority under the Commerce Clause, we stress that the task before us is a modest one. We need not determine whether respondents' activities, taken in the aggregate, substantially affect interstate commerce in fact, but only whether a "rational basis" exists for so concluding. That the regulation ensnares some purely intrastate activity is of no moment. As we have done many times before, we refuse to excise individual components of that larger scheme.

During-Reading Questions: Why doesn't it matter to the Court if the impact that the individual has on the Commerce Clause is insignificant when examined alone? What is the Court trying to prevent when just deciding on the rights of one individual?

IV

To support their contrary submission, respondents rely heavily on two of our more recent Commerce Clause cases. In their myopic focus, they overlook the larger context of modern-era Commerce Clause jurisprudence preserved by those cases. Moreover, even in the narrow prism of respondents' creation, they read those cases far too broadly.

The statutory scheme that the Government is defending in this litigation is at the opposite end of the regulatory spectrum. As explained above, the CSA, enacted in 1970 as part of the Comprehensive Drug Abuse Prevention and Control Act was a lengthy and detailed statute creating a comprehensive framework for regulating the production, distribution, and possession of five classes of "controlled substances." Most of those substances—those listed in Schedules II through V—"have a useful and legitimate medical purpose and are necessary to maintain the health and general welfare of the American people." The regulatory scheme is designed to foster the beneficial use of those medications, to prevent their misuse, and to prohibit entirely the possession or use of substances listed in Schedule I, except as a part of a strictly controlled research project.

While the statute provided for the periodic updating of the five schedules, Congress itself made the initial classifications. It identified 42 opiates, 22 opium derivatives, and 17 hallucinogenic substances as Schedule I drugs. Marijuana was listed as the 10th item in the third subcategory. That classification, unlike the discrete prohibition established by the Gun-Free School Zones Act of 1990, was merely one of many "essential part[s] of a larger regulation of economic activity, in which the regulatory scheme could be undercut unless the intrastate activity were regulated."

Unlike those at issue in *Lopez* and *Morrison*, the activities regulated by the CSA are quintessentially economic. "Economics" refers to "the production, distribution, and consumption of commodities." The CSA is a statute that regulates the production, distribution, and consumption of commodities for which there is an established, and lucrative, interstate market. Prohibiting the intrastate possession or manufacture of an article of commerce is a rational (and commonly utilized) means of regulating commerce in that product. Such prohibitions include specific decisions requiring that a drug be withdrawn from the market as a result of the failure to comply with regulatory requirements as well as decisions excluding Schedule I drugs entirely from the market. Because the CSA is a statute that directly regulates economic, commercial activity, our opinion in *Morrison* casts no doubt on its constitutionality.

The Court of Appeals was able to conclude otherwise only by isolating a "separate and distinct" class of activities that it held to be beyond the reach of federal power, defined as "the intrastate, noncommercial cultivation, possession and use of marijuana for personal medical purposes on the advice of a physician and in accordance with state law." The court characterized this class as "different in kind from drug trafficking." The differences between the members of a class so defined and the principal traffickers in Schedule I substances might be sufficient to justify a policy decision exempting the narrower class from the coverage of the CSA. The question, however, is whether Congress' contrary policy judgment, i.e., its decision to include this narrower "class of activities" within the larger regulatory scheme, was constitutionally deficient. We have no difficulty concluding that Congress acted rationally in determining that none of the characteristics making up the purported class, whether viewed individually or in the aggregate, compelled an exemption from the CSA; rather, the subdivided class of activities defined by the Court of Appeals was an essential part of the larger regulatory scheme.

First, the fact that marijuana is used "for personal medical purposes on the advice of a physician" cannot itself serve as a distinguishing factor. The CSA designates marijuana as contraband for any purpose; in fact, by characterizing marijuana as a Schedule I drug, Congress expressly found that the drug has no acceptable medical uses. Moreover, the CSA is a comprehensive regulatory regime specifically designed to regulate which controlled substances can be utilized for medicinal purposes, and in what manner. Indeed, most of the substances classified in the CSA "have a useful and legitimate medical purpose." Thus, even if respondents are correct that marijuana does have accepted medical uses and thus should be redesignated as a lesser schedule drug, the CSA would still impose controls beyond what is required by California law. The CSA requires manufacturers, physicians, pharmacies, and other handlers of controlled substances to comply with statutory and regulatory provisions mandating registration with the DEA, compliance with specific production quotas, security controls to guard against diversion, recordkeeping and reporting obligations, and prescription requirements. Furthermore, the dispensing of new drugs, even when doctors approve their use, must await federal approval. Accordingly, the mere fact that marijuana—like virtually every other controlled substance regulated by the CSA—is used for medicinal purposes cannot possibly serve to distinguish it from the core activities regulated by the CSA.

One need not have a degree in economics to understand why a nationwide exemption for the vast quantity of marijuana (or other drugs) locally cultivated for personal use (which presumably would include use by friends, neighbors, and family members) may have a substantial impact on the interstate market for this extraordinarily popular substance. The congressional judgment that an exemption for such a significant segment of the total market would undermine the orderly enforcement of the entire regulatory scheme is entitled to a strong presumption of validity. Indeed, that judgment is not only rational, but "visible to the naked eye," under any common sense appraisal of the probable consequences of such an open-ended exemption.

Second, limiting the activity to marijuana possession and cultivation "in accordance with state law" cannot serve to place respondents' activities beyond congressional reach. The Supremacy Clause unambiguously provides that if there is any conflict between federal and state law, federal law shall prevail. It is beyond peradventure that federal power over commerce is "superior to that of the States to provide for the welfare or necessities of their inhabitants," however legitimate or dire those necessities may be. Just as state acquiescence to federal regulation cannot expand the bounds of the Commerce Clause, so too state action cannot circumscribe Congress' plenary commerce power.

During-Reading Questions: What does the Court mean by "Congress' plenary commerce power"? What impact does that power have on the right for states to make decisions on their own?

Respondents acknowledge this proposition, but nonetheless contend that their activities were not "an essential part of a larger regulatory scheme" because they had been "isolated by the State of California, and [are] policed by the State of California," and thus remain "entirely separated from the market." The notion that California law has surgically excised a discrete activity that is hermetically sealed off from the larger interstate marijuana market is a dubious proposition, and, more importantly, one that Congress could have rationally rejected.

The exemption for physicians provides them with an economic incentive to grant their patients permission to use the drug. In contrast to most prescriptions for legal drugs, which limit the dosage and duration of the usage, under California law the doctor's permission to recommend marijuana use is open-ended. The authority to grant permission whenever the doctor determines that a patient is afflicted with "any other illness for which marijuana provides relief," is broad enough to allow even the most scrupulous doctor to conclude that some recreational uses would be therapeutic. And our cases have taught us that there are some unscrupulous physicians who overprescribe when it is sufficiently profitable to do so.

The exemption for cultivation by patients and caregivers can only increase the supply of marijuana in the California market. The likelihood that all such production will promptly terminate when patients recover or will precisely match the patients' medical needs during their convalescence seems remote; whereas the danger that excesses will satisfy some of the admittedly enormous demand for recreational use seems obvious. Moreover, that the national and international narcotics trade has thrived in the face of vigorous criminal enforcement efforts suggests that no small number of unscrupulous people will make use of the California exemptions to serve their commercial ends whenever it is feasible to do so. Taking into account the fact that California is only one of at least nine States to have authorized the medical use of marijuana, Congress could have rationally concluded that the aggregate impact on the national market of all the transactions exempted from federal supervision is unquestionably substantial.

So, from the "separate and distinct" class of activities identified by the Court of Appeals (and adopted by the dissenters), we are left with "the intrastate, noncommercial cultivation, possession and use of marijuana." Thus the case for the exemption comes down to the claim that a locally cultivated product that is used domestically rather than sold on the open market is not subject to federal regulation. Given the findings in the CSA and the undisputed magnitude of the commercial market for marijuana, our decisions in *Wickard v. Filburn* and the later cases endorsing its reasoning foreclose that claim.

V

Respondents also raise a substantive due process claim and seek to avail themselves of the medical necessity defense. These theories of relief were set forth in their complaint but were not reached by the Court of Appeals. We therefore do not address the question whether judicial relief is available to respondents on these alternative bases. We do note, however, the presence of another avenue of relief. As the Solicitor General confirmed during oral argument, the statute authorizes procedures for the reclassification of Schedule I drugs. But perhaps even more important than these legal avenues is the democratic process, in which the voices of voters allied with these respondents may one day be heard in the halls of Congress. Under the present state of the law, however, the judgment of the Court of Appeals must be vacated. The case is remanded for further proceedings consistent with this opinion.

It is so ordered.

Post-Reading Questions

1. Who does the Court say has to make the decision if the respondents want the growth and use of marijuana to be legal?
2. Do you think this case would have been decided differently if doctors were the ones growing the marijuana for use by their patients?
3. What are the federal penalties for growing and distributing marijuana? Read the Controlled Substances Act (CSA) to get more information on the penalties.

Further Explorations

Exploring the Story

Learn more about the defendant Angel Raich and what brought her to the Supreme Court on her website at http://www.angeljustice.org.

Exploring the Law

To further examine how the Commerce Clause has changed over time, see the following article: Street Law, Inc. and The Supreme Court Historical Society. (n.d.). How interpretation of the commerce power has changed over time. Retrieved from http://landmarkcases.org/en/Page/401/How_Interpretation_of_the_Commerce_Power_Has_Changed_over_Time

Explore the Online Library of Law and Liberty's website, which provides a number of articles that comment on the decision in *Gonzales v. Raich*, at http://www.libertylawsite.org/tag/gonzales-v-raich.

Exploring the Effects

1. What impact has the decision in *Gonzales v. Raich* had on the federal prosecution of marijuana cases since 2005?
2. Since the decision in *Gonzales v. Raich*, states including California, Oregon, and Colorado have moved to legalize marijuana for use in-state. How have surrounding states responded? How has the federal government responded under the CSA?

Activities for Extending the Learning

To learn more about the ability for states to reject federal laws, have students go to the Cato Institute website and read the following article: Levy, R. A. (2013, March 18). Yes, states can nullify some federal laws, not all. *CATO Institute*. Retrieved from https://www.cato.org/publications/commentary/yes-states-can-nullify-some-federal-laws-not-all

Have students explore other areas where state and federal law conflict—the death penalty, immigration, and gun laws. How are these issues treated differently in different states?

A NOTE FROM THE AUTHORS

This chapter presents some challenging material. As you read the cases, one core theme is that as time has passed in the United States, there has been an increase in governmental involvement in industry and business. This may not be readily apparent to students, but it certainly has an impact on their lives. In one way, government intrusion protected the country from monopolies and allowed the development of free markets, but with the Court continuing to revisit the Commerce Clause, some might argue that the government is taking an increasing role in dictating to American citizens what they can and cannot purchase and how they can or cannot have access to goods.

For a high school student, one topic this leads into is net neutrality—whether the government should be involved in these types of affairs. When the government gets involved, is it always a good thing or a bad thing for a consumer? What if it affects the access to media and antigovernment messages? Is that a fair result? These cases tend to be cases brought by one person or a few people with a result that affects society as a whole—that is, individual rights are not always the focus of the decision of the Court. This is an interesting phenomenon when the Court makes decisions that impact more than just an individual, but society as a whole. When has this been useful and when has it been harmful?

Chapter Ten

Science, Technology, and Society

Theme 8: *Social studies programs should include experiences that provide for the study of relationships among science, technology, and society.*
—*National Curriculum Standards for Social Studies* (2010), National Council for the Social Studies, p. 21

Theme 8 asks students to consider the role of science and technology in society. With the constant changes involved in scientific developments and the impact on culture as a result, this theme can be quite intriguing to today's students. Questions posed within this theme include:

> What can we learn from the past about how new technologies result in broader social change, some of which is unanticipated? Is new technology always better than that which it replaces? How can we cope with the ever-increasing pace of change, perhaps even the concern that technology might get out of control? How can we manage technology so that the greatest numbers of people benefit? How can we preserve fundamental values and beliefs in a world that is rapidly becoming one technology-linked village? How do science and technology affect our sense of self and morality? How are disparate cultures, geographically separated but impacted by global events, brought together by the technology that informs us about events, and offered hope by the science that may alleviate global problems (e.g., the spread of AIDS)? How can gaps in access to benefits of science and technology be bridged? (NCSS, 2010, p. 21)

Living in the United States during the next century promises to be a time of scientific breakthroughs, changes, and developments. Just think, since 1980 we've seen the invention of the smartphone, personal computers, tracking devices, fitness trackers, and wireless controls for the locks on a house. We carry our identity around with us on our smartphones and manage our finances through online websites. History has shown that science changes culture, beliefs, values, and productivity. In 1995, this was a nation without Facebook, Twitter, or iPhones. Today, breaking news is often reported first on Twitter before it reaches more traditional news sites. With these gains come potential drawbacks as technology is more pervasive and invasive than ever before. Citizens now must worry about identity theft, technologically based warfare, and personal privacy unlike any generation before the turn of the millennium.

United States v. American Library Association (2003) tackles Internet filtering on public library computers. As access to the Internet has increased, so too has access to pornographic or obscene material by children. This case highlights the government's attempt to control federal funding as a means to minimize exposure to such sites by children in the nation's libraries.

United States. v. Jones (2012) presents a case dealing with GPS monitoring and the ability of the police to place a GPS device on a potential criminal's car. Because electronic monitoring by the government is becoming more covert, secluded, and undiscoverable, it is likely that this type of surveillance will occur more frequently. As such, Fourth Amendment issues are a central focus of this chapter—that is, when can a citizen be assured the government is not impeding on areas he or she believes to be inherently private?

Maryland v. King (2013) explores the collection of an accused criminal's DNA prior to his conviction. With DNA advancements occurring quite rapidly, this case illustrates how Constitutionally complex something as simple as a cheek swab can be.

CASE #1: *UNITED STATES V. AMERICAN LIBRARY ASSOCIATION, INC.*

Pre-Reading Questions

1. Two main questions in this case are: (1) Does installing internet filters interfere with library patrons' First Amendment rights? and (2) Is the Children's Internet Protection Act (2000) unconstitutional? What First Amendment rights do library patrons have and why?
2. The Children's Internet Protection Act required installation of Internet filters in order for libraries to receive federal funding. Why is this an incentive or disincentive?

United States v. American Library Assn., Inc., 539 U.S. 194 (2003)

JUSTICE WILLIAM REHNQUIST delivered the opinion of the Court.

To address the problems associated with the availability of Internet pornography in public libraries, Congress enacted the Children's Internet Protection Act (CIPA). Under CIPA, a public library may not receive federal assistance to provide Internet access unless it installs software to block images that constitute obscenity or child pornography, and to prevent minors from obtaining access to material that is harmful to them. The District Court held these provisions facially invalid on the ground that they induce public libraries to violate patrons' First Amendment rights. We now reverse.

To help public libraries provide their patrons with Internet access, Congress offers two forms of federal assistance. First, the E-rate program established by the Telecommunications Act of 1996 entitles qualifying libraries to buy Internet access at a discount. In the year ending June 30, 2002, libraries received $58.5 million in such discounts. Second, pursuant to the Library Services and Technology Act (LSTA), the Institute of Museum and Library Services makes grants to state library administrative agencies to "electronically link libraries with educational, social, or information services," "assist libraries in accessing information through electronic networks," and "pay costs for libraries to acquire or share computer systems and telecommunications technologies." In fiscal year 2002, Congress appropriated more than $149 million in LSTA grants. These programs have succeeded greatly in bringing Internet access to public libraries: By 2000, 95% of the Nation's libraries provided public Internet access.

During-Reading Questions: How did the government attempt to incentivize libraries to install filtering software? Was this fair?

By connecting to the Internet, public libraries provide patrons with a vast amount of valuable information. But there is also an enormous amount of pornography on the Internet, much of which is easily obtained. The accessibility of this material has created serious problems for libraries, which have found that patrons of all ages, including minors, regularly search for online pornography. Some patrons also expose others to pornographic images by leaving them displayed on Internet terminals or printed at library printers.

During-Reading Questions: Public libraries seem like a free space for people to do whatever they want. Should this be the case? If not, who should make the rules?

Upon discovering these problems, Congress became concerned that the E-rate and LSTA programs were facilitating access to illegal and harmful pornography. Congress learned that adults "use library computers to access pornography that is then exposed to staff, passersby, and children," and that "minors access child and adult pornography in libraries."

But Congress also learned that filtering software that blocks access to pornographic websites could provide a reasonably effective way to prevent such uses of library resources. By 2000, before Congress enacted CIPA, almost 17% of public libraries used such software on at least some of their Internet terminals, and 7% had filters on all of them. A library can set such software to block categories of material, such as "Pornography" or "Violence." When a patron tries to view a site that falls within such a category, a screen appears indicating that the site is blocked. But a filter set to block pornography may sometimes block other sites that present neither obscene nor pornographic material, but that nevertheless trigger the filter. To minimize this problem, a library can set its software to prevent the blocking of material that falls into categories like "Education," "History," and "Medical." A library may also add or delete specific sites from a blocking category, and anyone can ask companies that furnish filtering software to unblock particular sites.

Responding to this information, Congress enacted CIPA. It provides that a library may not receive E-rate or LSTA assistance unless it has "a policy of Internet safety for minors that includes the operation of a technology protection measure . . . that protects against access" by all persons to "visual depictions" that constitute "obscenity" or "child pornography," and that protects against access by minors to "visual depictions" that are "harmful to minors." The statute defines a "technology protection measure" as "a specific technology that blocks or filters Internet access to material covered by" CIPA. CIPA also permits the library to "disable" the filter "to enable access for bona fide research or other lawful purposes. Under the E-rate program, disabling is permitted "during use by an adult." Under the LSTA program, disabling is permitted during use by any person.

During-Reading Question: While children are the targets of this Act, the Act does seem to admit that adults may be blocked from legitimate sites that are used for research purposes. How did the Act address this?

Appellees are a group of libraries, library associations, library patrons, and Web site publishers, including the American Library Association (ALA) and the Multnomah County Public Library in Portland, Oregon (Multnomah). They sued the United States and the Government agencies and officials responsible for administering the E-rate and LSTA programs in District Court, challenging the constitutionality of CIPA's filtering provisions. A three-judge District Court convened.

During-Reading Question: Why would a library object to installing filtering software under CIPA?

After a trial, the District Court ruled that CIPA was facially unconstitutional and enjoined the relevant agencies and officials from withholding federal assistance for failure to comply with CIPA. The District Court held that Congress had exceeded its authority under the Spending Clause, U.S. Const., because, in the court's view, "any public library that complies with CIPA's conditions will necessarily violate the First Amendment." The court acknowledged that "generally the First Amendment subjects libraries' content-based decisions about which print materials to acquire for their collections to only rational [basis] review." But it distinguished libraries' decisions to make certain Internet material inaccessible. "The central difference," the court stated, "is that by providing patrons with even filtered Internet access, the library permits patrons to receive speech on a virtually unlimited number of topics, from a virtually unlimited number of speakers, without attempting to restrict patrons' access to speech that the library, in the exercise of its professional judgment, determines to be particularly valuable." Reasoning that "the provision of Internet access within a public library . . . is for use by the public . . . for expressive activity," the court analyzed such access as a "designated public forum." The District Court also likened Internet access in libraries to "traditional public fora . . . such as sidewalks and parks" because it "promotes First Amendment values in an analogous manner."

During-Reading Question: The District Court analyzed the case using forum analysis. More can be read about that in the following article: First Amendment Schools. (2006). What is a public forum? Retrieved from http://www.firstamendmentschools.org/freedoms/faq.aspx?id=13012

Based on both of these grounds, the court held that the filtering software contemplated by CIPA was a content-based restriction on access to a public forum, and was therefore subject to strict scrutiny. Applying this standard, the District Court held that, although the Government has a compelling interest "in preventing the dissemination of obscenity, child pornography, or, in the case of minors, material harmful to minors," the use of software filters is not narrowly tailored to further those interests.

Congress has wide latitude to attach conditions to the receipt of federal assistance in order to further its policy objectives. But Congress may not "induce" the recipient "to engage in activities that would themselves be unconstitutional." To determine whether libraries would violate the First Amendment by employing the filtering software that CIPA requires, we must first examine the role of libraries in our society.

Public libraries pursue the worthy missions of facilitating learning and cultural enrichment. Appellee ALA's Library Bill of Rights states that libraries should provide "books and other . . . resources . . . for the interest, information, and enlightenment of all people of the community the library serves." To fulfill their traditional missions, public libraries must have broad discretion to decide what material to provide to their patrons. Although they seek to provide a wide array of information, their goal has never been to provide "universal coverage." Instead, public libraries seek to provide materials "that would be of the greatest direct benefit or interest to the community." To this end, libraries collect only those materials deemed to have "requisite and appropriate quality."

During-Reading Questions: Why is the Court thinking about the role and function of the public library in society? Do you agree or disagree with the ALA's Bill of Rights?

The public forum principles on which the District Court relied are out of place in the context of this case. Internet access in public libraries is neither a "traditional" nor a "designated" public forum. First, this resource—which did not exist until quite recently—has not "immemorially been held in trust for the use of the public and, time out of mind, . . . been used for purposes of assembly, communication of thoughts between citizens, and discussing public questions." *International Soc'y for Krishna Consciousness, Inc.* v. *Lee.* We have "rejected the view that traditional public forum status extends beyond its historic confines." The doctrines surrounding traditional public forums may not be extended to situations where such history is lacking.

Nor does Internet access in a public library satisfy our definition of a "designated public forum." To create such a forum, the government must make an affirmative choice to open up its property for use as a public forum. "The government does not create a public forum by inaction or by permitting limited discourse, but only by intentionally opening a non-traditional forum for public discourse."

The situation here is very different. A public library does not acquire Internet terminals in order to create a public forum for Web publishers to express themselves, any more than it collects books in order to provide a public forum for the authors of books to speak. It provides Internet access, not to "encourage a diversity of views from private speakers," but for the same reasons it offers other library resources: to facilitate research, learning, and recreational pursuits by furnishing materials of requisite and appropriate quality. As Congress recognized, "the Internet is simply another method for making information available in a school or library." It is "no more than a technological extension of the book stack."

During-Reading Question: Why do libraries offer Internet connections?

A library's failure to make quality-based judgments about all the material it furnishes from the Web does not somehow taint the judgments it does make. A library's need to exercise judgment in making collection decisions depends on its traditional role in identifying suitable and worthwhile material; it is no less entitled to play that role when it collects material from the Internet than when it collects material from any other source. Most libraries already exclude pornography from their print collections because they deem it inappropriate for inclusion. We do not subject these decisions to heightened scrutiny; it would make little sense to treat libraries' judgments to block online pornography any differently, when these judgments are made for just the same reason.

Moreover, because of the vast quantity of material on the Internet and the rapid pace at which it changes, libraries cannot possibly segregate, item by item, all the Internet material that is appropriate for inclusion from all that is not. While a library could limit its Internet collection to just those sites it found worthwhile, it could do so only at the cost of excluding an enormous amount of valuable information that it lacks the capacity to review. Given that tradeoff, it is entirely reasonable for public libraries to reject that approach and instead exclude certain categories of content, without making individualized judgments that everything they do make available has requisite and appropriate quality.

The E-rate and LSTA programs were intended to help public libraries fulfill their traditional role of obtaining material of requisite and appropriate quality for educational and informational purposes. Congress may certainly insist that these "public funds be spent for the purposes for which they were authorized." Especially because public libraries have traditionally excluded pornographic material from their other collections, Congress could reasonably impose a parallel limitation on its Internet assistance programs. As the use of filtering software helps to carry out these programs, it is a permissible condition under *Rust.*

Justice Stevens asserts the premise that "[a] federal statute penalizing a library for failing to install filtering software on every one of its Internet-accessible computers would unquestionably violate [the First] Amendment." But—assuming again that public libraries have First Amendment rights—CIPA does not "penalize" libraries that choose not to install such software, or deny them the right to provide their patrons with unfiltered Internet access. Rather, CIPA simply reflects Congress' decision not to subsidize their doing so. To the extent that libraries wish to offer unfiltered access, they are free to do so without federal assistance. "'A refusal to fund protected activity, without more, cannot be equated with the imposition of a 'penalty' on that activity."

Appellees mistakenly contend that CIPA's filtering conditions "distort the usual functioning of public libraries." Public libraries have no comparable role that pits them against the Government, and there is no comparable assumption that they must be free of any conditions that their benefactors might attach to the use of donated funds or other assistance.

Because public libraries' use of Internet filtering software does not violate their patrons' First Amendment rights, CIPA does not induce libraries to violate the Constitution, and is a valid exercise of Congress' spending power. Nor does CIPA impose an unconstitutional condition on public libraries. Therefore, the judgment of the District Court for the Eastern District of Pennsylvania is reversed.

Post-Reading Questions

1. How did the Court justify Congress' ability to withhold funding for libraries that failed to use filtering software?
2. Should public libraries have First Amendment rights, or are those reserved only for people to exercise?

Further Explorations

Exploring the Story

Since this case was decided in 2003, the Internet has continued to evolve and change. One issue that has arisen is the "connectivity gap," or the disparity that occurs when some have access to the Internet and others do not. Read more about that in this *Atlantic* article: Anderson, M. (2016, April 26). How Internet filtering hurts kids. *The Atlantic*. Retrieved from https://www.theatlantic.com/education/archive/2016/04/internet-filtering-hurts-kids/479907/

Exploring the Law

- Read the text of CIPA here: Children's Internet Protection Act. 47 U.S.C. § 54.520 *et seq.* (2000). Retrieved from http://ifea.net/cipa.pdf
- Two other laws passed by Congress were found to be unconstitutional: The Communications Decency Act and the Child Online Protection Act. Have students look at each of these and determine why each was found to be unconstitutional.

Exploring the Effects

- Since this decision, the American Library Association has argued that although the Children's Internet Protection Act allows library personnel to unblock some material for adults or minors (like sites that were erroneously filtered during a legitimate search for research articles), implementation of the processes needed to unblock sites can be arduous and simply take too long. Read their statement here: American Library Association. (2015, June 30). Internet filtering: An interpretation of the Library Bill of Rights. Retrieved from http://www.ala.org/advocacy/intfreedom/librarybill/interpretations/internet-filtering
- The ALA also argues that three long-term effects have taken place since this case was decided: (1) it widened disparities in access based on who can afford their own unfiltered Internet access and those who rely on public sources for Internet access; (2) when Internet filters are used, sometimes legitimate minority viewpoints are improperly blocked, thus, sometimes only presenting one side of an issue; and (3) when filters are used and block too much information, users are denied access to legitimate sources. Do you agree this is still the case today? If so, which reason is most compelling?
- The Rhode Island ACLU published "Access Still Denied" in 2017, documenting the overreach of Internet filtering software within the State's schools. That report can be read here: American Civil Liberties Union, Rhode Island. (2017, December). Access still denied: How school Internet filtering violates state law and hinders academic freedom. Retrieved from http://www.riaclu.org/images/uploads/ACLUInternetFilteringReportDec2017.pdf

Activities for Extending the Learning

In what other settings does Congress use the issue of funding to control or influence how a state or other entity acts or conducts business? Consider federal drug laws, highway funds, or funding for sanctuary cities. Have students investigate other instances where the government leverages its funding power in order to force compliance on a different issue.

CASE #2: *UNITED STATES V. JONES*

Pre-Reading Questions

1. What do you consider a search? Which other the following do you think is considered a search under the Fourth Amendment: A dog sniffing your backpack? A principal opening your locker for a search? Someone looking through your cell phone photos? Going through security screening at an airport?
2. What historical events were taking place or had taken place by the time of the drafting of the Constitution (the late 1780s) that made freedom from unlawful search and seizures an important principle to the Constitution drafters? Think back to the time when soldiers were regularly entering the homes of private citizens during times of war. Does this help shape why the Amendment was written in the manner it was?
3. Probable cause is reasonable grounds for making a search. So, what are reasonable grounds: A rumor about someone having drugs in his/her locker? A tweet stating a student has a knife? A student observing another student passing something in the bathroom? A teacher observing "suspicious behavior"?
4. Why is it important that any search warrant indicate specifics like the place, person, or things being searched? How could law enforcement officers misuse this? What other things might this phrase include? What about cell phones? Social media accounts? Do

police officers need search warrants to search your cell phone or to peruse your Facebook account?

United States v. Jones, 565 U.S. 400 (2012)

JUSTICE SCALIA delivered the opinion of the Court.

We decide whether the attachment of a Global-Positioning-System (GPS) tracking device to an individual's vehicle, and subsequent use of that device to monitor the vehicle's movements on public streets, constitutes a search or seizure within the meaning of the Fourth Amendment.

During-Reading Questions: Have you or someone you know ever been tracked by using some form of GPS device? Why would using a GPS device be a search and seizure? What sort of information would police be able to obtain from this device?

I

In 2004 respondent Antoine Jones, owner and operator of a nightclub in the District of Columbia, came under suspicion of trafficking in narcotics and was made the target of an investigation by a joint FBI and Metropolitan Police Department task force. Officers employed various investigative techniques, including visual surveillance of the nightclub, installation of a camera focused on the front door of the club, and a pen register and wiretap covering Jones's cellular phone.

Based in part on information gathered from these sources, in 2005 the Government applied to the United States District Court for the District of Columbia for a warrant authorizing the use of an electronic tracking device on the Jeep Grand Cherokee registered to Jones's wife. A warrant issued, authorizing installation of the device in the District of Columbia and within 10 days.

On the 11th day, and not in the District of Columbia but in Maryland, agents installed a GPS tracking device on the undercarriage of the Jeep while it was parked in a public parking lot. Over the next 28 days, the Government used the device to track the vehicle's movements, and once had to replace the device's battery when the vehicle was parked in a different public lot in Maryland. By means of signals from multiple satellites, the device established the vehicle's location within 50 to 100 feet, and communicated that location by cellular phone to a Government computer. It relayed more than 2,000 pages of data over the 4-week period.

The United States Court of Appeals for the District of Columbia Circuit reversed [the District Court's] conviction [life imprisonment for conspiracy] because of admission of the evidence obtained by warrantless use of the GPS device which, it said, violated the Fourth Amendment. The D. C. Circuit denied the Government's petition for rehearing en banc, with four judges dissenting We granted certiorari.

During-Reading Question: The Fourth Amendment states, "[t]he right of the people to be secure in their persons, houses, papers, and effects, against unreasonable searches and seizures, shall not be violated, and no Warrants shall issue, but upon probable cause, supported by Oath or affirmation, and particularly describing the place to be searched, and the persons or things to be seized." (U.S. Const. amend. IV.) How would placing a GPS on someone's car violate the Fourth Amendment?

II

The Fourth Amendment provides in relevant part that "[t]he right of the people to be secure in their persons, houses, papers, and effects, against unreasonable searches and seizures, shall not be violated." It is beyond dispute that a vehicle is an "effect" as that term is used in the Amendment. We hold that the Government's installation of a GPS device on a target's vehicle, and its use of that device to monitor the vehicle's movements, constitutes a "search."

It is important to be clear about what occurred in this case: The Government physically occupied private property for the purpose of obtaining information. We have no doubt that such a physical intrusion would have been considered a "search" within the meaning of the Fourth Amendment when it was adopted.

The text of the Fourth Amendment reflects its close connection to property, since otherwise it would have referred simply to "the right of the people to be secure against unreasonable searches and seizures"; the phrase "in their persons, houses, papers, and effects" would have been superfluous.

Consistent with this understanding, our Fourth Amendment jurisprudence was tied to common-law trespass, at least until the latter half of the 20th century. Thus, in *Olmstead* v. *United States*, we held that wiretaps attached to telephone wires on the public streets did not constitute a Fourth Amendment search because "[t]here was no entry of the houses or offices of the defendants."

During-Reading Question: List the factors the Court considers in determining whether a "search" occurred up until the latter half of the twentieth century.

Our later cases, of course, have deviated from that exclusively property-based approach. In *Katz* v. *United States*, we said that "the Fourth Amendment protects people, not places," and found a violation in attachment of an eavesdropping device to a public telephone booth. Our later cases have applied the analysis of Justice Harlan's concurrence in that case, which said that a violation occurs when government officers violate a person's "reasonable expectation of privacy."

The Government contends that no search occurred here, since Jones had no "reasonable expectation of privacy" in the area of the Jeep accessed by Government agents (its underbody) and in the locations of the Jeep on the public roads, which were visible to all. But we need not address the Government's contentions, because Jones's Fourth Amendment rights do not rise or fall with the *Katz* formulation. At bottom, we must "assur[e] preservation of that degree of privacy against government that existed when the Fourth Amendment was adopted." As explained, for most of our history the Fourth Amendment was understood to embody a particular concern for government trespass upon the areas ("persons, houses, papers, and effects") it enumerates. *Katz* did not repudiate that understanding. Less than two years later the Court upheld defendants' contention that the Government could not introduce against them conversations between *other* people obtained by warrantless placement of electronic surveillance devices in their homes.

During-Reading Question: Explain the State's reasoning that no search occurred here.

More recently, in *Soldal* v. *Cook County*, the Court unanimously rejected the argument that although a "seizure" had occurred "in a 'technical' sense" when a trailer home was forcibly removed, no Fourth Amendment violation occurred because law enforcement had not "invade[d] the [individuals'] privacy," the Court explained, established that "property rights are not the sole measure of Fourth Amendment violations," but did not "snuf[f] out the previously recognized protection for property." As Justice Brennan explained in his concurrence in *Knotts*, *Katz* did not erode the principle "that, when the Government *does* engage in physical intrusion of a constitutionally protected area in order to obtain information, that intrusion may constitute a violation of the Fourth Amendment." We have embodied that preservation of past rights in our very definition of "reasonable expectation of privacy" which we have said to be an expectation "that has a source outside of the Fourth Amendment, either by reference to concepts of real or personal property law or to understandings that are recognized and permitted by society." *Katz* did not narrow the Fourth Amendment's scope.

The Government contends that several of our post-*Katz* cases foreclose the conclusion that what occurred here constituted a search. It relies principally on two cases in which we rejected Fourth Amendment challenges to "beepers," electronic tracking devices that represent another form of electronic monitoring. The first case, *Knotts*, upheld against Fourth Amendment challenge the use of a "beeper" that had been placed in a container of chloroform, allowing law enforcement to monitor the location of the container. We said that there had been no infringement of Knotts' reasonable expectation of privacy since the information obtained—the location of the automobile carrying the container on public roads, and the location of the off-loaded container in open fields near Knotts' cabin—had been voluntarily conveyed to the public.

The second "beeper" case, *United States* v. *Karo*, does not suggest a different conclusion. There we addressed the question left open by *Knotts*, whether the installation of a beeper in a container amounted to a search or seizure. As in *Knotts*, at the time the beeper was installed the container belonged to a third party, and it did not come into possession of the defendant until later. Thus, the specific question we considered was whether the installation "*with the consent of the original owner* constitute[d] a search or seizure . . . when the container is delivered to a buyer having no knowledge of the presence of the beeper." We held not. The Government, we said, came into physical contact with the container only before it belonged to the defendant Karo; and the transfer of the container with the unmonitored beeper inside did not convey any information and thus did not invade Karo's privacy. That conclusion is perfectly consistent with the one we reach here. Karo accepted the container as it came to him, beeper and all, and was therefore not entitled to object to the beeper's presence, even though it was used to monitor the container's location. Jones, who possessed the Jeep at the time the Government trespassorily inserted the information-gathering device, is on much different footing.

During-Reading Questions: How are the circumstances in the two "beeper" cases different from the case at hand? What did the Court say distinguishes the cases?

The Government also points to our exposition in *New York* v. *Class*, that "[t]he exterior of a car . . . is thrust into the public eye, and thus to examine it does not constitute a 'search.'" That statement is of marginal relevance here since, as the Government acknowledges, "the officers in this case did *more* than conduct a visual inspection of respondent's vehicle." By attaching the device to the Jeep, officers encroached on a protected area. In *Class* itself we suggested that this would make a difference, for we concluded that an officer's momentary reaching into the interior of a vehicle did constitute a search.

During-Reading Questions: How does the Court distinguish this case from Class*? What other areas of one's vehicle could an officer inspect without a warrant? What can't an officer inspect without a warrant?*

III

The Government argues in the alternative that even if the attachment and use of the device was a search, it was reasonable—and thus lawful—under the Fourth Amendment because "officers had reasonable suspicion, and indeed probable cause, to believe that [Jones] was a leader in a large-scale cocaine distribution conspiracy." We have no occasion to consider this argument. The Government did not raise it below, and the D.C. Circuit therefore did not address it. We consider the argument forfeited.

During-Reading Questions: Explain, in your own words, what the Court is saying. What seems to be important to the Court? What do the Justices value?

The judgment of the Court of Appeals for the D.C. Circuit is affirmed.
It is so ordered.

Post-Reading Questions

1. One interesting note about this case is that the government did not raise the issue that even though the search may have been warrantless (as the Court decided), it did have probable cause and a reasonable suspicion that Jones was indeed involved in drug trafficking, based on its prior surveillance of him. How do you think the case would have been decided if the government had claimed it had reasonable suspicion to follow Jones without a warrant? Would the case have turned out differently?
2. Do you think Jones had a reasonable expectation of privacy while he was driving his wife's car around Washington, D.C., and Maryland? Why or why not? What is it within a person's car that might be considered a "private" area?
3. Had Jones been suspected of plotting terrorism instead of drug use, would that change the analysis by the Court? That is, are there levels of crime that require less privacy protections for those involved than those considered more minor or victimless crimes?
4. Realistically, today's police do not obtain warrants for many common events, including searching automobiles during a vehicle stop, detaining people on public streets, or conducting a search while an emergency is taking place. When are you comfortable allowing police the latitude to conduct searches without warrants? Why?

Further Explorations

Exploring the Story

- For more information on how police use GPS to track vehicles, read the following article: Brick House Security. (2014, July 18). How police use GPS for personal and vehicle tracking. Retrieved from https://www.brickhousesecurity.com/category/gps+tracking/gps+tracking+and+law+enforcement.do
- One of the Justices noted that technology may have changed our expectation of privacy—that is, because we are more active online and disclosing our phone numbers, web searches, and other information freely, we have a lowered expectation of privacy. How has technolo-

gy changed privacy? Consider cell phone technology, car tracking devices that provide roadside assistance, and surveillance video present on many streets. What is private today?

Exploring the Law

- The plain view doctrine as applied to Fourth Amendment cases basically says that if the police can see a crime being committed (or evidence of it) in plain view (out in the open, without obstruction), then the Fourth Amendment does not apply. The open fields doctrine allows the government to enter bodies of water, large fields of space, open woods, or pastures in order to search for criminal activity. Why did neither of these doctrines apply to Jones in this case?
- *Frontline* at pbs.org has an interactive online quiz called "Spot the Illegal Police Stop" that allows users to consider several real-life instance of police stops to determine whether they are in violation of the Fourth Amendment: Breslow, J. M. (2016, June 28). Quiz: Spot the illegal police stop. *Frontline, PBS*. Retrieved from http://www.pbs.org/wgbh/frontline/article/quiz-spot-the-illegal-police-stop/
- For more illustrative examples of the Fourth Amendment in real-life instances, read this article: Harris, A. (2012, July 11). What can "99 Problems" teach us about the Fourth Amendment? *browbeat, Slate.com*. Retrieved from http://www.slate.com/blogs/browbeat/2012/07/11/_99_problems_and_the_fourth_amendment_what_the_jay_z_song_can_teach_us_about_the_constitution_.html

Exploring the Effects

- What if the government had used a drone to monitor Jones' activities? Because a drone would not attach to any piece of Jones' personal property, would Jones have a reasonable expectation of privacy while he was out on city streets and in public venues?

  - Note, in 2012 the first case of an American citizen arrested with assistance from a drone arose in North Dakota. Read more about that case at: Gallagher, R. (2012, May 4). What a cattle-theft case could mean for U.S. law enforcement use of drones. *future tense, Slate.com*. Retrieved from http://www.slate.com/blogs/future_tense/2012/05/04/brossart_case_cattle_theft_allegations_and_law_enforcement_use_of_domestic_drones_.html

- Today, police are using drones and other electronic surveillance techniques to conduct investigations. Students can explore the issues entwined with these types of technology. A few suggested articles are:

  - K. K. (2015, March 19). Drones and privacy: A looming threat. *The Economist*. Retrieved from https://www.economist.com/blogs/democracyinamerica/2015/03/drones-and-privacy
  - Harris, A. (2012, July 11). What can "99 Problems" teach us about the Fourth Amendment? *browbeat, Slate.com*. Retrieved from http://www.slate.com/blogs/browbeat/2012/07/11/_99_problems_and_the_fourth_amendment_what_the_jay_z_song_can_teach_us_about_the_constitution_.html
  - Koerner, M. R. (2015). Drones and the Fourth Amendment: Redefining expectations of privacy. *Duke Law Journal, 64*(6), 1129–1172. Retrieved from https://scholarship.law.duke.edu/dlj/vol64/iss6/3/

- The U.S. Supreme Court heard a similar issue in 2017 when it considered whether police could track cell phone locations without a warrant. Still undecided at the time of this book's publication, the Court's decision will eventually be found when a decision in *Carpenter v. United States* is issued.

Activities for Extending the Learning

- Boarding an airplane today requires a search of a person's body, property, and personal effects, however no immediate need (probable cause) exists to search every single person. However, we accommodate this in order to, allegedly, make flying safer for everyone. What type of airport search would require a higher standard of probable cause? Have students determine where limits should be placed on this type of transportation.
- How does the United States keep its citizens safe and what methods are borderline intrusive in doing so? Have students consider what liberties they would forgo in order for improved safety and protection.

CASE #3: *MARYLAND V. KING*

Pre-Reading Questions

1. What constitutes a "search" under the Fourth Amendment?
2. Alonzo King was the person arrested on assault charges in this case and after his DNA was collected and analyzed, he was linked to a rape that occurred a decade prior to his arrest. Knowing this, do you support the DNA collection or do you think it was unfair?

Maryland v. King, 569 U.S. 435 (2013)

JUSTICE KENNEDY delivered the opinion of the Court.

In 2003 a man concealing his face and armed with a gun broke into a woman's home in Salisbury, Maryland. He raped her. The police were unable to identify or apprehend the assailant based on any detailed description or other evidence they then had, but they did obtain from the victim a sample of the perpetrator's DNA.

In 2009, Alonzo King was arrested in Wicomico County, Maryland, and charged with first- and second-degree assault for menacing a group of people with a shotgun. As part of a routine booking procedure for serious offenses, his DNA sample was taken by applying a cotton swab or filter paper—known as a buccal swab—to the inside of his cheeks. The DNA was found to match the DNA taken from the Salisbury rape victim. King was tried and convicted for the rape. Additional DNA samples were taken from him and used in the rape trial, but there seems to be no doubt that it was the DNA from the cheek sample taken at the time he was booked in 2009 that led to his first having been linked to the rape and charged with its commission.

The Court of Appeals of Maryland, on review of King's rape conviction, ruled that the DNA taken when King was booked for the 2009 charge was an unlawful seizure because obtaining and using the cheek swab was an unreasonable search of the person. It set the rape conviction aside.

I

When King was arrested on April 10, 2009, for menacing a group of people with a shotgun and charged in state court with both first- and second-degree assault, he was processed for detention in custody at the Wicomico County Central Booking facility. Booking personnel used a cheek swab to take the DNA sample from him pursuant to provisions of the Maryland DNA Collection Act (or Act).

On July 13, 2009, King's DNA record was uploaded to the Maryland DNA database, and three weeks later, on August 4, 2009, his DNA profile was matched to the DNA sample collected in the unsolved 2003 rape case. Once the DNA was matched to King, detectives presented the forensic evidence to a grand jury, which indicted him for the rape. Detectives obtained a search warrant and took a second sample of DNA from King, which again matched the evidence from the rape. He moved to suppress the DNA match on the grounds that Maryland's DNA collection law violated the Fourth Amendment. The Circuit Court Judge upheld the statute as constitutional. King pleaded not guilty to the rape charges but was convicted and sentenced to life in prison without the possibility of parole.

During-Reading Question: Why would King have objected to his DNA collection under the Fourth Amendment?

The majority concluded that a DNA swab was an unreasonable search in violation of the Fourth Amendment because King's "expectation of privacy is greater than the State's purported interest in using King's DNA to identify him."

During-Reading Questions: The lower court weighed King's expectation of privacy versus the State's interest in using his DNA to identify him for the rape and ruled that his expectation of privacy was greater. Do you agree? Why or why not?

Both federal and state courts have reached differing conclusions as to whether the Fourth Amendment prohibits the collection and analysis of a DNA sample from persons arrested, but not yet convicted, on felony charges.

II

The advent of DNA technology is one of the most significant scientific advancements of our era. The full potential for use of genetic markers in medicine and science is still being explored, but the utility of DNA identification in the criminal justice system is already undisputed. Since the first use of forensic DNA analysis to catch a rapist and murderer in England in 1986, law enforcement, the defense bar, and the courts have acknowledged DNA testing's "unparalleled ability both to exonerate the wrongly convicted and to identify the guilty. It has the potential to significantly improve both the criminal justice system and police investigative practices." *DA's Office* v. *Osborne*.

A

The current standard for forensic DNA testing relies on an analysis of the chromosomes located within the nucleus of all human cells. "The DNA material in chromosomes is composed of 'coding' and 'noncoding' regions. The coding regions are known as *genes* and contain the information necessary for a cell to make proteins. . . . Non-protein-coding regions . . . are not related directly to making proteins, [and] have been referred to as 'junk' DNA." The adjective "junk" may mislead the layperson, for in fact this is the DNA region used with near certainty to identify a person. The term apparently is intended to indicate that this particular noncoding region, while useful and even dispositive for purposes like identity, does not show more far-reaching and complex characteristics like genetic traits.

Many of the patterns found in DNA are shared among all people, so forensic analysis focuses on "repeated DNA sequences scattered throughout the human genome," known as "short tandem repeats" (STRs). The alternative possibilities for the size and frequency of these STRs at any given point along a strand of DNA are known as "alleles," and multiple alleles are analyzed in order to ensure that a DNA profile matches only one individual. Future refinements may improve present technology, but even now STR analysis makes it "possible to determine whether a biological tissue matches a suspect with near certainty."

The Act authorizes Maryland law enforcement authorities to collect DNA samples from "an individual who is charged with . . . a crime of violence or an attempt to commit a crime of violence; or . . . burglary or an attempt to commit burglary." Maryland law defines a crime of violence to include murder, rape, first-degree assault, kidnaping, arson, sexual assault, and a variety of other serious crimes. Once taken, a DNA sample may not be processed or placed in a database before the individual is arraigned (unless the individual consents). It is at this point that a judicial officer ensures that there is probable cause to detain the arrestee on a qualifying serious offense. If "all qualifying criminal charges are determined to be unsupported by probable cause . . . the DNA sample shall be immediately destroyed." DNA samples are also destroyed if "a criminal action begun against the individual . . . does not result in a conviction," "the conviction is finally reversed or vacated and no new trial is permitted," or "the individual is granted an unconditional pardon."

During-Reading Question: It appears that once DNA has been collected, it cannot always be processed. What are the requirements that must be met before it can be processed?

The Act also limits the information added to a DNA database and how it may be used. Specifically, "[o]nly DNA records that directly relate to the identification of individuals shall be collected and stored." No purpose other than identification is permissible: "A person may not willfully test a DNA sample for information that does not relate to the identification of individuals as specified in this subtitle." Tests for familial matches are also prohibited. The officers involved in taking and analyzing respondent's DNA sample complied with the Act in all respects.

During-Reading Question: Why would a prohibition on testing for familial matches be important?

Respondent's DNA was collected in this case using a common procedure known as a "buccal swab." "Buccal cell collection involves wiping a small piece of filter paper or a cotton swab similar to a Q-tip against the inside cheek of an individual's mouth to collect some skin cells." The procedure is quick and painless. The swab touches inside an arrestee's mouth, but it requires no "surgical intrusio[n] beneath the skin," and it poses no "threa[t] to the health or safety" of arrestees.

B

Respondent's identification as the rapist resulted in part through the operation of a national project to standardize collection and storage of DNA profiles. Authorized by Congress and supervised by the Federal Bureau of Investigation (FBI), the Combined DNA Index System (CODIS) connects DNA laboratories at the local, state, and national level. Since its authorization in 1994, the CODIS system has grown to include all 50 States and a number of federal agencies. CODIS collects DNA profiles provided by local laboratories taken from arrestees, convicted offenders, and forensic evidence found at crime scenes. To participate in CODIS, a local laboratory must sign a memorandum of understanding agreeing to adhere to quality standards and submit to audits to evaluate compliance with the federal standards for scientifically rigorous DNA testing.

One of the most significant aspects of CODIS is the standardization of the points of comparison in DNA analysis. In short, CODIS sets uniform national standards for DNA matching and then facilitates connections between local law enforcement agencies who can share more specific information about matched STR profiles.

All 50 States require the collection of DNA from felony convicts, and respondent does not dispute the validity of that practice. Twenty-eight States and the Federal Government have adopted laws similar to the Maryland Act authorizing the collection of DNA from some or all arrestees. Although those statutes vary in their particulars, such as what charges require a DNA sample, their similarity means that this case implicates more than the specific Maryland law. At issue is a standard, expanding technology already in widespread use throughout the Nation.

III

A

Although the DNA swab procedure used here presents a question the Court has not yet addressed, the framework for deciding the issue is well established. The Fourth Amendment, binding on the States by the Fourteenth Amendment, provides that "[t]he right of the people to be secure in their persons, houses, papers, and effects, against unreasonable searches and seizures, shall not be violated." It can be agreed that using a buccal swab on the inner tissues of a person's cheek in order to obtain DNA samples is a search. Virtually any "intrusio[n] into the human body," will work an invasion of "'cherished personal security' that is subject to constitutional scrutiny." The Court has applied the Fourth Amendment to police efforts to draw blood, scraping an arrestee's fingernails to obtain trace evidence, and even to "a breathalyzer test, which generally requires the production of alveolar or 'deep lung' breath for chemical analysis."

During-Reading Question: Why is a DNA swab considered a "search" under the Fourth Amendment?

A buccal swab is a far more gentle process than a venipuncture to draw blood. It involves but a light touch on the inside of the cheek; and although it can be deemed a search within the body of the arrestee, it requires no "surgical intrusions beneath the skin." The fact than an intrusion is negligible is of central relevance to determining reasonableness, although it is still a search as the law defines that term.

B

To say that the Fourth Amendment applies here is the beginning point, not the end of the analysis. "[T]he Fourth Amendment's proper function is to constrain, not against all intrusions as such, but against intrusions which are not justified in the circumstances, or which are made in an improper manner." *Schmerber*. "As the text of the Fourth Amendment indicates, the ultimate measure of the constitutionality of a governmental search is 'reasonableness.'" *Vernonia School Dist.*

In some circumstances, such as "[w]hen faced with special law enforcement needs, diminished expectations of privacy, minimal intrusions, or the like, the Court has found that certain general, or individual, circumstances may render a warrantless search or seizure reasonable." *Illinois* v. *McArthur*. Those circumstances diminish the need for a warrant, either because "the public interest is such that neither a warrant nor probable cause is required," or because an individual is already on notice, for instance because of his employment, or the conditions of his release from government custody, that some reasonable police intrusion on his privacy is to be expected. The need for a warrant is perhaps least when the search involves no discretion that could properly be limited by the "interpo[lation of] a neutral magistrate between the citizen and the law enforcement officer" *Treasury Employees* v. *Von Raab*.

During-Reading Question: Does the public interest in solving cold cases outweigh someone's privacy interest when considering the DNA swab?

The instant case can be addressed with this background. The Maryland DNA Collection Act provides that, in order to obtain a DNA sample, all arrestees charged with serious crimes must furnish the sample on a buccal swab applied, as noted, to the inside of the cheeks. The arrestee is already in valid police custody for a serious offense supported by probable cause. The DNA collection is not subject to the judgment of officers whose perspective might be "colored by their primary involvement in 'the often competitive enterprise of ferreting out crime.'" "Indeed, in light of the standardized nature of the tests and the minimal discretion vested in those charged with administering the program, there are virtually no facts for a neutral magistrate to evaluate." Here, the search effected by the buccal swab of respondent falls within the category of cases this Court has analyzed by reference to the proposition that the "touchstone of the Fourth Amendment is reasonableness, not individualized suspicion."

Even if a warrant is not required, a search is not beyond Fourth Amendment scrutiny; for it must be reasonable in its scope and manner of execution. Urgent government interests are not a license for indiscriminate police behavior. To say that no warrant is required is merely to acknowledge that "rather than employing a *per se* rule of unreasonableness, we balance the privacy-related and law enforcement–related concerns to determine if the intrusion was reasonable." *McArthur*. This application of "traditional standards of reasonableness" requires a court to weigh "the promotion of legitimate governmental interests" against "the degree to which [the search] intrudes upon an individual's privacy." *Wyoming* v. *Houghton*. An assessment of reasonableness to determine the lawfulness of requiring this class of arrestees to provide a DNA sample is central to the instant case.

IV

A

The legitimate government interest served by the Maryland DNA Collection Act is one that is well established: the need for law enforcement officers in a safe and accurate way to process and identify the persons and possessions they must take into custody. It is beyond dispute that "probable cause provides legal justification for arresting a person suspected of crime, and for a brief period of detention to take the administrative steps incident to arrest." Also uncontested is the "right on the part of the Government, always recognized under English and American law, to search the person of the accused when legally arrested." "The validity of the search of a person incident to a lawful arrest has been regarded as settled from its first enunciation, and has remained virtually unchallenged." *United States* v. *Robinson*. Even in that context, the

Court has been clear that individual suspicion is not necessary, because "[t]he constitutionality of a search incident to an arrest does not depend on whether there is any indication that the person arrested possesses weapons or evidence. The fact of a lawful arrest, standing alone, authorizes a search." *Michigan* v. *DeFillippo.*

The "routine administrative procedure[s] at a police station house incident to booking and jailing the suspect" derive from different origins and have different constitutional justifications than, say, the search of a place, for the search of a place not incident to an arrest depends on the "fair probability that contraband or evidence of a crime will be found in a particular place," *Illinois* v. *Gates*. The interests are further different when an individual is formally processed into police custody. Then "the law is in the act of subjecting the body of the accused to its physical dominion." *People* v. *Chiagles*. When probable cause exists to remove an individual from the normal channels of society and hold him in legal custody, DNA identification plays a critical role in serving those interests.

First, "[i]n every criminal case, it is known and must be known who has been arrested and who is being tried." *Hiibel* v. *Sixth Judicial Dist. Court of Nev., Humboldt Cty*. An individual's identity is more than just his name or Social Security number, and the government's interest in identification goes beyond ensuring that the proper name is typed on the indictment. Identity has never been considered limited to the name on the arrestee's birth certificate. In fact, a name is of little value compared to the real interest in identification at stake when an individual is brought into custody. "It is a well-recognized aspect of criminal conduct that the perpetrator will take unusual steps to conceal not only his conduct, but also his identity. Disguises used while committing a crime may be supplemented or replaced by changed names, and even changed physical features." *Jones* v. *Murray*. An "arrestee may be carrying a false ID or lie about his identity," and "criminal history records . . . can be inaccurate or incomplete." *Florence* v. *Bd. of Chosen Freeholders*.

A suspect's criminal history is a critical part of his identity that officers should know when processing him for detention. It is a common occurrence that "[p]eople detained for minor offenses can turn out to be the most devious and dangerous criminals. Hours after the Oklahoma City bombing, Timothy McVeigh was stopped by a state trooper who noticed he was driving without a license plate. Police stopped serial killer Joel Rifkin for the same reason. One of the terrorists involved in the September 11 attacks was stopped and ticketed for speeding just two days before hijacking Flight 93." Police already seek this crucial identifying information. They use routine and accepted means as varied as comparing the suspect's booking photograph to sketch artists' depictions of persons of interest, showing his mugshot to potential witnesses, and of course making a computerized comparison of the arrestee's fingerprints against electronic databases of known criminals and unsolved crimes. In this respect the only difference between DNA analysis and the accepted use of fingerprint databases is the unparalleled accuracy DNA provides.

During-Reading Question: The Court mentions how some terrorists were detained for minor offenses before being linked to their larger crimes. Why do you think the Court mentions these names?

The task of identification necessarily entails searching public and police records based on the identifying information provided by the arrestee to see what is already known about him. The DNA collected from arrestees is an irrefutable identification of the person from whom it was taken. Like a fingerprint, the 13 CODIS loci are not themselves evidence of any particular crime, in the way that a drug test can by itself be evidence of illegal narcotics use. A DNA profile is useful to the police because it gives them a form of identification to search the records already in their valid possession. In this respect the use of DNA for identification is no different than matching an arrestee's face to a wanted poster of a previously unidentified suspect; or matching tattoos to known gang symbols to reveal a criminal affiliation; or matching the arrestee's fingerprints to those recovered from a crime scene. DNA is another metric of identification used to connect the arrestee with his or her public persona, as reflected in records of his or her actions that are available to the police. Those records may be linked to the arrestee by a variety of relevant forms of identification, including name, alias, date and time of previous convictions and the name then used, photograph, Social Security number, or CODIS profile. These data, found in official records, are checked as a routine matter to produce a more comprehensive record of the suspect's complete identity. Finding occurrences of the arrestee's CODIS profile in outstanding cases is consistent with this common practice. It uses a different form of identification than a name or fingerprint, but its function is the same.

Second, law enforcement officers bear a responsibility for ensuring that the custody of an arrestee does not create inordinate "risks for facility staff, for the existing detainee population, and for a new detainee." *Florence*. DNA identification can provide untainted information to those charged with detaining suspects and detaining the property of any felon. For these purposes officers must know the type of person whom they are detaining, and DNA allows them to make critical choices about how to proceed.

Recognizing that a name alone cannot address this interest in identity, the Court has approved, for example, "a visual inspection for certain tattoos and other signs of gang affiliation as part of the intake process," because "[t]he identification and isolation of gang members before they are admitted protects everyone." *Florence.*

Third, looking forward to future stages of criminal prosecution, "the Government has a substantial interest in ensuring that persons accused of crimes are available for trials." *Bell* v. *Wolfish.* A person who is arrested for one offense but knows that he has yet to answer for some past crime may be more inclined to flee the instant charges, lest continued contact with the criminal justice system expose one or more other serious offenses. For example, a defendant who had committed a prior sexual assault might be inclined to flee on a burglary charge, knowing that in every State a DNA sample would be taken from him after his conviction on the burglary charge that would tie him to the more serious charge of rape. In addition to subverting the administration of justice with respect to the crime of arrest, this ties back to the interest in safety; for a detainee who absconds from custody presents a risk to law enforcement officers, other detainees, victims of previous crimes, witnesses, and society at large.

During-Reading Questions: Is the potential for DNA collection a deterrent to crime? Why or why not?

Fourth, an arrestee's past conduct is essential to an assessment of the danger he poses to the public, and this will inform a court's determination whether the individual should be released on bail. "The government's interest in preventing crime by arrestees is both legitimate and compelling." *United States* v. *Salerno*. DNA identification of a suspect in a violent crime provides critical information to the police and judicial officials in making a determination of the arrestee's future dangerousness. This inquiry always has entailed some scrutiny beyond the name on the defendant's driver's license. Knowing that the defendant is wanted for a previous violent crime based on DNA identification is especially probative of the court's consideration of "the danger of the defendant to the alleged victim, another person, or the community." Rule 4-216(f)(1)(G)

This interest is not speculative. In considering laws to require collecting DNA from arrestees, government agencies around the Nation found evidence of numerous cases in which felony arrestees would have been identified as violent through DNA identification matching them to previous crimes but who later committed additional crimes because such identification was not used to detain them.

Present capabilities make it possible to complete a DNA identification that provides information essential to determining whether a detained suspect can be released pending trial. Regardless of when the initial bail decision is made, release is not appropriate until a further determination is made as to the person's identity in the sense not only of what his birth certificate states but also what other records and data disclose to give that identity more meaning in the whole context of who the person really is. And even when release is permitted, the background identity of the suspect is necessary for determining what conditions must be met before release is allowed. If release is authorized, it may take time for the conditions to be met, and so the time before actual release can be substantial. For example, in the federal system, defendants released conditionally are detained on average for 112 days; those released on unsecured bond for 37 days; on personal recognizance for 36 days; and on other financial conditions for 27 days. During this entire period, additional and supplemental data establishing more about the person's identity and background can provide critical information relevant to the conditions of release and whether to revisit an initial release determination. The facts of this case are illustrative. Though the record is not clear, if some thought were being given to releasing respondent on bail on the gun charge, a release that would take weeks or months in any event, when the DNA report linked him to the prior rape, it would be relevant to the conditions of his release. The same would be true with a supplemental fingerprint report.

During-Reading Question: How does the Court justify using the DNA knowledge of prior crimes as a method for determining whether someone awaiting trial should be allowed out on bail or not?

Even if an arrestee is released on bail, development of DNA identification revealing the defendant's unknown violent past can and should lead to the revocation of his conditional release. Pretrial release of a person charged with a dangerous crime is a most serious responsibility. It is reasonable in all respects for the State to use an accepted database to determine if an arrestee is the object of suspicion in other serious crimes, suspicion that may provide a strong incentive for the arrestee to escape and flee.

Finally, in the interests of justice, the identification of an arrestee as the perpetrator of some heinous crime may have the salutary effect of freeing a person wrongfully imprisoned for the same offense. "[P]rompt [DNA] testing . . . would speed up apprehension of criminals before they commit additional crimes, and prevent the grotesque detention of . . . innocent people."

During-Reading Questions: Is the potential of freeing wrongfully imprisoned people justification for collecting DNA? Why or why not?

Because proper processing of arrestees is so important and has consequences for every stage of the criminal process, the Court has recognized that the "governmental interests underlying a station-house search of the arrestee's person and possessions may in some circumstances be even greater than those supporting a search immediately following arrest." *Lafayette*. The

Court has been reluctant to circumscribe the authority of the police to conduct reasonable booking searches.

B

DNA identification represents an important advance in the techniques used by law enforcement to serve legitimate police concerns for as long as there have been arrests, concerns the courts have acknowledged and approved for more than a century. Law enforcement agencies routinely have used scientific advancements in their standard procedures for the identification of arrestees. "Police had been using photography to capture the faces of criminals almost since its invention." Courts did not dispute that practice, concluding that a

> sheriff in making an arrest for a felony on a warrant has the right to exercise a discretion . . . , [if] he should deem it necessary to the safe-keeping of a prisoner, and to prevent his escape, or to enable him the more readily to retake the prisoner if he should escape, to take his photograph. *State ex rel. Bruns* v. *Clausmeier*.

By the time that it had become "the daily practice of the police officers and detectives of crime to use photographic pictures for the discovery and identification of criminals," the courts likewise had come to the conclusion that "it would be [a] matter of regret to have its use unduly restricted upon any fanciful theory or constitutional privilege." *Shaffer* v. *United States*.

Beginning in 1887, some police adopted more exacting means to identify arrestees, using the system of precise physical measurements pioneered by the French anthropologist Alphonse Bertillon. Bertillon identification consisted of 10 measurements of the arrestee's body, along with a "scientific analysis of the features of the face and an exact anatomical localization of the various scars, marks, &c., of the body."

> [W]hen a prisoner was brought in, his photograph was taken according to the Bertillon system, and his body measurements were then made. The measurements were made . . . and noted down on the back of a card or a blotter, and the photograph of the prisoner was expected to be placed on the card. This card, therefore, furnished both the likeness and description of the prisoner, and was placed in the rogues' gallery, and copies were sent to various cities where similar records were kept. *People ex rel. Jones* v. *Diehl*.

As in the present case, the point of taking this information about each arrestee was not limited to verifying that the proper name was on the indictment. These procedures were used to "facilitate the recapture of escaped prisoners," to aid "the investigation of their past records and personal history," and "to preserve the means of identification for . . . future supervision after discharge." *Hodgeman* v. *Olsen*.

> [C]riminal identification is said to have two main purposes: (1) The identification of the accused as the person who committed the crime for which he is being held; and (2) the identification of the accused as the same person who has been previously charged with, or convicted of, other offenses against the criminal law.

Perhaps the most direct historical analogue to the DNA technology used to identify respondent is the familiar practice of fingerprinting arrestees. From the advent of this technique, courts had no trouble determining that fingerprinting was a natural part of "the administrative steps incident to arrest." *County of Riverside* v. *McLaughlin*. By the middle of the 20th century, it was considered "elementary that a person in lawful custody may be required to submit to photographing and fingerprinting as part of routine identification processes." *Smith* v. *United States*.

DNA identification is an advanced technique superior to fingerprinting in many ways, so much so that to insist on fingerprints as the norm would make little sense to either the forensic expert or a layperson. The additional intrusion upon the arrestee's privacy beyond that associated with fingerprinting is not significant, and DNA is a markedly more accurate form of identifying arrestees. A suspect who has changed his facial features to evade photographic identification or even one who has undertaken the more arduous task of altering his fingerprints cannot escape the revealing power of his DNA.

The Respondent's primary objection to this analogy is that DNA identification is not as fast as fingerprinting, and so it should not be considered to be the 21st-century equivalent. But rapid analysis of fingerprints is itself of recent vintage. The FBI's vaunted Integrated Automated Fingerprint Identification System (IAFIS) was only "launched on July 28, 1999. Prior to this time, the processing of . . . fingerprint submissions was largely a manual, labor-intensive process, taking weeks or months to process a single submission." It was not the advent of this technology that rendered fingerprint analysis constitutional in a single moment. The question of how long it takes to process identifying information obtained from a valid search goes only to the efficacy of the search for its purpose of prompt identification, not the constitutionality of the search. Given the importance of DNA in the identification of police records pertaining to arrestees and the need to refine and confirm that identity for its important bearing on the decision to continue release on bail or to impose new conditions, DNA serves an essential purpose despite the existence of delays such as the one that occurred in this case. Even so, the delay in processing DNA from arrestees is being reduced to a substantial degree by rapid technical advances. And the FBI has already begun testing devices that will enable police to process the DNA of arrestees within 90 minutes. An assessment and understanding of the reasonableness of this minimally invasive search of a person detained for a serious crime should take account of these technical advances. Just as fingerprinting was constitutional for generations prior to the introduction of IAFIS, DNA identification of arrestees is a permissible tool of law enforcement today. New technology will only further improve its speed and therefore its effectiveness. And, as noted above, actual release of a serious offender as a routine matter takes weeks or months in any event. By identifying not only who the arrestee is but also what other available records disclose about his past to show who he is, the police can ensure that they have the proper person under arrest and that they have made the necessary arrangements for his custody; and, just as important, they can also prevent suspicion against or prosecution of the innocent.

In sum, there can be little reason to question "the legitimate interest of the government in knowing for an absolute certainty the identity of the person arrested, in knowing whether he is wanted elsewhere, and in ensuring his identification in the event he flees prosecution." To that end, courts have confirmed that the Fourth Amendment allows police to take certain routine "administrative steps incident to arrest—*i.e.,* . . . book[ing], photograph[ing], and fingerprint[ing]." *McLaughlin*. DNA identification of arrestees, of the type approved by the Maryland statute here at issue, is "no more than an extension of methods of identification long used in dealing with persons under arrest." *Kelly*. In the balance of reasonableness required by the Fourth Amendment, therefore, the Court must give great weight both to the significant government interest at stake in the identification of arrestees and to the unmatched potential of DNA identification to serve that interest.

V

A

By comparison to this substantial government interest and the unique effectiveness of DNA identification, the intrusion of a cheek swab to obtain a DNA sample is a minimal one. In considering those expectations in this case, however, the necessary predicate of a valid arrest for a serious offense is fundamental.

The reasonableness of any search must be considered in the context of the person's legitimate expectations of privacy. For example, when weighing the invasiveness of urinalysis of high school athletes, the Court noted that "[l]egitimate privacy expectations are even less with regard to student athletes. . . . Public school locker rooms, the usual sites for these activities, are not notable for the privacy they afford."

The expectations of privacy of an individual taken into police custody "necessarily [are] of a diminished scope." *Bell.* "[B]oth the person and the property in his immediate possession may be searched at the station house." *United States* v. *Edwards*. A search of the detainee's person when he is booked into custody may "involve a relatively extensive exploration," *Robinson*, including "requir[ing] at least some detainees to lift their genitals or cough in a squatting position," *Florence*.

The reasonableness inquiry here considers two other circumstances in which the Court has held that particularized suspicion is not categorically required: "diminished expectations of privacy [and] minimal intrusions." *McArthur*. This is not to suggest that any search is acceptable solely because a person is in custody. Some searches, such as invasive surgery, or a search of the arrestee's home, involve either greater intrusions or higher expectations of privacy than are present in this case. In those situations, when the Court must "balance the privacy-related and law enforcement-related concerns to determine if the intrusion was reasonable," *McArthur*, the privacy-related concerns are weighty enough that the search may require a warrant, notwithstanding the diminished expectations of privacy of the arrestee.

Here, by contrast to the approved standard procedures incident to any arrest detailed above, a buccal swab involves an even more brief and still minimal intrusion. A gentle rub along the inside of the cheek does not break the skin, and it "involves virtually no risk, trauma, or pain." *Schmerber*. "A crucial factor in analyzing the magnitude of the intrusion . . . is the extent to which the procedure may threaten the safety or health of the individual," *Winston*, and nothing suggests that a buccal swab poses any physical danger whatsoever. A brief intrusion of an arrestee's person is subject to the Fourth Amendment, but a swab of this nature does not increase the indignity already attendant to normal incidents of arrest.

B

In addition the processing of respondent's DNA sample's 13 CODIS loci did not intrude on respondent's privacy in a way that would make his DNA identification unconstitutional.

First, as already noted, the CODIS loci come from noncoding parts of the DNA that do not reveal the genetic traits of the arrestee. While science can always progress further, and those progressions may have Fourth Amendment consequences, alleles at the CODIS loci "are not at present revealing information beyond identification." The argument that the testing at issue in this case reveals any private medical information at all is open to dispute.

And even if noncoding alleles could provide some information, they are not in fact tested for that end. It is undisputed that law enforcement officers analyze DNA for the sole purpose of generating a unique identifying number against which future samples may be matched. If in the future police analyze samples to determine, for instance, an arrestee's predisposition for a particular disease or other hereditary factors not relevant to identity, that case would present additional privacy concerns not present here.

During-Reading Question: The Court seems to draw a line here that testing for purposes beyond criminal identification might raise additional privacy concerns. Why would that be?

Finally, the Act provides statutory protections that guard against further invasion of privacy. As noted above, the Act requires that "[o]nly DNA records that directly relate to the identification of individuals shall be collected and stored." No purpose other than identification is permissible: "A person may not willfully test a DNA sample for information that does not relate to the identification of individuals as specified in this subtitle." The Court need not speculate about the risks posed "by a system that did not contain comparable security provisions." In light of the scientific and statutory safeguards, once respondent's DNA was lawfully collected the STR analysis of respondent's DNA pursuant to CODIS procedures did not amount to a significant invasion of privacy that would render the DNA identification impermissible under the Fourth Amendment.

In light of the context of a valid arrest supported by probable cause respondent's expectations of privacy were not offended by the minor intrusion of a brief swab of his cheeks. By contrast, that same context of arrest gives rise to significant state interests in identifying respondent not only so that the proper name can be attached to his charges but also so that the criminal justice system can make informed decisions concerning pretrial custody. Upon these considerations the Court concludes DNA identification of arrestees is a reasonable search that can be considered part of a routine booking procedure. When officers make an arrest supported by probable cause to hold for a serious offense and they bring the suspect to the station to be detained in custody, taking and analyzing a cheek swab of the arrestee's DNA is, like fingerprinting and photographing, a legitimate police booking procedure that is reasonable under the Fourth Amendment.

The judgment of the Court of Appeals of Maryland is reversed.

It is so ordered.

Post-Reading Questions

1. Is DNA analysis a twenty-first century equivalent to fingerprinting? Why or why not?
2. It took almost four months for King's DNA to make its way through the labs and to return with his connection to the rape case. Does this support the idea that DNA is simply used to help identify someone (like a fingerprint) or does it lead to a bigger question about solving unsolved crimes (and using DNA to assist in solving those crimes)?

Further Explorations

Exploring the Story

One of the concerns after this case was decided was the idea that law enforcement could collect DNA from someone accused, but not convicted of a crime. Why does this make a difference? See this brief news report here for more information: Mass Tea Party—Wake Up America! (2013, June 4). Controversial Supreme Court ruling police can collect DNA from suspects. [Fox News program]. *YouTube.* Retrieved from https://youtu.be/RpgX-BNyoZ8

Exploring the Law

The U.S. Department of Justice describes how it uses DNA to solve crimes in the following article: United States Department of Justice. (2017, March 17). Advancing justice through DNA technology: Using DNA to solve crimes. Retrieved from https://www.justice.gov/archives/ag/advancing-justice-through-dna-technology-using-dna-solve-crimes

Exploring the Effects

- The Innocence Project is an entity seeking to reverse wrongful convictions using DNA testing. Visit their website here: https://www.innocenceproject.org and read about the various cases they have helped solve.
- The Brookings Institute offers some strong criticism for the Court's decision in *Maryland v. King.* One of the issues they raise is the racial disparity in arrest rates and how that may influence a disparity in whose DNA is actually collected. Read more about their concerns with the case in the following article: Lempert, R. (2013, June 6). *Maryland v. King*: An unfortunate Supreme Court decision on the collection of DNA samples. *Up Front, Brookings Institute.* Retrieved from https://www.brookings.edu/blog/up-front/2013/06/06/maryland-v-king-an-unfortunate-supreme-court-decision-on-the-collection-of-dna-samples/
- The Katie Sepich Enhanced DNA Collection Act was passed by Congress in 2010 to provide funding to states for enhanced DNA collection and testing. Read more about that Act here: GovTrack. (n.d.). H.R. 6014 (112th): Katie Sepich Enhanced DNA Collection Act of 2012. Retrieved from https://www.govtrack.us/congress/bills/112/hr6014

Activities for Extending the Learning

DNA analysis is widely advertised as a way to discover one's ancestry or familial connections. Are people who send their DNA to companies who do ancestry analysis (like Ancestry.com or 123me.com) lowering their expectation of privacy? Have students investigate how an innocent submission of DNA for these purposes might end up having unintended consequences.

A NOTE FROM THE AUTHORS

The use of science and technology will be a high-interest standard with which to link a U.S. Supreme Court case. Given the prevalence of electronic devices in the hands of today's students, in addition to the prevalence of information being shared on social media, this is a great opportunity to discuss exactly how one gains, loses, and protects one's own privacy. Use current events to highlight how technology is being used to enforce more laws (drones and GPS), to monitor citizen behavior (body cameras on police officers), and to increase efficiency within police departments (red light cameras that can issue a ticket to a driver based on a photo taken by a camera attached to the light).

Given the social nature of adolescents, privacy can be a sliding scale, so it is important to explicitly discuss how one's expectation to privacy may be eroded by oversharing on social media or being lax with sharing private information. Use these teachable moments to foster responsible sharing and appreciation for how technology can be a fantastic development or a massive intrusion into our personal lives.

Chapter Eleven

Global Connections

> Theme 9: *Social studies programs should include experiences that provide for the study of global connections and interdependence.*
> —*National Curriculum Standards for Social Studies* (2010), National Council for the Social Studies, p. 22)

The United States has long been seen as a global leader, and within that role the United States finds itself interacting with different countries all over the world. In dealing with different people and nations, how does the United States respond when the ideas and beliefs possessed by others come into conflict with those possessed in the United States? With global access becoming easier and easier due to technology, should we consider issues more globally, or should the United States put its needs and ideologies first?

Theme 9 asks students to look at the decision made in United States and to analyze our place in relation to other countries. Questions students should be able to answer include:

> What are the different types of global connections? What global connections have existed in the past, exist currently, and are likely in the future? How do ideas spread between societies in today's interconnected world? How does this result in change in those societies? What are the other consequences of global connections? How should people and societies balance global connectedness with local needs? (NCSS, 2010, p. 22)

Roper v. Simmons (2005) is a case examining whether the death penalty should be used against people under the age of eighteen. Why is it an important consideration of the Court to examine what the rest of the world is doing when it arrives at its decision?

Medellín v. Texas (2008) explores the decision of the International Court of Justice (ICJ) and whether it has any binding implications on someone who is convicted of a crime in the United States. This case examines whether the State of Texas is obligated to fulfill the ruling of the ICJ based on the Vienna Convention. Should Texas be allowed to execute a Mexican national who has been convicted of a particularly heinous murder?

Finally *Maslenjak v. United States* (2017) looks at the requirements of becoming a naturalized United States citizen and what could potentially cause that citizenship to be taken away. Not only does this case consider what constitutes a substantial reason for removing citizenship, but it also addresses the issues related to what type of person we want to allow to become a naturalized citizen of the United States.

CASE #1: *ROPER V. SIMMONS*

Pre-Reading Questions

1. At what age should a person be held criminally responsible for his or her actions?
2. What are the reasons for having a different juvenile court and an adult court? Do some research to explore the rationale and history behind the two systems.
3. During a sentencing in a capital criminal case, the Court will allow testimony for exacerbating and mitigating factors. What are these and why are they allowed?

Roper v. Simmons, 543 U. S. 551 (2005)

JUSTICE KENNEDY delivered the opinion of the Court.

This case requires us to address, for the second time in a decade and a half, whether it is permissible under the Eighth and Fourteenth Amendments to the Constitution of the United States to execute a juvenile offender who was older than 15 but younger than 18 when he committed a capital crime. In *Stanford v. Kentucky*, 492 U. S. 361 (1989), a divided Court rejected the proposition that the Constitution bars capital punishment for juvenile offenders in this age group. We reconsider the question.

I

At the age of 17, when he was still a junior in high school, Christopher Simmons, the respondent here, committed murder. About nine months later, after he had turned 18, he was tried and sentenced to death. There is little doubt that Simmons was the instigator of the crime. Before its commission Simmons said he wanted to murder someone. In chilling, callous terms he talked about his plan, discussing it for the most part with two friends, Charles Benjamin and John Tessmer, then aged 15 and 16 respectively. Simmons proposed to commit burglary and murder by breaking and entering, tying up a victim, and throwing the victim off a bridge. Simmons assured his friends they could "get away with it" because they were minors.

The three met at about 2 a.m. on the night of the murder, but Tessmer left before the other two set out. (The State later charged Tessmer with conspiracy, but dropped the charge in exchange for his testimony against Simmons.) Simmons and Benjamin entered the home of the victim, Shirley Crook, after reaching through an open window and unlocking the back door. Simmons turned on a hallway light. Awakened, Mrs. Crook called out, "Who's there?" In response Simmons entered Mrs. Crook's bedroom, where he recognized her from a previous car accident involving them both. Simmons later admitted this confirmed his resolve to murder her.

Using duct tape to cover her eyes and mouth and bind her hands, the two perpetrators put Mrs. Crook in her minivan and drove to a state park. They reinforced the bindings, covered her head with a towel, and walked her to a railroad trestle spanning the Meramec River. There they tied her hands and feet together with electrical wire, wrapped her whole face in duct tape and threw her from the bridge, drowning her in the waters below.

By the afternoon of September 9, Steven Crook had returned home from an overnight trip, found his bedroom in disarray, and reported his wife missing. On the same afternoon fishermen recovered the victim's body from the river. Simmons, meanwhile, was bragging about the killing, telling friends he had killed a woman "because the bitch seen my face."

The next day, after receiving information of Simmons' involvement, police arrested him at his high school and took him to the police station in Fenton, Missouri. They read him his

Miranda rights. Simmons waived his right to an attorney and agreed to answer questions. After less than two hours of interrogation, Simmons confessed to the murder and agreed to perform a videotaped reenactment at the crime scene.

The State charged Simmons with burglary, kidnaping, stealing, and murder in the first degree. As Simmons was 17 at the time of the crime, he was outside the criminal jurisdiction of Missouri's juvenile court system. He was tried as an adult. At trial the State introduced Simmons' confession and the videotaped reenactment of the crime, along with testimony that Simmons discussed the crime in advance and bragged about it later. The defense called no witnesses in the guilt phase. The jury having returned a verdict of murder, the trial proceeded to the penalty phase.

The State sought the death penalty. As aggravating factors, the State submitted that the murder was committed for the purpose of receiving money; was committed for the purpose of avoiding, interfering with, or preventing lawful arrest of the defendant; and involved depravity of mind and was outrageously and wantonly vile, horrible, and inhuman. The State called Shirley Crook's husband, daughter, and two sisters, who presented moving evidence of the devastation her death had brought to their lives.

In mitigation Simmons' attorneys first called an officer of the Missouri juvenile justice system, who testified that Simmons had no prior convictions and that no previous charges had been filed against him. Simmons' mother, father, two younger half brothers, a neighbor, and a friend took the stand to tell the jurors of the close relationships they had formed with Simmons and to plead for mercy on his behalf. Simmons' mother, in particular, testified to the responsibility Simmons demonstrated in taking care of his two younger half-brothers and of his grandmother and to his capacity to show love for them.

During closing arguments, both the prosecutor and defense counsel addressed Simmons' age, which the trial judge had instructed the jurors they could consider as a mitigating factor. Defense counsel reminded the jurors that juveniles of Simmons' age cannot drink, serve on juries, or even see certain movies, because "the legislatures have wisely decided that individuals of a certain age aren't responsible enough." Defense counsel argued that Simmons' age should make "a huge difference to [the jurors] in deciding just exactly what sort of punishment to make." In rebuttal, the prosecutor gave the following response: "Age, he says. Think about age. Seventeen years old. Isn't that scary? Doesn't that scare you? Mitigating? Quite the contrary I submit. Quite the contrary."

During-Reading Questions: How did the prosecutor use Simmons' age as an exacerbating factor in his initial trial? What was the prosecution trying to say to this jury with the above statement?

The jury recommended the death penalty after finding the State had proved each of the three aggravating factors submitted to it. Accepting the jury's recommendation, the trial judge imposed the death penalty.

Simmons obtained new counsel, who moved in the trial court to set aside the conviction and sentence. One argument was that Simmons had received ineffective assistance at trial. To support this contention, the new counsel called as witnesses Simmons' trial attorney, Simmons' friends and neighbors, and clinical psychologists who had evaluated him.

Part of the submission was that Simmons was "very immature," "very impulsive," and "very susceptible to being manipulated or influenced." The experts testified about Simmons' background including a difficult home environment and dramatic changes in behavior, accompanied by poor school performance in adolescence. Simmons was absent from home for long periods, spending time using alcohol and drugs with other teenagers or young adults. The contention by Simmons' postconviction counsel was that these matters should have been established in the sentencing proceeding.

The trial court found no constitutional violation by reason of ineffective assistance of counsel and denied the motion for postconviction relief. In a consolidated appeal from Simmons' conviction and sentence, and from the denial of postconviction relief, the Missouri Supreme Court affirmed. The federal courts denied Simmons' petition for a writ of habeas corpus.

After these proceedings in Simmons' case had run their course, this Court held that the Eighth and Fourteenth Amendments prohibit the execution of a mentally retarded person. *Atkins v. Virginia.* Simmons filed a new petition for state postconviction relief, arguing that the reasoning of Atkins established that the Constitution prohibits the execution of a juvenile who was under 18 when the crime was committed.

The Missouri Supreme Court agreed. It held that since *Stanford*,

> a national consensus has developed against the execution of juvenile offenders, as demonstrated by the fact that eighteen states now bar such executions for juveniles, that twelve other states bar executions altogether, that no state has lowered its age of execution below 18 since Stanford, that five states have legislatively or by case law raised or established the minimum age at 18, and that the imposition of the juvenile death penalty has become truly unusual over the last decade.

On this reasoning it set aside Simmons' death sentence and resentenced him to "life imprisonment without eligibility for probation, parole, or release except by act of the Governor."

We granted certiorari and now affirm.

II

The Eighth Amendment provides: "Excessive bail shall not be required, nor excessive fines imposed, nor cruel and unusual punishments inflicted." The provision is applicable to the States through the Fourteenth Amendment. As the Court explained in *Atkins*, the Eighth Amendment guarantees individuals the right not to be subjected to excessive sanctions. The right flows from the basic "precept of justice that punishment for crime should be graduated and proportioned to [the] offense." By protecting even those convicted of heinous crimes, the Eighth Amendment reaffirms the duty of the government to respect the dignity of all persons.

The prohibition against "cruel and unusual punishments," like other expansive language in the Constitution, must be interpreted according to its text, by considering history, tradition, and precedent, and with due regard for its purpose and function in the constitutional design. To implement this framework we have established the propriety and affirmed the necessity of referring to "the evolving standards of decency that mark the progress of a maturing society" to determine which punishments are so disproportionate as to be cruel and unusual.

In *Thompson v. Oklahoma*, 487 U. S. 815 (1988), a plurality of the Court determined that our standards of decency do not permit the execution of any offender under the age of 16 at the time of the crime. The plurality opinion explained that no death penalty State that had given express consideration to a minimum age for the death penalty had set the age lower than 16. The plurality also observed that

> [t]he conclusion that it would offend civilized standards of decency to execute a person who was less than 16 years old at the time of his or her offense is consistent with the views that have been expressed by respected professional organizations, by other nations that share our Anglo-American heritage, and by the leading members of the Western European community.

Bringing its independent judgment to bear on the permissibility of the death penalty for a 15-year-old offender, the *Thompson* plurality stressed that "[t]he reasons why juveniles are not trusted with the privileges and responsibilities of an adult also explain why their irresponsible conduct is not as morally reprehensible as that of an adult." According to the plurality, the lesser culpability of offenders under 16 made the death penalty inappropriate as a form of retribution, while the low likelihood that offenders under 16 engaged in "the kind of cost-benefit analysis that attaches any weight to the possibility of execution" made the death penalty ineffective as a means of deterrence. With Justice O'Connor concurring in the judgment on narrower grounds, the Court set aside the death sentence that had been imposed on the 15-year-old offender.

The next year, in *Stanford v. Kentucky*, the Court, over a dissenting opinion joined by four Justices, referred to contemporary standards of decency in this country and concluded the Eighth and Fourteenth Amendments did not proscribe the execution of juvenile offenders over 15 but under 18. The Court noted that 22 of the 37 death penalty States permitted the death penalty for 16-year-old offenders, and, among these 37 States, 25 permitted it for 17-year-old offenders. These numbers, in the Court's view, indicated there was no national consensus "sufficient to label a particular punishment cruel and unusual." A plurality of the Court also "emphatically reject[ed]" the suggestion that the Court should bring its own judgment to bear on the acceptability of the juvenile death penalty.

The same day the Court decided *Stanford*, it held that the Eighth Amendment did not mandate a categorical exemption from the death penalty for the mentally retarded. *Penry v. Lynaugh*, 492 U. S. 302 (1989). In reaching this conclusion it stressed that only two States had enacted laws banning the imposition of the death penalty on a mentally retarded person convicted of a capital offense. According to the Court, "the two state statutes prohibiting execution of the mentally retarded, even when added to the 14 States that have rejected capital punishment completely, [did] not provide sufficient evidence at present of a national consensus."

Three Terms ago the subject was reconsidered in *Atkins*. We held that standards of decency have evolved since *Penry* and now demonstrate that the execution of the mentally retarded is cruel and unusual punishment. The Court noted objective indicia of society's standards, as expressed in legislative enactments and state practice with respect to executions of the mentally retarded. When *Atkins* was decided only a minority of States permitted the practice, and even in those States it was rare. On the basis of these indicia the Court determined that executing mentally retarded offenders "has become truly unusual, and it is fair to say that a national consensus has developed against it."

The inquiry into our society's evolving standards of decency did not end there. The *Atkins* Court neither repeated nor relied upon the statement in *Stanford* that the Court's independent judgment has no bearing on the acceptability of a particular punishment under the Eighth Amendment. Instead we returned to the rule, established in decisions predating *Stanford*, that "the Constitution contemplates that in the end our own judgment will be brought to bear on the question of the acceptability of the death penalty under the Eighth Amendment." Mental retardation, the Court said, diminishes personal culpability even if the offender can distinguish right from wrong. The impairments of mentally retarded offenders make it less defensible to impose the death penalty as retribution for past crimes and less likely that the death penalty will have a real deterrent effect. Based on these considerations and on the finding of national consensus against executing the mentally retarded, the Court ruled that the death penalty constitutes an excessive sanction for the entire category of mentally retarded offenders, and that the Eighth Amendment "places a substantive restriction on the State's power to take the life of a mentally retarded offender."

Just as the *Atkins* Court reconsidered the issue decided in *Penry*, we now reconsider the issue decided in *Stanford*. The beginning point is a review of objective indicia of consensus, as expressed in particular by the enactments of legislatures that have addressed the question. This data gives us essential instruction. We then must determine, in the exercise of our own independent judgment, whether the death penalty is a disproportionate punishment for juveniles.

III

A

The evidence of national consensus against the death penalty for juveniles is similar, and in some respects parallel, to the evidence *Atkins* held sufficient to demonstrate a national consensus against the death penalty for the mentally retarded. When *Atkins* was decided, 30 States prohibited the death penalty for the mentally retarded. This number comprised 12 that had abandoned the death penalty altogether, and 18 that maintained it but excluded the mentally retarded from its reach. By a similar calculation in this case, 30 States prohibit the juvenile death penalty, comprising 12 that have rejected the death penalty altogether and 18 that maintain it but, by express provision or judicial interpretation, exclude juveniles from its reach. *Atkins* emphasized that even in the 20 States without formal prohibition, the practice of executing the mentally retarded was infrequent. Since *Penry,* only five States had executed offenders known to have an IQ under 70. In the present case, too, even in the 20 States without a formal prohibition on executing juveniles, the practice is infrequent. Since *Stanford*, six States have executed prisoners for crimes committed as juveniles. In the past 10 years, only three have done so: Oklahoma, Texas, and Virginia. In December 2003 the Governor of Kentucky decided to spare the life of Kevin Stanford, and commuted his sentence to one of life imprisonment without parole, with the declaration that "[w]e ought not be executing people who, legally, were children." By this act the Governor ensured Kentucky would not add itself to the list of States that have executed juveniles within the last 10 years even by the execution of the very defendant whose death sentence the Court had upheld in *Stanford v. Kentucky.*

There is, to be sure, at least one difference between the evidence of consensus in *Atkins* and in this case. Impressive in *Atkins* was the rate of abolition of the death penalty for the mentally retarded. Sixteen States that permitted the execution of the mentally retarded at the time of *Penry* had prohibited the practice by the time we heard *Atkins*. By contrast, the rate of change in reducing the incidence of the juvenile death penalty, or in taking specific steps to abolish it, has been slower. Five States that allowed the juvenile death penalty at the time of Stanford have abandoned it in the intervening 15 years—four through legislative enactments and one through judicial decision.

Though less dramatic than the change from *Penry* to *Atkins*, we still consider the change from *Stanford* to this case to be significant. The number of States that have abandoned capital punishment for juvenile offenders since *Stanford* is smaller than the number of States that abandoned capital punishment for the mentally retarded after *Penry*; yet we think the same consistency of direction of change has been demonstrated. Since *Stanford*, no State that previously prohibited capital punishment for juveniles has reinstated it. This fact, coupled with the trend toward abolition of the juvenile death penalty, carries special force in light of the general popularity of anticrime legislation, and in light of the particular trend in recent years toward cracking down on juvenile crime in other respects.

The slower pace of abolition of the juvenile death penalty over the past 15 years, moreover, may have a simple explanation. When we heard *Penry*, only two death penalty States had already prohibited the execution of the mentally retarded. When we heard *Stanford*, by contrast, 12 death penalty States had already prohibited the execution of any juvenile under 18, and 15 had prohibited the execution of any juvenile under 17. If anything, this shows that the impropriety of executing juveniles between 16 and 18 years of age gained wide recognition earlier than the impropriety of executing the mentally retarded. In the words of the Missouri Supreme Court:

> It would be the ultimate in irony if the very fact that the inappropriateness of the death penalty for juveniles was broadly recognized sooner than it was recognized for the mentally retarded were to become a reason to continue the execution of juveniles now that the execution of the mentally retarded has been barred.

During-Reading Question: Why do you think it was easier for more states to give up the execution of the mentally handicapped than it was to give up the execution of juveniles?

As in *Atkins*, the objective indicia of consensus in this case—the rejection of the juvenile death penalty in the majority of States; the infrequency of its use even where it remains on the books; and the consistency in the trend toward abolition of the practice—provide sufficient evidence that today our society views juveniles, in the words *Atkins* used respecting the mentally retarded, as "categorically less culpable than the average criminal."

B

A majority of States have rejected the imposition of the death penalty on juvenile offenders under 18, and we now hold this is required by the Eighth Amendment.

Because the death penalty is the most severe punishment, the Eighth Amendment applies to it with special force. Capital punishment must be limited to those offenders who commit "a narrow category of the most serious crimes" and whose extreme culpability makes them "the most deserving of execution." This principle is implemented throughout the capital sentencing process. States must give narrow and precise definition to the aggravating factors that can result in a capital sentence. In any capital case a defendant has wide latitude to raise as a mitigating factor "any aspect of [his or her] character or record and any of the circumstances of the offense that the defendant proffers as a basis for a sentence less than death." There are a number of crimes that beyond question are severe in absolute terms, yet the death penalty may not be imposed for their commission. The death penalty may not be imposed on certain classes of offenders, such as juveniles under 16, the insane, and the mentally retarded, no matter how heinous the crime. These rules vindicate the underlying principle that the death penalty is reserved for a narrow category of crimes and offenders.

Three general differences between juveniles under 18 and adults demonstrate that juvenile offenders cannot with reliability be classified among the worst offenders. First, as any parent knows and as the scientific and sociological studies respondent and his amici cite tend to confirm, "[a] lack of maturity and an underdeveloped sense of responsibility are found in youth more often than in adults and are more understandable among the young. These qualities often result in impetuous and ill-considered actions and decisions." It has been noted that "adolescents are overrepresented statistically in virtually every category of reckless behavior."

In recognition of the comparative immaturity and irresponsibility of juveniles, almost every State prohibits those under 18 years of age from voting, serving on juries, or marrying without parental consent.

The second area of difference is that juveniles are more vulnerable or susceptible to negative influences and outside pressures, including peer pressure. This is explained in part by the prevailing circumstance that juveniles have less control, or less experience with control, over their own environment.

The third broad difference is that the character of a juvenile is not as well formed as that of an adult. The personality traits of juveniles are more transitory, less fixed.

These differences render suspect any conclusion that a juvenile falls among the worst offenders. The susceptibility of juveniles to immature and irresponsible behavior means "their irresponsible conduct is not as morally reprehensible as that of an adult." Their own vulnerability and comparative lack of control over their immediate surroundings mean juveniles have a greater claim than adults to be forgiven for failing to escape negative influences in their whole environment. The reality that juveniles still struggle to define their identity means it is less supportable to conclude that even a heinous crime committed by a juvenile is evidence of irretrievably depraved character. From a moral standpoint it would be misguided to equate the failings of a minor with those of an adult, for a greater possibility exists that a minor's character deficiencies will be reformed. Indeed, "[t]he relevance of youth as a mitigating factor derives from the fact that the signature qualities of youth are transient; as individuals mature, the impetuousness and recklessness that may dominate in younger years can subside."

In *Thompson*, a plurality of the Court recognized the import of these characteristics with respect to juveniles under 16, and relied on them to hold that the Eighth Amendment prohibited the imposition of the death penalty on juveniles below that age. We conclude the same reasoning applies to all juvenile offenders under 18.

Once the diminished culpability of juveniles is recognized, it is evident that the penological justifications for the death penalty apply to them with lesser force than to adults. We have held there are two distinct social purposes served by the death penalty: "retribution and deterrence of capital crimes by prospective offenders." As for retribution, we remarked in Atkins that "[i]f the culpability of the average murderer is insufficient to justify the most extreme sanction available to the State, the lesser culpability of the mentally retarded offender surely does not merit that form of retribution.". The same conclusions follow from the lesser culpability of the juvenile offender. Whether viewed as an attempt to express the community's moral outrage or as an attempt to right the balance for the wrong to the victim, the case for retribution is not as strong with a minor as with an adult. Retribution is not proportional if the law's most severe penalty is imposed on one whose culpability or blameworthiness is diminished, to a substantial degree, by reason of youth and immaturity.

As for deterrence, it is unclear whether the death penalty has a significant or even measurable deterrent effect on juveniles, as counsel for the petitioner acknowledged at oral argument. In general we leave to legislatures the assessment of the efficacy of various criminal penalty schemes. Here, however, the absence of evidence of deterrent effect is of special concern because the same characteristics that render juveniles less culpable than adults suggest as well that juveniles will be less susceptible to deterrence. In particular, as the plurality observed in *Thompson*, "[t]he likelihood that the teenage offender has made the kind of cost-benefit analysis that attaches any weight to the possibility of execution is so remote as to be virtually nonexistent." To the extent the juvenile death penalty might have residual deterrent effect, it is worth noting that the punishment of life imprisonment without the possibility of parole is itself a severe sanction, in particular for a young person.

In concluding that neither retribution nor deterrence provides adequate justification for imposing the death penalty on juvenile offenders, we cannot deny or overlook the brutal crimes too many juvenile offenders have committed. Certainly it can be argued, although we by no means concede the point, that a rare case might arise in which a juvenile offender has sufficient psychological maturity, and at the same time demonstrates sufficient depravity, to merit a sentence of death. Indeed, this possibility is the linchpin of one contention pressed by petitioner and his amici. They assert that even assuming the truth of the observations we have made about juveniles' diminished culpability in general, jurors nonetheless should be allowed to consider mitigating arguments related to youth on a case-by-case basis, and in some cases to impose the death penalty if justified. A central feature of death penalty sentencing is a particular assessment of the circumstances of the crime and the characteristics of the offender. The system is designed to consider both aggravating and mitigating circumstances, including youth, in every case. Given this Court's own insistence on individualized consideration, petitioner maintains that it is both arbitrary and unnecessary to adopt a categorical rule barring imposition of the death penalty on any offender under 18 years of age.

During-Reading Question: The Court discusses the two reasons for having a death penalty—retribution and deterrence. In general, do you think either (or both) of these is a good reason to have a death penalty? Please explain your reasoning.

We disagree. The differences between juvenile and adult offenders are too marked and well understood to risk allowing a youthful person to receive the death penalty despite insufficient culpability. An unacceptable likelihood exists that the brutality or cold-blooded nature of any particular crime would overpower mitigating arguments based on youth as a matter of course, even where the juvenile offender's objective immaturity, vulnerability, and lack of true depravity should require a sentence less severe than death. In some cases a defendant's youth may even be counted against him. In this very case, as we noted above, the prosecutor argued Simmons' youth was aggravating rather than mitigating. While this sort of overreaching could be corrected by a particular rule to ensure that the mitigating force of youth is not overlooked, that would not address our larger concerns.

It is difficult even for expert psychologists to differentiate between the juvenile offender whose crime reflects unfortunate yet transient immaturity, and the rare juvenile offender whose crime reflects irreparable corruption. As we understand it, this difficulty underlies the rule forbidding psychiatrists from diagnosing any patient under 18 as having antisocial personality disorder, a disorder also referred to as psychopathy or sociopathy, and which is characterized by callousness, cynicism, and contempt for the feelings, rights, and suffering of others. If trained psychiatrists with the advantage of clinical testing and observation refrain, despite diagnostic expertise, from assessing any juvenile under 18 as having antisocial personality disorder, we conclude that States should refrain from asking jurors to issue a far graver condemnation—that a juvenile offender merits the death penalty. When a juvenile offender commits a heinous crime, the State can exact forfeiture of some of the most basic liberties, but the State cannot extinguish his life and his potential to attain a mature understanding of his own humanity.

Drawing the line at 18 years of age is subject, of course, to the objections always raised against categorical rules. The qualities that distinguish juveniles from adults do not disappear when an individual turns 18. By the same token, some under 18 have already attained a level of maturity some adults will never reach. For the reasons we have discussed, however, a line must be drawn. The plurality opinion in *Thompson* drew the line at 16. In the intervening years the *Thompson* plurality's conclusion that offenders under 16 may not be executed has not been challenged. The logic of *Thompson* extends to those who are under 18. The age of 18 is the point where society draws the line for many purposes between childhood and adulthood. It is, we conclude, the age at which the line for death eligibility ought to rest.

During-Reading Questions: The Court believes there is a distinct difference in the level of maturity between a sixteen-year-old and an eighteen-year-old. Do you agree with this? Why or why not?

In holding that the death penalty cannot be imposed upon juvenile offenders, we take into account the circumstance that some States have relied on *Stanford* in seeking the death penalty against juvenile offenders. This consideration, however, does not outweigh our conclusion that *Stanford* should no longer control in those few pending cases or in those yet to arise.

IV

Our determination that the death penalty is disproportionate punishment for offenders under 18 finds confirmation in the stark reality that the United States is the only country in the world that continues to give official sanction to the juvenile death penalty. This reality does not become controlling, for the task of interpreting the Eighth Amendment remains our responsibility. Yet at least from the time of the Court's decision in *Trop v. Dulles*, the Court has referred to the laws of other countries and to international authorities as instructive for its interpretation of the Eighth Amendment's prohibition of "cruel and unusual punishments."

During-Reading Question: Trop v. Dulles *was decided in 1958 and was a case where a natural-born citizen of the United States had been denied citizenship rights (the ability to obtain a passport) because he had deserted the army during World War II. Why do you think that the Court decided to look to other countries after this time to see what might constitute "cruel and unusual" punishment?*

As respondent and a number of amici emphasize, Article 37 of the United Nations Convention on the Rights of the Child, which every country in the world has ratified save for the United States and Somalia, contains an express prohibition on capital punishment for crimes committed by juveniles under 18. No ratifying country has entered a reservation to the provision prohibiting the execution of juvenile offenders. Parallel prohibitions are contained in other significant international covenants.

Respondent and his amici have submitted, and petitioner does not contest, that only seven countries other than the United States have executed juvenile offenders since 1990: Iran, Pakistan, Saudi Arabia, Yemen, Nigeria, the Democratic Republic of Congo, and China. Since then each of these countries has either abolished capital punishment for juveniles or made public disavowal of the practice. In sum, it is fair to say that the United States now stands alone in a world that has turned its face against the juvenile death penalty.

Though the international covenants prohibiting the juvenile death penalty are of more recent date, it is instructive to note that the United Kingdom abolished the juvenile death penalty before these covenants came into being. The United Kingdom's experience bears particular relevance here in light of the historic ties between our countries and in light of the Eighth Amendment's own origins. The Amendment was modeled on a parallel provision in the English Declaration of Rights of 1689, which provided: "[E]xcessive Bail ought not to be required nor excessive Fines imposed; nor cruel and unusual Punishments inflicted." As of now, the United Kingdom has abolished the death penalty in its entirety; but, decades before it took this step, it recognized the disproportionate nature of the juvenile death penalty; and it abolished that penalty as a separate matter. In 1930 an official committee recommended that the minimum age for execution be raised to 21. Parliament then enacted the Children and Young Person's Act of 1933, which prevented execution of those aged 18 at the date of the sentence. And in 1948, Parliament enacted the Criminal Justice Act, prohibiting the execution of any person under 18 at the time of the offense. In the 56 years that have passed since the United Kingdom abolished the juvenile death penalty, the weight of authority against it there, and in the international community, has become well established.

During-Reading Question: Even though all other countries in the world had abolished a juvenile death penalty at the time this case was decided, the Court spends more time considering what had been done in the United Kingdom. Why do you think it chose to place more focus on that country?

It is proper that we acknowledge the overwhelming weight of international opinion against the juvenile death penalty, resting in large part on the understanding that the instability and emotional imbalance of young people may often be a factor in the crime. The opinion of the world community, while not controlling our outcome, does provide respected and significant confirmation for our own conclusions.

Over time, from one generation to the next, the Constitution has come to earn the high respect and even, as Madison dared to hope, the veneration of the American people. The document sets forth, and rests upon, innovative principles original to the American experience, such as federalism; a proven balance in political mechanisms through separation of powers; specific guarantees for the accused in criminal cases; and broad provisions to secure individual freedom and preserve human dignity. These doctrines and guarantees are central to the American experience and remain essential to our present-day self-definition and national identity. Not the least of the reasons we honor the Constitution, then, is because we know it to be our own. It does not lessen our fidelity to the Constitution or our pride in its origins to acknowledge that the express affirmation of certain fundamental rights by other nations and peoples simply underscores the centrality of those same rights within our own heritage of freedom.

The Eighth and Fourteenth Amendments forbid imposition of the death penalty on offenders who were under the age of 18 when their crimes were committed. The judgment of the Missouri Supreme Court setting aside the sentence of death imposed upon Christopher Simmons is affirmed.

It is so ordered.

Post-Reading Questions

1. Go back and reread the third paragraph from the end of the decision that starts with "Over time, from one generation to the next . . ." What is the Court doing in this paragraph? Why do you think Justice Kennedy felt the need to include this paragraph/explanation? Who is the audience he is addressing?
2. Do you agree with the finding of the Court? Is eighteen years a good cutoff age to deny the imposition of the death penalty, or is it too high? Is it too low? Give the reasoning behind your answer.

Further Explorations

Exploring the Story

Visit the following article from the Death Penalty Information Center to learn about other juveniles facing execution at the time the *Simmons* case was decided: Death Penalty Information Center (n.d.). Juvnile offenders who were on death row. Retrieved from https://deathpenaltyinfo.org/juvenile-offenders-who-were-death-row. After reading about these cases, do you still think the Supreme Court made the correct decision?

Exploring the Law

Do some research into the history of juvenile law in the United States. What conclusions can you draw about the purpose of the juvenile law system? How is it different from the adult system? Do you think it is effective in the United States?

Exploring the Effects

Examine the similarities and differences between how the United States and other countries around the world use the death penalty as it applies to adults. What do other countries do? Pay particular attention to the use of the death penalty by the United Kingdom. Why is what the United Kingdom does very persuasive in this case but not when it comes to the execution of adults?

Activities for Extending the Learning

As a result of the decision in this case and others, members of the U.S. House of Representatives proposed a nonbinding resolution expressing that decisions of the Supreme Court should not be based on foreign laws or decisions. Do some research into the resolution and the reasoning behind it, and conduct a class debate on whether the United States should be influenced by other countries when it examines laws.

CASE #2: *MEDELLÍN V. TEXAS*

Pre-Reading Questions

1. Explore the history of the Vienna Convention. Why is this such an important treaty, and what rights does it guarantee?
2. What is a writ of habeas corpus? What purpose does this type of writ serve for someone accused of a crime?

Medellín v. Texas, 552 U. S. 491 (2008)

Chief Justice Roberts delivered the opinion of the Court.

The International Court of Justice (ICJ), located in the Hague, is a tribunal established pursuant to the United Nations Charter to adjudicate disputes between member states. In *The Case Concerning Avena and Other Mexican Nationals* (Mex. v. U. S.), 2004 I. J. 12, that tribunal considered a claim brought by Mexico against the United States. The ICJ held that, based on violations of the Vienna Convention, 51 named Mexican nationals were entitled to review and reconsideration of their state-court convictions and sentences in the United States. This was so regardless of any forfeiture of the right to raise Vienna Convention claims because of a failure to comply with generally applicable state rules governing challenges to criminal convictions.

In *Sanchez-Llamas v. Oregon*, 548 U. S. 331 (2006)—issued after *Avena* but involving individuals who were not named in the *Avena* judgment—we held that, contrary to the ICJ's determination, the Vienna Convention did not preclude the application of state default rules. After the *Avena* decision, President George W. Bush determined, through a Memorandum to the Attorney General, that the United States would "discharge its international obligations" under *Avena* "by having State courts give effect to the decision."

Petitioner José Ernesto Medellín, who had been convicted and sentenced in Texas state court for murder, is one of the 51 Mexican nationals named in the *Avena* decision. Relying on the ICJ's decision and the President's Memorandum, Medellín filed an application for a writ of habeas corpus in state court. The Texas Court of Criminal Appeals dismissed Medellín's application as an abuse of the writ under state law, given Medellín's failure to raise his Vienna Convention claim in a timely manner under state law. We granted certiorari to decide two questions. First, is the ICJ's judgment in *Avena* directly enforceable as domestic law in a state court in the United States? Second, does the President's Memorandum independently require the States to provide review and reconsideration of the claims of the 51 Mexican nationals named in *Avena* without regard to state procedural default rules? We conclude that neither *Avena* nor the President's Memorandum constitutes directly enforceable federal law that pre-empts state limitations on the filing of successive habeas petitions. We therefore affirm the decision below.

I

A

In 1969, the United States, upon the advice and consent of the Senate, ratified the Vienna Convention on Consular Relations and the Optional Protocol Concerning the Compulsory Settlement of Disputes to the Vienna Convention. The preamble to the Convention provides that its purpose is to "contribute to the development of friendly relations among nations." Toward that end, Article 36 of the Convention was drafted to "facilitat[e] the exercise of consular functions." It provides that if a person detained by a foreign country "so requests, the competent authorities of the receiving State shall, without delay, inform the consular post of the sending State" of such detention, and "inform the [detainee] of his righ[t]" to request assistance from the consul of his own state.

The Optional Protocol provides a venue for the resolution of disputes arising out of the interpretation or application of the Vienna Convention. Under the Protocol, such disputes "shall lie within the compulsory jurisdiction of the International Court of Justice" and "may accordingly be brought before the [ICJ] . . . by any party to the dispute being a Party to the present Protocol."

The ICJ is "the principal judicial organ of the United Nations." It was established in 1945 pursuant to the United Nations Charter. The ICJ Statute—annexed to the U. N. Charter—provides the organizational framework and governing procedures for cases brought before the ICJ. Statute of the International Court of Justice.

Under Article 94(1) of the U. N. Charter, "[e]ach Member of the United Nations undertakes to comply with the decision of the [ICJ] in any case to which it is a party." The ICJ's jurisdiction in any particular case, however, is dependent upon the consent of the parties. The ICJ Statute delineates two ways in which a nation may consent to ICJ jurisdiction: It may consent generally to jurisdiction on any question arising under a treaty or general international law, or it may consent specifically to jurisdiction over a particular category of cases or disputes pursuant to a separate treaty. The United States originally consented to the general jurisdiction of the ICJ when it filed a declaration recognizing compulsory jurisdiction under Art. 36(2) in 1946. The United States withdrew from general ICJ jurisdiction in 1985. By ratifying the Optional Protocol to the Vienna Convention, the United States consented to the specific jurisdiction of the ICJ with respect to claims arising out of the Vienna Convention. On March 7, 2005, subsequent to the ICJ's judgment in *Avena*, the United States gave notice of withdrawal from the Optional Protocol to the Vienna Convention.

During-Reading Questions: According to the Geneva Convention, what two things can a person from another country receive from a country who has detained them? According to the U.N. charter, what does a country have to do to agree to the jurisdiction of the International Court of Justice? At the time of this case, did the United States consent to the jurisdiction of the ICJ?

B

Petitioner José Ernesto Medellín, a Mexican national, has lived in the United States since preschool. A member of the "Black and Whites" gang, Medellín was convicted of capital murder and sentenced to death in Texas for the gang rape and brutal murders of two Houston teenagers.

On June 24, 1993, 14-year-old Jennifer Ertman and 16-year-old Elizabeth Pena were walking home when they encountered Medellín and several fellow gang members. Medellín attempted to engage Elizabeth in conversation. When she tried to run, petitioner threw her to the ground. Jennifer was grabbed by other gang members when she, in response to her friend's cries, ran back to help. The gang members raped both girls for over an hour. Then, to prevent their victims from identifying them, Medellín and his fellow gang members murdered the girls and discarded their bodies in a wooded area. Medellín was personally responsible for strangling at least one of the girls with her own shoelace.

Medellín was arrested at approximately 4 a.m. on June 29, 1993. A few hours later, between 5:54 and 7:23 a.m., Medellín was given Miranda warnings; he then signed a written waiver and gave a detailed written confession. Local law enforcement officers did not, however, inform Medellín of his Vienna Convention right to notify the Mexican consulate of his detention. Medellín was convicted of capital murder and sentenced to death; his conviction and sentence were affirmed on appeal. *Medellín v. State*.

Medellín first raised his Vienna Convention claim in his first application for state postconviction relief. The state trial court held that the claim was procedurally defaulted because Medellín had failed to raise it at trial or on direct review. The trial court also rejected the Vienna Convention claim on the merits, finding that Medellín had "fail[ed] to show that any non-notification of the Mexican authorities impacted on the validity of his conviction or punishment."

Medellín then filed a habeas petition in Federal District Court. The District Court denied relief, holding that Medellín's Vienna Convention claim was procedurally defaulted and that Medellín had failed to show prejudice arising from the Vienna Convention violation.

While Medellín's application for a certificate of appealability was pending in the Fifth Circuit, the ICJ issued its decision in *Avena*. The ICJ held that the United States had violated Article 36(1)(b) of the Vienna Convention by failing to inform the 51 named Mexican nationals, including Medellín, of their Vienna Convention rights. In the ICJ's determination, the United States was obligated "to provide, by means of its own choosing, review and reconsideration of the convictions and sentences of the [affected] Mexican nationals." The ICJ indicated that such review was required without regard to state procedural default rules.

The Fifth Circuit denied a certificate of appealability. The court concluded that the Vienna Convention did not confer individually enforceable rights. The court further ruled that it was in any event bound by this Court's decision in *Breard v. Greene*, which held that Vienna Convention claims are subject to procedural default rules, rather than by the ICJ's contrary decision in *Avena*.

This Court granted certiorari. Before we heard oral argument, however, President George W. Bush issued his Memorandum to the United States Attorney General, providing:

> I have determined, pursuant to the authority vested in me as President by the Constitution and the laws of the United States of America, that the United States will discharge its international obligations under the decision of the International Court of Justice in [*Avena*], by having State courts give effect to the decision in accordance with general principles of comity in cases filed by the 51 Mexican nationals addressed in that decision.

During-Reading Questions: What is the idea of comity as it relates to the law? How could the president's memorandum impact this case?

Medellín, relying on the President's Memorandum and the ICJ's decision in *Avena*, filed a second application for habeas relief in state court. Because the state-court proceedings might have provided Medellín with the review and reconsideration he requested, and because his claim for federal relief might otherwise have been barred, we dismissed his petition for certiorari as improvidently granted.

The Texas Court of Criminal Appeals subsequently dismissed Medellín's second state habeas application as an abuse of the writ. In the court's view, neither the *Avena* decision nor the President's Memorandum was "binding federal law" that could displace the State's limitations on the filing of successive habeas applications. We again granted certiorari.

During-Reading Questions: Medellín's case had many steps before it finally reached this case. What was the process that led to the Supreme Court hearing his case? While the initial case was about a writ of habeas corpus, what issue is the Court really deciding in this case?

II

Medellín first contends that the ICJ's judgment in *Avena* constitutes a "binding" obligation on the state and federal courts of the United States. He argues that "by virtue of the Supremacy Clause, the treaties requiring compliance with the *Avena* judgment are already the 'Law of the Land' by which all state and federal courts in this country are 'bound.' " Accordingly, *Medellín* argues, *Avena* is a binding federal rule of decision that pre-empts contrary state limitations on successive habeas petitions.

No one disputes that the *Avena* decision—a decision that flows from the treaties through which the United States submitted to ICJ jurisdiction with respect to Vienna Convention disputes—constitutes an international law obligation on the part of the United States. But not all international law obligations automatically constitute binding federal law enforceable in United States courts. The question we confront here is whether the *Avena* judgment has automatic domestic legal effect such that the judgment of its own force applies in state and federal courts.

This Court has long recognized the distinction between treaties that automatically have effect as domestic law, and those that—while they constitute international law commitments—do not by themselves function as binding federal law. The distinction was well explained by Chief Justice Marshall's opinion in *Foster v. Neilson*, which held that a treaty is "equivalent to an act of the legislature," and hence self-executing, when it "operates of itself without the aid of any legislative provision." When, in contrast, "[treaty] stipulations are not self-executing they can only be enforced pursuant to legislation to carry them into effect." *Whitney v. Robertson.* In sum, while treaties "may comprise international commitments . . . they are not domestic law unless Congress has either enacted implementing statutes or the treaty itself conveys an intention that it be 'self-executing' and is ratified on these terms."

A treaty is, of course, "primarily a compact between independent nations." It ordinarily "depends for the enforcement of its provisions on the interest and the honor of the governments which are parties to it."

Medellín and his amici nonetheless contend that the Optional Protocol, United Nations Charter, and ICJ Statute supply the "relevant obligation" to give the *Avena* judgment binding effect in the domestic courts of the United States. Because none of these treaty sources creates binding federal law in the absence of implementing legislation, and because it is uncontested that no such legislation exists, we conclude that the *Avena* judgment is not automatically binding domestic law.

During-Reading Questions: The last paragraph refers to the "amici" of Medellin. What are amici (or amicus) under the law and what purpose do they serve in the decision of a case? What does the Court say are the two things that can cause the provisions of a treaty to become enforceable?

A

The interpretation of a treaty, like the interpretation of a statute, begins with its text. Because a treaty ratified by the United States is "an agreement among sovereign powers," we have also considered as "aids to its interpretation" the negotiation and drafting history of the treaty as well as "the postratification understanding" of signatory nations.

As a signatory to the Optional Protocol, the United States agreed to submit disputes arising out of the Vienna Convention to the ICJ. The Protocol provides: "Disputes arising out of the interpretation or application of the [Vienna] Convention shall lie within the compulsory jurisdiction of the International Court of Justice." Of course, submitting to jurisdiction and agreeing to be bound are two different things. A party could, for example, agree to compulsory nonbinding arbitration. Such an agreement would require the party to appear before the arbitral tribunal without obligating the party to treat the tribunal's decision as binding.

The most natural reading of the Optional Protocol is as a bare grant of jurisdiction. It provides only that "[d]isputes arising out of the interpretation or application of the [Vienna] Convention shall lie within the compulsory jurisdiction of the International Court of Justice" and "may accordingly be brought before the [ICJ] . . . by any party to the dispute being a Party to the present Protocol." The Protocol says nothing about the effect of an ICJ decision and does not itself commit signatories to comply with an ICJ judgment. The Protocol is similarly silent as to any enforcement mechanism.

The obligation on the part of signatory nations to comply with ICJ judgments derives not from the Optional Protocol, but rather from Article 94 of the United Nations Charter—the provision that specifically addresses the effect of ICJ decisions. Article 94(1) provides that "[e]ach Member of the United Nations undertakes to comply with the decision of the [ICJ] in any case to which it is a party."

We agree with this construction of Article 94. The Article is not a directive to domestic courts. It does not provide that the United States "shall" or "must" comply with an ICJ decision, nor indicate that the Senate that ratified the U.N. Charter intended to vest ICJ decisions with immediate legal effect in domestic courts. Instead, "[t]he words of Article 94 . . . call upon governments to take certain action." In other words, the U. N. Charter reads like "a compact between independent nations" that "depends for the enforcement of its provisions on the interest and the honor of the governments which are parties to it."

The U. N. Charter's provision of an express diplomatic—that is, nonjudicial—remedy is itself evidence that ICJ judgments were not meant to be enforceable in domestic courts. And even this "quintessentially international remed[y]," is not absolute. First, the Security Council must "dee[m] necessary" the issuance of a recommendation or measure to effectuate the judgment. Second, as the President and Senate were undoubtedly aware in subscribing to the U. N. Charter and Optional Protocol, the United States retained the unqualified right to exercise its veto of any Security Council resolution.

If ICJ judgments were instead regarded as automatically enforceable domestic law, they would be immediately and directly binding on state and federal courts pursuant to the Supremacy Clause. Mexico or the ICJ would have no need to proceed to the Security Council to enforce the judgment in this case. Noncompliance with an ICJ judgment through exercise of the Security Council veto—always regarded as an option by the Executive and ratifying Senate during and after consideration of the U. N. Charter, Optional Protocol, and ICJ Statute—would no longer be a viable alternative. There would be nothing to veto. In light of the U.N. Charter's remedial scheme, there is no reason to believe that the President and Senate signed up for such a result.

Medellín argues that because the *Avena* case involves him, it is clear that he—and the 50 other Mexican nationals named in the *Avena* decision—should be regarded as parties to the *Avena* judgment. But cases before the ICJ are often precipitated by disputes involving particular persons or entities, disputes that a nation elects to take up as its own. That has never been understood to alter the express and established rules that only nation-states may be parties before the ICJ.

It is, moreover, well settled that the United States' interpretation of a treaty "is entitled to great weight." *Sumitomo Shoji America, Inc. v. Avagliano*. The Executive Branch has unfailingly adhered to its view that the relevant treaties do not create domestically enforceable federal law.

The pertinent international agreements, therefore, do not provide for implementation of ICJ judgments through direct enforcement in domestic courts, and "where a treaty does not provide a particular remedy, either expressly or implicitly, it is not for the federal courts to impose one on the States through lawmaking of their own."

B

Given our obligation to interpret treaty provisions to determine whether they are self-executing, we have to confess that we do think it rather important to look to the treaty language to see what it has to say about the issue. That is after all what the Senate looks to in deciding whether to approve the treaty.

The interpretive approach employed by the Court today—resorting to the text—is hardly novel. In two early cases involving an 1819 land-grant treaty between Spain and the United States, Chief Justice Marshall found the language of the treaty dispositive. In *Foster*, after distinguishing between self-executing treaties (those "equivalent to an act of the legislature") and non-self-executing treaties (those "the legislature must execute"), Chief Justice Marshall held that the 1819 treaty was non-self-executing. Four years later, the Supreme Court considered another claim under the same treaty, but concluded that the treaty was self-executing. The reason was not because the treaty was sometimes self-executing and sometimes not, but because "the language of" the Spanish translation (brought to the Court's attention for the first time) indicated the parties' intent to ratify and confirm the land-grant "by force of the instrument itself."

Our Framers established a careful set of procedures that must be followed before federal law can be created under the Constitution—vesting that decision in the political branches, subject to checks and balances. They also recognized that treaties could create federal law, but again through the political branches, with the President making the treaty and the Senate approving it.

To read a treaty so that it sometimes has the effect of domestic law and sometimes does not is tantamount to vesting with the judiciary the power not only to interpret but also to create the law.

C

Our conclusion that *Avena* does not by itself constitute binding federal law is confirmed by the "postratification understanding" of signatory nations. There are currently 47 nations that are parties to the Optional Protocol and 171 nations that are parties to the Vienna Convention. Yet neither *Medellín* nor his amici have identified a single nation that treats ICJ judgments as binding in domestic courts. In determining that the Vienna Convention did not require certain relief in United States courts in *Sanchez-Llamas*, we found it pertinent that the requested relief would not be available under the treaty in any other signatory country. So too here the lack of any basis for supposing that any other country would treat ICJ judgments as directly enforceable as a matter of their domestic law strongly suggests that the treaty should not be so viewed in our courts.

Moreover, the consequences of *Medellín*'s argument give pause. An ICJ judgment, the argument goes, is not only binding domestic law but is also unassailable. As a result, neither Texas nor this Court may look behind a judgment and quarrel with its reasoning or result. (We already know, from *Sanchez-Llamas*, that this Court disagrees with both the reasoning and result in *Avena*.) *Medellín*'s interpretation would allow ICJ judgments to override otherwise binding state law; there is nothing in his logic that would exempt contrary federal law from the same fate. And there is nothing to prevent the ICJ from ordering state courts to annul criminal convictions and sentences, for any reason deemed sufficient by the ICJ. Indeed, that is precisely the relief Mexico requested.

During-Reading Question: What does the Court say is the big problem with automatically saying that states must immediately follow the decision of the ICJ?

Even the dissent flinches at reading the relevant treaties to give rise to self-executing ICJ judgments in all cases. It admits that "Congress is unlikely to authorize automatic judicial enforceability of all ICJ judgments, for that could include some politically sensitive judgments and others better suited for enforcement by other branches." Our point precisely. But the lesson to draw from that insight is hardly that the judiciary should decide which judgments are politically sensitive and which are not.

D

Our holding does not call into question the ordinary enforcement of foreign judgments or international arbitral agreements. Indeed, we agree with *Medellín* that, as a general matter, "an agreement to abide by the result" of an international adjudication—or what he really means, an agreement to give the result of such adjudication domestic legal effect—can be a treaty obligation like any other, so long as the agreement is consistent with the Constitution. The point is that the particular treaty obligations on which *Medellín* relies do not of their own force create domestic law.

[W]hile the ICJ's judgment in Avena creates an international law obligation on the part of the United States, it does not of its own force constitute binding federal law that preempts state restrictions on the filing of successive habeas petitions. As we noted in *Sanchez-Llamas*, a contrary conclusion would be extraordinary, given that basic rights guaranteed by our own Constitution do not have the effect of displacing state procedural rules. Nothing in the text, background, negotiating and drafting history, or practice among signatory nations suggests that the President or Senate intended the improbable result of giving the judgments of an international tribunal a higher status than that enjoyed by "many of our most fundamental constitutional protections."

During-Reading Question: After reading section II, which do you think the Supreme Court would say is more important: the United States Constitution or the judgments of the International Court of Justice? Find at least three quotes from this section to support your position.

III

Medellín next argues that the ICJ's judgment in *Avena* is binding on state courts by virtue of the President's February 28, 2005 Memorandum. The United States contends that while the *Avena* judgment does not of its own force require domestic courts to set aside ordinary rules of procedural default, that judgment became the law of the land with precisely that effect pursuant to the President's Memorandum and his power "to establish binding rules of decision that preempt contrary state law." Accordingly, we must decide whether the President's declaration alters our conclusion that the *Avena* judgment is not a rule of domestic law binding in state and federal courts.

A

The United States maintains that the President's constitutional role "uniquely qualifies" him to resolve the sensitive foreign policy decisions that bear on compliance with an ICJ decision and "to do so expeditiously." In this case, the President seeks to vindicate United States interests in ensuring the reciprocal observance of the Vienna Convention, protecting relations with foreign governments, and demonstrating commitment to the role of international law. These interests are plainly compelling.

Such considerations, however, do not allow us to set aside first principles. The President's authority to act, as with the exercise of any governmental power, "must stem either from an act of Congress or from the Constitution itself." *Youngstown Sheet & Tube Co. v. Sawyer*.

Justice Jackson's familiar tripartite scheme provides the accepted framework for evaluating executive action in this area. First, "[w]hen the President acts pursuant to an express or implied authorization of Congress, his authority is at its maximum, for it includes all that he possesses in his own right plus all that Congress can delegate." Second, "[w]hen the President acts in absence of either a congressional grant or denial of authority, he can only rely upon his own independent powers, but there is a zone of twilight in which he and Congress may have concurrent authority, or in which its distribution is uncertain." In this circumstance, Presidential authority can derive support from "congressional inertia, indifference or quiescence." Finally, "[w]hen the President takes measures incompatible with the expressed or implied will of Congress, his power is at its lowest ebb," and the Court can sustain his actions "only by disabling the Congress from acting upon the subject."

B

The United States marshals two principal arguments in favor of the President's authority "to establish binding rules of decision that preempt contrary state law." The Solicitor General first argues that the relevant treaties give the President the authority to implement the *Avena* judgment and that Congress has acquiesced in the exercise of such authority. The United States also relies upon an "independent" international dispute-resolution power wholly apart from the asserted authority based on the pertinent treaties. *Medellín* adds the additional argument that the President's Memorandum is a valid exercise of his power to take care that the laws be faithfully executed.

1

The United States maintains that the President's Memorandum is authorized by the Optional Protocol and the U. N. Charter. That is, because the relevant treaties "create an obligation to comply with *Avena*," they "implicitly give the President authority to implement that treaty-based obligation." As a result, the President's Memorandum is well grounded in the first category of the *Youngstown* framework.

We disagree. The President has an array of political and diplomatic means available to enforce international obligations, but unilaterally converting a non-self-executing treaty into a self-executing one is not among them. The responsibility for transforming an international obligation arising from a non-self-executing treaty into domestic law falls to Congress. As this Court has explained, when treaty stipulations are "not self-executing they can only be enforced pursuant to legislation to carry them into effect." Moreover, "[u]ntil such act shall be passed, the Court is not at liberty to disregard the existing laws on the subject."

The requirement that Congress, rather than the President, implement a non-self-executing treaty derives from the text of the Constitution, which divides the treaty-making power between the President and the Senate. The Constitution vests the President with the authority to "make" a treaty. If the Executive determines that a treaty should have domestic effect of its own force, that determination may be implemented "in mak[ing]" the treaty, by ensuring that it contains language plainly providing for domestic enforceability. If the treaty is to be self-executing in this respect, the Senate must consent to the treaty by the requisite two-thirds vote, *ibid.*, consistent with all other constitutional restraints.

Once a treaty is ratified without provisions clearly according it domestic effect, however, whether the treaty will ever have such effect is governed by the fundamental constitutional principle that "[t]he power to make the necessary laws is in Congress; the power to execute in the President." As already noted, the terms of a non-self-executing treaty can become domestic law only in the same way as any other law—through passage of legislation by both Houses of Congress, combined with either the President's signature or a congressional override of a Presidential veto. Indeed, "the President's power to see that the laws are faithfully executed refutes the idea that he is to be a lawmaker." *Youngstown.*

A non-self-executing treaty, by definition, is one that was ratified with the understanding that it is not to have domestic effect of its own force. That understanding precludes the assertion that Congress has implicitly authorized the President—acting on his own—to achieve precisely the same result. We therefore conclude, given the absence of congressional legislation, that the non-self-executing treaties at issue here did not "express[ly] or implied[ly]" vest the President with the unilateral authority to make them self-executing. Accordingly, the President's Memorandum does not fall within the first category of the *Youngstown* framework.

The United States nonetheless maintains that the President's Memorandum should be given effect as domestic law because "this case involves a valid Presidential action in the context of Congressional 'acquiescence.'" Under the *Youngstown* tripartite framework, congressional acquiescence is pertinent when the President's action falls within the second category—that is, when he "acts in absence of either a congressional grant or denial of authority." Here, however, as we have explained, the President's effort to accord domestic effect to the *Avena* judgment does not meet that prerequisite.

None of this is to say, however, that the combination of a non-self-executing treaty and the lack of implementing legislation precludes the President from acting to comply with an international treaty obligation. It is only to say that the Executive cannot unilaterally execute a non-self-executing treaty by giving it domestic effect. That is, the non-self-executing character of a treaty constrains the President's ability to comply with treaty commitments by unilaterally making the treaty binding on domestic courts. The President may comply with the treaty's obligations by some other means, so long as they are consistent with the Constitution. But he may not rely upon a non-self-executing treaty to "establish binding rules of decision that preempt contrary state law."

2

We thus turn to the United States' claim that—independent of the United States' treaty obligations—the Memorandum is a valid exercise of the President's foreign affairs authority to resolve claims disputes with foreign nations. The United States relies on a series of cases in which this Court has upheld the authority of the President to settle foreign claims pursuant to an executive agreement. In these cases this Court has explained that, if pervasive enough, a history of congressional acquiescence can be treated as a "gloss on 'Executive Power' vested in the President by §1 of Art. II."

This argument is of a different nature than the one rejected above. Rather than relying on the United States' treaty obligations, the President relies on an independent source of authority in ordering Texas to put aside its procedural bar to successive habeas petitions. Nevertheless, we find that our claims-settlement cases do not support the authority that the President asserts in this case.

The claims-settlement cases involve a narrow set of circumstances: the making of executive agreements to settle civil claims between American citizens and foreign governments or foreign nationals. They are based on the view that "a systematic, unbroken, executive practice, long pursued to the knowledge of the Congress and never before questioned," can "raise a presumption that the [action] had been [taken] in pursuance of its consent." As this Court explained in *American Ins. Assn. v. Garamendi*, "Making executive agreements to settle claims of American nationals against foreign governments is a particularly longstanding practice. . . . Given the fact that the practice goes back over 200 years, and has received congressional acquiescence throughout its history, the conclusion that the President's control of foreign relations includes the settlement of claims is indisputable."

Even still, the limitations on this source of executive power are clearly set forth and the Court has been careful to note that "[p]ast practice does not, by itself, create power."

The President's Memorandum is not supported by a "particularly longstanding practice" of congressional acquiescence, but rather is what the United States itself has described as "unprecedented action," Indeed, the Government has not identified a single instance in which the President has attempted (or Congress has acquiesced in) a Presidential directive issued to state courts, much less one that reaches deep into the heart of the State's police powers and compels state courts to reopen final criminal judgments and set aside neutrally applicable state laws. The Executive's narrow and strictly limited authority to settle international claims disputes pursuant to an executive agreement cannot stretch so far as to support the current Presidential Memorandum.

3

Medellín argues that the President's Memorandum is a valid exercise of his "Take Care" power. *Brief for Petitioner 28*. The United States, however, does not rely upon the President's responsibility to "take Care that the Laws be faithfully executed." *U. S. Const., Art. II, §3*. We think this a wise concession. This authority allows the President to execute the laws, not make them. For the reasons we have stated, the *Avena* judgment is not domestic law; accordingly, the President cannot rely on his Take Care powers here.

The judgment of the Texas Court of Criminal Appeals is affirmed.

It is so ordered.

Post-Reading Questions

1. Not only did this case decide whether a ruling of the ICJ had any weight in the United States, but it also decided a Presidential Memorandum for the enforcement of an ICJ ruling was outside of President Bush's presidential powers. Take a look at Article 2 of the United States Constitution. How does this case interpret the president's power?
2. What impact do you think the *Medellin* decision might have on citizens of the United States if they find themselves imprisoned in other countries? Should the United States Supreme Court be concerned with the opinion of other countries? Why or why not?

Further Explorations

Exploring the Story

- What happened to Jose Medellín after this decision? What was the international reaction to what happened to Medellín?
- Do some research on the International Court of Justice. What types of cases does it hear? What impact does its ruling have on those who come before it?

Exploring the Law

Research the *Avena* case decided by the ICJ. What was the background of the case and what was the underlying issue that the ICJ was addressing? What is it about that underlying issue that is so sensitive in the United States?

Exploring the Effects

Compare the decision in *Avena* (and Medellín as a party to the *Avena* decision) to the earlier decision in *Roper v. Simmons*. Why do you think the Court gives great weight to what the rest of the world does in reference to the death penalty for juveniles, but it discounts the judgment of the International Court of Justice (speaking for representatives of other countries) when it comes to the people represented in *Avena*. What are the distinctions between the two situations?

Activities for Extending the Learning

Go to the U.S. State Department website at www.state.gov and research the "Treaties in Force" that the United States currently has with other countries. Can you find any other treaties that might have implications for state's rights or implementation issues?

CASE #3: *MASLENJAK V. UNITED STATES*

Pre-Reading Questions

1. Do some research on the ethnic-based war in Bosnia from 1992 to 1995. Who were the groups involved in the wars? What were the issues? How did the different ethnic groups treat each other? What kind of immigration impact did it have on the United States as a result of the war in Bosnia?
2. What requirements do you think a person should have to meet to be allowed residence in the United States as a refugee? Should the process for a refugee to become a naturalized citizen be different from those who are seeking to immigrate to the United States under other circumstances?

Maslenjak v. United States, 582 U.S. ___ (2017)

Justice Kagan delivered the opinion of the Court.

A federal statute, 18 U. S. C. §1425(a), makes it a crime to "knowingly procure[ ], contrary to law, the naturalization of any person." And when someone is convicted under §1425(a) of unlawfully procuring her own naturalization, her citizenship is automatically revoked. See 8 U. S. C. §1451(e). In this case, we consider what the Government must prove to obtain such a conviction. We hold that the Government must establish that an illegal act by the defendant played some role in her acquisition of citizenship. When the illegal act is a false statement, that means demonstrating that the defendant lied about facts that would have mattered to an immigration official, because they would have justified denying naturalization or would predictably have led to other facts warranting that result.

I

Petitioner Divna Maslenjak is an ethnic Serb who resided in Bosnia during the 1990's, when a civil war between Serbs and Muslims divided the new country. In 1998, she and her family (her husband Ratko Maslenjak and their two children) met with an American immigration official to seek refugee status in the United States. Interviewed under oath, Maslenjak explained that the family feared persecution in Bosnia from both sides of the national rift. Muslims, she said, would mistreat them because of their ethnicity. And Serbs, she testified, would abuse them because her husband had evaded service in the Bosnian Serb Army by absconding to Serbia—where he remained hidden, apart from the family, for some five years. Persuaded of the Maslenjaks' plight, American officials granted them refugee status, and they immigrated to the United States in 2000.

Six years later, Maslenjak applied for naturalization. Question 23 on the application form asked whether she had ever given "false or misleading information" to a government official while applying for an immigration benefit; question 24 similarly asked whether she had ever "lied to a[ ] government official to gain entry or admission into the United States." *Id., at 72a.* Maslenjak answered "no" to both questions, while swearing under oath that her replies were true. She also swore that all her written answers were true during a subsequent interview with an immigration official. In August 2007, Maslenjak was naturalized as a U. S. citizen.

But Maslenjak's professions of honesty were false: In fact, she had made up much of the story she told to immigration officials when seeking refuge in this country. Her fiction began to unravel at around the same time she applied for citizenship. In 2006, immigration officials confronted Maslenjak's husband Ratko with records showing that he had not fled conscription during the Bosnian civil war; rather, he had served as an officer in the Bosnian Serb Army. And not only that: He had served in a brigade that participated in the Srebrenica massacre—a slaughter of some 8,000 Bosnian Muslim civilians. Within a year, the Government convicted Ratko on charges of making false statements on immigration documents. The newly naturalized Maslenjak attempted to prevent Ratko's deportation. During proceedings on that matter, Maslenjak admitted she had known all along that Ratko spent the war years not secreted in Serbia but fighting in Bosnia.

As a result, the Government charged Maslenjak with knowingly "procur[ing], contrary to law, [her] naturalization," in violation of 18 U. S. C. §1425(a). According to the Government's theory, Maslenjak violated §1425(a) because, in the course of procuring her naturalization, she broke another law: 18 U. S. C. §1015(a), which prohibits knowingly making a false statement under oath in a naturalization proceeding. The false statements the Government invoked were Maslenjak's answers to questions 23 and 24 on the citizenship application (stating that she had not lied in seeking refugee status) and her corresponding statements in the citizenship interview. Those statements, the Government argued to the District Court, need not have affected the naturalization decision to support a conviction under §1425(a). The court agreed: over Maslenjak's objection, it instructed the jury that a conviction was proper so long as the Government "prove[d] that one of the defendant's statements was false"—even if the statement was not "material" and "did not influence the decision to approve [her] naturalization." The jury returned a guilty verdict; and the District Court, based on that finding, stripped Maslenjak of her citizenship.

The United States Court of Appeals for the Sixth Circuit affirmed the conviction. As relevant here, the Sixth Circuit upheld the District Court's instructions that Maslenjak's false statements need not have influenced the naturalization decision. If, the Court of Appeals held, Maslenjak made false statements violating §1015(a) and she procured naturalization, then she also violated §1425(a)—irrespective of whether the false statements played any role in her obtaining citizenship. See 821 F. 3d 675, 685–686 (2016). That decision created a conflict in the Circuit Courts.[1] We granted certiorari to resolve it, 580 U.S. ___ (2017), and we now vacate the Sixth Circuit's judgment.

During-Reading Questions: The lower courts found that because Maslenjak lied about lying, that this was enough to revoke her citizenship. Do you agree with the lower courts? Why or why not?

II

A

Section 1425(a), the parties agree, makes it a crime to commit some other illegal act in connection with naturalization. But the parties dispute the nature of the required connection. Maslenjak argues that the relationship must be "causal" in kind: A person "procures" her naturalization "contrary to law," she contends, only if a predicate crime in some way "contribut[ed]" to her gaining citizenship. By contrast, the Government proposes a basically chronological link: Section 1425(a), it urges, "punishes the commission of other violations of law in the course of procuring naturalization"—even if the illegality could not have had any effect on the naturalization decision. We conclude that Maslenjak has the better of this argument.

We begin, as usual, with the statutory text. In ordinary usage, "to procure" something is "to get possession of" it. *Webster's Third New International Dictionary* 1809 (2002); accord, *Black's Law Dictionary* 1401 (10th ed. 2014) (defining "procure" as "[t]o obtain (something), esp. by special effort or means"). So to "procure . . . naturalization" means to obtain naturalization (or, to use another word, citizenship). The adverbial phrase "contrary to law," wedged in between "procure" and "naturalization," then specifies how a person must procure naturalization so as to run afoul of the statute: in contravention of the law—or, in a word, illegally. Putting the pieces together, someone "procure[s], contrary to law, naturalization" when she obtains citizenship illegally.

During-Reading Questions: What is the Court doing here? Why is it important to determine what the meaning of words are in this case?

What, then, does that whole phrase mean? The most natural understanding is that the illegal act must have somehow contributed to the obtaining of citizenship. Consider if someone said to you: "John obtained that painting illegally." You might imagine that he stole it off the walls of a museum. Or that he paid for it with a forged check. Or that he impersonated the true buyer when the auction house delivered it. But in all events, you would imagine illegal acts in some kind of means-end relation—or otherwise said, in some kind of causal relation—to the painting's acquisition. If someone said to you, "John obtained that painting illegally, but his unlawful acts did not play any role in his obtaining it," you would not have a clue what the statement meant. You would think it nonsense—or perhaps the opening of a riddle. That is because if no illegal act contributed at all to getting the painting, then the painting would not have been gotten illegally. And the same goes for naturalization. If whatever illegal conduct occurring within the naturalization process was a causal dead-end—if, so to speak, the ripples from that act could not have reached the decision to award citizenship—then the act cannot support a charge that the applicant obtained naturalization illegally. The conduct, though itself illegal, would not also make the obtaining of citizenship so. To get citizenship unlawfully, we understand, is to get it through an unlawful means—and that is just to say that an illegality played some role in its acquisition.

The Government's contrary view—that §1425(a) requires only a "violation[ ] of law in the course of procuring naturalization"—falters on the way language naturally works. Return for a moment to our artwork example. Imagine this time that John made an illegal turn while driving to the auction house to purchase a painting. Would you say that he had "procured the painting illegally" because he happened to violate the law in the course of obtaining it? Not likely. And again, the same is true with respect to naturalization. Suppose that an applicant for citizenship fills out the necessary paperwork in a government office with a knife tucked away in her handbag (but never mentioned or used). She has violated the law—specifically, a statute criminalizing the possession of a weapon in a federal building. And she has surely done so "in the course of" procuring citizenship. But would you say, using English as you ordinarily would, that she has "procure[d]" her citizenship "contrary to law" (or, as you would really speak, "illegally")? Once again, no. That is because the violation of law and the acquisition of citizenship are in that example merely coincidental: The one has no causal relation to the other.

During-Reading Questions: Usually in Supreme Court cases, the Court relies on legal precedent (i.e., cases similar to the case at hand) to help guide its decision. However in this case, the Court is doing something else. What is it doing to help make its point? How convincing is it? What does it also say about the issues presented in this case?

The Government responds to such examples by seeking to define them out of the statute, but that effort falls short for multiple reasons. According to the Government, the laws to which §1425(a) speaks are only laws "pertaining to naturalization." But to begin with, that claim fails on its own terms. The Government's proposed limitation has no basis in §1425(a)'s text (which refers to "law" generally); it is a deus ex machina—rationalized only by calling it "necessary," and serving only to get the Government out of a tight interpretive spot. Indeed, the Government does not really buy its own argument: at another point, it asserts that an applicant for citizenship can violate §1425(a) by bribing a government official, even though the law against that conduct has nothing in particular to do with naturalization. And still more important, the Government's (sometime) carve-out does nothing to alter the linguistic understanding that gives force to the examples the Government would exclude—and that applies just as well to every application that would remain. Laws pertaining to naturalization, in other words, are subject to the same rules of language usage as laws concerning other subjects. And under those rules, as we have shown, §1425(a) demands a means-end connection between a legal violation and naturalization. Take §1015(a)'s bar on making false statements in connection with naturalization—the prototypical §1425(a) predicate, and the one at issue here. If such a statement (in an interview, say) has no bearing at all on the decision to award citizenship, then it cannot render that award illegally gained.

The broader statutory context reinforces that point, because the Government's reading would create a profound mismatch between the requirements for naturalization on the one hand and those for denaturalization on the other. The immigration statute requires all applicants for citizenship to have "good moral character," and largely defines that term through a list of unlawful or unethical behaviors. On the Government's theory, some legal violations that do not justify denying citizenship under that definition would nonetheless justify revoking it later. Again, false statements under §1015(a) offer an apt illustration. The statute's description of "good moral character" singles out a specific class of lies—"false testimony for the purpose of obtaining [immigration] benefits"—as a reason to deny naturalization. By contrast, "[w]illful misrepresentations made for other reasons, such as embarrassment, fear, or a desire for privacy, were not deemed sufficiently culpable to brand the applicant as someone who lacks good moral character"—and so are not generally disqualifying. *Kungys v. United States*, 485 U. S. (1988). But under the Government's reading of §1425(a), a lie told in the naturalization process—even out of embarrassment, fear, or a desire for privacy—would always provide a basis for rescinding citizenship. The Government could thus take away on one day what it was required to give the day before.

And by so wholly unmooring the revocation of citizenship from its award, the Government opens the door to a world of disquieting consequences—which we would need far stronger textual support to believe Congress intended. Consider the kinds of questions a person seeking citizenship confronts on the standard application form. Says one: "Have you EVER been . . . in any way associated with[ ] any organization, association, fund, foundation, party, club, society, or similar group[?]" Asks another: "Have you EVER committed . . . a crime or offense for which you were NOT arrested?" Suppose, for reasons of embarrassment or what-have-you, a person concealed her membership in an online support group or failed to disclose a prior speeding violation. Under the Government's view, a prosecutor could scour her paperwork and bring a §1425(a) charge on that meager basis, even many years after she became a citizen. That would give prosecutors nearly limitless leverage—and afford newly naturalized Americans precious little security. Small wonder that Congress, in enacting §1425(a), did not go so far as the Government claims. The statute it passed, most naturally read, strips a person of citizenship not when she committed any illegal act during the naturalization process, but only when that act played some role in her naturalization.

B

That conclusion leaves us with a more operational question: How should §1425(a)'s requirement of causal influence apply in practice, when charges are brought under that law? Because the proper analysis may vary with the nature of the predicate crime, we confine our discussion of that issue to the kind of underlying illegality alleged here: a false statement made to government officials. Such conduct can affect a naturalization decision in a single, significant way—by distorting the Government's understanding of the facts when it investigates, and then adjudicates, an application. So the issue a jury must decide in a case like this one is whether a false statement sufficiently altered those processes as to have influenced an award of citizenship.

The answer to that question, like the naturalization decision itself, turns on objective legal criteria. Congress has prescribed specific eligibility standards for new citizens, respecting such matters as length of residency and "physical[ ] presen[ce]," understanding of English and American government, and (as previously mentioned) "good moral character," with all its many specific components. Government officials are obligated to apply that body of law faithfully—granting naturalization when the applicable criteria are satisfied, and denying it when they are not. And to ensure right results are reached, a court can reverse such a determination, at an applicant's request, based on its "own findings of fact and conclusions of law." The entire system, in other words, is set up to provide little or no room for subjective preferences or personal whims. Because that is so, the question of what any individual decisionmaker might have done with accurate information is beside the point: The defendant in a §1425(a) case should neither benefit nor suffer from a wayward official's deviations from legal requirements. Accordingly, the proper causal inquiry under §1425(a) is framed in objective terms: To decide whether a defendant acquired citizenship by means of a lie, a jury must evaluate how knowledge of the real facts would have affected a reasonable government official properly applying naturalization law.

During-Reading Question: The Court has said that the requirements of naturalization are set up to prevent people from receiving citizenship based on the whims or preferences of a government official. What subjective quality preferences of an individual could the government be trying to prevent when allocating citizenship?

If the facts the defendant misrepresented are themselves disqualifying, the jury can make quick work of that inquiry. In such a case, there is an obvious causal link between the defendant's lie and her procurement of citizenship. To take an example: An applicant for citizenship must be physically present in the United States for more than half of the five-year period preceding her application. Suppose a defendant misrepresented her travel history to convey she had met that requirement, when in fact she had not. The Government need only expose that lie to establish that she obtained naturalization illegally—for had she told the truth instead, the official would have promptly denied her application. Or consider another, perhaps more common case stemming from the "good moral character" criterion. That phrase is defined to exclude any person who has been convicted of an aggravated felony. If a defendant falsely denied such a conviction, she too would have gotten her citizenship by means of a lie—for otherwise the outcome would have been different. In short, when the defendant misrepresents facts that the law deems incompatible with citizenship, her lie must have played a role in her naturalization.

But that is not the only time a jury can find that a defendant's lie had the requisite bearing on a naturalization decision. For even if the true facts lying behind a false statement would not "in and of themselves justify denial of citizenship," they could have "led to the discovery of other facts which would" do so. *Chaunt v. United State*s, 364 U. S. 350. We previously addressed that possibility when considering the civil statute that authorizes the Government to revoke naturalization. As we explained in that context, a person whose lies throw investigators off a trail leading to disqualifying facts gets her citizenship by means of those lies—no less than if she had denied the damning facts at the very end of the trail.

When relying on such an investigation-based theory, the Government must make a two-part showing to meet its burden. As an initial matter, the Government has to prove that the misrepresented fact was sufficiently relevant to one or another naturalization criterion that it would have prompted reasonable officials, "seeking only evidence concerning citizenship qualifications," to undertake further investigation. If that much is true, the inquiry turns to the prospect that such an investigation would have borne disqualifying fruit. As to that second link in the causal chain, the Government need not show definitively that its investigation would have unearthed a disqualifying fact (though, of course, it may). Rather, the Government need only establish that the investigation "would predictably have disclosed" some legal disqualification. If that is so, the defendant's misrepresentation contributed to the citizenship award in the way we think §1425(a) requires.

That standard reflects two real-world attributes of cases premised on what an unhindered investigation would have found. First is the difficulty of proving that a hypothetical inquiry would have led to some disqualifying discovery, often several years after the defendant told her lies. As witnesses and other evidence disappear, the Government's effort to reconstruct the course of a "could have been" investigation confronts ever-mounting obstacles. Second, and critical to our analysis, is that the defendant—not the Government—bears the blame for that evidentiary predicament. After all, the inquiry cannot get this far unless the defendant made an unlawful false statement and, by so doing, obstructed the normal course of an investigation.

Even when the Government can make its two-part showing, however, the defendant may be able to overcome it. Section 1425(a) is not a tool for denaturalizing people who, the available evidence indicates, were actually qualified for the citizenship they obtained. When addressing the civil denaturalization statute, this Court insisted on a similar point: We provided the defendant with an opportunity to rebut the Government's case "by showing, through a preponderance of the evidence, that the statutory requirement as to which [a lie] had a natural tendency to produce a favorable decision was in fact met." Or said otherwise, we gave the defendant a chance to establish that she was qualified for citizenship, and held that she could not be denaturalized if she did so—even though she concealed or misrepresented facts that suggested the opposite. And indeed, all our denaturalization decisions share this crucial feature: We have never read a statute to strip citizenship from someone who met the legal criteria for acquiring it. Whatever the Government shows with respect to a thwarted investigation, qualification for citizenship is a complete defense to a prosecution brought under §1425(a).

III

Measured against all we have said, the jury instructions in this case were in error. As earlier noted, the District Court told the jury that it could convict based on any false statement in the naturalization process, no matter how inconsequential to the ultimate decision. But as we have shown, the jury needed to find more than an unlawful false statement. Recall that Maslenjak's lie in the naturalization process concerned her prior statements to immigration officials: She swore that she had been honest when applying for admission as a refugee, but in fact she had not. The jury could have convicted if that earlier dishonesty (i.e., the thing she misrepresented when seeking citizenship) were itself a reason to deny naturalization—say, because it counted as "false testimony for the purpose of obtaining [immigration] benefits" and thus demonstrated bad moral character. Or else, the jury could have convicted if (1) knowledge of that prior dishonesty would have led a reasonable official to make some further investigation (say, into the circumstances of her admission), (2) that inquiry would predictably have yielded a legal basis for rejecting her citizenship application, and (3) Maslenjak failed to show that (notwithstanding such an objective likelihood) she was in fact qualified to become a U. S. citizen. This jury, however, was not asked to—and so did not—make any of those determinations. Accordingly, Maslenjak was not convicted by a properly instructed jury of "procur[ing], contrary to law, [her] naturalization."

During-Reading Question: The Court touches on the fact that there are other problems with Maslenjak's application for naturalization. What is the Court referring to?

The Government asserts that any instructional error in this case was harmless.

"Had officials known the truth," the Government asserts, "it would have affected their decision to grant [Maslenjak] citizenship." Unsurprisingly, Maslenjak disagrees. In keeping with our usual practice, we leave that dispute for resolution on remand.

For the reasons stated, we vacate the judgment of the Court of Appeals and remand the case for further proceedings consistent with this opinion.

It is so ordered.

Post-Reading Questions

1. The issue before the Court arose due to the jury instruction that stated the jury only needed to find that Maslenjek lied in order to revoke her citizenship. The Government argues that there are other reasons the jury could have made the decision it made, but the Supreme Court doesn't rule on that issue. What is the next step for the Government to take?
2. Go to the United States State Department website and explore the process a person must go through to become a refugee, starting with the following article: U.S. Depart-

ment of State. (n.d.). Refugee admissions. Retrieved from https://www.state.gov/j/prm/ra/. How easy is it to become a refugee in the United States?

Further Explorations

Exploring the Story

Listen to the oral arguments in this case before the Supreme Court in this video: C-SPAN. (2017, April 26). *Maslenjak v. United States* oral argument. [Streaming video]. *Campaign 2016.* Retrieved from https://www.c-span.org/video/?425470-1/maslenjak-v-united-states-oral-argument. How are oral arguments different from what you have come to expect from a criminal trial?

Exploring the Law

Do some research to find out what happened to Divna Maslenjak after this decision. Was she ultimately stripped of her citizenship and deported?

Exploring the Effects

Read more about the impact the *Maslenjak* case could have on revoking citizenship, as well as other legal issues around immigration in the following article from *The Atlantic*: Ford, M. (2017, May 2). Will the Supreme Court defend citizenship? *The Atlantic.* Retrieved from https://www.theatlantic.com/politics/archive/2017/05/supreme-court-citizenship-maslenjak/525000/

Activities for Extending the Learning

- Do you know what it actually takes to become a United States citizen? Read the following information from USA.gov and research the different ways a person can legally become a U.S. citizen: USA.gov (2018, March 2). How to apply for U.S. citizenship. Retrieved from https://www.usa.gov/become-us-citizen
- Did you know that a person born the United States can lose his or her citizenship? Research the Immigration and Naturalization Act, § 349 to find out what seven things can cause a U.S.-born citizen to be "expatriated."

A NOTE FROM THE AUTHORS

The United States is a powerful player in the global community. Students may see the country as an independent entity, yet in reality, many decisions rely on other countries. How do we decide who we want to "partner" with the United States in terms of policy, immigration regulations, or economic developments?

In these cases, one discusses the death penalty for those under the age of eighteen in which the Court used a rationale that the global community tends to have a similar standard in not executing those under a certain age. However, when it came to the use of the findings of an adult convicted of the death penalty, the Court did not use the same global community mind-set in making its decision. When do we look at the world as a whole and when do we stand alone as a nation? When we consider immigration, when are the gates open and when are they closed? Why?

Ultimately, this goes back to the "big idea" that the United States sees itself as unique and special and tends to make its own decisions independent of the global community. Many decisions are made without consulting the global community at all. Is this the best way to function? When does it benefit the nation and when does it harm it? Is the United States a global citizen? Why or why not? Where does the United States fit as a global citizen? Are we making decisions just to be different from the rest of the world, or are the decisions we make considerate of the larger global community?

Chapter Twelve

Civic Ideals and Practices

> Theme 10: *Social studies programs should include experiences that provide for the study of the ideals, principles, and practices of citizenship in a democratic republic.*
> —*National Curriculum Standards for Social Studies* (2010), National Council for the Social Studies, p. 23

Theme 10 asks teachers to have students learn the ideas and practices of a democratic republic—that "students acquire a historical and contemporary understanding of the basic freedoms and rights of citizens in a democracy, and learn about the institutions and practices that support and protect these freedoms and rights . . ." (NCSS, 2010, p. 23). The most important protector of these rights is the Supreme Court of the United States and the most important documents to learn about that protection are Supreme Court cases. Theme 10 wants students to explore such questions as:

> What are the democratic ideals and practices of a constitutional democracy? What is the balance between rights and responsibilities? What is civic participation? How do citizens become involved? What is the role of the citizen in the community and the nation, and as a member of the world community? Students will explore how individuals and institutions interact. They will also recognize and respect different points of view. Students learn by experience how to participate in community service and political activities and how to use democratic processes to influence public policy. Courses dealing with civics, history, political science, cultural anthropology, and fields such as global studies and law-related education, while also drawing upon content from the humanities. (NCSS, 2010, p. 23)

The cases in this chapter revolve around the balance of rights, civic participation, and political activities—the right to vote, the freedom of political speech, and the right to assembly. These cases give the students the opportunity to recognize and respect different sides of an issue.

Edwards v. South Carolina (1963) also revolves around the balancing of the individual's right with the state's interest. The right to assembly was essential in promoting social growth during the civil rights era. This case easily connects to current issues in our democracy and the opportunity to explore how the right to assembly is promoting social change today.

In *Texas v. Johnson* (1989), a man burns a flag in protest during the 1984 Republican National Convention. What is the state's interest in preventing this desecration? Students can examine the balancing of the rights of the individual with the interests of the state. How are those two sides balanced?

Shelby County v. Holder (2013) allows the opportunity to discuss how the right to vote hasn't always been a right for everyone. The case challenges the Voting Rights Act of 1965. How has our society progressed so that it no longer needs some of the protections of the Act? What current obstacles are there for people to vote?

CASE# 1: *EDWARDS V. SOUTH CAROLINA*

Pre-Reading Questions

1. Discuss the right to assembly articulated in the First Amendment. Why was/is this an important right? What limitations should the government be able to put on this right?
2. How has the right to assembly been important in our history to encourage social progress?

***Edwards v. South Carolina*, 372 U.S. 229 (1963)**

MR. JUSTICE STEWART delivered the opinion of the Court.

The petitioners, 187 in number, were convicted in a magistrate's court in Columbia, South Carolina, of the common law crime of breach of the peace. Their convictions were ultimately affirmed by the South Carolina Supreme Court. We granted certiorari to consider the claim that these convictions cannot be squared with the Fourteenth Amendment of the United States Constitution.

During-Reading Question: Why is this a Fourteenth Amendment issue?

There was no substantial conflict in the trial evidence. Late in the morning of March 2, 1961, the petitioners, high school and college students of the Negro race, met at the Zion Baptist Church in Columbia. From there, at about noon, they walked in separate groups of about 15 to the South Carolina State House grounds, an area of two city blocks open to the general public. Their purpose was

> to submit a protest to the citizens of South Carolina, along with the Legislative Bodies of South Carolina, our feelings and our dissatisfaction with the present condition of discriminatory actions against Negroes in general, and to let them know that we were dissatisfied, and that we would like for the laws which prohibited Negro privileges in this State to be removed.

Already on the State House grounds when the petitioners arrived were 30 or more law enforcement officers, who had advance knowledge that the petitioners were coming. Each group of petitioners entered the grounds through a driveway and parking area known in the record as the "horseshoe." As they entered, they were told by the law enforcement officials that "they had a right, as a citizen, to go through the State House grounds, as any other citizen has, as long as they were peaceful." During the next half hour or 45 minutes, the petitioners, in the same small groups, walked single file or two abreast in an orderly way, through the grounds, each group carrying placards bearing such messages as "I am proud to be a Negro" and "Down with segregation."

During this time, a crowd of some 200 to 300 onlookers had collected in the horseshoe area and on the adjacent sidewalks. There was no evidence to suggest that these onlookers were anything but curious, and no evidence at all of any threatening remarks, hostile gestures, or offensive language on the part of any member of the crowd. The City Manager testified that he recognized some of the onlookers, whom he did not identify, as "possible troublemakers," but his subsequent testimony made clear that nobody among the crowd actually caused or threatened any trouble. There was no obstruction of pedestrian or vehicular traffic within the State House grounds. No vehicle was prevented from entering or leaving the horseshoe area. Although vehicular traffic at a nearby street intersection was slowed down somewhat, an officer was dispatched to keep traffic moving. There were a number of bystanders on the public sidewalks adjacent to the State House grounds, but they all moved on when asked to do so, and there was no impediment of pedestrian traffic. Police protection at the scene was at all times sufficient to meet any foreseeable possibility of disorder.

In the situation and under the circumstances thus described, the police authorities advised the petitioners that they would be arrested if they did not disperse within 15 minutes. Instead of dispersing, the petitioners engaged in what the City Manager described as "boisterous," "loud," and "flamboyant" conduct, which, as his later testimony made clear, consisted of listening to a "religious harangue" by one of their leaders, and loudly singing "The Star Spangled Banner" and other patriotic and religious songs, while stamping their feet and clapping their hands. After 15 minutes had passed, the police arrested the petitioners and marched them off to jail.

During-Reading Question: Prepare a flowchart to illustrate the sequence of events.

Upon this evidence, the state trial court convicted the petitioners of breach of the peace, and imposed sentences ranging from a $10 fine or five days in jail to a $100 fine or 30 days in jail. In affirming the judgments, the Supreme Court of South Carolina said that, under the law of that State, the offense of breach of the peace "is not susceptible of exact definition," but that the "general definition of the offense" is as follows:

> In general terms, a breach of the peace is a violation of public order, a disturbance of the public tranquility, by any act or conduct inciting to violence . . . , it includes any violation of any law enacted to preserve peace and good order. It may consist of an act of violence or an act likely to produce violence. It is not necessary that the peace be actually broken to lay the foundation for a prosecution for this offense. If what is done is unjustifiable and unlawful, tending with sufficient directness to break the peace, no more is required. Nor is actual personal violence an essential element in the offense. . . .

During-Reading Question: Prepare an argument that the protesters did violate this statute.

"By 'peace,' as used in the law in this connection, is meant the tranquility enjoyed by citizens of a municipality or community where good order reigns among its members, which is the natural right of all persons in political society." 239 S.C. at 343–344, 123 S.E.2d at 249.

The petitioners contend that there was a complete absence of any evidence of the commission of this offense, and that they were thus denied one of the most basic elements of due process of law. Whatever the merits of this contention, we need not pass upon it in the present case. The state courts have held that the petitioners' conduct constituted breach of the peace under state law, and we may accept their decision as binding upon us to that extent. But it nevertheless remains our duty in a case such as this to make an independent examination of the whole record. And it is clear to us that, in arresting, convicting, and punishing the petitioners under the circumstances disclosed by this record, South Carolina infringed the petitioners' constitutionally protected rights of free speech, free assembly, and freedom to petition for redress of their grievances.

During-Reading Question: Distinguish the question the Court is deciding from the question they do not need to decide.

It has long been established that these First Amendment freedoms are protected by the Fourteenth Amendment from invasion by the States. The circumstances in this case reflect an exercise of these basic constitutional rights in their most pristine and classic form. The petitioners felt aggrieved by laws of South Carolina which allegedly "prohibited Negro privileges in this State." They peaceably assembled at the site of the State Government, and there peaceably expressed their grievances "to the citizens of South Carolina, along with the Legislative Bodies of South Carolina."

Not until they were told by police officials that they must disperse on pain of arrest did they do more. Even then, they but sang patriotic and religious songs after one of their leaders had delivered a "religious harangue." There was no violence or threat of violence on their part, or on the part of any member of the crowd watching them. Police protection was "ample."

This, therefore, was a far cry from the situation in *Feiner v. New York*, where two policemen were faced with a crowd which was "pushing, shoving and milling around," where "at least one member of the crowd threatened violence if the police did not act," where "the crowd was pressing closer around petitioner and the officer," and where "the speaker passes the bounds of argument or persuasion and undertakes incitement to riot." And the record is barren of any evidence of "fighting words."

During-Reading: Compare and contrast the facts of this case to the facts in Feiner v. New York.

We do not review in this case criminal convictions resulting from the evenhanded application of a precise and narrowly drawn regulatory statute evincing a legislative judgment that certain specific conduct be limited or proscribed. If, for example, the petitioners had been convicted upon evidence that they had violated a law regulating traffic, or had disobeyed a law reasonably limiting the periods during which the State House grounds were open to the public, this would be a different case. These petitioners were convicted of an offense so generalized as to be, in the words of the South Carolina Supreme Court, "not susceptible of exact definition." And they were convicted upon evidence which showed no more than that the opinions which they were peaceably expressing were sufficiently opposed to the views of the majority of the community to attract a crowd and necessitate police protection.

The Fourteenth Amendment does not permit a State to make criminal the peaceful expression of unpopular views.

> [A] function of free speech under our system of government is to invite dispute. It may indeed best serve its high purpose when it induces a condition of unrest, creates dissatisfaction with conditions as they are, or even stirs people to anger. Speech is often provocative and challenging. It may strike at prejudices and preconceptions, and have profound unsettling effects as it presses for acceptance of an idea. That is why freedom of speech . . . is . . . protected against censorship or punishment, unless shown likely to produce a clear and present danger of a serious substantive evil that rises far above public inconvenience, annoyance, or unrest. . . . There is no room under our Constitution for a more restrictive view. For the alternative would lead to standardization of ideas either by legislatures, courts, or dominant political or community groups" *Terminiello v. Chicago.*

As in the *Terminiello* case, the courts of South Carolina have defined a criminal offense so as to permit conviction of the petitioners if their speech "stirred people to anger, invited public dispute, or brought about a condition of unrest. A conviction resting on any of those grounds may not stand."

As Chief Justice Hughes wrote in *Stromberg v. California,*

> The maintenance of the opportunity for free political discussion to the end that government may be responsive to the will of the people and that changes may be obtained by lawful means, an opportunity essential to the security of the Republic, is a fundamental principle of our constitutional system. A statute which, upon its face and as authoritatively construed, is so vague and indefinite as to permit the punishment of the fair use of this opportunity is repugnant to the guaranty of liberty contained in the Fourteenth Amendment. . . .

For these reasons, we conclude that these criminal convictions cannot stand.

Reversed.

Post-Reading Questions

What kind of restrictions can the government place on the right to assembly? For questions to discuss regarding the right to assembly, see: Newseum Institute. (n.d.). Frequently asked questions: Freedom of assembly. Retrieved from http://www.newseuminstitute.org/about/faq/category/freedom-of-assembly/

Further Explorations

Exploring the Story

To hear the story behind the protest that led to the case, see: Hudson. D. L. (2017, January 30). Freedom of assembly and *Edwards v. South Carolina*: Protecting the peaceful expression of unpopular views. *Newseum*. Retrieved from http://www.newseuminstitute.org/2017/01/30/freedom-of-assembly-and-edwards-v-south-carolina-protecting-the-peaceful-expression-of-unpopular-views/

Exploring the Law

For further understanding and discussion of the case, see the comprehension and critical thinking questions at: Bill of Rights Institute. (n.d.). *Edwards v. South Carolina* (1963). [Lesson plan]. In *Landmark Supreme Court Cases eLessons*. Retrieved from http://www.billofrightsinstitute.org/educate/educator-resources/lessons-plans/landmark-supreme-court-cases-elessons/edwards-v-south-carolina-1963/

Exploring the Effects

To explore the freedom of assembly today, have students look at current news events using the resources listed in this article: Bill of Rights Institute. (n.d.). Freedom of Assembly and Freedom of Petition. In *Teaching with Current Events*. Retrieved from http://www.billofrightsinstitute.org/educate/educator-resources/headlines/assembly-and-petition

Activities for Extending the Learning

For an extension activity that has students respond in writing to a quotation about the First Amendment, see: Bill of Rights Institute. (n.d.). *Edwards v. South Carolina* (1963). [Lesson plan]. In *Landmark Supreme Court Cases eLessons.* Retrieved from http://www.billofrightsinstitute.org/educate/educator-resources/lessons-plans/landmark-supreme-court-cases-elessons/edwards-v-south-carolina-1963

CASE #2: *TEXAS V. JOHNSON*

Pre-Reading Questions

1. Read and discuss the rights articulated in the First Amendment. Discuss what would be included in "speech" or symbolic speech?
2. Discuss the idea of a flag. What is the denotation and connotation of the flag? What are society's "rules" regarding the handling of a flag? Why? What is considered disrespectful in our society regarding the flag?

Texas v. Johnson, 491 U.S. 397 (1989)

JUSTICE BRENNAN delivered the opinion of the Court.

After publicly burning an American flag as a means of political protest, Gregory Lee Johnson was convicted of desecrating a flag in violation of Texas law. This case presents the question whether his conviction is consistent with the First Amendment. We hold that it is not.

I

While the Republican National Convention was taking place in Dallas in 1984, respondent Johnson participated in a political demonstration dubbed the "Republican War Chest Tour." As explained in literature distributed by the demonstrators and in speeches made by them, the purpose of this event was to protest the policies of the Reagan administration and of certain Dallas-based corporations. The demonstrators marched through the Dallas streets, chanting political slogans and stopping at several corporate locations to stage "die-ins" intended to dramatize the consequences of nuclear war. On several occasions they spray-painted the walls of buildings and overturned potted plants, but Johnson himself took no part in such activities. He did, however, accept an American flag handed to him by a fellow protestor who had taken it from a flagpole outside one of the targeted buildings.

The demonstration ended in front of Dallas City Hall, where Johnson unfurled the American flag, doused it with kerosene, and set it on fire. While the flag burned, the protestors chanted, "America, the red, white, and blue, we spit on you." After the demonstrators dispersed, a witness to the flag burning collected the flag's remains and buried them in his backyard. No one was physically injured or threatened with injury, though several witnesses testified that they had been seriously offended by the flag burning.

During-Reading Question: Why is the context of the flag burning significant?

II

Johnson was convicted of flag desecration for burning the flag, rather than for uttering insulting words. This fact somewhat complicates our consideration of his conviction under the First Amendment. We must first determine whether Johnson's burning of the flag constituted expressive conduct, permitting him to invoke the First Amendment in challenging his conviction.

During-Reading Question: Why does the conviction of flag desecration rather than uttering insulting words complicate the issue?

The First Amendment literally forbids the abridgment only of "speech," but we have long recognized that its protection does not end at the spoken or written word. While we have rejected "the view that an apparently limitless variety of conduct can be labeled 'speech' whenever the person engaging in the conduct intends thereby to express an idea," *United States v. O'Brien,* we have acknowledged that conduct may be "sufficiently imbued with elements of communication to fall within the scope of the First and Fourteenth Amendments," *Spence v. Washington.*

In deciding whether particular conduct possesses sufficient communicative elements to bring the First Amendment into play, we have asked whether "[a]n intent to convey a particularized message was present, and [whether] the likelihood was great that the message would be understood by those who viewed it" *United States v. Nixon.* Hence, we have recognized the expressive nature of students' wearing of black armbands to protest American military involvement in Vietnam, *Tinker v. Des Moines Independent Community School Dist.*

Especially pertinent to this case are our decisions recognizing the communicative nature of conduct relating to flags.

> [T]he flag salute is a form of utterance. Symbolism is a primitive but effective way of communicating ideas. The use of an emblem or flag to symbolize some system, idea, institution, or personality, is a shortcut from mind to mind. Causes and nations, political parties, lodges and ecclesiastical groups seek to knit the loyalty of their followings to a flag or banner, a color or design. *West Virginia State Board of Education v. Barnette.*

Pregnant with expressive content, the flag as readily signifies this Nation as does the combination of letters found in "America." We have not automatically concluded, however, that any action taken with respect to our flag is expressive. Instead, in characterizing such action for First Amendment purposes, we have considered the context in which it occurred.

Johnson burned an American flag as part—indeed, as the culmination—of a political demonstration that coincided with the convening of the Republican Party and its renomination of Ronald Reagan for President. The expressive, overtly political nature of this conduct was both intentional and overwhelmingly apparent. At his trial, Johnson explained his reasons for burning the flag as follows: "The American Flag was burned as Ronald Reagan was being renominated as President. And a more powerful statement of symbolic speech, whether you agree with it or not, couldn't have been made at that time. It's quite a just position [juxtaposition]. We had new patriotism and no patriotism." In these circumstances, Johnson's burning of the flag was conduct "sufficiently imbued with elements of communication," *Spence v. Washington* to implicate the First Amendment.

During-Reading Questions: What criteria does the Court consider in determining whether something is "speech"? What criteria would you use?

III

Thus, although we have recognized that, where "'speech' and 'nonspeech' elements are combined in the same course of conduct, a sufficiently important governmental interest in regulating the nonspeech element can justify incidental limitations on First Amendment freedoms,"*United States v. O'Brien*, we have limited the applicability of *O'Brien*'s relatively lenient standard to those cases in which "the governmental interest is unrelated to the suppression of free expression."

In order to decide whether *O'Brien*'s test applies here, therefore, we must decide whether Texas has asserted an interest in support of Johnson's conviction that is unrelated to the suppression of expression. If we find that an interest asserted by the State is simply not implicated on the facts before us, we need not ask whether *O'Brien*'s test applies. The State offers two separate interests to justify this conviction: preventing breaches of the peace and preserving the flag as a symbol of nationhood and national unity. We hold that the first interest is not implicated on this record, and that the second is related to the suppression of expression.

During-Reading Question: The O'Brien test allows the government to limit an individual's First Amendment right when there is a sufficiently important governmental issue and that interest is unrelated to the suppression of free expression. Brainstorm some "sufficiently important governmental issues" that would pass this test.

A

Texas claims that its interest in preventing breaches of the peace justifies Johnson's conviction for flag desecration. However, no disturbance of the peace actually occurred or threatened to occur because of Johnson's burning of the flag. The State's emphasis on the protestors' disorderly actions prior to arriving at City Hall is not only somewhat surprising, given that no charges were brought on the basis of this conduct, but it also fails to show that a disturbance of the peace was a likely reaction to Johnson's conduct. The only evidence offered by the State at trial to show the reaction to Johnson's actions was the testimony of several persons who had been seriously offended by the flag burning.

The State's position, therefore, amounts to a claim that an audience that takes serious offense at particular expression is necessarily likely to disturb the peace, and that the expression may be prohibited on this basis. Our precedents do not countenance such a presumption. On the contrary, they recognize that a principal "function of free speech under our system of government is to invite dispute. It may indeed best serve its high purpose when it induces a condition of unrest, creates dissatisfaction with conditions as they are, or even stirs people to anger."

Thus, we have not permitted the government to assume that every expression of a provocative idea will incite a riot, but have instead required careful consideration of the actual circumstances surrounding such expression, asking whether the expression "is directed to inciting or producing imminent lawless action and is likely to incite or produce such action." *Brandenburg v. Ohio* (reviewing circumstances surrounding rally and speeches by Ku Klux Klan). To accept Texas' arguments that it need only demonstrate "the potential for a breach of the peace," *Brief for Petitioner*, and that every flag burning necessarily possesses that potential, would be to eviscerate our holding in *Brandenburg.* This we decline to do.

During-Reading Question: The State has an interest in preventing breaches of peace. What actual circumstances would the State need to show?

Nor does Johnson's expressive conduct fall within that small class of "fighting words" that are "likely to provoke the average person to retaliation, and thereby cause a breach of the peace." *Chaplinsky v. New Hampshire*. No reasonable onlooker would have regarded Johnson's generalized expression of dissatisfaction with the policies of the Federal Government as a direct personal insult or an invitation to exchange fisticuffs.

We thus conclude that the State's interest in maintaining order is not implicated on these facts. The State need not worry that our holding will disable it from preserving the peace. We do not suggest that the First Amendment forbids a State to prevent "imminent lawless action." *Brandenburg v. Ohio*. And, in fact, Texas already has a statute specifically prohibiting breaches of the peace which tends to confirm that Texas need not punish this flag desecration in order to keep the peace.

IV

It remains to consider whether the State's interest in preserving the flag as a symbol of nationhood and national unity justifies Johnson's conviction.

As in *Spence,* "[w]e are confronted with a case of prosecution for the expression of an idea through activity," and "[a]ccordingly, we must examine with particular care the interests advanced by [petitioner] to support its prosecution." Johnson was not, we add, prosecuted for the expression of just any idea; he was prosecuted for his expression of dissatisfaction with the policies of this country, expression situated at the core of our First Amendment values.

Moreover, Johnson was prosecuted because he knew that his politically charged expression would cause "serious offense." If he had burned the flag as a means of disposing of it because it was dirty or torn, he would not have been convicted of flag desecration under this Texas law: federal law designates burning as the preferred means of disposing of a flag "when it is in such condition that it is no longer a fitting emblem for display," and Texas has no quarrel with this means of disposal. *Brief for Petitioner 45*. The Texas law is thus not aimed at protecting the physical integrity of the flag in all circumstances, but is designed instead to protect it only against impairments that would cause serious offense to others. Texas concedes as much: "Section 42.09(b) reaches only those severe acts of physical abuse of the flag carried out in a way likely to be offensive. The statute mandates intentional or knowing abuse, that is, the kind of mistreatment that is not innocent, but rather is intentionally designed to seriously offend other individuals."

Whether Johnson's treatment of the flag violated Texas law thus depended on the likely communicative impact of his expressive conduct. Our decision in *Boos v. Barry,* tells us that this restriction on Johnson's expression is content-based. In *Boos,* we considered the constitutionality of a law prohibiting "the display of any sign within 500 feet of a foreign embassy if that sign tends to bring that foreign government into 'public odium' or 'public disrepute.'" Rejecting the argument that the law was content-neutral because it was justified by "our international law obligation to shield diplomats from speech that offends their dignity," we held that "[t]he emotive impact of speech on its audience is not a secondary effect" unrelated to the content of the expression itself.

According to the principles announced in *Boos,* Johnson's political expression was restricted because of the content of the message he conveyed. We must therefore subject the State's asserted interest in preserving the special symbolic character of the flag to "the most exacting scrutiny" *Boos v. Barry.*

Texas argues that its interest in preserving the flag as a symbol of nationhood and national unity survives this close analysis. According to Texas, if one physically treats the flag in a way that would tend to cast doubt on either the idea that nationhood and national unity are the flag's referents or that national unity actually exists, the message conveyed thereby is a harmful one, and therefore may be prohibited.

We have not recognized an exception to this principle even where our flag has been involved.

Texas' focus on the precise nature of Johnson's expression, moreover, misses the point of our prior decisions: their enduring lesson, that the government may not prohibit expression simply because it disagrees with its message, is not dependent on the particular mode in which one chooses to express an idea. If we were to hold that a State may forbid flag burning wherever it is likely to endanger the flag's symbolic role, but allow it wherever burning a flag promotes that role—as where, for example, a person ceremoniously burns a dirty flag—we would be saying that when it comes to impairing the flag's physical integrity, the flag itself may be used as a symbol—as a substitute for the written or spoken word or a "short cut from mind to mind"—only in one direction. We would be permitting a State to "prescribe what shall be orthodox" by saying that one may burn the flag to convey one's attitude toward it and its referents only if one does not endanger the flag's representation of nationhood and national unity. We never before have held that the Government may ensure that a symbol be used to express only one view of that symbol or its referents.

We perceive no basis on which to hold that the principle underlying our decision in *Schacht* does not apply to this case. To conclude that the government may permit designated symbols to be used to communicate only a limited set of messages would be to enter territory having no discernible or defensible boundaries. Could the government, on this theory, prohibit the burning of state flags? Of copies of the Presidential seal? Of the Constitution? In evaluating these choices under the First Amendment, how would we decide which symbols were sufficiently special to warrant this unique status? To do so, we would be forced to consult our own political preferences, and impose them on the citizenry, in the very way that the First Amendment forbids us to do.

There is, moreover, no indication—either in the text of the Constitution or in our cases interpreting it—that a separate juridical category exists for the American flag alone. Indeed, we would not be surprised to learn that the persons who framed our Constitution and wrote the Amendment that we now construe were not known for their reverence for the Union Jack. The First Amendment does not guarantee that other concepts virtually sacred to our Nation as a whole—such as the principle that discrimination on the basis of race is odious and destructive—will go unquestioned in the marketplace of ideas. We decline, therefore, to create for the flag an exception to the joust of principles protected by the First Amendment.

It is not the State's ends, but its means, to which we object. It cannot be gainsaid that there is a special place reserved for the flag in this Nation, and thus we do not doubt that the government has a legitimate interest in making efforts to "preserv[e] the national flag as an unalloyed symbol of our country" *Spence v. Washington.* We reject the suggestion, urged at oral argument by counsel for Johnson, that the government lacks "any state interest whatsoever" in regulating the manner in which the flag may be displayed. Congress has, for example, enacted precatory regulations describing the proper treatment of the flag, and we cast no doubt on the legitimacy of its interest in making such recommendations. To say that the government has an interest in encouraging proper treatment of the flag, however, is not to say that it may criminally punish a person for burning a flag as a means of political protest. "National unity as an end which officials may foster by persuasion and example is not in question. The problem is whether, under our Constitution, compulsion as here employed is a permissible means for its achievement" *West Virginia Board of Education v. Barnette.*

We are fortified in today's conclusion by our conviction that forbidding criminal punishment for conduct such as Johnson's will not endanger the special role played by our flag or the feelings it inspires. To paraphrase Justice Holmes, we submit that nobody can suppose that this one gesture of an unknown man will change our Nation's attitude towards its flag.

We are tempted to say, in fact, that the flag's deservedly cherished place in our community will be strengthened, not weakened, by our holding today. Our decision is a reaffirmation of the principles of freedom and inclusiveness that the flag best reflects, and of the conviction that our toleration of criticism such as Johnson's is a sign and source of our strength. Indeed, one of the proudest images of our flag, the one immortalized in our own national anthem, is of the bombardment it survived at Fort McHenry. It is the Nation's resilience, not its rigidity, that Texas sees reflected in the flag—and it is that resilience that we reassert today.

The way to preserve the flag's special role is not to punish those who feel differently about these matters. It is to persuade them that they are wrong. "To courageous, self-reliant men, with confidence in the power of free and fearless reasoning applied through the processes of popular government, no danger flowing from speech can be deemed clear and present unless the incidence of the evil apprehended is so imminent that it may befall before there is opportunity for full discussion. If there be time to expose through discussion the falsehood and fallacies, to avert the evil by the processes of education, the remedy to be applied is more speech, not enforced silence" *Whitney v. California.* And, precisely because it is our flag that is involved, one's response to the flag-burner may exploit the uniquely persuasive power of the flag itself. We can imagine no more appropriate response to burning a flag than waving one's own, no better way to counter a flag burner's message than by saluting the flag that burns, no surer means of preserving the dignity even of the flag that burned than by—as one witness here did—according its remains a respectful burial. We do not consecrate the flag by punishing its desecration, for in doing so we dilute the freedom that this cherished emblem represents.

During-Reading Question: Summarize the Court's reasoning in determining that one can not be punished for desecrating the flag.

V

Johnson was convicted for engaging in expressive conduct. The State's interest in preventing breaches of the peace does not support his conviction, because Johnson's conduct did not threaten to disturb the peace. Nor does the State's interest in preserving the flag as a symbol of nationhood and national unity justify his criminal conviction for engaging in political expression. The judgment of the Texas Court of Criminal Appeals is therefore

Affirmed. [The Texas Court of Criminal Appeals reversed Johnson's conviction, holding that the State could not, consistent with the First Amendment, punish Johnson for burning the flag in these circumstances.]

Post-Reading Questions

1. The Court talks about "content-based" speech. Why does the Court have an increased interest when the government limits content-based speech?
2. Further discussion questions can be found at: Bill of Rights Institute. (n.d.). *Texas v. Johnson* (1989). In *Landmark Supreme Court Cases eLessons*. Retrieved from http://billofrightsinstitute.org/educate/educator-resources/lessons-plans/landmark-supreme-court-cases-elessons/texas-v-johnson-1989/

Further Explorations

Exploring the Story

To learn about the precedent that led to the *Texas v. Johnson* decision and a glimpse into the Court's thinking, have students read: Bomboy, S. (2015, June 14). Inside the Supreme Court's flag burning decision. *Constitution Daily*. Retrieved from https://constitutioncenter.org/blog/inside-the-supreme-courts-flag-burning-decision

Exploring the Law

To better understand the two sides of flag burning, see this lesson: A burning issue: A structured academic controversy concerning flag desecration. [Lesson plan]. (n.d.). McCormick Tribune Freedom Museum. Retrieved from http://documents.mccormickfoundation.org/lesson-plans/1/burning_issue.pdf

Exploring the Effects

To explore First Amendment Rights, see the following article: Would you fight for all five? Weighing our First Amendment freedoms. [Lesson plan]. (n.d.). *Newseum*. Retrieved from https://www.ribar.com/UserFiles/1b(1).pdf See also: Newseum Institute. (n.d.). The first five. [Podcast series]. In *First Amendment Center*. Newseum Institute. Retrieved from http://www.newseuminstitute.org/first-amendment-center/podcast/

See also: Newseum Institute. (n.d.). The first five. [Podcast series]. In *First Amendment Center*, Newseum Institute. Retrieved from http://www.newseuminstitute.org/first-amendment-center/podcast/

Activities for Extending the Learning

For students to apply the law and reasoning to recent issues including Colin Kaepernick kneeling for the national anthem and a history teacher stomping on the American flag, see the following website: Bill of Rights Institute. (ca. 2016). An anthem, a flag and individual liberties. [Lesson plan]. Retrieved from http://billofrightsinstitute.org/anthem-flag-individual-liberties/

CASE #3: *SHELBY COUNTY V. HOLDER*

Pre-Reading Questions

1. Discuss the rights articulated in the Fifteenth Amendment.
2. The Tenth Amendment protects states' rights. Why is this important?
3. *Shelby County v. Holder* deals with the Voting Rights Act of 1965. Describe what the Act did, and what was its purpose?

Shelby County v. Holder, 570 U.S. 529 (2013)

CHIEF JUSTICE ROBERTS delivered the opinion of the Court.

The Voting Rights Act of 1965 employed extraordinary measures to address an extraordinary problem. Section 5 of the Act required States to obtain federal permission before enacting any law related to voting—a drastic departure from basic principles of federalism. And §4 of the Act applied that requirement only to some States—an equally dramatic departure from the principle that all States enjoy equal sovereignty. This was strong medicine, but Congress determined it was needed to address entrenched racial discrimination in voting. . . .

Nearly 50 years later, they are still in effect; indeed, they have been made more stringent, and are now scheduled to last until 2031. There is no denying, however, that the conditions that originally justified these measures no longer characterize voting in the covered jurisdictions.

At the same time, voting discrimination still exists; no one doubts that. The question is whether the Act's extraordinary measures, including its disparate treatment of the States, continue to satisfy constitutional requirements. As we put it a short time ago, "the Act imposes current burdens and must be justified by current needs" *Northwest Austin Municipal Utility District No. One v. Holder*.

During-Reading Question: What is evidence that the measures of the Voting Rights Act of 1965 are still justified?

I

A

The Fifteenth Amendment was ratified in 1870, in the wake of the Civil War. It provides that "[t]he right of citizens of the United States to vote shall not be denied or abridged by the United States or by any State on account of race, color, or previous condition of servitude," and it gives Congress the "power to enforce this article by appropriate legislation."

"The first century of congressional enforcement of the Amendment, however, can only be regarded as a failure." In the 1890s, Alabama, Georgia, Louisiana, Mississippi, North Carolina, South Carolina, and Virginia began to enact literacy tests for voter registration and to employ other methods designed to prevent African-Americans from voting. Congress passed statutes outlawing some of these practices and facilitating litigation against them, but litigation remained slow and expensive, and the States came up with new ways to discriminate as soon as existing ones were struck down. Voter registration of African-Americans barely improved.

During-Reading Question: How have states denied the right to vote to African Americans?

Inspired to action by the civil rights movement, Congress responded in 1965 with the Voting Rights Act. Section 2 was enacted to forbid, in all 50 States, any "standard, practice, or procedure . . . imposed or applied . . . to deny or abridge the right of any citizen of the United States to vote on account of race or color." The current version forbids any "standard, practice, or procedure" that "results in a denial or abridgement of the right of any citizen of the United States to vote on account of race or color." Both the Federal Government and individuals have sued to enforce §2, and injunctive relief is available in appropriate cases to block voting laws from going into effect.

Other sections targeted only some parts of the country. At the time of the Act's passage, these "covered" jurisdictions were those States or political subdivisions that had maintained a test or device as a prerequisite to voting as of November 1, 1964, and had less than 50 percent voter registration or turnout in the 1964 Presidential election. Such tests or devices included literacy and knowledge tests, good moral character requirements, the need for vouchers from registered voters, and the like. A covered jurisdiction could "bail out" of coverage if it had not used a test or device in the preceding five years "for the purpose or with the effect of denying or abridging the right to vote on account of race or color." In 1965, the covered States included

Alabama, Georgia, Louisiana, Mississippi, South Carolina, and Virginia. The additional covered subdivisions included 39 counties in North Carolina and one in Arizona.

During-Reading Question: How were targeted jurisdictions chosen?

In those jurisdictions, §4 of the Act banned all such tests or devices. Section 5 provided that no change in voting procedures could take effect until it was approved by federal authorities in Washington, D. C.—either the Attorney General or a court of three judges. A jurisdiction could obtain such "preclearance" only by proving that the change had neither "the purpose [nor] the effect of denying or abridging the right to vote on account of race or color."

Sections 4 and 5 were intended to be temporary; they were set to expire after five years. In *South Carolina v. Katzenbach*, we upheld the 1965 Act against constitutional challenge, explaining that it was justified to address "voting discrimination where it persists on a pervasive scale."

During-Reading Question: Summarize Sections 4 and 5 of the Voting Rights Act of 1965 .

B

Shelby County is located in Alabama, a covered jurisdiction. It has not sought bailout, as the Attorney General has recently objected to voting changes proposed from within the county. Instead, in 2010, the county sued the Attorney General in Federal District Court in Washington, D. C., seeking a declaratory judgment that sections 4(b) and 5 of the Voting Rights Act are facially unconstitutional, as well as a permanent injunction against their enforcement.

II

In *Northwest Austin Municipal Utility District No. One v. Holder*, we stated that "the Act imposes current burdens and must be justified by current needs." And we concluded that "a departure from the fundamental principle of equal sovereignty requires a showing that a statute's disparate geographic coverage is sufficiently related to the problem that it targets." These basic principles guide our review of the question before us.

A

The Constitution and laws of the United States are "the supreme Law of the Land." State legislation may not contravene federal law. The Federal Government does not, however, have a general right to review and veto state enactments before they go into effect. A proposal to grant such authority to "negative" state laws was considered at the Constitutional Convention, but rejected in favor of allowing state laws to take effect, subject to later challenge under the Supremacy Clause.

Outside the strictures of the Supremacy Clause, States retain broad autonomy in structuring their governments and pursuing legislative objectives. Indeed, the Constitution provides that all powers not specifically granted to the Federal Government are reserved to the States or citizens.

Not only do States retain sovereignty under the Constitution, there is also a "fundamental principle of equal sovereignty" among the States.

The Voting Rights Act sharply departs from these basic principles.

B

In 1966, we found these departures from the basic features of our system of government justified. The "blight of racial discrimination in voting" had "infected the electoral process in parts of our country for nearly a century" *South Carolina v. Katzenbach*. Several States had enacted a variety of requirements and tests "specifically designed to prevent" African-Americans from voting. Case-by-case litigation had proved inadequate to prevent such racial discrimination in voting, in part because States "merely switched to discriminatory devices not covered by the federal decrees," "enacted difficult new tests," or simply "defied and evaded court orders." Shortly before enactment of the Voting Rights Act, only 19.4 percent of African-Americans of voting age were registered to vote in Alabama, only 31.8 percent in Louisiana, and only 6.4 percent in Mississippi. Those figures were roughly 50 percentage points or more below the figures for whites.

In short, we concluded that "[u]nder the compulsion of these unique circumstances, Congress responded in a permissibly decisive manner." We also noted then and have emphasized since that this extra-ordinary legislation was intended to be temporary, set to expire after five years.

C

Nearly 50 years later, things have changed dramatically. Shelby County contends that the preclearance requirement, even without regard to its disparate coverage, is now unconstitutional. Its arguments have a good deal of force. In the covered jurisdictions, "[v]oter turnout and registration rates now approach parity. Blatantly discriminatory evasions of federal decrees are rare. And minority candidates hold office at unprecedented levels." *Northwest Austin v. Holder*. The tests and devices that blocked access to the ballot have been forbidden nationwide for over 40 years.

Those conclusions are not ours alone. Congress said the same when it reauthorized the Act in 2006, writing that "[s]ignificant progress has been made in eliminating first generation barriers experienced by minority voters, including increased numbers of registered minority voters, minority voter turnout, and minority representation in Congress, State legislatures, and local elected offices."

The provisions of §5 apply only to those jurisdictions singled out by §4. We now consider whether that coverage formula is constitutional in light of current conditions.

III

A

When upholding the constitutionality of the coverage formula in 1966, we concluded that it was "rational in both practice and theory" *South Carolina v. Katzenbach*. The formula looked to cause (discriminatory tests) and effect (low voter registration and turnout), and tailored the remedy (preclearance) to those jurisdictions exhibiting both.

By 2009, however, we concluded that the "coverage formula raise[d] serious constitutional questions." *Northwest Austin Municipal Utility District No. One v. Holder*. As we explained, a statute's "current burdens" must be justified by "current needs," and any "disparate geographic coverage" must be "sufficiently related to the problem that it targets." The coverage formula met that test in 1965, but no longer does so.

Coverage today is based on decades-old data and eradicated practices. The formula captures States by reference to literacy tests and low voter registration and turnout in the 1960s and early 1970s. But such tests have been banned nationwide for over 40 years. And voter registration and turnout numbers in the covered States have risen dramatically in the years since. Racial disparity in those numbers was compelling evidence justifying the preclearance remedy and the coverage formula. There is no longer such a disparity.

In 1965, the States could be divided into two groups: those with a recent history of voting tests and low voter registration and turnout, and those without those characteristics. Congress based its coverage formula on that distinction. Today the Nation is no longer divided along those lines, yet the Voting Rights Act continues to treat it as if it were.

But history did not end in 1965. By the time the Act was reauthorized in 2006, there had been 40 more years of it. In assessing the "current need" for a preclearance system that treats States differently from one another today, that history cannot be ignored. During that time, largely because of the Voting Rights Act, voting tests were abolished, disparities in voter registration and turnout due to race were erased, and African-Americans attained political office in record numbers. And yet the coverage formula that Congress reauthorized in 2006 ignores these developments, keeping the focus on decades-old data relevant to decades-old problems, rather than current data reflecting current needs.

The Fifteenth Amendment commands that the right to vote shall not be denied or abridged on account of race or color, and it gives Congress the power to enforce that command. The Amendment is not designed to punish for the past; its purpose is to ensure a better future.

During-Reading Question: Make an argument that Section 4(b) and 5 do ensure for a better future.

Striking down an Act of Congress "is the gravest and most delicate duty that this Court is called on to perform." *Blodgett v. Holden.* We do not do so lightly. That is why, in 2009, we took care to avoid ruling on the constitutionality of the Voting Rights Act when asked to do so, and instead resolved the case then before us on statutory grounds. But in issuing that decision, we expressed our broader concerns about the constitutionality of the Act. Congress could have updated the coverage formula at that time, but did not do so. Its failure to act leaves us today with no choice but to declare §4(b) unconstitutional. The formula in that section can no longer be used as a basis for subjecting jurisdictions to preclearance.

Our decision in no way affects the permanent, nationwide ban on racial discrimination in voting found in §2. We issue no holding on §5 itself, only on the coverage formula. Congress may draft another formula based on current conditions. Such a formula is an initial prerequisite to a determination that exceptional conditions still exist justifying such an "extraordinary departure from the traditional course of relations between the States and the Federal Government." *Presley v. Georgia.* Our country has changed, and while any racial discrimination in voting is too much, Congress must ensure that the legislation it passes to remedy that problem speaks to current conditions.

The judgment of the Court of Appeals is reversed.

It is so ordered.

Post-Reading Questions

1. Since the *Shelby* decision, states have enacted photo ID requirements for voting, which had been previously forbidden. Discuss whether this is discriminatory.
2. The Court's decision was a 5–4 decision. Write a dissent to the majority opinion in which you respond to their reasoning.

Further Explorations

Exploring the Story

In order to think about the importance of a person's right to vote, use the film series *The Voters* with the lesson plans provided by PBS News Hour in: To vote or not to vote—lesson plan. (2016, October 25). *PBS NewsHour Extra*. Retrieved from http://www.pbs.org/newshour/extra/lessons-plans/to-vote-or-not-to-vote-lesson-plan/

Exploring the Law

To gain a better understanding of the case, students can explore the *New York Times'* annotated case: Schwartz, J. (2013, June 25). Between the lines of the Voting Rights Act opinion. *New York Times*. Retrieved from http://www.nytimes.com/interactive/2013/06/25/us/annotated-supreme-court-decision-on-voting-rights-act.html

Exploring the Effects

For a connection to the Selma march, look to the following Flocabulary lesson which incorporates a video: Flocabulary. (n.d.). Voting Rights Act and Selma March [Lesson plan]. Retrieved from https://www.flocabulary.com/unit/voting-rights-act-selma-march/.

In addition, students depict a skit or rap to show their understanding of change or continuity in voting rights, in the following lesson plan: Flocabulary. (n.d.). Voting rights then and now. [Lesson plan]. Retrieved from https://www.flocabulary.com/lesson/voting-rights-history-lesson-plan/

Activities for Extending the Learning

In order to further explore the history of voting rights and the government's role in securing those rights, check out this lesson (one of a 3-part series) that includes videos, news clips from 1965, graphs, and documents for students to explore these issues: The Voting Rights Act, 1965 and Beyond. [Lesson plan]. (n.d.). In *Teaching Tolerance*. Retrieved from https://www.tolerance.org/classroom-resources/tolerance-lessons/the-voting-rights-act-1965-and-beyond

A NOTE FROM THE AUTHORS

The rights, sometimes duties, of a citizen may not be fully realized by secondary students, yet remain some of the most important concepts they will identify with as adults. Questions that arise with these cases include: What is your duty to be involved in civic discourse? How do you decide how to express yourself? How do we protect these rights and how does the government protect the rights for us? How do we encourage citizens to exercise these rights? It is one thing for the government to grant you a right (e.g., the right to protest, the right to burn a flag), but it is the individual's duty to use that right.

Using your rights granted by the government is in and of itself patriotic, so whether your patriotism appears to be in favor or in protest of the government, the action of protest itself is a democratic embrace of the Constitution. To question government is a good thing—we must continually reinforce this with today's students. This is why the authors of the Constitution gave us those rights—to be active with the rights to protect the democracy. As teachers, we should encourage students to use these rights provided by the government (the right to vote, the right to assemble, the right to speak out, etc.). As teenagers, they must realize they still have rights, particularly as they move from adolescence into adulthood. Being a citizen means more than espousing our own ideals, but understanding those who disagree with us and using words and protest in a productive way.

Bibliography

Adler v. Bd. of Educ. of City of New York, 342 U.S. 485 (1952).
Brandenburg v. Ohio, 395 U.S. 444 (1969).
Brown v. Bd. of Educ. of Topeka, 347 U.S. 483 (1954).
Colonial Williamsburg Foundation. (2006). *Using primary sources*. Retrieved from https://socialstudies.madison.k12.wi.us/files/socialstudies/docs/using_primary_sources.pdf
County of Allegheny v. American Civil Liberties Union, 492 U.S. 573 (1989).
Edwards v. South Carolina, 372 U.S. 229 (1963).
Gideon v. Wainwright, 372 U.S. 335 (1963).
Gonzales v. Raich, 545 U.S. 1 (2005).
In re Gault, 387 U.S. 1 (1967).
Kelo v. City of New London, 545 U.S. 469 (2005).
Korematsu v. United States., 323 U.S. 214 (1944).
Lee, B. T. (2002, January). Teaching the Amistad. *Saint Louis University Law Journal*, *46*, 775. Retrieved from http://ideaexchange.uakron.edu/cgi/viewcontent.cgi?article=1135&context=ua_law_publications
Library of Congress. (n.d.). *Why use primary sources?* Retrieved from http://www.loc.gov/teachers/usingprimarysources/whyuse.html
Loving v. Virginia, 388 U.S. 1 (1967).
Marbury v. Madison, 5 U.S. 137 (1803).
Maryland v. King, 569 U.S. 435 (2013).
Maslenjak v. United States, 582 U.S. ___ (2017).
Medellin v. Texas, 552 U.S. 491 (2008).
Meyer v. Nebraska, 262 U.S. 390 (1923).
Michigan v. Environmental Protection Agency, 576 U.S. ___ (2015).
Miranda v. Arizona, 364 U.S. 436 (1966).
National Archives. (2016). *History in the raw*. (para. 4). Retrieved from https://www.archives.gov/education/history-in-the-raw.html
National Council for the Social Studies. (2010). *National curriculum standards for social studies: A framework for teaching, learning, and assessment.* Silver Spring, MD: Third Publishing.
Neumann, D. J. (2010, August). "What is the text doing?" Preparing pre-service teachers to teach primary sources effectively. *The History Teacher, 43*(4), 489–511.
Payne v. Tennessee, 501 U.S. 808 (1991).
Roper v. Simmons, 543 U.S. 551 (2005).
Shanahan, T. & Shanahan, C. (2008). Teaching disciplinary literacy to adolescents: Rethinking content-area literacy. *Harvard Educational Review, 78*(1), 40–59.
Shanahan, T. & Shanahan, C. (2017). Disciplinary literacy: Just the FAQs. *Educational Leadership, 74*(5), 18–22.
Shelby County v. Holder, 570 U.S. 529 (2013).
Sherbert v. Verner, 374 U.S. 398 (1963).
South Carolina v. Gathers, 490 U.S. 805 (1989).
Swift & Co. v. United States, 196 U.S. 375 (1905).
Texas v. Johnson, 491 U.S. 397 (1989).
Tinker v. Des Moines Indep. Cmty. Sch. Dist., 393 U.S. 503 (1969).
U.S. Const. amend. IV.
U.S. Const. amend. XIV, § 1.
United States. v. The Amistad, 40 U.S. 518 (1841).

United States v. 95 Barrels of Vinegar, 265 U.S. 438 (1924).
United States v. American Library Ass'n., Inc., 539 U.S. 194 (2003).
United States v. Jones, 565 U.S. 400 (2012).
Whitney v. California, 274 U.S. 357 (1927).
Wisconsin v. Yoder, 406 U.S. 205 (1972).
Yale University. (n.d.). *Primary sources at Yale*. Retrieved from https://primarysources.yale.edu/

Index

About the Authors

Gretchen Oltman, J.D., Ph.D., has spent over a decade in education as a high school teacher, university professor, and program administrator. Oltman earned a bachelor of arts in English from the University of Nebraska-Lincoln, a master of arts in teaching from the University of Louisville, a juris doctorate from the University of Nebraska College of Law, and a Ph.D. in educational studies from the University of Nebraska. She is a licensed attorney in the state of Nebraska. Oltman currently serves as an assistant professor in the Interdisciplinary Studies Department and as program director for the Masters and Bachelors Leadership Programs at Creighton University in Omaha, Nebraska. She was awarded the 2010 Dr. Ted Sizer High School Level Dissertation of the Year by the National Association of Secondary School Principals. Her first book, *Violence in Student Writing: A Guide for School Administrators*, was published in 2013. Her second text, a coauthored book, *Law Meets Literature: A Novel Approach for the English Classroom,* was published in 2015. She regularly presents at national conferences including those hosted by the National Council of Teachers of English and the Education Law Association.

Johnna L. Graff, J.D., earned a bachelor of arts in English from Nebraska Wesleyan University and a juris doctorate with distinction from the University of Nebraska College of Law. She is a licensed attorney in the state of Nebraska. Graff currently serves as the English Department chair at Lincoln Southeast High School in Lincoln, Nebraska. Her teaching assignment includes "Law and Literature." In addition, she is an adjunct instructor at Nebraska Wesleyan University and Doane University. She coauthored her first book, *Law Meets Literature: A Novel Approach for the English Classroom,* which was published in 2015. She presents at national conventions including the AP Annual Conference, National Council of Teachers of English, and Conference on English Leadership.

Cynthia Wood Maddux, J.D., earned a bachelor of arts in English from the University of Nebraska-Lincoln and a juris doctorate from the University of Nebraska College of Law. After spending nearly seven years as a practicing attorney and a nonprofit executive director, she received her postbaccalaureate teaching certification and began teaching high school English in 2000. Along with Gretchen Oltman and Johnna Graff, Maddux coauthored her first book in 2015, *Law Meets Literature: A Novel Approach for the English Classroom*. She is currently an English teacher at Lincoln North Star High School in Lincoln, Nebraska, and also serves as an adjunct instructor at Nebraska Wesleyan University. Maddux regularly presents at national conferences including the National Council of Teachers of English, the Advanced Placement Annual Conference, and the Conference on English Leadership.

www.ingramcontent.com/pod-product-compliance
Ingram Content Group UK Ltd.
Pitfield, Milton Keynes, MK11 3LW, UK
UKHW051932150926
475560UK00005B/360

9 781475 836066